EARTH
SCIENCE
for Christian Schools®

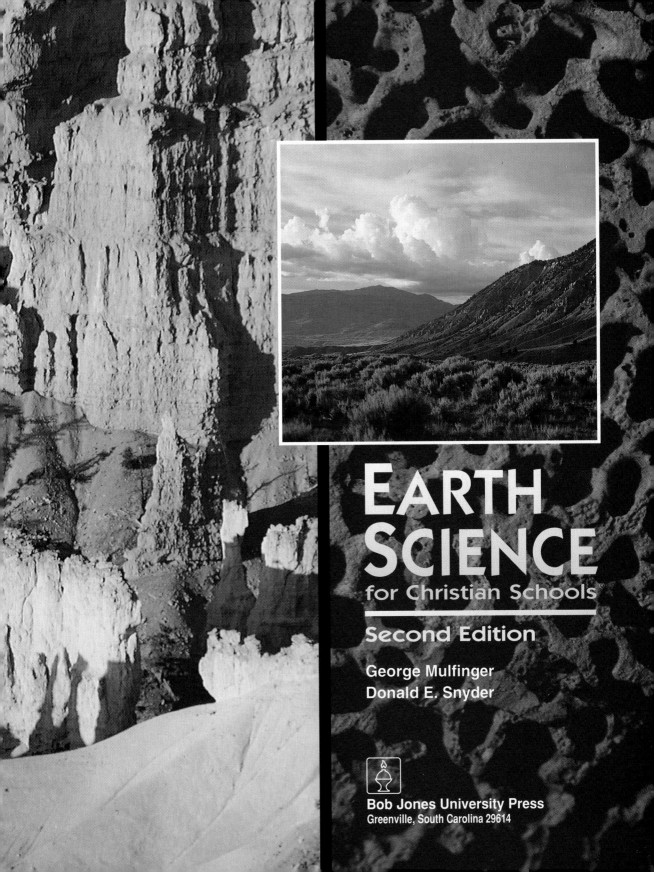

EARTH SCIENCE
for Christian Schools®

Second Edition

George Mulfinger
Donald E. Snyder

Bob Jones University Press
Greenville, South Carolina 29614

EARTH SCIENCE for Christian Schools®

Second Edition

George Mulfinger, Jr., M.S.
Donald E. Snyder, M.Ed.

Revised by
David Anderson, Ph.D.
Rosemary Lasell

© 1992, 1995 Bob Jones University Press
Greenville, South Carolina 29614

Printed in the United States of America
All rights reserved

ISBN 0-89084-612-X

15   14   13   12   11   10   9   8   7   6   5

Contents

Unit III   The Lithosphere

Unit IV   The Hydrosphere

Appendixes

Glossary

Index

Introduction

"Where do you live?" Your answer to this question is closely related to your maturity level. An infant, for example, is aware of a very limited area such as a bedroom. However, as he matures, he realizes that he lives in a house and that his house is in a neighborhood. By the time the child is in elementary school, he has developed the concept of a city and a state. Junior high students have developed to the point of realizing that they live in a country and on a planet. The expansion continues, until finally he realizes that he lives in the solar system and that it is part of the universe.

What is it that broadens our concept of where we live? The most important factor is the *discoveries* we make that demonstrate to us that our lives are influenced by our *environment,* or surroundings. The more discoveries we make, the more we realize that where we live is a relative concept; that is, it all depends upon how we look at it.

For this reason, when we study a particular object or organism, it also will be important for us to study its environment. Sharks, for example, would make an interesting study. But to thoroughly understand a shark, a student would need to know a great deal about the environment of the shark. This might include such things as the composition of ocean water, the other organisms present in the ocean, the ocean currents, and even the contour of the ocean floor.

You will use a similar process in your study of earth science this year. In order for you to develop a clear understanding of the planet on which you live, you also must get a view of the environment in which it is found. This study of earth science begins with a study of space because the planets, stars, and all other heavenly bodies "float" in the "ocean of space," and these bodies affect one another.

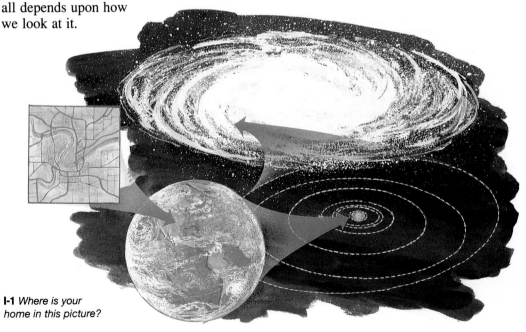

I-1 *Where is your home in this picture?*

Science and the Bible

For the Christian, earth science is a study of God's creation. As such, it is subject to God's infallible Word, the Bible. The final authority for the Christian is not man's observation, but God's revelation. Man's senses are so easily fooled that it is impossible to trust in observations alone.

The Christian researcher is aware that God has communicated many important scientific truths to man in His written Word, the Bible. Although the Bible is not intended primarily to be a science textbook, it is nevertheless an extremely valuable source of information. Being the inspired Word of God, it can be trusted to be correct in every point. Where could we get more accurate information about the heavens, the earth, and everything in them, than from the one who brought them into existence? There are many statements in the Bible about the beginning of the universe, how it is sustained, and God's plan for new heavens and a new earth in the future. To a great extent this information is beyond the realm of science. We would know far less about the world we live in if God had not revealed these important truths to us in His Word.

The thoughtful Christian researcher uses the statements of Scripture to guide his thinking. He puts different portions of Scripture

I-2 *The beauty of nature testifies to the existence of God.*

together and draws up a broad outline of truth that is called the Bible-derived framework. This framework is the "skeleton" upon which he later places the "flesh," the detailed findings from his scientific investigations. If his findings fail to fit the framework, he immediately suspects that he has made a mistake in his research. Realizing that he is a fallible human being, he reviews and carefully checks his work. He knows, whatever else may happen, that his framework is correct and that true science will fit that framework. Anything that does not fit the Bible-derived framework must come under the heading of "science falsely so called" (I Tim. 6:20). True science always agrees with the Bible.

Science and Its Limitations

People sometimes get exaggerated ideas of what science is and what it is capable of doing. We do not wish to curb anyone's enthusiasm, but it is necessary to point out some of the limitations of science.

First, *science deals only with the physical universe.* Science is unable to deal with the spiritual domain, ultimate origins (where things originated), or other nonobservable events. **Science*** is usually defined as the study of observable facts or events. All other topics are outside the realm of true science and are **philosophy*** (the pursuit of wisdom through avenues other than observation). Suppose, for example, that a person attempted a research project on the subject of prayer. He is interested in finding out how prayer is transmitted. Are there "prayer waves" of some kind? He would find himself wondering where to begin. He cannot build a detector for such supposed waves if he does not know what they are, and he cannot find out what they are until he can detect them. Such a problem may discourage the researcher be-

science: (L. SCIENS, to know)
philosophy: philo- (Gk. PHILOS, loving) + -sophy (Gk. SOPHOS, wisdom)

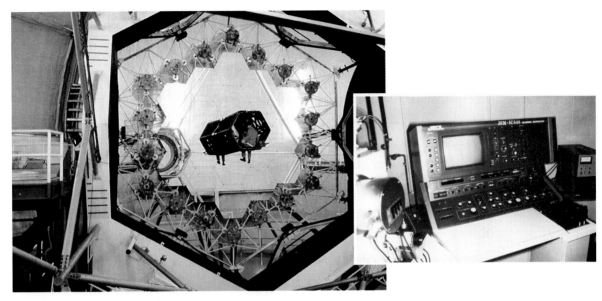

I-3 *Telescopes are limited in what they tell us about the heavens. We are unable to tell, for example, whether every star has planets orbiting it* (left). *Even the most powerful electron microscope is unable to let us see the inside of an atom* (right).

fore his research project ever gets under way. Science will never be able to give answers to such questions. Likewise, the origin of the universe lies outside the realm of science, since no human observer was present to view the process.

Another limitation of science is *its inability to prove a universal negative.* A universal negative is a blanket statement of denial. Suppose someone makes the statement "There is no such thing as a sea monster." How would a person go about proving or disproving this claim? He probably would investigate reports of large, unclassified marine creatures, carcasses that had been washed ashore, footprints on beaches, and similar clues. Suppose he can discredit every clue he is given. In each instance he is able to show that the report is either a mis-identification of some commonplace creature or an outright hoax. He still has not proved what he set out to prove. To prove that sea monsters do not exist, he would have to search every bit of seawater, at all depths, over the entire globe. Not only that, he would have to observe each region at the same time because while he was looking in one place, the slippery sea monster could have gone somewhere else. Statements such as "There is no God" and "Science has disproved the existence of miracles" are universal negatives and lie outside the realm of science.

Another shortcoming of science is *its inability to make value judgments.* Value is the worth that we attach to an object. How much is a gallon of gasoline worth? It appears that it is worth about as much as someone is willing to pay. But can science determine what a person will pay for something? No, what someone will pay depends upon his desire to have the object and his ability to purchase it. A person with a half tank of gas out in a desert would pay very little for gas if he knew he could make it safely out of the desert. On the other hand, another person may be willing to pay ten times the normal cost if his tank is nearly empty. Someone else may be willing to pay any amount for gas but may be unable to pay for it because he has no money. Science would be unable to establish the value of gasoline in these examples.

Moral judgments are also outside the realm of scientific research. Science may be able to establish a method of developing atomic energy, but decisions regarding the moral use of that energy are beyond the range of science. Moral judgments deal with the rightness or wrongness of an act. Atomic energy can be used to make bombs to destroy people, or it can be used to make electricity to provide energy for use in our homes. Science can determine how to do both, but it is unable to determine when it should be used for bombs or when it should be used for electricity.

Another limitation of science is its *inability to produce final answers.* In fact, one scientist has estimated that for each question science is able to answer, ten new questions are raised. Whenever someone invents the "ultimate computer," it is not long before someone invents one just a little bit better. This is one reason that science is so changeable. Change in science might be somewhat discouraging for the young student of science until he realizes that this situation is according to the plan of God. As we study God's handiwork and seek to find out the ordinances that govern our physical world, we should develop a deep sense of humility. We should realize that we cannot understand everything, for man is totally incapable of thinking on God's level (Isa. 55:9).

In the early 1900s, someone suggested closing the patent office since all things that could possibly be invented had already been invented. This error was made because some-

I-4 *Many would-be aviators learned the hard way that science is fallible. Both before and after the invention of the airplane, errors in aerodynamics resulted in many injuries and loss of life.*

one failed to recognize that science is unable to produce final answers.

As we can see, *scientific work is fallible and prone to error.* Scientists often make mistakes because their senses are limited. Perhaps you have experienced some of the optical illusions that are published in books. Or perhaps you have been fooled by some "brain teaser" that took advantage of the tendency of the human mind to be distracted by irrelevant data. These shortcomings of the human being make science fallible, and this is another reason science changes.

As strange as it may seem, science is limited by the fact that *it is often forced to deal with models rather than with reality.* What a scientist dreams up in his mind is not necessarily what really exists. Remember, his senses are fallible, and he cannot understand God's creation fully or correctly. He sees everything through a clouded glass (I Cor. 13:12). He does not always study matter; he often studies his ideas of matter (models). For instance, the atomic theory is based on a model, and the scientist studies the atom using his model, even though he feels certain it is not a completely accurate model. For lack of a better model, however, he will use it because it is capable of explaining some of the things observed about atoms. A good model is a *workable* model, though it may not be thoroughly accurate. A model should be discarded, however, when a better model is found.

Science is bound by certain God-ordained restrictions. Genesis 8:22 places definite limits on the ability to modify the weather, the alternation of day and night, and the processes of decay that are found in nature. Matthew 26:11 and Hebrews 9:27 clearly state that poverty and death will never be eradicated.

I-5 *Just as a two-year-old child would have difficulty understanding algebra, so man has difficulty understanding how God created the universe.*

Finally, perhaps the most subtle of the limitations of science is *the scientist's prejudices.* Often a scientist's prejudices (likes and dislikes) will determine what type of model

he will choose or develop. A creationist will choose a different model than an evolutionist will to explain origins. The authors of this book are Bible-believing Christians who accept the creation account as recorded in the Scriptures. They have "prejudiced" this series toward creation and God's Word. But keep in mind that education is a process of prejudicing. The most highly educated person is a very prejudiced person. A civil engineer,

I-6 *Scientists' prejudices often affect their judgment.*

for example, has been prejudiced in his education against using lead to build a bridge. He has learned that lead "creeps" under its own weight and is therefore not a good structural material. A prejudiced engineer would not use lead to build a bridge; an unprejudiced engineer might do so, however, and be rather surprised at the finished product.

These limitations of science should not make us say, "Well, if this is the case, science is worthless." Absolutely not! Science is very useful. Look at all the modern conveniences and medical advances wrought by scientists. The next time we work with a calculator or computer or the next time we take a dose of some "wonder drug," we should remember that this is a result of a scientific effort. If something works in science, we use it; if it does not work, we do not use it.

Science and the Christian

As a scientist studies the world about him, he is often at the frontier of human knowledge. Only a relatively small number of people—his fellow scientists—understand the work he is doing. Occasionally he will find out something new that his colleagues do not yet know about. Because he now knows something that other men do not, he may become puffed up with pride. However, a scientist who is a Christian studies God's handiwork with an attitude of reverence and humility. He realizes his limitations as a human being and interprets his findings as evidence of God's greatness and goodness rather than his own cleverness. This understanding makes the Christian realize that it is a privilege to learn about God's universe. With this privilege comes the responsibility

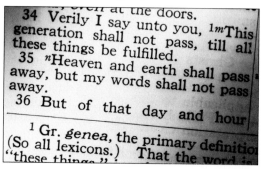

I-7 Years of detailed calculations were required for Kepler to develop his three laws of planetary motion.

of spreading the knowledge of God's glory to others. The famous Christian astronomer Johannes Kepler attempted to learn more about the Creator's purposes as he carried out his investigations. After years of detailed calculations and study, he was able to develop his laws of planetary motion. He was careful to give God the glory for his discoveries.

> 34 Verily I say unto you, [1m]This generation shall not pass, till all these things be fulfilled.
> 35 [n]Heaven and earth shall pass away, but my words shall not pass away.
> 36 But of that day and hour
>
> [1] Gr. genea, the primary definition (So all lexicons.) That the word is "these things."

I-8 Unlike heaven and earth, Jesus' words are permanent and unchanging.

In view of the uncertainty of science, is it not strange that some people choose to worship science rather than God? The Christian puts his faith and trust in the one who is "the same yesterday, and to day, and for ever" (Heb. 13:8). With God there is "no variableness, neither shadow of turning" (James 1:17). His Word represents absolute truth, which stands unchanged from one generation to the next. The unbeliever, on the other hand, places his faith in that which is constantly changing. How much better for a person to have his faith grounded on the solid Rock than on shifting sand!

Earth Science and Its Elements

The elements that make up a study of earth science are **space,** sometimes called the **celestial sphere;** the **atmosphere,*** the layers of air surrounding the earth; the **lithosphere,*** the solid part of the earth; and the

---

atmosphere: atmo- (Gk. ATMOS, vapor) + -sphere (Gk. SPHAIRA, sphere, ball)

lithosphere: litho- (Gk. LITHOS, stone) + -sphere

hydrosphere, * the water that covers nearly three-fourths of the earth's surface.

In your study of the celestial sphere, you also will study the instruments used by scientists to examine the outer regions of space. You will study the stars, planets, comets, and many other celestial objects, and you will have the opportunity of studying the laws that keep everything in their respective places.

You will also study the atmosphere. Weather forecasting and violent weather are an interesting part of this unit. You will study the colorful aurora and will find out why hail can form even on a hot summer day. Life on the earth would not be possible without the blanket of air that God has wrapped around the earth. This is one of the characteristics of the earth that makes it exceptional to any other planet.

The solid part of the earth, the lithosphere, is a fascinating study. Rocks and minerals will take on a new meaning as you examine the beauty found beneath the surface of the ground. Volcanoes and earthquakes are two topics that will capture your attention as you realize that the earth is a restless planet.

Finally, your study will end with the topic of the hydrosphere. You will examine water, a characteristic of the earth that makes it exceptional among the planets. No other planet has water in abundance like the earth. Water is vital to life as we know it, and you will learn how God has put into effect one of the greatest recycling units. No other areas on earth have been explored less than the oceans, and yet they are filled with prospects for future energy, food, and riches beyond our comprehension.

It is the desire of the staff at the Bob Jones University Press that this study of earth science be exciting and profitable and be a challenge for you to seek the Lord's will for your future vocation. Perhaps your choice of a vocation will be influenced by some of the information that you study this year. You might consider the field of meteorology (study of the weather), astronomy (study of the heavens), geology (study of the earth and its processes), oceanography (study of the oceans), or seismology (study of earthquakes). These are just a few of the hundreds of possible choices that await your exploration.

Pronunciation Key

The pronunciations given in this text are designed to be self-evident and should give the average reader an acceptable pronunciation of the singular form of the word. For precise pronunciations, consult a good dictionary. This sample pronunciation key may help those who have difficulty with the symbols used.

Stressed syllables appear in large capital letters. Syllables with secondary stress and one-syllable words appear in small capital letters. Unstressed syllables are in lowercase letters. Most consonants and combinations of consonants *(ng, sh)* make the sounds normally associated with them.

Symbols, Key Words, and Examples

a	cat = KAT, laugh = LAF	i-e	might = MITE
a-e	cape = KAPE,	ih	pity = PIH tee
	reign = RANE	oh	potion = POH shun,
ah	father = FAH thur		own = OHN
ar	car = KAR	o-e	groan = GRONE
aw	all = AWL,	oo	tune = TOON
	caught = KAWT	*oo*	foot = F*OO*T
ay	neigh = NAY,	ow	loud = LOWD
	paint = PAYNT	oy	toil = TOYL
e	jet = JET	th	thin = THIN
ee	fiend = FEEND	*th*	then = *TH*EN
eh	rebel = REH bul,	u, uh	above = uh BUV
	care = KEHR	ur	person = PUR suhn
eye	ivory = EYE vuh ree	wh	where = WHEHR
i	women = WIM un	y	mighty = MY tee

hydrosphere: hydro- (Gk. HUDOR, water) + -sphere

THE CELESTIAL SPHERE

UNIT I

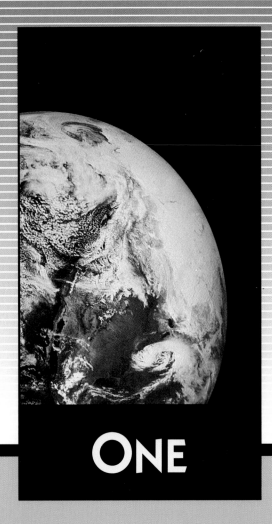

THE EARTH'S MOTIONS

ONE

1A-Does the Earth Move?

Does the earth move? The ground under your feet seems solidly immovable. You feel no sensation of movement. But when you ride in a good car at a steady speed, movement is also difficult to feel. How do you know that the car is moving? You observe movement by looking at your surroundings. In the same way, the earth's surroundings—the heavens—can show whether the earth is moving.

The Geocentric Theory

When you stand outside looking at the night sky, you may get the impression that you are at the center of a large dome. All the stars seem to be attached to the dome. As you watch the sky for a time, the dome appears to be turning. When you come back the following night and look again, the sky seems to have made one complete turn and come back to the position where you saw it the previous night. You may decide that the sky is not just a dome but is a whole sphere (like the inside of a hollow ball) that surrounds you. Ancient observers drew this conclusion. From such observations they reasoned that the earth is stationary and that the sky turns around it.

1A-1 *In this time exposure, the stars appear to move counterclockwise around the North Star.*

Yet early star watchers noticed that seven heavenly bodies were different from the others. These seven bodies were the sun, the moon, and five planets: Mercury, Venus, Mars, Jupiter, and Saturn. When the ancients observed these bodies over several weeks, they saw them move slowly among the stars. How could these objects move among the stars if they were attached to the same sphere as the stars? Early astronomers decided that each heavenly body must be turning on its own separate sphere. The spheres must be hollow shells, they reasoned, made of something transparent such as glass so that they would not hide the sky.

The ancient description of the universe is called the **geocentric*** (JEE oh SEN trik) **theory.** According to this theory, the earth is at the center; the moon occupies the innermost crystal sphere; Mercury, the second sphere; and Venus, the third, followed by the sun, Mars, Jupiter, and Saturn in consecutive spheres. The stars occupy the outermost

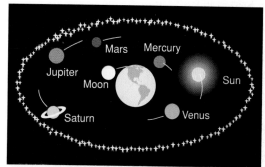

1A-2 *A model of the geocentric theory of the solar system. The ancients, not knowing the true sizes of the objects, pictured an oversized earth. The objects circling the earth are the moon, Mercury, Venus, the sun, Mars, Jupiter, and Saturn. Ancient astronomers were not aware of the existence of Uranus, Neptune, or Pluto.*

sphere. In modern terminology we call this a **model** of the universe. A model is a simplified picture that a scientist uses to represent what he is studying.

Ancient astronomers thought that the sun's sphere turned once each day. The other spheres turned nearly once each day. The moon's sphere, they explained, turned much slower than the others, allowing the moon to change its position rapidly among the stars. This explained why the moon rises about fifty minutes later each night. The planets' spheres

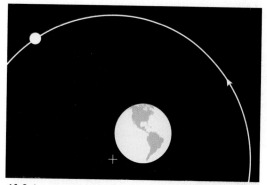

1A-3 *An attempt to make the geocentric model "work." Because a planet sometimes appears closer and other times farther away, it was suggested that perhaps the earth is not at the very center of a planet's circular orbit.*

---

geocentric: geo- (Gk. GE, earth) + -centric (Gk. KENTRON, center)

turned at slightly different rates, explaining their independent paths among the stars.

Different Greek philosophers and astronomers of several centuries contributed to the geocentric view of the universe. Most notable were Hipparchus (hih PAR kus) in the second century B.C. and Ptolemy (TOLE uh mee) in the second century A.D. Ptolemy played such a large role in attempting to improve the geocentric theory that it is sometimes called the **Ptolemaic theory.**

Several problems with the geocentric model bothered the ancient astronomers. One is that the planets sometimes appear to be large, bright, and close; at other times they seem smaller, dimmer, and farther away. Ptolemy tried to solve this problem by shifting each planet's sphere so that the earth was no longer at its center. Such an off-center circle is called **eccentric.*** This would make the planet on the sphere closer to the earth at times and farther from the earth at other times. This solution offended the ancient sense of beauty because it was not symmetrical, but it helped to make the model closer to reality.

Another problem with the geocentric view is that the planets sometimes slow down in their motion among the stars, stop, and then back up. After tracing out a backward loop, they resume their forward motion. How could the model explain these variations in motion? Could the crystal spheres slow down, stop, and reverse their motion? They could, but that would make the heavens seem somewhat disorderly. Ptolemy preferred to think that the spheres turned at a constant rate. He imagined that the planets moved around small circles called **epicycles*** while each epicycle went around the earth on the crystal sphere. He then called the crystal sphere the **deferent** (DEF ur unt) to distinguish it from the epicycles. With this ap-

1A-4 *Epicycles, small loops in an orbit, were added in an attempt to correct the geocentric model.*

proach he could explain a backward loop as the planet's moving rapidly backward in its epicycle as the epicycle itself was moving slowly forward around the deferent.

Although astronomers tried juggling the distances as well as the speeds in their model, the resulting system was still disappointingly inaccurate. In spite of a total of more than seventy separate motions for the seven bodies, a careful observer could find discrepancies between his observations and the model. Two major objections to the geocentric theory are its inaccuracy and complexity. The inaccuracy of the model hinders its ability to

eccentric: ec- (Gk. EK-, out) + -centric (center)

epicycle: epi- (Gk. EPI, on) + -cycle (Gk. KUKLOS, circle)

predict where the heavenly bodies would be at a given time, while the complexity of the model makes solving even simple problems time consuming. Complexity is undesirable in a scientific model because it reduces efficiency. However, if no simple explanation exists, a complex model is better than none. Some of God's creations are extremely complex, and oversimplification of them would be an error. So for centuries astronomers used the geocentric model because it was the only mathematical model available.

Section Review Questions 1A-1

1. Besides the stars, what seven heavenly bodies were ancient astronomers able to observe?
2. What is the name of the ancient theory of the universe that states that the earth is at the center and all heavenly bodies revolve around it?
3. What person in the second century A.D. is most noted for his work on improving and promoting the above theory?
4. What did the above astronomer call the transparent spheres in his theory?
5. Some astronomers believed the planets moved in circular loops within their spheres. What were these loops called?

The Heliocentric Theory

The fourteenth, fifteenth, and sixteenth centuries brought the great rebirth of learning called the Renaissance. A renewed interest in every area of culture—art, literature, music, drama, geography, science, and medicine—swept across Europe. There was also a re-awakening of interest in the Bible. With Gutenberg's movable-type printing process, the

1A-5 *The Copernican model of the solar system (left) is sun-centered. The planets are arranged outward from the sun in the following order: Mercury, Venus, Earth, Mars, Jupiter, and Saturn. Only the moon orbits the earth. Nicolaus Copernicus (right), a Polish astronomer, formulated this heliocentric theory.*

Bible and many other books became more available. The printed books stimulated new thought, reopening the question "Does the earth move?"

Copernicus

Nicolaus Copernicus (koh PUR nuh kus) (1473–1543), a Polish astronomer, was born during this exciting time. A full-time student until age thirty-three, Copernicus had time to study mathematics, astronomy, medicine, law, and theology at several prominent universities. Later, when he was the attending physician at his wealthy uncle's castle, Copernicus began to study the heavens seriously. He observed the motions of the planets and studied the writings of Ptolemy. As he became disillusioned with the many "tricks" that forced the geocentric theory to work, he began to suspect that a stationary sun and a moving earth would give a simpler and more accurate model.

For many years Copernicus labored, collecting facts and arguments that he finally compiled into a large work called *Six Books Concerning the Revolutions of the Heavenly Spheres,* or *The Revolutions* for short. In this book he answered many of the arguments people had used against the idea of a moving earth. For example, opponents had said that a spinning earth would fly apart. Copernicus answered that a rotating sky would be far more likely to fly apart, because its greater size required greater speed. Opponents claimed that birds in flight would be left behind if the earth were spinning. His reply was that the earth drags along the atmosphere, including birds, as it turns. Skeptics argued that if the earth were revolving around the sun, the nearer stars would seem to shift their positions among the more distant stars when viewed from different places in the earth's orbit. Copernicus's reply, which has proved to be correct, was that the stars are too far away for observers to see the shift. The shift can be seen with strong telescopes, but Copernicus died before the telescope was invented.

1A-6 *Copernicus showed that a moving earth catching up with and passing a slower planet like Mars makes the slower planet appear to go backward.*

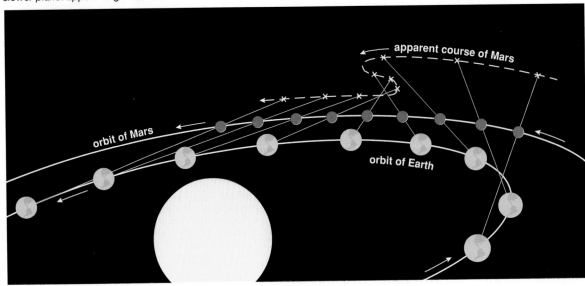

Copernicus also explained why the planets seem to go backward at times. Normally, a planet's own motion carries it eastward among the stars. Copernicus, however, showed that a moving earth catching up with and passing a slower planet such as Mars or Jupiter would make the slower planet *appear* to go backward. During the brief period that the earth is passing it, the slower planet *appears* to be drifting back toward the west. When the earth moves far enough ahead of the planet, the planet's own motion predominates, and its normal eastward movement is observed again.

Copernicus published *The Revolutions* in 1543, the year he died. A hundred years later his theory became accepted by most scientists. Although astronomers have changed some of its details, they still accept Copernicus's model of the solar system. The model is called the **heliocentric*** (HEE lee oh SEN trik) or **Copernican theory.** Today, when we speak of the "solar system," which includes the sun and everything that orbits it, we are continuing the tradition of Copernicus.

Tycho

Tycho (TY koh) Brahe (BRAH hee) (1546–1601), a Danish nobleman, was one of the most accurate astronomical observers in history. Although he did not accept the Copernican theory, his observations helped establish the heliocentric theory as correct. With a grant from the king of Denmark, Tycho built a palatial* observatory on the Isle of Hveen near Copenhagen. For the next twenty years, Tycho made and recorded remarkably precise observations of the positions of stars and planets. Later, when he went to Prague to become Imperial Mathematician, he began analyzing his numerous volumes of data with a team of assistants. But not until Johannes Kepler joined Tycho's staff in the year 1600

1A-7 *Tycho Brahe, one of the most accurate astronomical observers in history, and a view of his observatory, Uraniborg*

was any significant progress made toward understanding the motions of the solar system.

Kepler

Johannes (yoh HAH nus) Kepler (KEP lur) (1571–1630), a German astronomer, was an outstanding Christian and a brilliant mathematician. Because of his clear-cut testimony, he was severely persecuted. Still he proved God's promise that "all things work together for good to them that love God, to them who are the called according to his purpose" (Rom. 8:28). When Protestants were persecuted and forced out of Austria, Kepler went to work for Tycho in Prague. Kepler recog-

---

heliocentric: helio- (Gk. HELIOS, sun) + -centric (center)

palatial: (L. PALATIUM, palace; *thus, like a palace*)

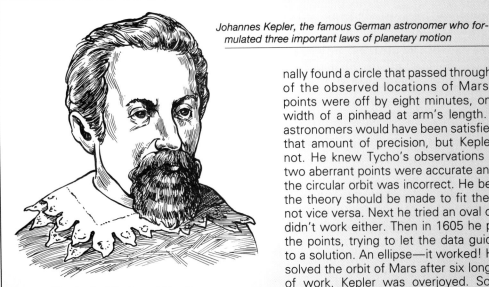

Johannes Kepler, the famous German astronomer who formulated three important laws of planetary motion

Kepler's Work and Testimony

Soon after Kepler joined Tycho's staff in Prague, in 1600, Tycho lay on his deathbed. Giving his precious observations to Kepler, he charged Kepler with finishing the work he had begun. Kepler promised he would.

Kepler began by trying to solve the problem of the motion of Mars. Eccentric circles did not fit the planet's path. Kepler wondered if the earth also traveled in an eccentric path, changing its speed as it circled the sun. This made the calculations much more difficult, since Tycho's observations would then have been made from an irregularly moving earth. Calculations needed to be made and the model needed to be tested. It took Kepler seventy different trials and over nine hundred pages of calculations! He fi-

nally found a circle that passed through most of the observed locations of Mars. Two points were off by eight minutes, only the width of a pinhead at arm's length. Many astronomers would have been satisfied with that amount of precision, but Kepler was not. He knew Tycho's observations of the two aberrant points were accurate and thus the circular orbit was incorrect. He believed the theory should be made to fit the facts, not vice versa. Next he tried an oval orbit. It didn't work either. Then in 1605 he plotted the points, trying to let the data guide him to a solution. An ellipse—it worked! He had solved the orbit of Mars after six long years of work. Kepler was overjoyed. Soon he showed that the other planets traveled in elliptical orbits as well.

Kepler could see the hand of God in his work. It was fortunate that he had started with Mars, since Mars has the most eccentric orbit of the planets he could observe. He had been given the privilege of discovering laws governing the heavens. At the conclusion of the book that contains his third law, he wrote:

> Great is God our Lord, great is His power and there is no end to His wisdom. Praise Him, you heavens, glorify Him, sun and moon and you planets. For out of Him, through Him, and in Him are all things. . . . We know, oh, so little. To him be the praise, the honor and the glory from eternity to eternity.

nized this arrangement as providential and once said, "I see how God let me be bound with Tycho through an unalterable fate and did not let me be separated from him by the most oppressive hardships."

Soon after Kepler's arrival in Prague, he began to study Tycho's observations of Mars. Other members of Tycho's staff had already

tried to make sense of them and had failed. After several years of work involving hundreds of pages of calculations, Kepler devised three laws that described planetary motion. He published the first two laws in a book called *New Astronomy* in 1609. His third law came later, in 1618. Kepler's major contribution to the Copernican theory was his mathematical proof that the orbits of the planets are not circular, but elliptical (like a squashed circle).

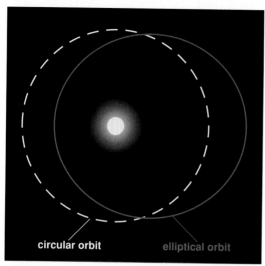

1A-8 *Kepler proved mathematically that the orbits of the planets are not circular but elliptical.*

Kepler's life is a forceful demonstration of what a dedicated Christian man of science can accomplish. In spite of great hardships in his life, he was able to succeed and give God the glory. Kepler saw himself as an instrument in God's hands for revealing more of His handiwork to men. He believed that the primary goal of science is to lead men to God. Today's Christians should follow his example.

Galileo

The same year that Kepler published his book *New Astronomy*, Galileo (GAL uh LEE oh) Galilei (GAL uh LAY ee) (1564–1642) designed a telescope. He was the first person to use it for astronomy. He observed that Venus has phases like the moon. Not only does it appear as a crescent at times and nearly full at others, but its size also appears to change. According to the geocentric theory, its ap-

parent size should not change noticeably. Galileo also spotted something protruding from the sides of Saturn. He was looking at the rings, but he could not see them clearly enough to understand what they were.

Galileo was especially fascinated by his discovery of the four largest moons of Jupiter. As he observed these moons from night to night, Galileo realized that they were traveling in orbits around the planet. He considered this to be good evidence for the heliocentric theory of the solar system: they proved that not every body orbits the earth. Furthermore, these moons were small bodies traveling around a more massive body; the heliocentric theory required that the smaller earth orbit the more massive sun. From these observations Galileo became an active supporter of the heliocentric theory. He promoted and defended the model until the Roman Catholic church forced him to stop.

1A-9 *Galileo Galilei was the first person to use a telescope for astronomy.*

FACETS OF ASTRONOMY

1A-1

Religious Opposition to the Heliocentric Theory

In the sixteenth and seventeenth centuries, astronomers who accepted the heliocentric theory were often subjected to religious persecution. In the thirteenth century, an Italian philosopher named Thomas Aquinas (1225–74) claimed that he could harmonize (fit together) the science of the ancient Greek philosophers with Christianity. He proposed that reason can operate within faith, yet according to its own laws. The Roman Catholic church recognized his work and accepted the geocentric theory as part of its official doctrine. This made teaching the heliocentric theory equivalent to teaching heresy.

Copernicus, a member of a Roman Catholic religious community, realized that the heliocentric theory explained in his book *The Revolutions* would be extremely controversial. He held the manuscript for ten years before publishing it. Copernicus once said, "I do not want to be hissed off the stage. What I know, the public does not approve, and what it approves, I know to be error." Shortly before his death, friends convinced him to have the book published. A well-meaning friend who helped Copernicus publish the book added a phony

9/27/10

preface signing Copernicus's name to it. The preface stated that the heliocentric theory lacked reality; it was only a mathematical way of figuring celestial events more easily. Copernicus's friend feared that the ideas in the book would lead to persecution. Copernicus died soon after the published book was brought to him. He did not live to suffer persecution resulting from his "heretical" ideas.

Kepler was the first major scientist after Copernicus to dare support the heliocentric view in print. While he was training for the ministry, he was warned that the Copernican theory was dangerous for a Lutheran clergyman to hold. Luther himself had expressed his firm belief that the earth was stationary, at the center of the universe. As it turned out, Kepler left the theological school before finishing in order to teach mathematics. As much as he wanted to study theology, he sensed that God was leading him to study the heavens.

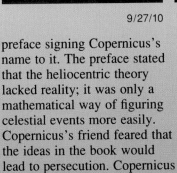

6/10/10

Throughout his life, Kepler did not hesitate to make his beliefs known. When his first book, *Cosmic Mystery,* was published, he sent a copy to Galileo. Galileo wrote back:

> I adopted the teachings of Copernicus many years ago. . . . However, so far I have not dared bring it into public light, frightened by the fate of Copernicus himself. It is deplorable that there are so few who seek the truth. I would certainly dare to approach the public with my ways of thinking if there were more people of your mind. As this is not the case, I shall refrain from doing so.

Kepler replied to Galileo, urging him to make his views public. Galileo remained silent until he observed the heavens with the telescope he had designed. Then, in 1610 he published the *Message from the Stars,* a book in which he described his observations through the telescope. His observations made him bolder.

However, Galileo's reluctance to make his views known

These photos of Venus at various positions in its orbit, but at the same magnification, show that Venus appears to change in size as it orbits. These observations support the heliocentric theory and were once considered heretical.

10/24/27   9/25/19   6/19/64

turned out to be well founded. By 1615 the Roman Catholic church examined Copernicus's book *The Revolutions* and declared it heretical, banning sales of the book. The following year Galileo was ordered to stop teaching Copernican heresies.

Galileo complied but over the next fifteen years collected information that he published in 1632 under the title *Dialogue on the Two Chief World Systems*. The pope was furious and insisted that Galileo come to the Inquisition at Rome on the

charge of heresy. He was made to recant his Copernican views under threat of torture and then was put under house arrest where he remained until his death in 1643. More than a century would pass before the Roman Catholic church would accept Galileo's visible proofs of the heliocentric theory.

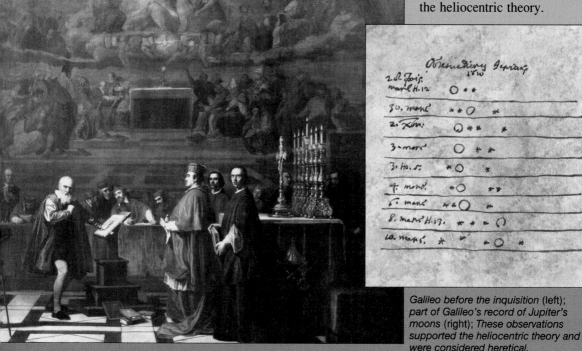

Galileo before the inquisition (left); part of Galileo's record of Jupiter's moons (right); These observations supported the heliocentric theory and were considered heretical.

1A-10
Sir Isaac Newton, the English mathematician and scientist who formulated the law of gravitation

Newton

Until the late 1600s, astronomers worked out models and laws for the solar system but said very little about what kept the planets in their orbits. They described what was happening instead of telling how it happened. The task of explaining how the solar system worked remained for the English mathematician and scientist Isaac Newton (1642–1727), who devised the **law of gravitation** to describe the force between the sun and the bodies around it.

While he was sitting in the garden of his family's estate, Newton received the inspiration he needed to devise his theory. As he sat thinking about the moon and its orbit, he saw an apple fall from a nearby tree. Could the force that made the apple fall be the same force that kept the moon in its orbit? Preliminary calculations suggested that it was. After much additional work, Newton showed mathematically that the more massive a body is, the more attraction it has for another body. He also discovered that the attraction between two bodies decreases as the distance between them increases. Newton stated his findings in the law of gravitation: "Any two bodies attract each other with a force pro-

portional to the product of their masses and inversely proportional to the square of the distance between them." Gravity provides the force that holds the planets in orbit around the sun and the moons around the planets.

What Newton accomplished was a mathematical description of the force that holds the planets and other members of the solar system in their orbits. He also answered for modern scientists the question "Does the earth move?" Yes it does, because the force of gravity causes a lighter body, such as the earth, to orbit a more massive body, such as the sun. To say that the sun orbits the earth is to contradict the theory of gravity and all the observations that support it.

1A-11 *Newton pondering the nature of the force that causes objects to fall to the ground*

Section Review Questions 1A-2

1. What positions do the sun, moon, earth, planets, and stars occupy according to the heliocentric theory?
2. Who was the first person to seriously question the accuracy of the geocentric theory?
3. How did Copernicus explain why birds in flight would not be left behind if the earth is rotating?
4. In his book *The Revolutions,* how did Copernicus answer the skeptics' argument that if the earth revolved around the sun, the nearer stars would seem to shift their positions among the more distant stars?
5. Who developed the three laws of planetary motion?
6. What observations did Galileo make of Venus, Saturn, and Jupiter with his new invention, the telescope?
7. Who developed the law of gravitation?
8. Why did the Roman Catholic church oppose the heliocentric theory?
9. Who claimed he could harmonize the science of the ancient Greek philosophers with Christianity?
10. Why was Kepler not satisfied with the circle he calculated to fit most of the observed locations of Mars?

1B–Evidence That the Earth Moves

The earth's motion has two components. It **rotates** on its **axis,** the imaginary line about which the earth is spinning, and it **revolves** around the sun in its orbit. Scientists can prove both motions from their observations.

Rotation

Many observations show that the earth is rotating. The sun, moon, planets, and stars rise in the east and set in the west because the earth rotates. Moreover, observers in the Northern Hemisphere see the northern stars move counterclockwise in circles centered on the North Star. Yet, these observations can be explained not only by a rotating earth but also by a stationary earth with a movable sky. In contrast to these evidences, the following evidences can be explained *only* by a rotating earth.

1B-1 *The setting of the sun in the west indicates that something is moving, but is it the earth or the sky?*

The earth's bulging shape is evidence of its motion. Because it is slightly flattened at the poles and bulged at the equator, the distance through the earth at its equator is 12,760 km (7,930 mi.), but from one pole to the other is only 12,720 km (7,900 mi.). Other planets also have bulging shapes. Jupiter and Saturn, the fastest-spinning planets, show this bulging effect most. Even through a small telescope the casual observer can notice that these planets are not round. On the other hand, Mercury and Venus, the planets that spin the slowest, are the most nearly spherical. Physicists explain this effect by the tendency of matter to keep moving in the same direction. This tendency is called **inertia** (in UR shuh). If the matter making up the planet were not held in place by the planet's gravity, it would fly out from the rotating planet like mud from a spinning wheel. The planet's surface is moving fastest at its equator where its matter bulges out against the inward pull of gravity. The earth's bulge at its equator can be explained by its rotation.

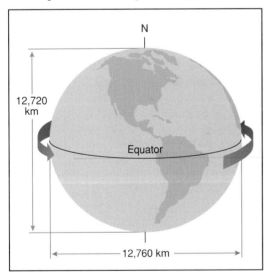

1B-2 *The bulging shape of the earth is shown somewhat exaggerated in this drawing. The earth is 40 km "wider" than it is "high."*

Another evidence of the earth's rotation comes from its wind patterns. If the earth were not spinning, the wind patterns would be much simpler. The heated air at the equator would move toward the poles, and the cold air from the higher latitudes would move back toward the equator. The motion would be straight north and south. However, we actually observe a diagonal wind pattern because the earth's rotation deflects the wind.

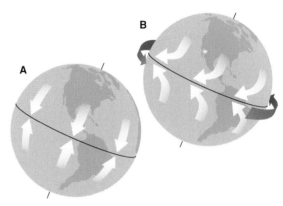

1B-3 (a) *If the earth were not rotating, the wind on the earth's surface would travel directly to the equator from the poles. (b) We actually see a diagonal wind pattern because the earth's rotation deflects the wind.*

Bullets, cannonballs, missiles, and even spacecraft experience the same deflection that affects the wind. Unless the launchers make allowance for this deflection, any of these projectiles may miss its target. This deflection occurs because the surface of the earth moves at different speeds at different latitudes. Suppose your target is on the equator. In twenty-four hours it would move the length of the earth's circumference—40,200 km (25,000 mi.). Its speed is therefore about 1,700 km/hr. (1,000 mph). If you are located at 35° N latitude, your speed is 1,400 km/hr. (870 mph). Your target is moving faster than you are. Unless you fire the missile ahead of your target, you will miss it. The deflection

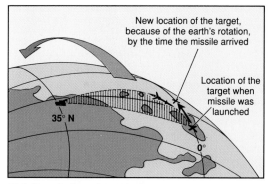

1B-4 *If a missile at 35° N is fired directly at a target on the equator, it will miss its target.*

of projectiles and winds show that the earth is rotating.

An important evidence of the earth's rotation is the behavior of a **Foucault** (foo KOH) **pendulum** (PEN juh lum). This special kind of pendulum was named for the French physicist Jean Foucault (1819–68), who made the first one in 1851. Foucault hung a 60-m (200-ft.) wire inside the dome of the famous Pantheon building in Paris. At the end of the wire, he attached a 25-kg (55-lb.) iron ball. Within a few minutes after he started the ball swinging back and forth,

1B-5 *A Foucault pendulum's direction of swing will appear to change; however, it is actually the earth which has moved beneath the pendulum.*

those who were watching could see that the direction of its swing was changing. By that time scientists knew the principle of inertia, that a moving object keeps moving in the same direction unless an outside force acts on it. Foucault had hung his wire by a single-point suspension so that no outside force could act on the pendulum. Thus the pendulum's swing could not be changing; the earth had to be turning while the pendulum continued swinging in the same direction.

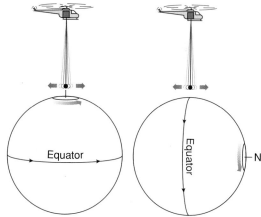

1B-6 *A Foucault pendulum appears to swing differently at the North Pole than at the equator, but it is actually the earth-bound observer's movements that are different.*

You probably can understand the Foucault pendulum better if you picture it set up at one of the poles. Imagine the pendulum hanging from a helicopter that is hovering directly over the North Pole. As the pendulum continues to swing back and forth in the same direction, the earth turns under it at the rate of 15° per hour. After six hours the earth has turned through a right angle. After twenty-four hours the earth has turned 360°, one complete rotation.

If you tried this same experiment at the equator, the pendulum would not turn. If the helicopter stayed over the same spot on the earth, you would notice no change. However,

the helicopter would be traveling at the same rate the earth is turning. As you move away from the equator with a Foucault pendulum, you start to notice the earth's turning. This effect grows until it reaches a maximum at the poles. The Foucault pendulum is probably the most spectacular demonstration of the earth's rotation. Planetariums and museums often include a Foucault pendulum.

1B-7 *A view from* Apollo 11 *as it orbited the moon. Astronauts saw the earth rotating.*

Finally, we know by direct observation that the earth is rotating. Astronauts on the moon saw the earth's entire surface in each twenty-four-hour day. The moon does not revolve around the earth once each day. The earth must therefore be rotating.

Section Review Questions 1B-1
1. What is the tendency of matter to keep moving in the same direction called?
2. What aspect of the earth's shape is evidence of its rotation?
3. World wind patterns and the paths of projectiles are evidence of what type of earth movement?
4. What type of pendulum is used to demonstrate the earth's rotation?
5. What is the most recent evidence that shows the earth's rotation?

Revolution

For the earth's revolution, as well as for its rotation, there are two kinds of evidence: evidence that can be explained either by the earth's moving or by the sun's moving and evidence that can be explained only by the earth's moving. Evidences that can be explained by either the geocentric or the heliocentric theory include the sun's apparent path through the stars and the earth's seasons.

The sun changes its position among the stars throughout the year. We cannot see which stars are around the sun because we cannot see the stars in the daytime. However, if we observe a particular star carefully, we notice that it rises above the eastern horizon about four minutes earlier each evening. If we could observe the stars in relation to the sun, we would see that the sun appears to move slowly along a path through the stars. After a year the sun returns to the same place

relative to the stars. This apparent path of the sun among the stars is called the **ecliptic** (ih KLIP tik). It can be explained by our changing point of view on the moving earth. You can see how this works by walking around a campfire. You see the fire against a changing background as you walk around the fire. Similarly, we see the sun from the moving earth against the changing background of the stars.

How does the earth's orbit produce seasons? Are we closer to the sun in the summertime? If distance to the sun causes seasons, both the Northern and Southern Hemispheres would have summer in January when the earth is closest to the sun. Then why are the coldest months in the Northern Hemisphere when the earth is nearest the sun?

1B-8 *Because of the earth's motion along its orbit, the sun seems to move along a path through the stars called the ecliptic.*

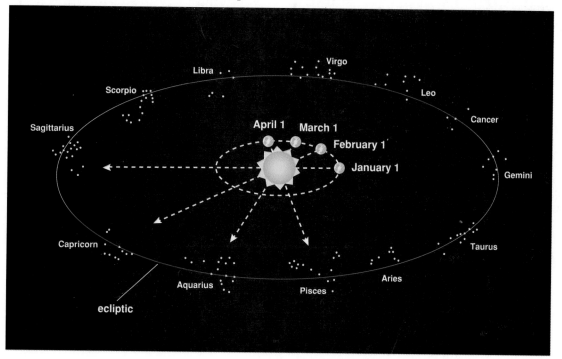

1B-9 *When the sun's rays are direct, the sun's energy is more concentrated and less of it is lost as the rays pass a shorter distance through the earth's atmosphere.*

You probably know that the number of hours of daylight is greater in the summer, and you may have noticed that the sun is higher in the sky in the summertime. There are three reasons it is warmer in the summer: First, because of the greater number of daylight hours, the earth has more time each day to absorb the sun's heat. Second, because the direct rays of the sun are more concentrated, the amount of energy per square kilometer is greater. Finally, the direct rays of the sun lose less energy to the atmosphere as they pass a shorter distance through the atmosphere to the earth.

Both the longer days and the change in the sun's position in the sky are caused by the earth's tilt and revolution. The earth's axis is always tilted at the same angle, $23\frac{1}{2}°$ from vertical. The north end of the axis, the North Pole, always points toward the North Star,

1B-10 *In the Northern Hemisphere, the number of daylight hours is greatest when the north pole tilts toward the sun.*

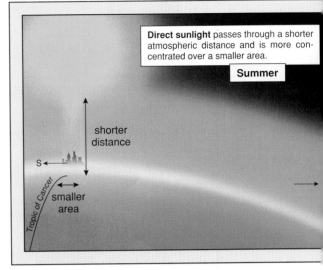

Direct sunlight passes through a shorter atmospheric distance and is more concentrated over a smaller area.

Summer

shorter distance

smaller area

no matter where in its orbit the earth may be. In the Northern Hemisphere's summer, the North Pole tilts toward the sun. In the Northern Hemisphere's winter, the North Pole tilts away from the sun. As seen in Figure 1B-11, the tilt of the earth's axis affects the directness of the sun's light striking the earth.

The sun appears to move north and south as well as around the earth. This motion is

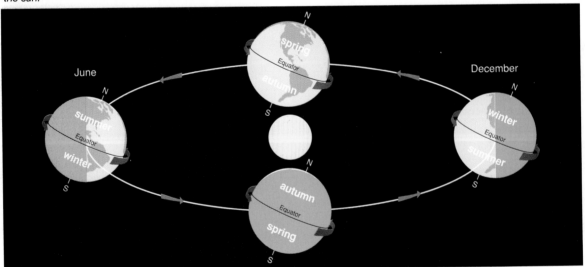

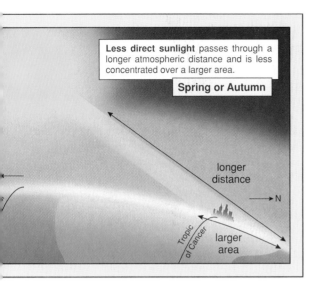

related to the earth's tilt. About June 21, when the North Pole tilts toward the sun, the sun appears to be standing still. It is directly over the **Tropic of Cancer,** an imaginary line on the earth's surface at $23\frac{1}{2}°$ N latitude. This event is called **summer solstice.*** The sun then appears to move southward until about December 21, when the South Pole tilts toward the sun. The sun again appears to

stop, this time directly over the **Tropic of Capricorn,** an imaginary line at $23\frac{1}{2}°$ S latitude. After this **winter solstice,** the sun appears to move northward.

Midway between each pair of solstices is a day in which the number of daylight and dark hours are about equal. On this day, the sun is directly over the equator. These days are called **equinoxes.*** The spring or **vernal equinox** occurs around March 21, and the fall or **autumnal equinox** occurs around September 22. These dates may vary by a day because of leap year. The terms *solstice* and *equinox* can refer to the dates or to the apparent position of the sun in the sky.

The seasons are evidences of the earth's revolution, but they are not conclusive. The earth's revolution is not easy to demonstrate. Science did not progress to the point where it could prove the earth's revolution until the 1800s. However, with the aid of more powerful telescopes, the heliocentric theory

1B-11 *The sun's rays strike the summertime hemisphere more directly. The longest day in the Northern Hemisphere occurs on the summer solstice when the sun is directly over the Tropic of Cancer.*

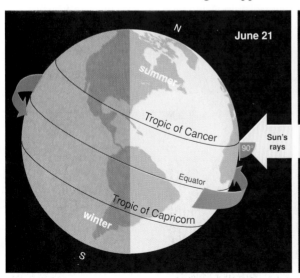
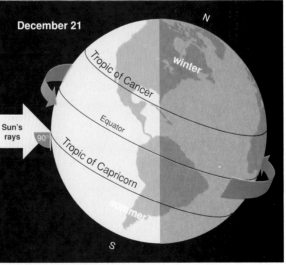

solstice: sol- (L. SOL, sun) + -stice (L. SISTERE, to stand)

equinox: equi- (L. AEQUUS, equal) + -nox (L. NOX, night)

FACETS OF ASTRONOMY

Calendars

The earliest timepiece was the earth itself. When the Bible says, "The evening and the morning were the first day" (Gen. 1:5), it is using the earth to reckon time. The day is an important time unit for us. Most of our short-term plans are based on days; for example, you may plan to practice basketball tomorrow or bake a cake three days from now. God set aside one day in seven for rest and worship.

For longer plans, you need a longer unit, the week. Your schedule is based on the week. You go to school five days each week, your church may have services on two days of each week, and so on. Your teacher may plan an earth science test for a week from Friday.

A third time unit comes from the changes in the appearance of the moon. About every thirty days the cycle of changes begins

again. This unit is called the month, which comes from the word *moon*. Another cycle we can use to reckon time is the seasons: spring, summer, fall, and winter. One cycle of seasons is called a year, and it marks the time that is required for the earth to orbit the sun once. Ancient astronomers noticed that a year is about twelve months. They devised a schedule called a *calendar* to keep track of the years.

The first calendars had 12 months of 30 days each, for a total of 360 days. They usually started in spring and ended in winter. Astronomers soon found that their calendars did not reflect the sun's and the moon's motions accurately. The moon really needs only $29\frac{1}{2}$ days to complete its phase cycle, so the month was a little long. Instead of beginning at new moon, a month began $\frac{1}{2}$ day late, the next began 1 day late, and by the end of the year

the month was starting 6 days later than it should. Furthermore, the earth actually orbits the sun in about $365\frac{1}{4}$ days, so the year was too short. The new year thus began about 5 days too early. The next year began 10 days early, the next 15, and soon the months were in the wrong season. Astronomers found three different ways to correct the calendar.

The first way to solve the problem was to ignore the solar year and concentrate on the moon's changes. Moslems chose this solution and produced a **lunar** (moon) **calendar.** This calendar has 12 months. Half the months have 29 days, and the other half have 30 days, for a total of 354 days. The months correspond to the moon's cycle, but not to any particular season. The same month in different years will be in different seasons.

Another solution is to consider both the solar year and the lunar

month. The Hebrew calendar is such a **lunisolar** (moon-sun) **calendar.** It has 6 months with 29 days and 6 months with 30 days, like the lunar calendar. To keep in step with the sun, every few years it includes an extra 29-day month. Thus the months reflect the moon's cycle and yet remain in the same season.

The third solution to the problem is to ignore the moon's cycle and adjust the calendar to the solar year. All nations now use this **solar** (sun) **calendar** for government business. Our current calendar is descended from this Roman calendar. In the first century B.C. Julius Caesar reorganized the Roman calendar. The calendar originally had 365 days each year, a little less than the solar year. Caesar added an extra day every four years to make a **leap year** and keep the calendar in

step with the seasons. His calendar had 12 months with 30 or 31 days: Januarius (31), Februarius (30), Martius (31), Aprilis (30), Maius (31), Junius (30), Quinctilis (30), Sextilis (30), September (30), October (31), November (30), and December (31).

The next Caesar, Augustus, modified the calendar. Augustus changed the name of Quinctilis to Julius to honor Julius Caesar and the name of Sextilis to Augustus to honor himself. To make these months as long as the longest months, he took two days from Februarius and gave one to each renamed month. This Julian calendar, was used in Europe for the next fifteen centuries.

The Julian calendar was a little too long; the solar year is shorter

by three days every four centuries. By the time of Pope Gregory XIII the calendar was beginning 10 days late each year. The vernal equinox was in April rather than March, and the dates of church holidays no longer corresponded to the earth's motion as they had in the past. The pope corrected the problem in 1582 by advancing the date by 10 days. He prevented future problems by leaving out three leap years every four centuries. Now century years (1900, 2000, 2100, etc.) are leap years only if they are evenly divisible by 400. Thus the years 1900 and 2100 are not leap years, but 2000 is. Our current calendar is this Gregorian calendar.

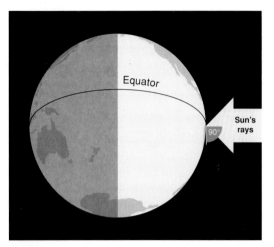

1B-12 *On the autumnal and vernal equinoxes the sun's rays are directly over the equator.*

gained the much needed scientific evidence for conclusive support.

One evidence of the earth's revolution that can be explained by only the heliocentric theory is the **parallax** of stars, the apparent shift of nearby stars among farther stars as the earth's position around the sun changes. Have you ever noticed that your sighting of a pencil against the far side of a room seems to shift when you sight it with one eye and then the other? This shifting demonstrates the parallax effect. The difference is caused by the distance between your eyes.

For many years, skeptics refused to believe that the earth revolves around the sun because they could observe no parallax for the nearby stars. After all, they said, if our locations on opposite sides of our orbit are really 300 million km (186 million mi.) apart, we should be able to see some change in position, at least for the closest stars. But the skeptics had not realized how far away the stars are and thus how small the effect is.

Because of the enormous distance to the stars, you need a powerful telescope to observe the shift. Not until the 1800s was a

strong enough telescope developed. Friedrich Bessel (1784–1846), a German mathematician, first discovered a star's parallax in 1838. The star he observed was 61 Cygni, a star approximately 106 trillion km (66 trillion mi.) from the earth. Since Bessel's time, parallaxes have been observed for about six thousand stars. If the earth is not revolving, we must somehow explain why each of these stars moves back and forth in exactly one year.

1B-13 *When sighting a pencil against the far side of a room, the pencil seems to shift position when sighted first with one eye, then with the other. This effect is called parallax.*

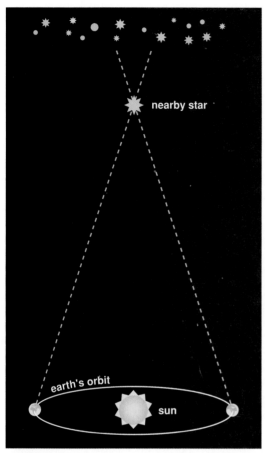

1B-14 *Parallax of a nearby star—when viewed through a telescope the position of a nearby star in relation to the background stars appears to shift as the earth moves along its orbit.*

Another evidence that the earth is revolving is that meteors are generally brighter and more plentiful after midnight than before midnight. This difference stems from the fact that an observer after midnight is on the leading side of the earth as it races through its orbit. That there should be more collisions on the "front" side than on the "back" side of the earth is only logical. When you drive through the rain, you observe more raindrops hitting the windshield than the rear window, especially if the car is going fast. So it is with the earth. Meteors bombard the earth more frequently on its forward side. If the earth were stationary, this observation would be difficult to explain.

Whenever an astronomer makes measurements, he must know the nature of his vantage point. We have seen in this chapter evidences that an earth-based astronomer works from a moving vantage point—one that is both spinning and traveling through space. An observer's vantage point produces important effects on his opinion of what he observes.

Section Review Questions 1B-2

1. At what season of the year in the Northern Hemisphere is the earth the closest in its approach to the sun?
2. List three reasons that summer is warmer than winter.
3. How much is the earth tilted?
4. What is the meaning of the word *equinox? solstice?*
5. An apparent shift in position of background objects due to a change in viewing position is called by what name?
6. What are two observations that are difficult to explain if the earth is not revolving around the sun?

Chapter 1B

Terms

autumnal equinox
axis
Copernican theory
deferent
eccentric
ecliptic
epicycle
equinox
Foucault pendulum

geocentric theory
heliocentric theory
inertia
law of gravitation
leap year
lunar calendar
lunisolar calendar
model
parallax

Ptolemaic theory
revolve
rotate
solar calendar
summer solstice
Tropic of Cancer
Tropic of Capricorn
vernal equinox
winter solstice

What Did You Learn?

1. How did the development of more accurate methods of observing the heavens affect the acceptance of the heliocentric theory?
2. What is exemplary about Kepler's life and work?
3. Who wrote *The Revolutions* and why was it important?
4. Explain why the earth's tilt causes the seasons.
5. How does the Gregorian calendar differ from the Julian calendar?
6. How does the Moslem calendar work?

What Do You Think?

1. On most maps the shortest distance from Rome, Italy, to New York City appears to be a straight line near and parallel to 40° N latitude. However, the shortest route from Rome to New York is actually through the middle of France, over the North Atlantic, past Newfoundland, through Nova Scotia, and then to New York. Why is this curved route shorter than a straight line?
2. The heliocentric theory is generally accepted as fact today but was at first ridiculed. Many currently accepted facts were at first unpopular. Likewise, many readily accepted ideas were later proved false. How should a Christian react to new ideas?
3. Suppose the earth rotated slower than it does now. Other than longer days and nights, what else would be different on the earth?
4. Suppose the earth's axis was tilted 30° instead of $23\frac{1}{2}°$. What effect would this have on seasons, lengths of days, deflection of winds, position of the Tropics of Cancer and Capricorn, and dates of solstices and equinoxes?

THE GLORY OF THE STARS

TWO

2A-Tools for Studying the Stars

On a clear night the unaided eye can see thousands of stars. The telescope seems the obvious tool to use to study astronomy. However, many other instruments have been used by both ancient and modern astronomers. With the variety of tools available, astronomers can record and measure position, distance, movement, composition, size, shape, color, brightness, and temperature.

Early Methods

History does not tell us of the people who first studied the stars and grouped them into patterns called **constellations.*** Soon after creation men must have realized the need to study the heavens. Constellations are mentioned in the book of Job (38:31-32), which many scholars believe is one of the earliest books written in the Bible. The Greeks were

---

constellation: con- (L. COM-, together) + -stellation (L. STELLA, star)

familiar with similar constellations. Homer's *Odyssey*, written about 800 B.C., mentions that Ulysses navigated his ship homeward by observing constellations. He gazed ''with fixed eye on the Pleiades, on Bootes setting late, and on the Larger Bear.'' Apparently the constellations were common knowledge to ancient peoples. A knowledge of the heavens was necessary in order to guide travelers and to keep accurate calendars.

Ancient astronomers developed several devices to help them determine the position and motion of the heavenly bodies. One of these old devices, the **gnomon** (NOH mun), cast shadows in sunlight. The gnomon was an upright pole, a column of stones, a pyramid, or a tall stone pillar. Astronomers used the daily movement of the gnomon's shadow to estimate the time of day and the changes in the length of the shadow to estimate the time of year. The instrument thus served as a crude clock and calendar and gave astronomers their first opportunity to judge the mo-

2A-1 *This eighteenth-century, state-of-the-art sundial was used on a ship. The compass was used to adjust the sundial's position. The projecting pin is the gnomon.*

tion of the sun and stars. Later astronomers added a numbered dial to the gnomon to make a sundial.

Astronomers used many instruments that helped them locate the stars or the sun by sighting along fixed points. Early sighting

2A-2 *At the summer solstice, the sun rises above a pointed rock framed by the massive pillars of Stonehenge.*

"instruments" included natural features such as mountain peaks as well as stones or buildings set up to align with a star or the sun at a particular time of year. Primitive observatories often were set up to view the sun at the beginning instant of summer or winter (at the summer or winter solstice). Stonehenge, a ring of stones in England, is apparently an observatory for determining the summer solstice. Later instruments included scales to measure a star's position. The **quadrant** (KWAHD runt) used a dial and a movable

2A-3 *Quadrants were used to read the angle a star made with the horizons.*

sight. When an astronomer had sighted a star, he could read from the dial the angle it made with the horizon.

Clocks were also important to ancient astronomers. Most people used the sun to measure time, but astronomers wanted to time the sun's motion. The first clocks that did not rely on the sun included water clocks and sand clocks (hourglasses). These measured the time by the amount of water or sand that had flowed through a hole. Candles of uniform size measured time by the amount that the candle shortened. These clocks were inaccurate because the water and sand did not flow at a constant rate, and the candles did not burn at a constant rate. Nevertheless, these clocks gave ancient astronomers some idea of the stars' and planets' rates of motion.

Ptolemy, a Greek astronomer of the second century A.D., recorded the observations of astronomers who used such equipment. His thirteen-volume work, called the *Almagest* (AL muh JEST), included a two-volume cat-

alogue of the stars. This was the main reference work for almost fifteen hundred years and was used by such great astronomers as Nicolaus Copernicus and Tycho Brahe.

The great Danish astronomer Tycho Brahe was probably the best pre-telescope observer. He equipped his observatory, Uraniborg, with instruments to plot the positions and movements of the sun, moon, comets, and planets. These instruments and his powers of observation combined to make his measurements extremely accurate. Tycho died in 1601, eight years before Galileo pointed his first telescope toward the heavens.

2A-4 *Water clocks were among the first clocks that did not rely on the sun.*

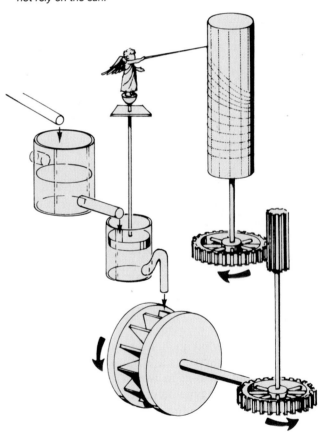

2A-5 *At his palatial observatory on the isle of Hveen, Tycho and his assistants used the most up-to-date instruments to record remarkably precise observations of the positions of stars and planets.*

Section Review Questions 2A-1

1. Who were the first people who studied the stars and grouped them into patterns called constellations?
2. What two assets did a knowledge of the heavens give to early civilizations?
3. What was the name given to an early device that was used to cast shadows in sunlight?
4. What was the above instrument called when a numbered dial was added?
5. What early work used by Copernicus and Tycho contained a catalogue of stars? Who was the author?

Telescopes

Refracting Telescopes

Roger Bacon (1214–94) was one of the first to investigate the use of lenses. By the 1300s, spectacles were available in Italy. The first telescopes began to appear in Holland in 1608, probably as a result of the work of Jan Lippershey, a Dutch spectacle maker. He discovered that two lenses, when placed appropriate distances apart, made objects appear to be much closer. He envisioned the telescope as a military aid, but not for astronomical use.

Galileo Galilei was the first astronomer to build a telescope for viewing the heavens.

His telescope consisted of two lenses, one mounted at each end of a tube that could adjust to focus the image. It was a **refractor* telescope** because it used only lenses to magnify an image. The lenses on the refractor telescope bend light from a star to make it appear larger and closer. The first lens refracts the light from the star to make a small image, and the second lens magnifies that image. Thus, the refractor telescope is a combination of a light-gathering lens (objective lens) and a magnifying lens (eyepiece). Astronomers use the diameter of the refractor's objective lens to indicate its size. The largest refractor telescope in the world is the 102-cm (40-in.) telescope at the Yerkes Observatory at Williams Bay, Wisconsin.

While light gathering and magnification are two important functions of a telescope, a third function is also of importance. **Resolution** is the ability of a telescope to bring out details in an image. This is determined by the quality of the glass and the degree to which the lenses or mirrors are accurately ground. Many "stars" that our eye sees as one star are really two, three, or even large groups of stars. A good telescope can resolve them

2A-6 *Galileo demonstrates one of his telescopes* (left). *The long telescope* (below) *built by Galileo can magnify 20×.*

refract: re- (L. RE-, back) + -fract (L. FRANGERE, to break)

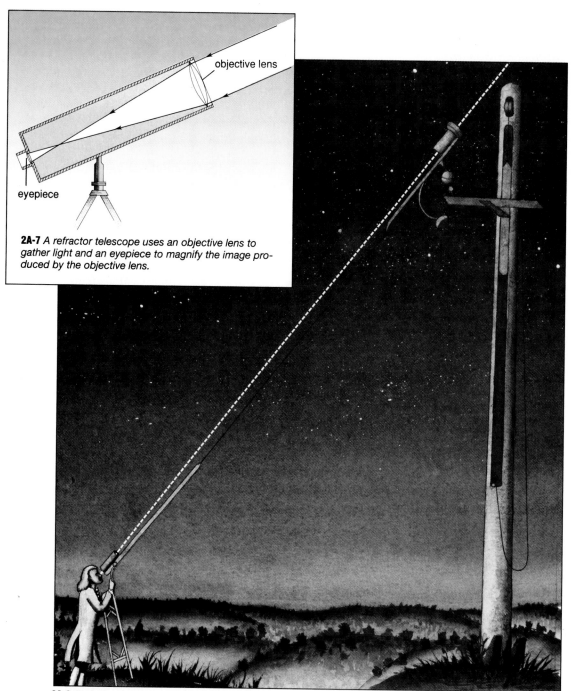

2A-7 *A refractor telescope uses an objective lens to gather light and an eyepiece to magnify the image produced by the objective lens.*

2A-8 *Christian Huygens, nearly fifty years after Galileo, built a tubeless telescope that was 123 feet long. He discovered the rings of Saturn with it.*

2A-9 *The world's largest refractor, with a 40-in. objective, is located at Yerkes Observatory in Williams Bay, Wisconsin. Because of the weight of the objective lens, a refracting telescope larger than this would not be practical.*

into individual stars; a poor telescope may make the image large, but it will still look like only one star.

The news of Galileo's instrument quickly spread across Europe, and many scientists began making telescopes. They found ways to make telescopes with greater magnifications. As they obtained greater magnification, however, they found a serious problem with refractors: the lenses produced a distortion of color around the image. For example, often a false halo of orange and yellow surrounded a white object. This color distortion was called **chromatic* aberration,*†** false color.

An early solution to the problem of chromatic aberration used thin objective lenses that did not bend the light enough to cause much distortion of color. These thin lenses required long telescopes—as long as 61 m (200 ft.). Some telescopes had no tubes, only the two lenses on pole supports. This allowed the telescope to be very long without being very expensive.

Early observers did not know why white light coming through a lens should produce colors. Then Sir Isaac Newton discovered that white light is made up of various colors. Each color has a different wavelength and a slightly different angle of refraction. Instead of refracting to the same point, these colors bend so that each focuses at a slightly different point. The result is chromatic aberration around the magnified image. Modern refractors avoid chromatic aberration by using special compound lenses that focus all the colors at the same point.

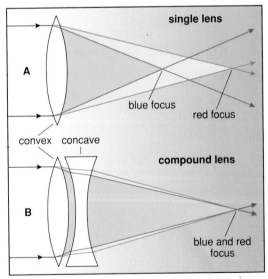

2A-10 (a) *Chromatic abberation occurs when various colors of light are refracted differently.* (b) *The unequal refraction can be corrected with an additional concave lens.*

---

chromatic: (Gk. KHROMA, color)
aberration: ab- (L. AB-, from) +
-erration (L. ERRARE, to stray)

† Spherical aberration is a problem of both lenses and mirrors. Flaws in the curvature cause rays to be focused at different points. This causes fuzzy images.

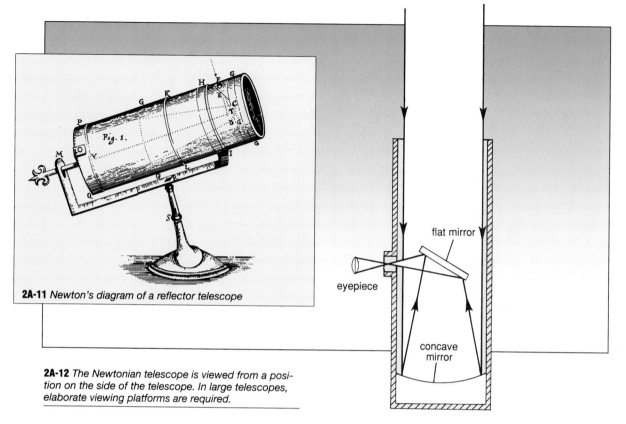

2A-11 *Newton's diagram of a reflector telescope*

flat mirror

eyepiece

concave mirror

2A-12 *The Newtonian telescope is viewed from a position on the side of the telescope. In large telescopes, elaborate viewing platforms are required.*

Section Review Questions 2A-2

1. Who was the first astronomer to build a telescope for viewing the heavens?
2. What does the word *refract* mean?
3. What are the three functions of a telescope?
4. What does a refractor telescope use to accomplish these three functions?
5. What is the color distortion caused by lenses called?
6. Give two ways to reduce this color distortion.

Reflecting Telescopes

Newton decided to build a telescope that would avoid chromatic aberration by eliminating refraction. In the middle of the eighteenth century, he developed the **reflector telescope,** which replaced the refractor's objective lens with a mirror. His first telescope reflected light from a 2.5-cm (1-in.) concave mirror at the lower end of the tube and formed an image at the upper end of the tube. A flat mirror there reflected the image through a hole in the side of the tube, where the eyepiece magnifiers were attached to receive the image. This arrangement in which the enlarged image is viewed through the side of the tube is called a Newtonian reflector.

Another arrangement that allows for greater magnification is called the Cassegrainian

2A-13 *The Hale Telescope, a 200-in. reflector in California, can be viewed from the Newtonian or Cassegrainian position as well as from a position in a cage within the tube near the top called the prime position.*

(KAS uh GRAY nee un) reflector. Its large concave mirror reflects light to a convex mirror. The convex mirror reflects light back through a hole in the center of the concave mirror. When a Cassegrainian reflector is used, the image can be seen from behind the base of the tube.

The size of a reflector telescope is rated by the diameter of its concave mirror. The large, 5-m (200-in.) Hale telescope on Mount Palomar in California has a concave mirror that alone weighs nearly 16 tons! The Hale telescope was designed so that it can be used as a Newtonian reflector or a Cassegrainian re-

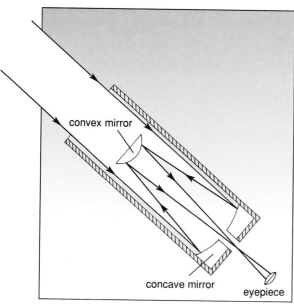

2A-14 *The Cassegrainian telescope allows for viewing from below the telescope and provides the design necessary for a longer focal length.*

flector. This telescope was the ''giant'' of telescopes in the United States until the early 1990s.

The huge telescopes of the 1990s, however, came into being with the development of three basic advances in telescope mirror design. One of these design improvements was the **honeycomb mirror,** first scheduled for use on the Multiple Mirror Telescope Conversion to be located on Mount Hopkins in Arizona. This design uses a process called **spin casting** to produce a mirror over a honeycomb-shaped structure. The molten glass spins in a huge oven, and centrifugal (spinning) force molds the concave shape. This process reduces the costly and time-consuming process of grinding a mirror's surface.

The Keck telescope on Mauna Kea, Hawaii, is a **segmented mirror** that combines thirty-six mirrors that fit together like hexagonal (six-sided) ceramic tiles to make a mirror 10 m (400 in.) in diameter. The mirror segments are monitored by a computer and aligned by special sensors.

The third advance in design was a **meniscus** (muh NIS kus) **mirror** that is so thin that it needs computer-controlled devices called actuators to keep the mirror in the proper

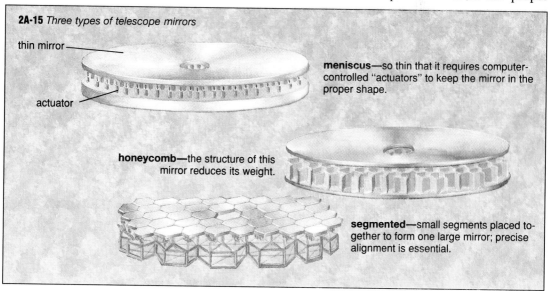

2A-15 *Three types of telescope mirrors*

thin mirror

actuator

meniscus—so thin that it requires computer-controlled "actuators" to keep the mirror in the proper shape.

honeycomb—the structure of this mirror reduces its weight.

segmented—small segments placed together to form one large mirror; precise alignment is essential.

shape. These mirrors rest on a bed of sensor-controlled actuators that constantly push or pull on the mirror. The Very Large Telescope (VLT) of the European Southern Observatory was first scheduled to be constructed with four telescopes, each having an 8-m (312-in.) meniscus mirror, giving the entire telescope the equivalent of one 630-inch mirror.

These advances, along with the advances made in glass production and the discovery of zero expansion glass equivalents in the early 1960s, have provided astronomers with a better view of the heavens than was ever before possible.

2A-16 *The back of a modern honeycomb mirror developed by Itek Optical Systems*

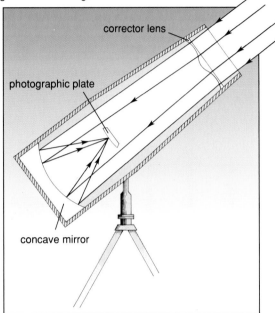

2A-17 *The Schmidt telescope is a composite telescope using both a lens and a mirror. The lens helps correct some of the distortion caused by the mirror, and it also gives the advantage of a wider field of view.*

corrector lens

photographic plate

concave mirror

A twentieth-century innovation is the **composite telescope,** a telescope that uses both mirrors and an objective lens to gather light. One example is the Schmidt telescope, which shows fine detail over a wide field. Astronomers use these to make wide-angle photographs of the heavens. Because large refractors or reflectors have narrow views, astronomers often use a Schmidt telescope for finding objects and a larger reflecting telescope for magnifying the object.

Section Review Questions 2A-3

1. Who developed the reflector telescope?
2. What does the reflector telescope use to accomplish the three functions of a telescope?
3. What type of reflector telescope is viewed from the same position as the refractor?
4. How is the size of a reflecting telescope rated?
5. List the three advances in mirror design that made the giant telescopes of the 1990s possible.
6. A telescope that uses both lenses and mirrors to gather light is called by what name?

Nonoptical Telescopes

So far we have mentioned only optical telescopes, telescopes that use visible light. But stars give out more than visible light; they emit radio waves, infrared waves, ultraviolet rays, x-rays, and gamma rays as well. Our atmosphere blocks most of these emissions, but radio waves can pass through. **Radio telescopes** reflect these waves to a focal point, where a special receiver picks up the desired signals and records their intensity.

An advantage of radio telescopes is that they can be larger than optical telescopes and so can detect fainter stars. While the largest optical telescope is the 10.95-m (35.9-ft.) Keck telescope, the largest single radio telescope is 300 m (1,000 ft.). Furthermore, radio telescopes that are far apart can work together to form a sharper picture of a celestial object.

Another advantage of radio telescopes is that they can send, as well as receive, radio waves. Astronomers use them as "radar" to explore nearby planets.

2A-18 *X-ray telescope prior to installation in a satellite*

2A-19 *The 305-m (1000-ft.) fixed disk radio telescope antenna near Arecibo, Puerto Rico, has its focal point on a truss that can be controlled to steer the beam anywhere within 20° of the zenith.*

Astronomers use instruments to detect other infrared, ultraviolet, x-ray, and gamma radiation as well. These are carried above most of our atmosphere by balloons, aircraft, and rockets. Some satellites carry instruments to detect radiation that our atmosphere blocks. Using all the radiation arriving from a star, astronomers can learn more about it.

Telescope Mounts

The telescope mount is an important part of the telescope. A telescope must be able to move both vertically and horizontally so that it can be pointed in any direction. Early telescopes had **altazimuth*** (al TAZ uh muth) **mounts** with separate controls for horizontal and vertical motions. A large telescope was suspended between two wooden frames, to which pulleys and ropes were attached for raising and lowering the tube, and sometimes the entire frame was on a rotating platform to move the telescope horizontally. Unfortunately, the astronomer had to move the telescope in two motions continually to keep a particular star in view.

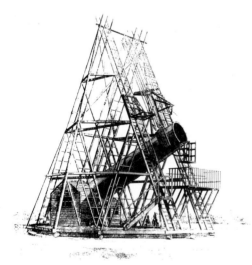

2A-20 *Herschel's altazimuth mount attained altitude by pulleys and azimuth compass direction by rotating the entire structure on rollers under the base.*

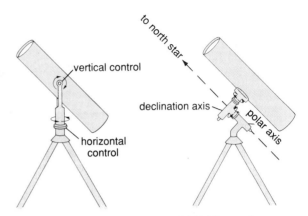

2A-21 *Altazimuth* (left) *and equatorial* (right) *mounts*

The **equatorial mount,** introduced in the early 1800s, was a great improvement. This mount takes advantage of the fact that the heavens appear to rotate around the celestial poles. The supporting shaft points at the nearest pole, and the telescope tube can rotate around this shaft to follow the star. Thus the telescope can follow a star with only one motion. An astronomer can easily turn the tube for a small telescope to follow a star, and for a large telescope the turning can be done by a machine.

Recording Telescope Images

An important accessory for a telescope is a camera. Optical astronomers glean most of their information from black-and-white photographic plates. These have several advantages. Unlike the human eye, photographic plates accumulate a stronger image as light continues to shine on them. Exposures of several hours thus can record images that the eye could never see. As an exposure is being made, the telescope slowly moves with the stars to prevent star streaks on the photographic plate. The camera thus shows faint stars and gives greater detail of faraway objects. Such pictures often require hours and even several successive nights of exposure of an object on the same film.

altazimuth: alt- (*from* altitude) + -azimuth (Arabic AS-SUMUT, the compass bearing)

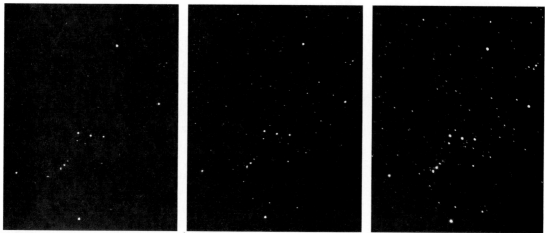

2A-22 *More stars are revealed in the same area of the sky as camera exposure time is increased.*

Photographs not only show dim objects that would be unknown without them, but they also provide an objective record of what an astronomer has seen. The photographic plate can be seen at any time, by any person. Thus several scientists can check an observation. Scientists also can measure celestial objects precisely in a photograph. They can analyze a star's light by using film that is sensitive to a particular color of light. By comparing photographic plates, they can tell how much a star is changing in brightness. These plates can be saved for additional study and comparison.

For radio astronomers, records usually take the form of strip charts or magnetic tapes. Strip charts, or continuous graphs, plot the strength of the radio waves in each part of the sky. Computers can turn this infor-

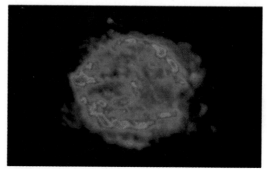

2A-23 *A radio image of Cas A, a supernova remnant in the constellation Cassiopeia*

mation into a picture of the sky for astronomers to compare with photographs. Computers store information magnetically on tapes or disks. These records can be compared with data from other radio telescopes to improve the detail that radio astronomers can discern.

Section Review Questions 2A-4
1. Name a common type of nonoptical telescope in use on the earth today.
2. How can nonoptical telescopes detect the kind of radiation that is filtered out by the atmosphere?
3. List two types of telescope mounts.
4. How are images from optical telescopes most often recorded?
5. How are images from nonoptical telescopes usually recorded?

2B–Mapping the Stars

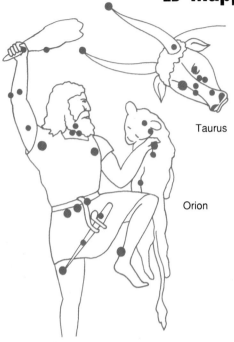

Taurus

Orion

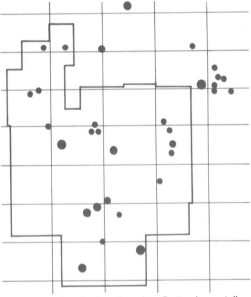

2B-1 *The ancient* (top) *and modern* (bottom) *constellation Orion*

When you want to tell a foreign friend where you live, you can do it in one of two ways. First, you can give the country, state, or city you live in, for example, Dallas, Texas, USA. If your friend is familiar with the country, state, or city, that would be enough for him to be able to locate your home on the globe. However, he might not know where the United States is located on the globe. The second way to say where you live is to give the **latitude** (distance in degrees north or south of the equator) and **longitude** (distance in degrees east or west of Greenwich, England). For example, Dallas, Texas, is at 33° N and 97° W. Then your friend could follow the lines on the globe to find where you live. Similarly, astronomers have two ways of locating stars. They can tell what constellation the star is in, or they can give its coordinates, the astronomical equivalent of latitude and longitude.

Using Constellations

For modern astronomers a constellation is an area in the sky, not a picture imagined from a group of stars. In 1928 astronomers agreed on boundaries for eighty-eight constellations that completely cover the sky. The boundaries are straight lines running north, south, east, and west, and they do not necessarily follow the outline of the ancient constellations.

In 1603 John Bayer introduced an orderly system for identifying particular stars within a constellation. His system is still being used today, although some stars are now in different constellations. Bayer assigned each star a Greek or Roman letter along with the possessive form of its constellation name. Modern astronomers also use numbers because most constellations contain too many stars to fit into Bayer's system.

Bayer began by assigning Greek letters to the most prominent stars. Usually *alpha* (α) is the brightest star in the constellation, *beta* (β) the next brightest, and so on. Thus the brightest star in the constellation Centaurus (sen TAWR us) is Alpha Centauri. Sometimes Bayer relied on position for assigning names to stars. For example, although the star at the lip of the Big Dipper is not the brightest in the constellation Ursa (UR suh) Major, it is a logical star to begin letter assignments. Thus, it is Alpha Ursae Majoris.

Bright or unusual stars may have a proper name as well as the name Bayer gave them. For example, the star at the end of the Big Dipper (in Ursa Major) has the proper name Alkaid (AL kade). It is the seventh star in the Big Dipper pattern, so it corresponds to the seventh letter of the Greek alphabet, *eta* (η). Thus Alkaid is also called Eta Ursae Majoris. Similarly, the star at the end of the Little Dipper (in Ursa Minor) has the proper name Polaris as well as the name Alpha Ursae Minoris (because it is the brightest star in Ursa Minor). The latter name helps astronomers locate the star by telling in what area of the sky—what constellation—the star is found.

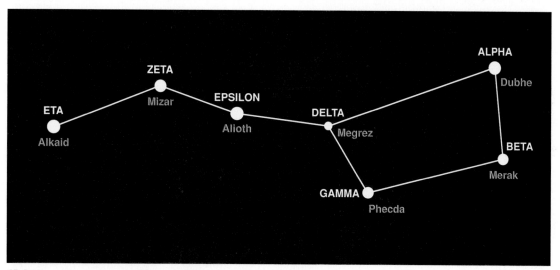

2B-2 *The proper names and Bayer names of the stars in the Big Dipper*

Section Review Questions 2B-1

1. What two methods do astronomers have for describing where in the sky an object may be found?
2. An area in the sky with imaginary boundaries running north, south, east, and west is called by what name?
3. Who introduced an orderly system for identifying particular stars within a constellation?
4. How many constellations are there?
5. How did Bayer generally designate the brightest star in a constellation?
6. What is another name for Eta Ursae Majoris?

Using Coordinates

Star charts, like maps of the earth, have numbered grid lines to show star location. The heavens are divided in half by the **celestial equator,** which is simply the plane of the earth's equator projected into the sky. A star's angular distance north or south of the celestial equator is its **declination.** Astronomers use a plus sign for stars north of the celestial equator and a minus sign for stars south of it. Thus the declination of Hamal (huh MAHL) (Alpha Arietis), 23° north of the celestial equator, is written as +23°.

On earth, longitude is measured in degrees east or west of a line passing through the poles and Greenwich, England. Although a star's **right ascension** corresponds to longitude, there are several differences. First, right ascension is usually given in hours, not degrees. The earth turns 15° each hour, so one hour equals 15°. Second, right ascension is measured only east from its starting line. A star may have a right ascension up to 24 hours (360°). Third, the starting line for right ascension is the **prime hour circle,** a line passing through the celestial poles and a point called the vernal equinox. This line appears to move around the earth each day. Actually, the earth rotates. The earth's motion does not affect the declination or right ascension of a star.

If you know a star's declination and right ascension, you can locate it easily on a star chart. For example, if you were looking for Sirius (SIR ee us) (Alpha Canis Majoris) and knew its location to be –16.7°, 6 hours 44 minutes, you could simply move along the celestial equator on the chart to 6 hours, 44 minutes and move down to –16.7° to locate the star.

Finding the star in the sky is more difficult, since a point's position in the sky changes

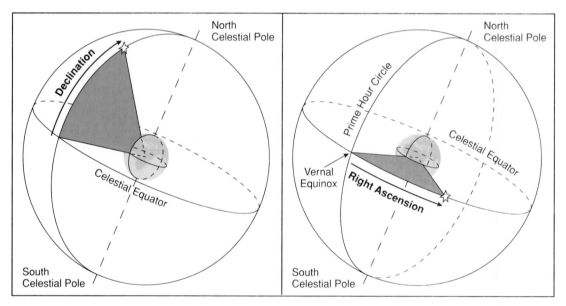

2B-3 *Declination (Dec.): the angular distance between the celestial equator and a celestial object in degrees north or south*

2B-4 *Right ascension (R.A.): the angular distance between the prime hour circle and a celestial object, measured in hours and minutes east of the vernal equinox*

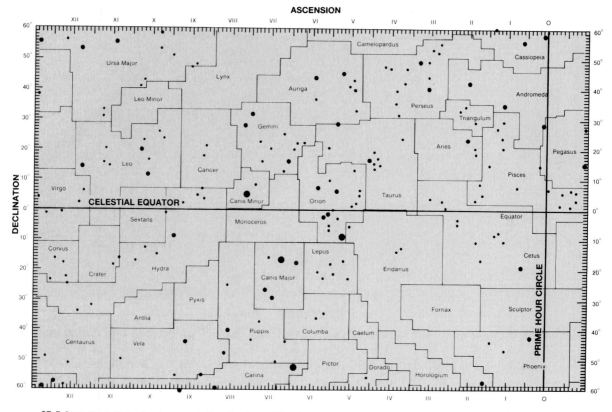

2B-5 *Star chart. This chart covers only a fraction of the sky.*

constantly. The easiest way to locate a star in the sky is to use the constellations. If you can find a star on a chart, the chart will show the star's constellation. You can find its approximate location in the sky by locating its constellation.

Section Review Questions 2B-2

1. Celestial latitude, or the angular distance between the celestial equator and a celestial object in degrees north or south, is called by what other name?
2. What math symbol is used for areas of the sky north of the celestial equator? south?
3. What is the term that refers to celestial longitude? What units is it measured in?
4. As the earth turns one hour, how many degrees does it turn?
5. What is the starting line for right ascension called?

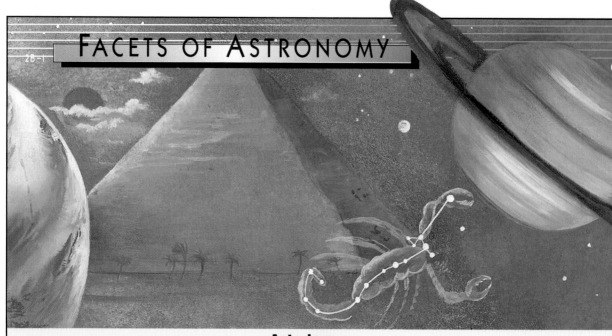

FACETS OF ASTRONOMY

Astrology

Do not confuse astronomy with astrology. Astronomy is a science. Astrology is a superstition closely related to magic and the black arts. Astrology was one of the false religions of the ancients. It flourished in Babylon, Egypt, China, and India as early as 2500 B.C. Its advocates taught that the sun, moon, and stars ruled people and events on earth. To them the earth was at the center of the universe; near the earth the various heavenly bodies gave off positive and negative vibrations that influenced people for good or for evil.

The teaching of astrology suffered a major setback when astronomers discovered the immense distances of these bodies from us. This discovery made nonsense of the claim that they

influence us by vibrations. Our recent studies of the moon and nearby planets show that they contain the same elements as the earth. Why then would their vibrations influence us more than the earth on which we live?

You are probably most familiar with the form of astrology called the horoscope. Daily papers often carry columns in which an astrologer advises readers to "Settle accounts," "Face limitations honestly," "Avoid self-deception," "Play it safe," or "Protect home and family interests." This advice is supposedly tailored to the needs of those born under a particular sign. Astrologers often win over their readers with flatteries, describing the wonderful traits possessed by all those born un-

der a certain sign. Twins born under the same sign would be expected to have the same traits. However, this is easily refuted by citing Jacob and Esau, the twin sons of Isaac, who were as different as night and day.

Astrologers make predictions, usually stated in such a way that they will obviously come true: "You will need patience this week" or "Brighter horizons ahead." Occasionally you will hear about an astrologer making a correct prediction about a famous person. This is usually a coincidence. In many cases, the astrologer, acting as a medium in contact with a spirit guide (demon), is parroting (channeling) what this evil spirit believes must happen in the future. The astrologer is seeking

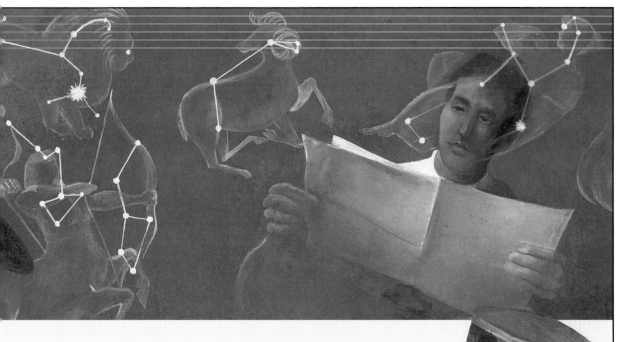

occult (hidden) knowledge. What you do not usually hear about are the hundreds of incorrect predictions made by the same astrologer. We know that such a person is not a prophet of God, for God's man always speaks truth. (See Deut. 18:22.)

The heathen neighbors of Israel were grossly superstitious, interpreting every eclipse or comet as an evil omen of a coming invasion, plague, or other natural calamity. However, God, who created these heavenly bodies, assures His people that there is no cause for alarm. "Be not dismayed at the signs of heaven," He told them in Jeremiah 10:2. If a person has come to a saving knowledge of Jesus Christ, he has the promise from the Creator of the heavens that "all things work together for good" (Rom. 8:28). Instead of the motions of planets and stars, the Christian has the Bible to guide him. It is more sure than the stars, which the Scriptures say are only temporary. "Heaven and earth shall pass away: but my words shall not pass away" (Mark 13:31). The Christian should hold the Bible as his daily guide and trust the Word about the future. Horoscopes are proved by the Scriptures to be false and against God's command. God commands us never to seek knowledge of the future from mediums and channelers (Isa. 8:19-20; Deut. 18:9-15). A Christian should never use them, even for amusement. (See also Isa. 47:13-14 and Deut. 18:9-22.)

2C–Describing the Stars

You can see by looking at the night sky that the stars are different. Some are bright, some are dim. Some are reddish, while others look pure white. We can describe stars by their characteristics as well as by their location.

Ordinary Stars

Star Brightness

One obvious characteristic of the stars is their brightness. The **magnitude** of a star is a measure of its brightness. Hipparchus, the Greek astronomer, established the system of assigning magnitude. He divided the stars into six levels of brightness. The brightest stars were first magnitude, the next brightest were second magnitude, and so on. The sixth magnitude consisted of the faintest stars he could see.

Today, astronomers still use Hipparchus's scale, with changes to make it more precise. Astronomers have divided the scale into smaller parts and added to both ends to describe objects brighter and dimmer than those Hipparchus considered. As they refined the scale, astronomers realized that some stars were too bright to be included with other "first magnitude" stars. They added 0 and negative numbers for brighter stars. For example, Sirius, Vega, and Spica are first magnitude stars according to Hipparchus. In the more precise modern scale, Sirius has a magnitude of –1.4; Vega, +0.04; Spica, +0.96. Sirius is the brightest star in the night sky. Brighter objects include the full moon at a magnitude of –12 and the sun at –27. The faintest objects recorded through telescopes have magnitudes of +25.

Star Distance

Star brightness depends on two things: the amount of light the star emits and its distance from us. Sirius, for example, appears bright because it is near us. Emitting twenty-five times as much light as the sun, Sirius is impressive. Rigel (RY jel), in contrast, appears to be less bright (only +0.08). Rigel emits about fifty thousand times as much light as the sun, but it is so far away that it cannot rival Sirius in our sky. Thus, when we describe a star, we should include its distance as well as its brightness.

Early astronomers thought the stars were much closer than they are. Today we have more accurate measurements, but because the distances are so much greater than anything we have experienced, they are still hard to understand. The stars are so far away that their distances dwarf our ordinary units of length. The nearest star is Proxima Centauri

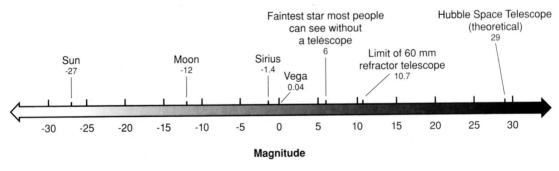

2C-1 *Hipparchus's scale now modified*

(PRAHKS ih mah • sen TAWR ee), one of the three stars in the Alpha Centauri system. It is 40 trillion km (25 trillion mi.) away. Such measurements are cumbersome to work with. Astronomers chose a new unit, the **light-year,** to express the distances to the stars. The light-year is the distance that light travels in a year, about 9.6 trillion km (6 trillion mi.). The nearest star is thus 4.2 light-years away.

"Nearby" suggests longer distances to an astronomer than to most people. Sirius is considered a close neighbor, but it is 8.8 light-years away. Whether a star is near depends on what you compare it to. Sirius is near compared to Rigel, which is 810 light-years away. Rigel is close compared to the Andromeda (an DRAHM uh duh) galaxy, over 2 million light-years away. Some ob-

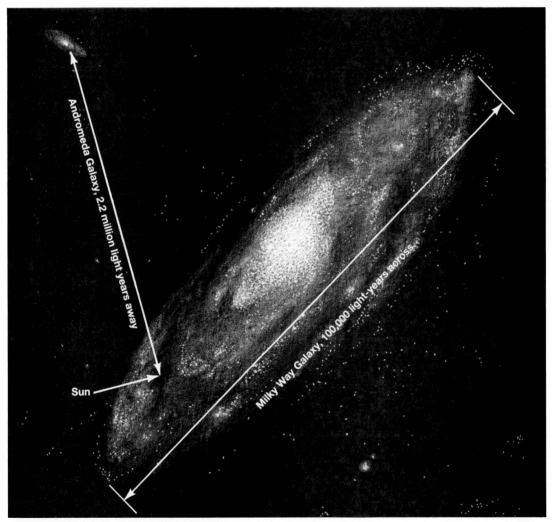

Andromeda Galaxy, 2.2 million light years away

Sun

Milky Way Galaxy, 100,000 light-years across.

2C-2 *A light-year (approximately 9.6 trillion km) is the unit astronomers use to express the great distances to the stars. In this drawing, one light-year is about 0.001 mm.*

jects seem to be billions of light-years away. We can see objects as far away as the Andromeda galaxy only if they are unusually bright. We can calculate the approximate distances to those stars within about 325 light-years by measuring their parallax and using geometry. Astronomers try to estimate the distances to farther stars by analyzing the light from the stars.

Star Motion

Another characteristic of stars is their motion. If a star is moving, perhaps the distance to it and its apparent brightness is changing. How much are the stars moving?

If you look at the stars for several hours, you can see that they change position. The stars appear to circle the earth daily from east to west. A few stars simply rotate around the celestial pole and thus are visible all night. Other stars rise and set like the sun. These motions are actually a result of the earth's rotation. Some stars are visible for only part of the year. If we were to observe a star rising early in the morning before dawn, and then observe it the next morning, we would find that it rises four minutes earlier. This would continue day after day until eventually the star would rise in the evening. If we were to continue our observation, we would find our observations hindered because the star would rise even before dark. As darkness approached each evening, the star would be seen farther to the west each day until it would no longer be visible in the evening. At that point, it would again be visible early in the morning in the east to repeat its cycle.

Do the stars have any real motion? Yes, stars do move. For convenience, astronomers separate a star's real motion into **proper motion,** movement across the sky as we see it, and **radial motion,** movement directly toward or away from us. Proper motions are so small that they are hard to detect. Edmund Halley (HAL ee) was the first man to detect proper motion when he saw that some stars were not in the position that Ptolemy had recorded fifteen hundred years earlier. The largest difference was equal to about twice the distance across the full moon. Since no careful astronomer would make such a large mistake, the stars must have moved. Astronomers now can compare photographs of star groups taken several years apart to see whether any stars have moved.

Radial motion is even harder to detect, since it does not cause the stars to change their positions. Astronomers finally found a way to study radial motion by examining the star's light. By this method they have found that about half the stars in our galaxy are moving toward us and about half are moving away from us. Stars moving toward us have a positive radial motion; those moving away, negative. Almost all other galaxies are moving away from us.

2C-3 *Barnard's star showing proper motion over a period of ten years*

Star Color and Size

As astronomers observed the stars using better instruments, they realized that stars vary greatly in color and size. Some appear blue-white in color, whereas others are white, cream, yellow, orange, and red. The color of a star is the result of its surface temperature. Hotter stars are bluish in color; the cooler stars are red. In general the hotter brighter stars are also larger and denser. However, there are many exceptions. Betelgeuse (BEET el JOOZ), the brightest star in the constellation Orion, is a red star that is five hundred times bigger than the sun. It is sometimes referred to as a *supergiant*. Some very hot, blue-white stars are relatively small. Called *white dwarfs,* they generally have a diameter half to four times the earth's diameter. Though small, these stars are extremely dense, on the average two million times the density of the sun. Sirius has a companion star that is a white dwarf. The variety of stars appears to be limitless, each one different from all the others.

2C-4	Classifying the Stars	
Class†	Color	Surface Temp. (° C)
O	blue	30,000+
B	blue-white	20,000
A	white	11,000
F	yellow-white	7,500
G	yellow	6,000
K	orange	4,200
M	red	3,000

† Each class is subdivided into ten parts, from 0 to 9. Our sun is G2.

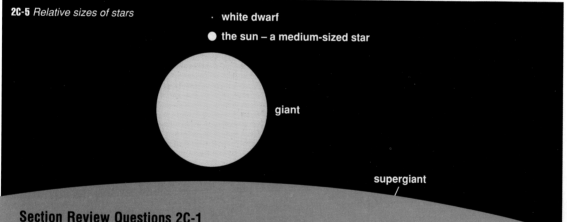

2C-5 *Relative sizes of stars*

white dwarf

the sun – a medium-sized star

giant

supergiant

Section Review Questions 2C-1

1. What is the measure of a star's brightness called?
2. Who devised a scale to rate stars according to their brightness?
3. What do negative numbers on the modern scale used by astronomers indicate about the star's brightness? What do positive numbers indicate?
4. What two things determine a star's apparent brightness?
5. What unit have astronomers chosen to measure the distance to stars?
6. What are the two kinds of motion that describe stars' actual movements?
7. List the different colors that a star may exhibit.

Unusual Stars

Among the vast number of stars of various colors and sizes are some even more unusual stars. As scientists have developed stronger and more sophisticated telescopes, they have discovered that some objects that look like stars are really something quite different. These unusual stars and starlike objects are actually quite common in the night sky.

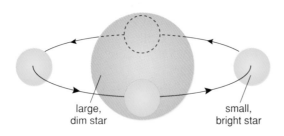

2C-6 *The eclipsing binary Algol. When the stars are side by side, Algol is at its brightest. When the small bright star is behind the large dim star, Algol is at its dimmest.*

large, dim star

small, bright star

Some stars appear to vary in brightness from night to night. Algol (AL GAHL), "eye of the demon," in Perseus (PUR see us) blinks from bright to dim. Algol is actually two stars revolving around each other, one bright and one dim. When the dimmer star is nearer to the earth, Algol is dim. When the stars are side by side, Algol is bright. Variable stars like Algol are **eclipsing binaries.**

Another type of star changes in brightness because it expands and contracts regularly. As the star grows, it emits more light and thus becomes brighter. When it shrinks, it emits less light and becomes dimmer. One star that expands and contracts regularly is Delta Cephei. Other stars like it are called **Cepheid** (SEE fee id) **variables.** The period of these stars—how long they take to go from one bright spurt to the next—is thought to be related to the total amount of light they emit. If an astronomer knows a star's period, he can estimate how much light the star actually emits. Then by comparing the amount of light the star emits to the apparent brightness of the star, he can calculate how far away the star is.

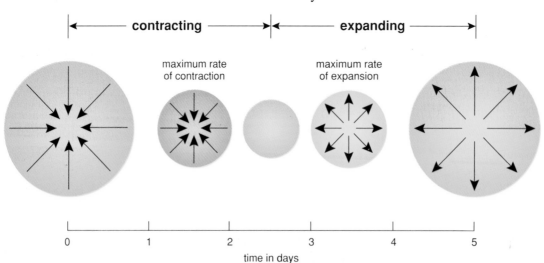

← contracting → ← expanding →

maximum rate of contraction

maximum rate of expansion

0   1   2   3   4   5

time in days

2C-7 *Cepheid variables are brighter while they are expanding and dimmer while they are contracting.*

FACETS OF ASTRONOMY

2C-1

What Is the New Age Movement?

Most local bookstores and record shops have added a new category—the New Age. At first glance, these books and records seem ''nice.'' They claim to help you to relax and meditate. They claim to promote healing and inner peace.

But the New Age movement is overtly anti-Christian. It perverts modern science to spread paganism throughout the world. It cloaks astrology and ancient Eastern mysticism in modern terms. The ''new age'' refers to a phenomenon in astrology— the rise of the constellation Aquarius and the descent of Pisces. The pisces, or fish, symbolizes the age of Christianity. The age of Aquarius, or water, symbolizes a fluid unity of all things. According to astrologers, vibrations from the stars are slowly changing the world to conform to this new age.

New Age writers and musicians believe that everything in the world is *one*. This *oneness* is referred to by such names as the ''cosmic source,'' ''universal energy,'' or a ''force.'' Modern physics teaches that all matter is a manifestation of energy. New Age leaders say that this energy is God; thus we are all manifestations of God. They ar-

gue, against God's Word, that man is basically good but that he fails to reach his potential. In the new age of Aquarius, they believe people will learn to tap into this ''energy'' source. Through a series of techniques, mankind will come into touch with his higher self and develop his highest potential—godhood. The nations of the world will unite in a time of peace and harmony. New Age music and various forms of meditation are just two methods suggested by the New Age movement for people to reach an altered or higher state of consciousness through relaxation and mental ''centering'' or focusing. Those who are in touch with the god

that lies within them can be at unity with their environment and with one another.

Christians must avoid and condemn these ''doctrines of devils'' (I Tim. 4:1). The New Age promotes a false hope of salvation, teaching that man's hope is that he is a sleeping god who needs to be awakened. The Bible teaches that salvation comes by believing that God became man to die for man's sin. In I Corinthians 10:20, Paul plainly says that false worship, no matter how good it sounds, is demonic. He warns us not to have ''fellowship with devils.'' Christians must have nothing to do with the music, books, or ways of this evil movement.†

† See II Corinthians 6:14-17.

2C-8 *Nova Cygni 1975, showing decline in brightness from magnitude 2* (top), *to magnitude 15* (bottom).

Occasionally an astronomer studying the sky will see a star that no one has recorded before. The star will be visible for several months or years; then it will fade away. Such a star is called a **nova*** because astronomers of the past thought that novae were new stars. Recently astronomers studying the light from novae concluded that they were stars that exploded. During a nova explosion a star's brightness may increase ten magnitudes. The star loses only a small percentage of its material in a nova explosion. It returns to normal after the explosion and may explode again later. Thus a star too dim for astronomers to see may become visible during an explosion, then fade away. Sometimes the star may increase its brightness by twenty magnitudes in an explosion that practically destroys the star. This type of exploding star is called a **supernova.** Astronomers can see individual supernovae in distant galaxies. In 1604 astronomers reported a new star that was visible in daylight for a short time. This bright star was probably a nearby supernova.

When a supernova explodes, it is thought to leave behind a cloud of dust and a **neutron star.** This is an extremely dense, small star in which atomic particles (electrons and protons) have combined to form neutrons. Since these neutron stars appear to be spinning rapidly and emitting radio waves at regular intervals, they are often referred to as pulsars.

Section Review Questions 2C-2

1. What is the name given to two stars that revolve around each other so that one star crosses in front of the other?
2. What is the name given to a star that varies in brightness because it expands and contracts regularly?
3. What is the name given to a star that increases in brightness for a few months and then returns to its original brightness?
4. An explosion that nearly destroys a star is called by what name?
5. An extremely dense, small star that is thought to be the remnant of a supernova is called by what name?

nova: (L. NOVUS, new)

Groups of Stars

Some objects in the night sky that look like stars are not. These are often fuzzy rather than clear points of light. Charles Messier, a French astronomer, was concerned that these objects might be confused with new comets. In 1781 he drew up a catalogue of over one hundred of these objects and assigned each a number to identify it. For example, he called a fuzzy spot in Orion "M 42."

Messier's observations were limited by the size of his telescope. He made a few mistakes and, of course, missed many objects his telescopes could not reveal. In 1887 J. L. Dreyer published his first *New General Catalogue,* listing over thirteen thousand objects. Dreyer assigned his own number to each of these objects, and professional astronomers usually use Dreyer's NGC numbers. Thus M 42 is also called NGC 1976. Many objects that Dreyer and Messier catalogued are groups of stars.

Astronomers can tell whether stars that appear to be near each other are in the same group by analyzing their proper and radial motions. If several stars have the same motions, they are a **star cluster.** Open clusters have stars that are relatively far apart. Often we can see several separate stars in a nearby open cluster. The stars in an open cluster may be arranged in any shape. Globular clusters, on the other hand, usually appear to be a single star. A globular cluster is a globe made of thousands of closely spaced stars.

A **galaxy** consists of millions of stars. Our sun is in the Milky Way galaxy, orbiting the galaxy's center as the planets orbit the sun. Although cosmic dust hides the galaxy's center from us, scientists believe the galaxy is a flat disk of stars with extending spiral arms. It rotates in space like a giant pinwheel. Its estimated diameter is 100,000 light-years. Until the 1900s astronomers believed that the Milky Way was the only galaxy. Improved telescopes showed that many of the objects in Dreyer's catalogue are galaxies. Galaxies are classified by their shape: elliptical, spiral, barred spiral, and irregular. Like the Milky Way, the Andromeda galaxy is a large spiral galaxy. Elliptical galaxies are probably the most common. They have shapes ranging from nearly spherical to quite flat, and they have stars that are fairly evenly distributed. Irregular galaxies may have any shape. The two Magellanic clouds in the Southern Hemisphere's sky are irregular galaxies.

2C-9
Open cluster— Abell 5

2C-10 *Globular cluster—M3 (NGC 5272)*

2C-11 *Elliptical, spiral, and barred spiral galaxies*

EXPLORING NEBULAS

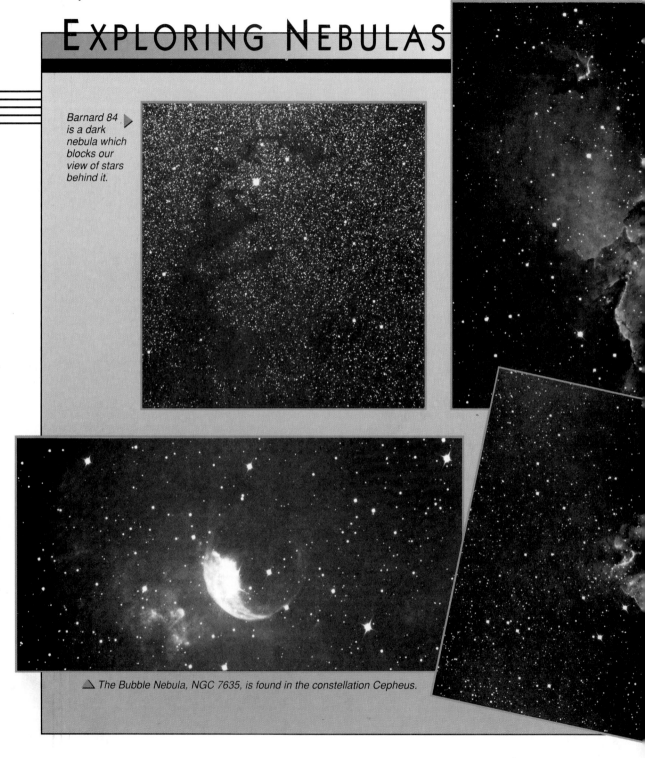

Barnard 84 is a dark nebula which blocks our view of stars behind it.

△ The Bubble Nebula, NGC 7635, is found in the constellation Cepheus.

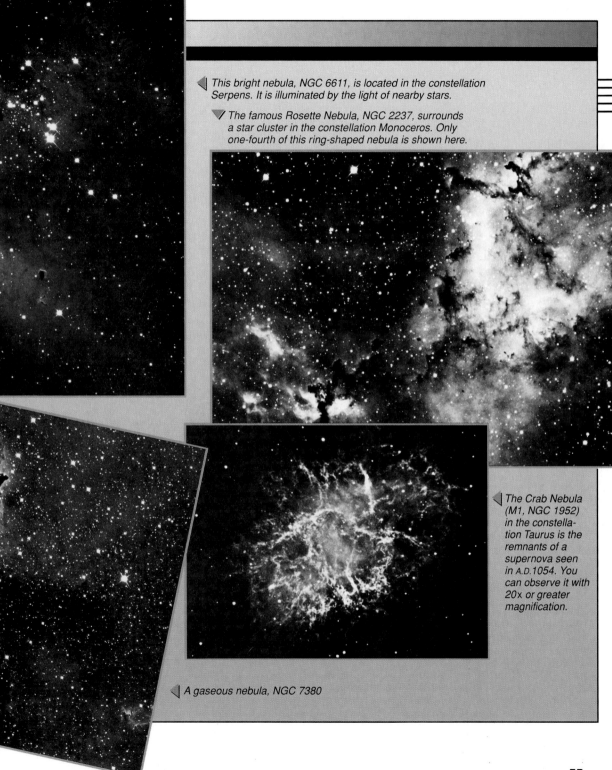

This bright nebula, NGC 6611, is located in the constellation Serpens. It is illuminated by the light of nearby stars.

The famous Rosette Nebula, NGC 2237, surrounds a star cluster in the constellation Monoceros. Only one-fourth of this ring-shaped nebula is shown here.

The Crab Nebula (M1, NGC 1952) in the constellation Taurus is the remnants of a supernova seen in A.D.1054. You can observe it with 20x or greater magnification.

A gaseous nebula, NGC 7380

2C-12 *The Great Nebula of Orion, a bright nebula*

Nebulae

Many of the objects that Messier and Dreyer catalogued are clouds of gas and dust called **nebulae** (NEB yuh LEE). Nebulae can be either bright or dark and, except for planetary nebulae, are irregularly shaped. A bright nebula is near a group of stars whose radiation causes the gas and dust to shine. If the stars are extremely hot, they cause the gases to glow. Nebulae around cooler stars reflect the light of the stars much like the halo around street lights on a foggy night. The Great Nebula of Orion, designated M 42 or NGC 1976, is a bright nebula. Sometimes these nebulae are the remnants of a supernova. The Crab Nebula in Taurus comes from a supernova observed in A.D. 1054. Dark nebulae lack nearby stars to cause them to shine. Astronomers see them because they block the light from the stars behind them. The Northern Coal Sack in Cygnus and the Horsehead Neb-

2C-13 *The Horsehead Nebula, a dark nebula in Orion*

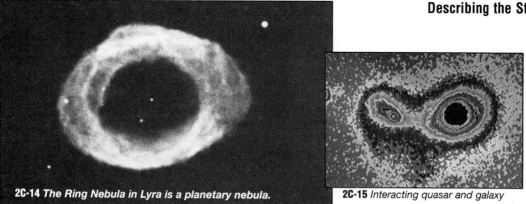

2C-14 *The Ring Nebula in Lyra is a planetary nebula.*

2C-15 *Interacting quasar and galaxy*

ula in Orion are dark nebulae. Planetary nebulae are ring-shaped, disk-shaped, or spherical envelopes of gases that are expanding outward from a central dense hot star. Through a telescope they often look disk-shaped rather than like a point of light. The Ring Nebula in the constellation Lyra is a planetary nebula.

Quasars

Astronomers cannot always explain what an object is. One group of mysterious objects is called quasi-stellar objects, or **quasars** (KWAY ZAR). Radio astronomers discovered strong radio emissions from an area with no bright stars. Working with optical astronomers, they discovered that the emissions came from faint starlike objects. Studying the light from quasars, scientists decided that

they must be moving away from us at astonishing speeds. Most objects that move rapidly away from us are very far away. Thus quasars were thought to be farther away than anything astronomers had found before them. Then scientists began calculating the size of the quasars and found them to be only a few light-years in diameter. A galaxy, thousands of light-years in diameter, would be invisible at the distance the quasars seemed to be. How could a small quasar give off enough light to be seen? Scientists do not agree. Some say that the quasars are closer than their speed would indicate or that their speed has been miscalculated. Others say that the quasars are far away but are more energetic than anything we have encountered so far. Scientists must study quasars more before they can hope to explain what they are.

Section Review Questions 2C-3

1. Who made the first catalogue of celestial objects that did not appear to be stars?
2. Who published the *New General Catalogue?*
3. Stars that have the same motions are called by what general name?
4. List four types of galaxies.
5. Clouds of gas and dust in space are referred to by what name?
6. List the classifications of nebulae.
7. What is the name given to objects that give off strong radio emissions from areas with no bright stars?
8. What major discovery about our solar system and universe caused a major setback for astrology?
9. To what phenomenon in astrology does the ''new age'' refer?

Chapter 2C

Terms

altazimuth mount	latitude	radial motion
celestial equator	light-year	radio telescope
Cepheid variable	longitude	reflector telescope
chromatic aberration	magnitude	refractor telescope
composite telescope	meniscus mirror	resolution
constellation	nebula	right ascension
declination	neutron star	segmented mirror
eclipsing binary	nova	spin casting
equatorial mount	prime hour circle	star cluster
galaxy	proper motion	supernova
gnomon	quadrant	
honeycomb mirror	quasar	

What Did You Learn?

1. Hebrews 1:11 states that the heavens ''shall wax old as doth a garment.'' What evidence of this degeneration can be observed in the heavens?
2. Explain how Newton's reflector solved the problem of chromatic aberration.
3. How are ascension and declination used to locate stars on a star chart?
4. Which is brighter, a star with a magnitude of −0.3 or one with a magnitude of +0.03?
5. Why are some nebulae bright and some dark?

What Do You Think?

1. What factors present in today's society hamper the accurate observations that were characteristic of some of the early astronomers? What factors helped overcome some of these problems?
2. What would be different today if lenses had never been invented?
3. What advantages would a telescope in orbit around the earth have over an earth-bound one? What disadvantages?
4. How would a permanent space station aid scientists in examining nonvisible electromagnetic (light) waves from distant objects? Would it be worth the cost?
5. Would coordinates be sufficient to locate an object in space if extended space travel becomes possible? Why or why not?
6. Suppose the earth orbited Proxima Centauri instead of the sun. What would be different about our star charts? our location in the Milky Way? What would be the same?
7. What would happen if the sun became a nova?
8. Psalm 19:1 states, ''The heavens declare the glory of God.'' What glory of God do you see in the celestial objects discussed in this chapter?

THE SUN: THE GREATER LIGHT

THREE

3A–General Description of the Sun

Although compared to other stars the sun may seem ordinary, it is a special star. The sun is the star that the Lord has ordained to be the source of heat and light for His creatures on the earth. It is the star that illumined the Judean hillside as Christ instructed His disciples. It is the star whose light was shut out as He hung on the cross (Matt. 27:45). It will continue to be "the greater light to rule the day" (Gen. 1:16) until He creates the new heaven and the new earth; then the sun will no longer be needed (Rev. 21:23).

The Sun's Position

Is the sun moving through space? Is there one part of the sky toward which it appears to be moving? The answer to these questions is yes. By studying the motions of many other

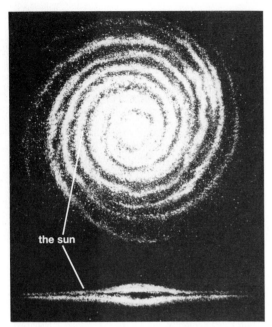

the sun

3A-1 *The sun is located in one of the spiral arms of the Milky Way galaxy.*

stars, astronomers have calculated that the sun is traveling toward a point in the constellation Hercules. The sun is traveling away from a point in the constellation Columba, which is a little to the southwest of Canis Major.

Although the sun is moving, it is not wandering. The sun is a star in the **Milky Way** galaxy, a vast, disk-shaped assemblage of stars that slowly turns like a giant pinwheel. Each star travels in its own orbit around the center of the galaxy, just as each planet in the solar system travels in its orbit around the sun. The sun's orbit is in a spiral arm of the galaxy, about three-fifths of the way from the center to the edge.

The Sun's Size

The sun is so enormous that its size is difficult to comprehend. Its diameter is about 1.4

million km (868,000 mi.); this is about 109 times the diameter of the earth. You may wonder why the sun does not look larger in the sky. The answer is simple: the sun is 150 million km (93 million mi.) away. The moon looks as large as the sun from the earth because although its diameter is only $\frac{1}{400}$ the sun's, it is 400 times closer to the earth than the sun is.

The sun's size is about midway between two extremes. Some stars, called giants and supergiants, are much larger than the sun. A red giant, for example, may have a diameter greater than that of the earth's orbit. Other stars, such as white dwarfs and neutron stars, are much smaller than the sun. Some white dwarfs are no larger than the earth, although they are much more dense. Neutron stars are much smaller and denser. Though the sun's size may be average, we have seen that the sun is by no means ordinary in its significance.

The sun contains over 99 per cent of all the matter in the entire solar system. It is about 330,000 times as massive as the earth. Expressed in metric tons, the mass of the sun would be a 2 followed by twenty-seven zeros. Not only does this great amount of ma-

Earth

3A-2 *The size of the sun compared to the size of the earth*

terial enable the sun to hold the planets in their orbits, but also it serves as the fuel that heats and lights the solar system.

The Sun's Energy

Imagine that you could build a bridge of ice from the earth to the sun. Picture a solid bar of ice 3 km (2 mi.) wide and 1.6 km (1 mi.) thick. If the energy of the sun could be concentrated in the direction of the ice bridge, it would melt the bridge completely in only one second.

About 97 per cent of the sun's energy output is in the form of **electromagnetic** (ih LEK troh mag NET ik) **waves,** such as light, x-rays, and radio waves. The other 3 per cent of its energy, it is theorized, is emitted as **neutrinos** (noo TREE noh), tiny particles that apparently travel at the speed of light and can easily penetrate ordinary matter. Most neutrinos that strike the earth go through it as though it were not there.

The light that is emitted by the sun consists of tiny waves that resemble waves in water. The distance from the crest (top) of one wave to the crest of the next is the **wavelength.** Different colors of light represent different wavelengths. The human eye can see light

3A-3 *If the earth were about the size of a BB, then on the same scale the sun would be the size of a basketball—about 27 meters away.*

from about 0.0004 mm (violet) to about 0.00075 mm (red). Ultraviolet waves, with wavelengths less than 0.0004 mm, are too short for the eye to detect. These are the rays that cause sunburn. Infrared waves, or heat waves, have wavelengths more than 0.00075 mm and are too long for the eye to detect. The sun also emits radio waves, which have wavelengths longer than infrared waves, and x-rays, which have wavelengths shorter than ultraviolet waves.

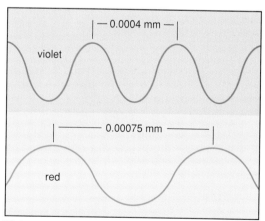

3A-4 *Light and other electromagnetic waves emitted by the sun differ in the distances from one wave crest to the next—wavelengths.*

FACETS OF ASTRONOMY

3A–1

Spectroscope

A spectroscope* (SPEK truh SKOPE) is an instrument used to identify specific colors (wavelengths) in light. The earliest spectroscopes used prisms to separate light into its component wavelengths, its spectrum.† (A prism produces a spectrum in much the same way that raindrops produce a spectrum called a rainbow.) Depending on the light source, certain wavelengths in the spectrum appeared relatively brighter or darker. The wavelengths that were more abundant in the light were brighter, and those which were less abundant were dimmer.

In most modern spectroscopes wavelengths are separated by a **diffraction grating.** A diffraction grating is a series of thousands of microscopic lines ruled or molded onto a transparent surface such as celluloid. The lines are tiny enough to interfere with the minuscule waves of light, and they separate the light by wavelengths. This produces a spectrum much like that produced by a prism, but it allows precise wavelength identification.

As seen through a modern spectroscope, a spectrum looks like a series of thin, bright lines. Each line is a separate wavelength of light. Elements in a light source can be identified by the pattern of bright lines that makes the spectrum. Each element has its own "signature," or pattern of lines. Astronomers can substitute a spectroscope for the eyepiece or camera on a telescope to study the spectrum of a star in detail. The elements in the star and their proportions can be identified from the star's spectrum.

There are two basic kinds of spectra produced by spectroscopes. A *bright-line spectrum* is produced directly from light emitted by an object. A *dark-line spectrum* is produced when particular wavelengths from a light source are absorbed by elements between the source and the spectroscope. The wavelengths absorbed are identical with those that would have been emitted by those intervening elements. Thus, a dark-line spectrum is like a negative of a bright-line spectrum. What we see in a star spectrum are dark-line spectra formed by gases in the star's atmosphere absorbing

Elements in a light source emit specific wavelengths (thin bright lines) in a bright-line spectrum. In a dark-line spectrum, the same elements absorb the wavelengths they would have emitted (thin dark lines).

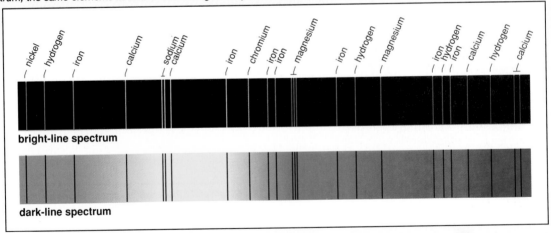

bright-line spectrum

dark-line spectrum

spectroscope: spectro- (L. SPECTRUM, appearance) + -scope (Gk. SKOPEIN, to see)

† A spectrum is all the wavelengths that make up light.

Joseph Fraunhofer (1787–1826), inventor of the spectroscope, was the first to measure and designate the dark lines of the solar spectrum.

light emitted from the star. The combined patterns from the different absorptions of the many elements in the star's atmosphere make a very complex dark-line spectrum. By patient work, astronomers can sort the patterns out and identify the elements present in the star's atmosphere. The chemical composition of the main body of the star is also identified since the composition of the star is probably similar to that of its atmosphere.

The light from the sun and other stars contains energy of all wavelengths and thus includes all the colors of the rainbow. In fact, the rainbow is sunlight that raindrops have separated into its component colors. However, as we discussed in Chapter 2, each star emits different amounts of each color. The amount of each color depends on the temperature of the star. The hotter stars emit more light with shorter wavelengths; so they are bluish in color. The cooler stars emit more light with longer wavelengths; so they are red. The sun is between these two extremes.

If all the colors in the sun's light were equally strong, the light from the sun would be white. But the colors toward the middle of the spectrum are more intense than those toward the edges of the spectrum, and hence the sun has an overall yellow color. Moreover, the human eye has its greatest sensitivity toward the middle of the visible spectrum, so that yellow is the color we see best. Furthermore, visible light, especially yellow, is the light that our atmosphere allows to pass most easily. Thus God made the sun, the eye, and the atmosphere to function together efficiently so that we can see.

3A-5	**Major Star Types**		
Class	**Color**	**Surface Temp °C**	**Surface Temp °F**
O	blue-white	>30,000	>55,000
B	blue-white	20,000	36,000
A	white	11,000	20,000
F	yellow-white	7,500	13,500
G	yellow	6,000	11,000
K	orange	4,200	7,500
M	red	3,000	5,500

This classification shows the relationship between the color of a star and its surface temperature.

The Sun's Composition

What is the sun made of? You might think that it is too far away for us to learn its true make-up. However, astronomers have a tool called the **spectroscope** that "fingerprints" the light coming from stars and planets. The spectroscope not only helps us determine what elements are present but also gives us an indication of how much of an element is there. It can even indicate whether an object is moving toward us or away from us.

The spectroscope has shown that the sun contains the same elements as the earth, but in different proportions. The most abundant element in the sun is hydrogen; the second most abundant is helium. These two elements make up about 96 per cent to 99 per cent of the sun's mass. The remaining mass com-

prises several dozen other elements. More than 60 of the 105 known elements have been identified in the sun; others may be present that are more difficult to observe. Interestingly, the element helium was found in the sun (1868) before it was found on the earth (1895). This element's name comes from the Greek *helios*, meaning "sun."

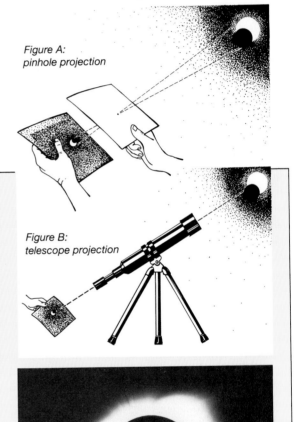

Figure A:
pinhole projection

Figure B:
telescope projection

solar eclipse

Observing the Sun

Though the sun's light is necessary for life on earth, it can be harmful in large doses. Never look directly at the sun. Its intense rays can damage your eyes. The proper way to observe the sun is indirectly—for example, by projecting its image on a white card. For this purpose, you can use either a second card with a pinhole in it or a telescope. A pinhole will give a small image, but with it you can easily observe a solar eclipse.

A telescope will show not only an eclipse but also sunspots and other features of the sun's surface. However, looking directly at the sun through a telescope can blind you in less than a second. To view the sun using a telescope, arrange your telescope as indicated in Figure B. Never position a telescope so that the sun's rays might focus to a pinpoint on a flammable object, since the object may ignite.

Section Review Questions 3A

1. Where is the sun located?
2. Why do the sun and the moon appear the same size in the sky when the sun's diameter is four hundred times greater than the diameter of the moon?
3. How much of the solar system's matter is in the sun?
4. In what form of energy is most of the sun's energy emitted?
5. What are the tiny particles of matter that travel at the speed of light and have the ability to penetrate ordinary matter?
6. List three reasons that the sun appears yellow to us.
7. What two elements make up more than 95 per cent of the sun's mass?
8. What is used in a spectroscope to separate light into its different wavelengths?

3B–The Sun's Structure

The sun is more than simply a ball of hot hydrogen and helium. It has regions of different temperature; it has several magnetic areas; it has an atmosphere. Phenomena on its surface cause radiation from the sun to vary in intensity and composition. In short, the sun is not simple; it has *structure* which we are just beginning to understand.

The Surface

Of all the stars in the universe, the sun is the only one close enough for astronomers to see surface detail. Great eruptions, brighter and darker areas, and an atmosphere can be observed on only this special star. These observations are then used to hint at the conditions that might be found in the interior of the sun and other stars.

Appearance

The sun's surface is **plasma,** superheated matter that is neither solid, liquid, nor gas. Even if you could tolerate the heat (and you could not, regardless of how much insulation you had), you could not stand on the sun's surface. You would fall through the surface to the hotter plasma. You would fall rapidly,

because the sun's gravity is twenty-eight times as strong as the earth's.

The visible surface of the sun is called the **photosphere.** Its temperature is about 6,000° C (10,800° F). The sun's surface is not plain and featureless; rather, it is divided into small cells called **granules.** A typical granule is several hundred kilometers in diameter and lasts for about five minutes. New ones are continually forming. Scientists believe that granules are "bubbles" caused by hotter plasma from the sun's interior coming to the surface.

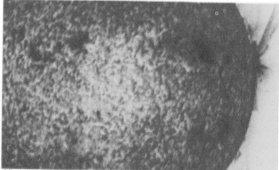

3B-1 *Granules on the sun's surface; an average granule is several hundred kilometers in diameter.*

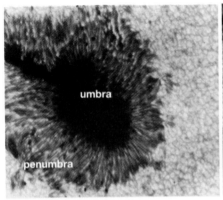
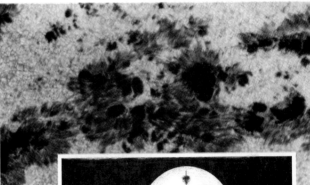
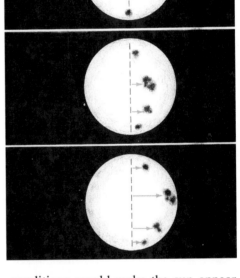

3B-2 *A large sun spot showing the umbra and penumbra (top left); a large group of sunspots photographed from New Mexico (top right); a six-day sequence showing how sunspots near the equator move faster than those near the poles, which demonstrates the sun's rotation (bottom right).*

Sunspots

From time to time small dark areas called **sunspots** appear on the sun's surface. Astronomers have noticed that these markings move across the sun's disk from east to west,† or left to right as we observe the sun in the southern sky. A sunspot that disappears at the western **limb** (edge) reappears at the eastern limb in about two weeks. These observations show that the sun is rotating.

Because the sun is a ball of plasma, its entire mass does not all rotate at the same speed. The rotation period is about twenty-five days at the equator, twenty-seven days at latitudes of 40° N and S, and thirty-five days close to the poles. The sun rotates on an axis that is tilted 7° from the earth's orbit, slightly more than the tilt of the moon's axis ($6\frac{1}{2}°$) but much less than the earth's ($23\frac{1}{2}°$).

The Chinese annals record that the ancients saw sunspots. They apparently observed unusually large sunspots when the sun was low in the sky on a hazy day. These conditions would make the sun appear dim and red. Around A.D. 1610 in Germany, Johannes Fabricius (fah BREE syoos) observed sunspots, using a pinhole arrangement. About the same time Galileo began observing sunspots by projecting the sun's image on a screen with his telescope.

No one knows exactly what sunspots are. The Bible says, "Yea, the stars are not pure in his sight" (Job 25:5). Could it be that this verse refers to "blemishes" such as sunspots

---

† When we discuss "east" and "west" based on observations on earth, we mean toward the earth's east and west, not toward the east or west for an observer on the sun.

in the sun and other stars? We do know that these are regions of reduced efficiency compared to the rest of the sun's surface. Sunspot temperatures are 1,500° C (2,700° F) cooler than the surrounding photosphere. A typical sunspot is about 4,500° C (8,100° F). This is still hotter than molten lava. Only because we see them against such a bright background do sunspots look dark. If you could see one by itself, it would be surprisingly bright.

A sunspot usually has two parts: a dark inner portion called the **umbra*** (UM bruh) and a brighter outer portion called the **penumbra*** (pih NUM bruh). Sunspots often occur in pairs, with one being a magnetic north pole and the other a magnetic south pole. The magnetic field in a sunspot is about 1,000 times stronger than the sun's average field. One theory is that the pair of sunspots is connected by a U-shaped bridge of material beneath the sun's surface. Sunspots usually last from a few days to a few weeks.

Solar observatories all over the world record the number, size, and groupings of sunspots. When astronomers plot the number of sunspots against time, they see a pattern, with the number of sunspots reaching a maximum every eleven years on the average.

Sunspots directly affect our shortwave radio transmissions. During maximum sunspot activity, shortwave radio broadcasts travel much farther than they do during minimum activity. This is true because sunspots eject charged particles at high speeds. Some of these particles strike the outer levels of our atmosphere and **ionize** (remove electrons from) the atoms in the atmosphere. There is usually an ionized layer called the ionosphere already present in the upper atmosphere. Short waves bouncing off this layer back to the ground can travel great distances. The additional ionizing caused by solar particles makes the ionosphere reflect better. When there are more sunspots, more ionizing takes place, and short radio waves are reflected better.

Scientists also suspect that sunspots may affect the weather. Tree rings show that reduced sunspot activity is historically linked to drought and cold weather. Increased sunspot activity, on the other hand, seems to accompany more favorable weather conditions. For

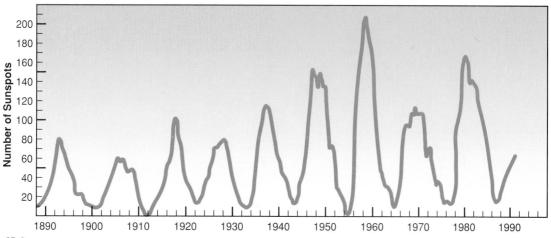

3B-3 *More than a century of sunspots cycles; the peaks, on the average, occur eleven years apart.*

---

umbra: (L. UMBRA, shadow)

penumbra: pen- (L. PAENE, almost) + -umbra (shadow)

example, extremely cold weather occurred during the reign of Louis XIV in France, when sunspot activity was slow. The drought in the 1930s also occurred during such a period. However, scientists are still unsure of the relationship between sunspots and the weather.

Solar Flares

At times there are severe storms on the sun called **solar flares,** which can hinder radio reception on the earth. A solar flare is a sudden energetic outburst that emits both rays and particles, and it shows itself as a brightening over a small region of the sun's surface. The rays given off by a solar flare include x-rays that temporarily destroy portions of the ionosphere and thus disrupt a variety of radio communications.

The particles given off by a solar flare include protons, electrons, and the nuclei of various atoms. These particles, sent in "bursts" or "clouds," are dangerous for astronauts in space who are not adequately protected. A day or two after an intense flare, there are spectacular displays of northern lights (aurora borealis) and southern lights (aurora australis) caused by particles from the solar flare disturbing atoms in the earth's ionosphere.

Solar flares are still mysterious. We do not know which part of the sun generates them, and we do not know why they occur; so we cannot predict them. We do know that they are somehow connected with sunspots because they usually occur near sunspots. They also occur most frequently during the peaks of sunspot activity.

3B-4 Solar flares are violent eruptions on the sun and last less than an hour.

3B-5 Aurora appear in the northern and southern skies a few days after solar flares.

Section Review Questions 3B-1

1. Superheated matter that is neither solid, liquid, nor gas is called by what name?
2. What is the name given to the visible surface of the sun?
3. What are the areas of the sun's surface that appear to be bubbles?
4. Small dark areas on the surface of the sun with much cooler temperatures than the surrounding areas are called by what name?
5. List the two regions of a sunspot.
6. List the two things on the earth that are most likely to be affected by sunspot activity.
7. What is the name given to severe storms on the sun?

The Sun's Atmosphere

The sun has an extensive atmosphere that extends upward from the photosphere. The solar atmosphere consists of two parts: the thin **chromosphere** and the more extensive **corona** (kuh ROH nuh). Though it is usually invisible, scientists have found various ways to learn about it.

To observe either part of the sun's atmosphere, the astronomer needs either a total solar eclipse or an artificial eclipse produced by an instrument called a **coronagraph.** Using these tools, astronomers have learned that the lower atmosphere, the chromosphere, is a layer of heated plasma less than 10,000 km (6,200 mi.) high. Its temperature ranges from 1,000,000° C (1,800,000° F) near the top to 6,000° C (10,800° F) at the bottom. The top divides into many pointed jets called **spicules** (SPIK yool). Spicules look rather like grass growing on the sun.

The corona begins at the top of the chromosphere and continues outward from the sun for millions of kilometers in all directions. It has no clear-cut outer edge. The **solar wind,** a flow of mostly protons and electrons from the sun, is a continuation of the corona. The corona's temperature can reach 2 million° C (3.6 million° F), much higher than the chromosphere or photosphere can reach. The shape of the corona changes continuously. If you study photographs of total solar eclipses, you will see that the corona never looks the same twice.

While observing the corona, you might be fortunate enough to see a **prominence** (PRAHM uh nunce), a spectacular display resembling fireworks. Prominences are streams of material that rise into the corona and then gradually fall back. As they move, they follow graceful curves that show the influence of the sun's magnetism. Prominences may be quiescent or eruptive. The

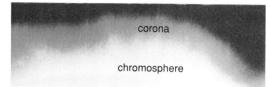

3B-6 *The sun's atmosphere*

3B-7 *Corona*

3B-8 *Spicules*

3B-9 *Large loop-shaped prominence*

3B-10 *Solar eruption*

smaller quiescent prominences seem to hang in the corona for several days, while the more impressive eruptive prominences change rapidly and last for only a few hours. The largest known prominence, which occurred in 1946, reached a height of 483,000 km (300,000 mi.) and was 113,000 km (70,000 mi.) wide.

The Sun's Interior

Astronomers cannot see the interior of the sun; so they have devised a model based upon observations that have been made from the earth and from satellites. Many guesses have also been added to their observations. The most widely accepted model today is that the sun has three interior sections: a core, a radiative zone, and a convective zone.

The **core,** the innermost section, is the site of thermonuclear reactions, which generate the sun's energy. Most scientists believe that hydrogen atoms combine to form helium—a process that releases tremendous amounts of energy. This nuclear reaction resembles that of a hydrogen bomb. Calculations indicate that the core has the unimaginable temperature of 14 million° C (25 million° F). If you heated the head of a pin to that temperature on earth, everything for miles around would be burned from the radiating heat.

After leaving the core, the sun's energy travels outward through the **radiative zone** as electromagnetic waves. As it reaches the **convective zone,** the energy heats the plasma in the lower part of this zone. This hot plasma rises to the surface of the photosphere, where it can be seen as granules.

If the thermonuclear model† of the sun's interior is correct, the sun converts 655 million tons of hydrogen to 650 million tons of helium each second. The 5 million "lost" tons become the energy that radiates away from the sun. The sun also loses about 1 million tons of particles in the solar wind

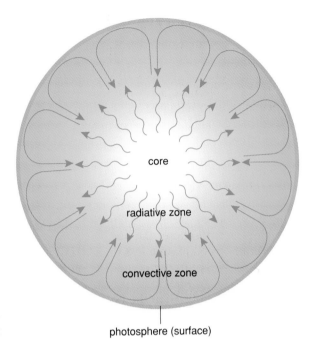

core

radiative zone

convective zone

photosphere (surface)

3B-11 *Model of the sun's interior; energy leaves the core and travels through the radiative zone as electromagnetic waves (radiation). Once it reaches the convective zone, it heats plasma which rises to the surface, cools, and returns to be heated again.*

each second. Thus the sun loses about 6 million tons of matter every second. Like all stars, it is slowly wearing out. Some stars will last longer than others, but all stars will eventually die. Their thermonuclear reactions will cease, and they will cool. We see here a good example of the Biblical principle that the heavens are wearing out like a garment (Heb. 1:11).

Could the sun always have been running down? Obviously not. At one time in the past the energy that is now leaving the sun must have been put into it. This "winding up" or "charging" process was a part of the miraculous creative act of God. No natural processes could have energized the sun. All evolutionary theories fail in an attempt to explain the origin of stars.

---

† Recent evidence suggests that the thermonuclear model of the sun may be incorrect. Scientists have tried unsuccessfully to detect the neutrinos that should result from the reactions. Likewise, recent evidence has discredited a theory that the sun produces energy by shrinking.

Section Review Questions 3B-2

1. What are the two parts of the sun's atmosphere?
2. What is the name given to streams of materials that rise into the corona and then fall gradually back?
3. List the two types of prominences.
4. List the three regions of the sun's interior.
5. About how much of the sun's mass is lost through radiation and the solar wind each second?
6. Does any evolutionary theory adequately explain the origin of stars?

3C–Harnessing Solar Energy

The sun's energy may help to supply the world's energy needs directly. Although it probably will not be a cure-all, this energy could theoretically supplement fossil fuels and nuclear energy. It is especially useful for heating water and for heating and cooling homes, although it also can generate electricity.

Solar energy has both disadvantages and advantages. One disadvantage is that it is diffuse (spread out). Remember that the sun's rays spread out in all directions and fill more space as they move away from the sun. At the earth's distance of 150 million km (93 million mi.), the rays are already quite spread out. This means that solar collectors must have large areas to gather a significant amount of energy. Furthermore, the sun's energy is not always available. A fossil fuel plant or nuclear reactor can operate around the clock, but the sun's energy is available only during the daytime. It is also weaker in the morning and evening than at midday, and much less energy reaches the earth on a cloudy day.

Solar energy is high-quality energy, however. That is, it converts readily to work. Another attractive feature of solar energy is its cleanness. It has no waste products like the smoke from fossil fuels or the radioactive wastes from nuclear fission.

Heating

Our greatest success so far in using solar energy has been in heating homes. This process uses a large collecting surface on a slanted roof to gather the sun's energy. The collecting surface is often black sheet metal, since a black surface readily absorbs energy.

3C-1 Rooftop solar water heaters are one of the most popular solar heating devices. In the Northern Hemisphere collectors face south to gather the most sunlight.

A black surface also radiates energy, but it radiates longer wavelengths than it absorbs. These longer waves cannot pass through glass; thus the collector is covered by a glass plate to prevent the energy from escaping. The absorbed energy heats water that is circulating in pipes beneath the sheet metal, and the water travels to a storage tank. The hot water can then circulate through the house to heat it or provide hot tap water. Homeowners, especially those in California and Florida, have used this system with success.

Electricity

Another use for solar energy is to produce electricity. **Solar cells** (photoelectric* cells) can convert light directly to electricity. A solar cell is a small, flat, waferlike device that is usually less than an inch square. Light is allowed to shine on one side. Specially prepared minerals—for example, cadmium sulfide, silicon, and gallium arsenide—respond to the light by producing a small voltage. By connecting many cells, we can use their combined electricity to charge storage batteries. These batteries in turn furnish electricity for useful work. The question is whether a given location receives enough sunlight to produce useful amounts of electrical energy.

Most current solar cells are expensive and inefficient. A typical residential installation probably could not supply the needs of a modern home with its many electrical appliances. At best, solar units could only supplement the electricity bought from the local power company.

In the near future, solar energy's chief promise seems to be in heating and cooling buildings in moderate climates. Its use for electricity is less certain. It will probably never replace fossil fuel or nuclear energy but will only supplement them. However, as

we continue to learn more about this part of God's creation, we may someday be able to use solar energy efficiently and economically.

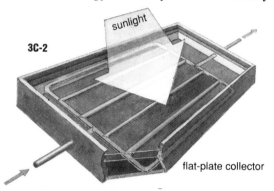

3C-2

sunlight

flat-plate collector

photoconductive cell (automatically turns streetlights on and off)

solar panel on the **Upper Atmosphere Research Satellite (UARS)**

---

photoelectric: photo- (Gk. PHOT-, light) + -electric (Gk. ELEKTRON, amber, *which produces electricity when rubbed*)

Section Review Questions 3C

1. List three things energy from the sun is most commonly used for.
2. What are two hindrances to using solar energy?
3. What device is used to convert the sun's energy directly to electricity?

Terms

chromosphere	limb	solar flare
convective zone	Milky Way	solar wind
core	neutrino	spectroscope
corona	penumbra	spicule
coronagraph	photosphere	sunspot
diffraction grating	plasma	umbra
electromagnetic waves	prominence	wavelength
granule	radiative zone	
ionize	solar cell	

What Did You Learn?

1. How do the sun's position, size, and energy compare to those of other stars?
2. What is the thermonuclear model of the sun's interior?
3. What is the evidence of the sun's rotation?
4. How does the sun affect radio broadcasts on the earth?

What Do You Think?

1. Why is the sun a special star?
2. How might sunspots cause drought or cold weather? How would you determine which climatic changes are caused by sunspots and which are caused by other factors?
3. One reason for studying the sun is to learn more about thermonuclear reactions. What changes would you expect if man is able to find a way to control thermonuclear reactions and put them to use as energy sources here on the earth?
4. Solar cells are used on satellites orbiting the earth. Why might solar cells be more useful in space than on earth? What limits the usefulness of solar cells on the earth? on satellites? on deep space probes?

THE NINE PLANETS

FOUR

4A–**Characteristics of the Planets**

As ancient astronomers watched the sky, they noticed that the stars stayed in permanent patterns, but there were seven exceptions. The sun, the moon, and five bright ''stars'' that the Greeks called wanderers, or **planets,*** moved slowly among the fixed stars. The motions of the planets were hard to explain. Three of them occasionally reversed their motion, and all five changed in brightness. Later astronomers found that a planet appears as a definite disk through a telescope, while a star looks like a pinpoint of light even with high magnification.

We now know that these five planets—Mercury, Venus, Mars, Jupiter, and Saturn—along with the earth and the three planets discovered by telescope—Uranus, Neptune, and Pluto—are dark bodies that orbit the sun.

---

planet: (Gk. PLANASTHAI, to wander)

74

Their usual order of increasing distance from the sun is Mercury, Venus, Earth, Mars, Jupiter, Saturn, Uranus, Neptune, Pluto. From 1979 to 1999, however, Pluto is closer to the sun than Neptune. We see the planets by the sunlight they reflect. Because they orbit the sun, the planets have varying distances from the earth. Thus their brightness changes.

The nine planets are often referred to as the sun's family. The planets, like family members, have much in common, but each has unique characteristics.

Orbits

One aspect in which the planets strongly resemble each other is their orbits. As seen from the earth, all the planets stay close to the *ecliptic,* the sun's apparent path through the stars. That means that the planets orbit almost in the same plane. However, Pluto's orbit is quite different, with an inclination of about 17° from the ecliptic. This similarity makes the planets easy to observe. Instead of searching the entire sky, you need only identify the ecliptic and search a small band for a planet.

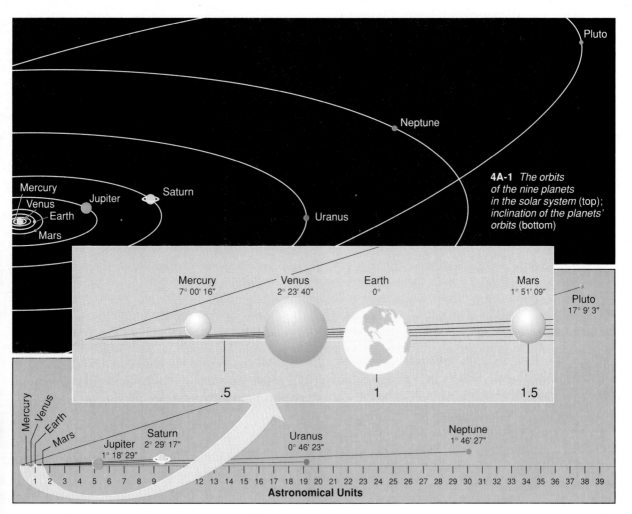

4A-1 *The orbits of the nine planets in the solar system* (top); *inclination of the planets' orbits* (bottom)

Mercury 7° 00' 16"
Venus 2° 23' 40"
Earth 0°
Mars 1° 51' 09"
Pluto 17° 9' 3"

.5 1 1.5

Jupiter 1° 18' 29"
Saturn 2° 29' 17"
Uranus 0° 46' 23"
Neptune 1° 46' 27"

1 2 3 4 5 6 7 8 9 12 13 14 15 16 17 18 19 20 21 22 23 24 25 26 27 28 29 30 31 32 33 34 35 36 37 38 39
Astronomical Units

Another characteristic of the planets' orbits is their shape. Planets travel in *elliptical,* or "ellipse-shaped," orbits. What is an **ellipse?** You can construct an ellipse with a piece of string, two thumbtacks, a pencil, and a piece of corrugated cardboard. Tie the two ends of the string together to form a circle that has a diameter larger than the distance between the two tacks. Place the loop over the tacks. Catch the point of the pencil in the string. Then trace out the curve, taking care to keep the string tight on both sides of the pencil. Each thumbtack forms what is called a **focus** (plural, foci) of the ellipse. The closer the foci are to each other, the more the ellipse will be like a circle. The farther apart they are, the more "unround," or eccentric, the figure will be.

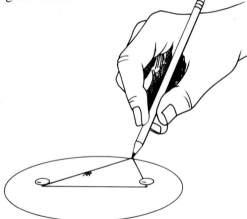

4A-2 *Drawing an ellipse with a pencil, two thumbtacks, and a piece of cardboard*

The famous German astronomer Johannes Kepler discovered three laws to describe the motions of the planets. These laws were published in the early 1600s and have been verified by many different types of observations. In recent years, Kepler's laws have become important in the space program because they apply not only to the planets but also to the moons and manmade satellites. They have been used to chart routes to the other planets. Kepler's laws are usually stated as follows:

1. Planets move in ellipses with the sun at one focus.
2. An imaginary line from the center of the sun to the center of a planet always sweeps over an equal area in equal time. (This means simply that when a planet is closer to the sun, it will be traveling faster along its orbit; as it moves farther from the sun, it will be traveling more slowly.)
3. The squares of the periods (the time it takes to make one orbit) of the planets are proportional to the cubes of their distances from the sun; thus a distant planet will have a longer period and go more slowly than a planet that is nearer the sun.

Though the orbits of planets are elliptical, most planets have nearly circular orbits.

4A-3 *Kepler's three laws: (a) elliptical orbits—the sun is one focus of the ellipse; (b) law of areas—a line between the sun and planet will cover equal areas during any equal orbital time; (c) period-distance relationship—the time required for a planet to orbit the sun is proportional to its distance from the sun*

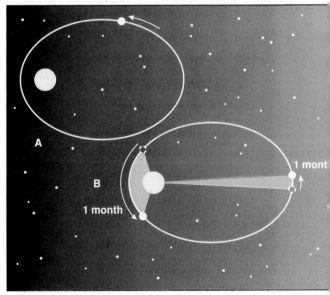

Some orbits are more nearly circular than others; Venus's and Neptune's are most nearly round, and Pluto's is the most eccentric. Because none of the orbits are exactly circular, the distance from a planet to the sun changes. When a planet is closest to the sun, it is at the **perihelion*** (PER uh HEE lee un); when it is farthest from the sun, it is at the **aphelion*** (uh FEE lee un). The distance from the sun that is given in most tables is an average. The earth's average distance from the sun, about 150 million km (93 million mi.), is called one **astronomical unit,** or A.U., and other planets' distances are usually measured in relation to it.

The distances of the planets to the sun range from 0.387 A.U. for Mercury to 39.5 A.U. for Pluto. Pluto is more than one hundred times as far from the sun as Mercury.

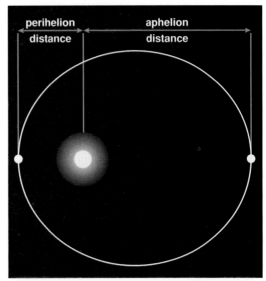

4A-4 *The point in a planet's orbit that is nearest the sun is called perihelion; the point that is most distant from the sun is aphelion.*

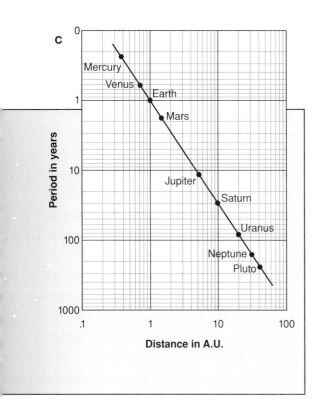

Light from the sun reaches Mercury in about $3\frac{1}{2}$ minutes; it takes the light about $8\frac{1}{2}$ minutes to reach the earth and over 5 hours to reach Pluto.

Brightness

As you might suspect, the magnitude (brightness) of a planet is related to its distance from the earth. Mars looks brighter when it is closer to the earth and dimmer when it is farther away. Another factor also affects magnitude, however, and that is the ability of the surface or atmosphere to reflect light. This reflective ability is called the planet's **albedo** (al BEE doh). Albedo is expressed as a decimal. Venus has an albedo of 0.76, meaning that its dense atmosphere reflects 76 per cent of the light it receives. A third factor that affects the magnitude of a planet is its size. Jupiter is the largest planet and therefore is very bright even though it is a great distance from the earth.

perihelion: peri- (Gk. PERI-, near) + -helion (sun)

aphelion: ap- (Gk. APO, away from) + -helion (sun)

Mass

The planets exhibit a variety of masses. **Mass** is a measure of the amount of material the planet contains. Mass is related to weight but is not quite the same thing. For example, an object in orbit is weightless, but it still has mass. A planet's size and mass together determine its **surface gravity,** the downward pull the planet exerts on objects at its surface. The two extreme cases for the planets are Pluto and Jupiter. On Pluto you would weigh only 5 per cent of your earth weight; on Jupiter you would weigh 2.6 times your earth weight. Thus, if you weigh 445 N† (100 lb.) on the earth, you would weigh 22 N (5 lb.) on Pluto and 1,157 N (260 lb.) on Jupiter.

Planets also vary in their **density.** Density is the mass of a certain material per volume. Density is usually compared to water. Water has a density of 1 gram for every cubic centimeter (1 g/cm³), or for simplicity, we usually say the density of water is 1. Rock is heavier than water and therefore has a density greater than 1. Wood, on the other hand, is lighter than water and has a density less than 1. The density of the earth is about 5.5 g/cm³, but Saturn is only about 0.7 g/cm³. We conclude, therefore, that Saturn is probably mostly gaseous. Jupiter has an average density of about 1.3 g/cm³; so it contains more liquid or possibly a small solid core with a thick gaseous atmosphere.

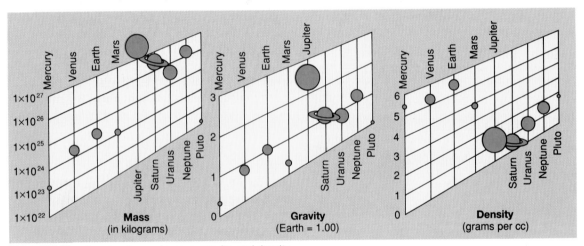

4A-5 *The nine planets vary in mass, gravity, and density.*

Section Review Questions 4A

1. What did the ancient Greeks call the planets?
2. List the nine planets in order from the sun outward.
3. What is the name given to the sun's apparent path through the stars?
4. What is the characteristic shape of a planet's orbit?
5. What is the term for the point in a planet's orbit when it is nearest the sun? farthest from the sun?
6. What is the ability of a planet to reflect light called?
7. What three factors affect the apparent magnitude of a planet?

† N = Newton. Chapter 6 (p. 122) has a discussion of the units used to measure weight.

4B–Classifying the Planets

Planets with similar characteristics can be grouped together to aid their study. The characteristics commonly used to classify the planets include their position and size.

By Position

Perhaps the most obvious grouping of the planets is by their position. In this system, the planets whose orbits are between the earth's orbit and the sun—Mercury and Venus—are called the **inferior planets.** When viewed from the earth, inferior planets have two characteristics caused by their orbits. Like the moon, they show phases; however, we can see the phases only when the planet is far enough east or west of the sun as viewed from the earth. They also undergo **transits** (TRAN sit). In a transit, a planet passes directly between the earth and the sun so that through a solar telescope we see its dark silhouette against the sun's bright disk.

Planets whose orbits are farther from the sun than the earth's orbit—Mars, Jupiter, Saturn, Uranus, Neptune, and Pluto—are **superior planets.** Because the superior planets move more slowly than the earth, the earth frequently catches up with and passes them. You can easily understand how this happens if you observe two athletes running at different speeds on a track. The faster runner is on the inside lane of the track, and the slower runner is on the outside lane. Since the runner

on the inside lane of the track goes faster over a shorter lap, he will soon lap the other runner. That is, he will pass the slower runner and be a full lap ahead of him. Similarly, the earth "laps" the superior planets by completing more orbits in a given time.

As the earth passes a superior planet, the superior planet seems to go backward. This is called **retrograde*** (RET ruh GRADE) **motion.** When most astronomers believed that the earth was the center of the solar system, they found retrograde motion baffling. What could make a planet go backward? Now that

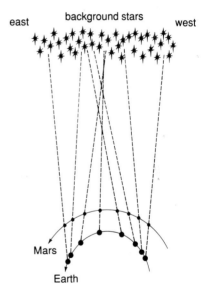

4B-2 *Retrograde motion. As viewed from the earth, the slower-moving superior planets will appear to move backward as the earth progresses through its orbit.*

we know the earth is a planet, we understand that retrograde motion is an illusion caused by the earth's motion. To understand the illusion, consider passing a car that is going in the same direction as you are on the highway at night. As you approach the other car, you can see its lights moving forward ahead of

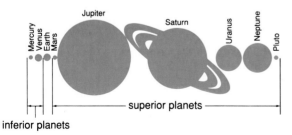

4B-1 *Inferior and superior planets*

retrograde: retro- (L. RETRO-, back) + -grade (L. GRADUS, step)

you. Because you are going faster than the other car, you pass it. While you are beside the car, its lights slip behind you and thus appear to be going backward.

By Size

Another way to classify the planets is by size and density. Planets that are the earth's size or smaller have about the same density as the earth. These are called **terrestrial*** (tuh RES tree ul), or earthlike, **planets.** Mercury, Venus, Earth, Mars, and probably Pluto are terrestrial planets. Although the other terrestrial planets resemble the earth in size and density, they are different in one important respect.

The earth has oxygen in its atmosphere and liquid water on its surface, but the other terrestrial planets have neither. Oxygen and water are essential for life as we know it.

Planets that are larger than the earth tend to have low densities. These planets—Jupiter, Saturn, Uranus, and Neptune—are called **Jovian** (JOH vee un), or Jupiter-like, planets. They have large, gaseous atmospheres that are so deep that even space probes have been unable to locate the planets' surfaces. Because they are mostly gaseous, they are sometimes called **gas giants.** Although they have thick atmospheres, these planets have no free oxygen and no water. Life as we know it could not exist on a Jovian planet.

4B-3 *Terrestrial planets are those that are about the same size and density as the earth. Jovian planets are much larger and less dense than the earth.*

Section Review Questions 4B
1. What is the term used to indicate that a planet is passing between the earth and the sun?
2. What is the difference between a superior planet and an inferior one?
3. Which planets undergo transits as viewed from the earth?
4. What is the name given to the apparent backward motion of a slow-moving planet as the earth passes it?
5. What is a Jovian planet?
6. What is a terrestrial planet?

---

terrestrial: (L. TERRA, earth)

4C–**Close-up of the Planets**

While grouping together planets with similar characteristics helps us to understand some observations, each planet still has its own special characteristics. Each planet is a unique creation of God with its own curious features. The magnificence of each planet's design speaks of the glory and magnificence of the Creator.

Mercury

Mercury is a difficult planet to observe with the naked eye. You must know exactly where to look, and you must look at just the right time. Much of the time Mercury is too close to the sun for us to see. Only when the planet nears the "ends" of its orbit—moves far enough east or west of the sun as viewed from the earth—do we get a chance to view it. Even then it is never viewed at an angle larger than 28° from the sun.

With its diameter of about 4,800 km (3,000 mi.), Mercury is the second smallest planet. Its mass is one-eighteenth of the earth's mass, and its gravity is too small to hold much of an atmosphere. It has an extremely thin atmosphere, composed of hydrogen, helium, and trace amounts of carbon dioxide. These gases produce an atmospheric pressure of only one-ten thousandth of the atmospheric pressure at the surface of the earth. Photos of Mercury sent back to the earth by space probes show its surface to be full of craters, much like the surface of the moon. Mercury has no known moons.

Mercury, which was named after the speedy messenger of the Roman gods, travels at an average speed of almost 48 km/s (30 mi./s). The length of Mercury's year (the time for a complete orbit) is only eighty-eight days. Although it moves through its orbit at great speed, Mercury spins slowly on its axis,

4C-1 *The surface of Mercury is heavily cratered, much like our own moon*

FACETS OF ASTRONOMY

4C-1

Voyages of Discovery

Imagine discovering an exotic new world unlike anything ever seen on earth. Modern scientists, through the eyes of space probes, have witnessed scenes never before seen by human eyes. The information they have gathered has revolutionized the way we see the universe. The surprising complexity of our solar system has shattered scientists' neat evolutionary theories. Astronomers are awed by the bewildering complexity of God's universe, which they cannot explain.

A

The exploration of other planets and their moons has revealed that each is a unique, remarkable creation. The photographs here were taken by various space probes: (A) close-up of Mercury's craters; (B) Mercury photographed by Mariner 10; (C) Olympus Mons on Mars photographed by Mariner 9; (D) Mars terrain photographed by Viking 1; (E) Callisto, a moon of Jupiter photographed by Voyager 2.

Mariner

The *Mariner* series of space probes focused on the earth's nearest neighbors. The first mission failed, but in 1962 *Mariner 2* came within 35,400 km (22,000 mi.) of Venus and reported surface temperatures of 427° C (800° F), hot enough to melt lead. *Mariner 3* was aborted when its solar panels failed to open, but in 1965 after a $7\frac{1}{2}$-month trip, *Mariner 4* made twenty-one close-up pictures of Mars. Widespread craters were found, but virtually no magnetic field, no vegetation, and no artificial waterways from a "dead civilization." *Mariner 5* went back to Venus, and 6 and 7 went back to Mars for further quick flyby studies.

Mariner 8 was aborted after take-off, but *Mariner 9* entered orbit around Mars. Scientists were at first worried that they might not get good pictures because a raging 160-km/hr. (100-mph) dust storm had engulfed the planet. More than a month later, the dust cleared and the probe successfully photographed much of Mars's surface with its television cameras. Among the many features it discovered was the largest sandy desert in the solar system, surrounding Mars's north pole. The tenth probe flew by Mercury three times, coming to within

694 km (431 mi.) of it. It added greatly to our knowledge of that broiling, crater-pocked planet, which had previously appeared as a tantalizing dot of light on telescopes.

Pioneer

The *Pioneer* series, originally a lunar probe, eventually reached the outer limits of the solar system. After almost two years in flight, *Pioneer 10* became the first probe to fly past Jupiter (1973). The vehicle included twelve instruments to measure Jupiter's atmosphere and radiation belt. The radiation belt

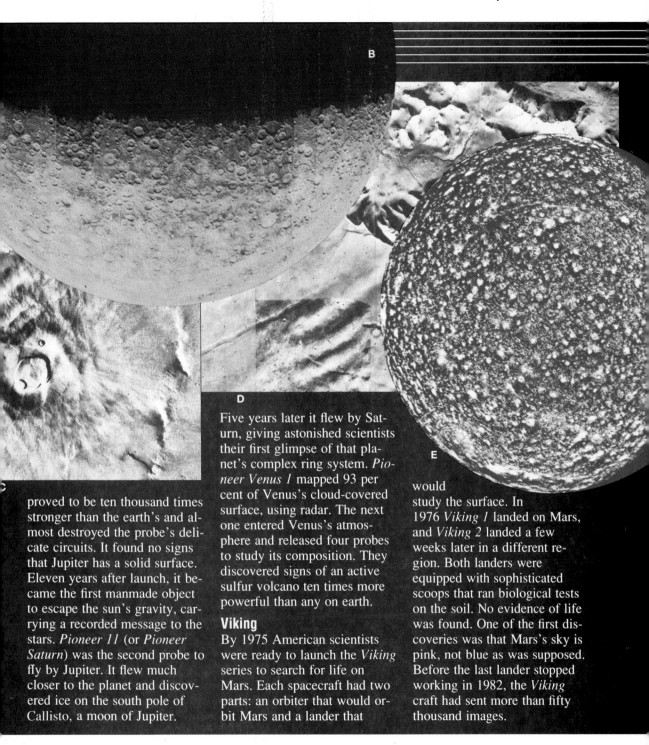

proved to be ten thousand times stronger than the earth's and almost destroyed the probe's delicate circuits. It found no signs that Jupiter has a solid surface. Eleven years after launch, it became the first manmade object to escape the sun's gravity, carrying a recorded message to the stars. *Pioneer 11* (or *Pioneer Saturn*) was the second probe to fly by Jupiter. It flew much closer to the planet and discovered ice on the south pole of Callisto, a moon of Jupiter.

Five years later it flew by Saturn, giving astonished scientists their first glimpse of that planet's complex ring system. *Pioneer Venus 1* mapped 93 per cent of Venus's cloud-covered surface, using radar. The next one entered Venus's atmosphere and released four probes to study its composition. They discovered signs of an active sulfur volcano ten times more powerful than any on earth.

Viking

By 1975 American scientists were ready to launch the *Viking* series to search for life on Mars. Each spacecraft had two parts: an orbiter that would orbit Mars and a lander that would study the surface. In 1976 *Viking 1* landed on Mars, and *Viking 2* landed a few weeks later in a different region. Both landers were equipped with sophisticated scoops that ran biological tests on the soil. No evidence of life was found. One of the first discoveries was that Mars's sky is pink, not blue as was supposed. Before the last lander stopped working in 1982, the *Viking* craft had sent more than fifty thousand images.

Saturn photographed from Voyager 1 (above); Iapetus, a satellite of Saturn as seen from Voyager 2 (right); Jupiter's moon Europa (below).

Voyager

Using the information from earlier probes, scientists launched the historic *Voyager* series, costing a total of $1 billion. Astronomers expected to confirm their theories that the outer planets had been shaped by predictable evolutionary processes. When *Voyager 1* flew by the gas giant Jupiter, scientists expected its moons to be crater pocked by four billion years of meteorite strikes. They discovered that Europa has the smoothest surface in the solar

system and that the moon Io, covered by sulfur dust from at least a dozen active volcanoes, has no meteorite craters. They theorized that only Saturn could have rings, but one last shot looking back showed a ghostly ring around Jupiter. Expecting Saturn to support their simple explanations, they were dumbstruck by its thousands of rings within rings.

Voyager 2 discovered Uranus's nine dark rings, Neptune's five arclike rings, the bizarre landscape of Uranus's moon Miranda, and the magnetic field and planetlike methane atmosphere of Neptune's moon Triton. Expecting the planets to grow increasingly calm in the near absolute zero weather, scientists found Neptune covered by a raging atmosphere with perhaps the highest winds in the solar system, 1,770 km/hr. (1,100 mph).

The 7.1 billion-km (4.4 billion-mi.) trip to Neptune would

normally have taken thirty-two years. It was reduced to less than twelve years because all the planets had lined up (as they do once every 176 years), enabling the probe to use each planet's gravity as a slingshot to the next planet. Zooming at 98,408 km/hr. (61,148 mph), *Voyager 2* edged to within 4,905 km (3,048 mi.) of Neptune (only 34 km [21 mi.] from its planned point of contact). At that distance radio signals from earth took four hours to reach the probe. The signals from the probe were only one-one quadrillionth of a watt when they reached the earth. *Voyager 2* alone has provided scientists enough information to fill 6,000 sets of encyclopedias. Both Voyagers are now searching for the heliopause (HEE lee oh PAWZ), the limit of the solar wind and the beginning of interstellar wind.

The Search Continues

The United States has begun a new generation of probes to study the solar system. In 1990 it sent the *Magellan* probe to map cloud-covered Venus with radar one hundred times more powerful than the resolution of *Pioneer Venus*. The *Galileo* spacecraft includes an orbiter to map Jupiter and a probe designed to parachute into the Jovian clouds. Pluto, however, will remain almost a complete mystery for decades to come.

taking about fifty-nine days to make one complete rotation. This slow rotation as well as its closeness to the sun gives Mercury temperatures as high as 430° C (806° F) at noon on its equator. However, with practically no atmosphere to hold the heat in, cooling takes place rapidly on the planet's dark side, and temperatures plunge to as low as –173° C (–279° F).

4C-3 *Color photo of Venus from* Voyager II

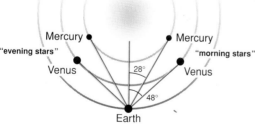

4C-2 *Crater on Mercury photographed by* Mariner 10 *space probe* (top); *the inferior planets, Venus and Mercury, can be viewed only in the early evening or morning. At other times the sun obscures them* (bottom).

Venus

Unlike Mercury, Venus is easy to observe. As earth's nearest neighboring planet, Venus outshines all other celestial bodies except the sun, the moon, and occasional bright comets and meteors. At its greatest brilliance, Venus is fifteen times as bright as Sirius, the brightest star. Venus was named after the Roman goddess of beauty and love.

A telescope or good binoculars reveal Venus's phases. When it is nearest the earth, Venus is a crescent. When it is almost full, it is farthest from the earth. But we can never see a full Venus because that phase always occurs when Venus is hidden behind the sun. Galileo first observed the phases of Venus in the early 1600s. Like Mercury, Venus can be either an ''evening star'' or a ''morning star.'' At one side of its orbit, we can see Venus only in the evening; at the other extreme, we can see it only in the early morning.

Of all the planets, Venus is most like the earth in size and mass. Its diameter is about

95 per cent of the earth's diameter, and its mass is about 82 per cent of the earth's. Like

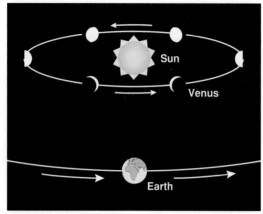

4C-4 The phases of Venus are explainable by its position in its orbit relative to an earth based observer (top). Venus appears as a thin crescent when it is in the part of its orbit nearest to the earth. Photos of Venus (bottom) were taken on four different nights within one month.

the earth, Venus has enough gravity to hold an atmosphere—a hot, dense atmosphere that our most powerful telescopes cannot penetrate. Venus is covered with clouds containing sulfuric acid. These reflect 76 per cent of the sunlight striking them, giving the planet a dazzling white appearance.

Radar studies and space probes have given us important facts about the planet. Probes that landed on Venus showed that its surface temperature is around 500° C (900° F). This high temperature results from the thick atmosphere, which traps heat inside it like a blanket. The probes also revealed an atmospheric pressure about one hundred times that of the earth. Venus's atmosphere is mostly carbon dioxide with traces of other substances and is only one-tenth as dense as water.

Section Review Questions 4C-1

1. Which planet is closest to the sun?
2. What is the length of time required for Mercury to complete its orbit around the sun?
3. How long does it take Mercury to make one complete rotation about its axis?
4. What planet is noted for its extreme brightness?
5. Why can't we observe Venus in its ''full'' phase?
6. What is the atmosphere of Venus like?
7. Which probes landed on Mars?

Mars

Continuing outward from the sun, we now come to the superior planets. Mars, named after the Roman god of war, is easy to identify because of its reddish color. Though not as bright as Venus, Mars at its best is brighter than all the other planets and stars. The planet has two tiny moons, Phobos (FOH BAHS) and Deimos (DY mahs), named after the attendants of the Greek god of war.

Mars has a diameter that is only 53 per cent of the earth's and a mass that is only 11 per cent of the earth's. Because of its low mass, you would weigh only 38 per cent of

4C-5 *The planet Mars* (below); *Deimos* (inset), *is only 12 km in diameter and is the smaller of Mars's two moons.*

FACETS OF ASTRONOMY

UFOs: Messengers of the Stars?

Alien landing strips discovered in England! In the late 1980s farmers in England found huge geometric forms where crops had suddenly wilted but did not die. Newsmen set up cameras to detect the cause, but they found nothing. The day after they removed the equipment, the weird designs reappeared.

UFOs (Unidentified Flying Objects) first gained popularity in 1947. Newspapers reported that a pilot had seen ''flying saucers'' near Mount Rainier, Washington. Many people scoff at these accounts, but UFO reports continue with full force in this scientific age. UFO sighters are not just crackpots and tricksters. Groups of respectable citizens have seen and photographed UFOs. President Carter saw one in 1969.

There are several causes of UFO reports:

- airplane
- weather balloon
- satellite
- rare atmospheric phenomenon (especially high clouds)
- meteor
- bright planet (especially Venus)
- star

Most UFOs are easy to explain. A famous UFO in 1984 turned out to be a group of planes flying in formation, each

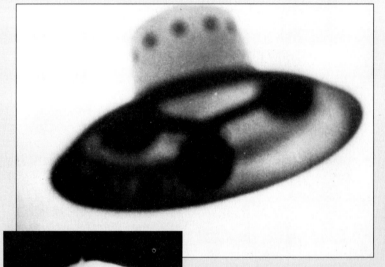

painted black on the bottom so that only the lights could be seen from the ground. When citizens complained to the Federal Aviation Administration, it responded, ''If the pilot is up there with a clearance and at the right altitude, we don't care what planet he comes from.''

Even if you know what you are looking for, your eyes can still play tricks on you. Without a reference point in the sky, you cannot estimate size or distance. A plane can appear as far away as a star. Furthermore, the moon and stars can appear to follow you as you move. If you stare at a stationary object for a while, the natural movements within your eye will cause the object to appear to flutter erratically.

Some common explanations for UFO reports are as follows:

- hoax
- exaggeration
- self-deception
- optical illusion
- freakish coincidence
- unknown natural process

How do you explain something like the crop incident? Admittedly a few UFOs currently have no scientific explanation. Perhaps these events may be attributed to a freakish coincidence (like a tornado or gust of wind) or a natural process that we do not yet understand. It is rash to attribute everything we cannot explain to visitors from outer space.

your earth weight on Mars. The temperature of the surface of Mars varies greatly. Although Mars is comfortable at the equator at high noon, 21°to 26° C (70° to 80° F), it is extremely cold at night, about –73° C (–100° F).† Considering that Mars is farther from the sun and that its atmosphere is too thin to be a good thermal blanket, we can understand the low temperatures.

Although the largest earth-based telescopes have given us some information about the surface of Mars, much of our knowledge has come from space probes that have transmitted pictures back to the earth from the planet. Mars has craters, volcanic mountains, canyons, and polar caps containing large amounts of solid carbon dioxide, or "dry ice." The planet's surface also has a large amount of dust that periodically becomes airborne in the Martian winds. Astronomers first observed these dust storms through telescopes.

Jupiter

Jupiter, the largest of the planets, is named after the leader of the Roman gods. Although never brighter than Venus, Jupiter is an impressive object in the night sky. Not only is Jupiter brighter than the brightest star, but it also has four large moons that show up clearly with even a small telescope. Because Galileo discovered these moons, they are called the **Galilean moons.**

Jupiter is truly gigantic in both size and mass. Its diameter is about eleven times that of the earth. With 318 times as much mass as the earth, Jupiter contains more material than all the other planets combined. As a result of this great mass, it has such a strong gravitational pull that many comets passing near it have their orbits permanently changed.

Nobody has ever seen the surface of Jupiter. All we can see are features of the planet's

extensive atmosphere. The most prominent of these features are the bands of turbulent clouds that extend around the planet parallel to the equator. The **Great Red Spot,** another feature, is a reddish-colored, oval-shaped area that astronomers have been trying to explain for centuries. Most of them agree that it is a gigantic storm of some sort.

Jupiter has many moons, and more are discovered by each space probe that passes it. Currently the official count is sixteen. Most of these are very small; some are less than 16 km (10 mi.) in diameter. The Galilean moons are large, however. Ganymede (GAN uh MEED) is larger than the planets Mercury and Pluto. Perhaps the most spectacular of Jupiter's moons is Io. Photographs sent back by the *Voyager 1* space probe in 1979 show several volcanoes erupting on its surface. *Voyager 1* also discovered that Jupiter has a thin ring, which astronomers cannot see from earth because it is so faint.

Europa   Io   Callisto   Ganymede

4C-6 *The relative sizes of the four largest moons of Jupiter which were seen by Galileo; Ganymede is the largest moon and Callisto is the outermost. Ganymede and Callisto are both larger than the planet Mercury.*

Jupiter holds the record as the fastest-spinning planet. Although it is far larger than the earth, the planet rotates in less than ten hours. This rapid turning has affected the shape of the planet: it is flattened at the poles and bulged at the equator.

---

† These equatorial temperatures are estimates, not actual measurements.

4C-7 *Swirling cloud belts and the Great Red Spot of Jupiter—the Great Red Spot is a gigantic storm.*

Section Review Questions 4C-2

1. What is the feature of Mars that makes it easy to identify?
2. What are the names of the two moons of Mars?
3. Describe the temperature at the equator on the surface of Mars.
4. Which planet is the largest?
5. What is the name given to the four moons of Jupiter?
6. List three distinguishing features of Jupiter's surface.
7. What makes Jupiter's moon Io so spectacular?

Saturn

The planet Saturn, named for the Roman god of agriculture, was the most distant planet known to the ancients. Even so, it is as bright as the brightest stars. Because of its magnificent system of rings, Saturn is a beautiful planet.

In many respects Saturn is like Jupiter. It has bands of clouds in its atmosphere parallel to the equator. It spins rapidly and thus is flattened at the poles and bulged at the equator. Saturn has temporary small spots like Jupiter's Red Spot. Like Jupiter, it has many moons, officially seventeen, with some astronomers reporting twenty-one or more. Titan, Saturn's largest moon, is unique among Saturn's moons in having an atmosphere. This atmosphere is mostly nitrogen and contains the poisonous gas methane and is extremely cold.

Saturn's rings are exceedingly thin. We can often see stars shining through them. These rings consist of a myriad of particles, each in its own orbit around the planet. Through telescopes, astronomers counted three or four rings, but space probes show

4C-8 *Saturn's rings are actually thousands of individual rings composed of a myraid of particles orbiting the planet. The ring system casts a shadow near Saturn's equator.*

4C-9	Physical Properties of the Planets†								
Property	Mercury	Venus	Earth	Mars	Jupiter	Saturn	Uranus	Neptune	Pluto
Mean distance from the sun (A.U.)	0.39	0.72	1.00	1.52	5.20	9.54	19.18	30.06	39.44
Diameter (km) (mi.)	4,877 3,031	12,101 7,521	12,755 7,927	6,793 4,222	143,800 89,372	120,660 74,990	51,118 31,770	49,500 30,764	2,294 1,425
Volume, compared to Earth's	0.06	0.92	1.00	0.15	1,324	736	64	58	0.01
Mass, compared to Earth's	0.056	0.820	1.000	0.110	318	95.1	14.5	17.2	0.002
Density (g/cm³)	5.4	5.2	5.5	3.9	1.3	0.7	1.2	1.7	1.8
Temperature (° C) (s = surface; c = top of clouds)	−173 to +430 (s)	+472 (s)	−50 to +50 (s)	−140 to +20 (s)	−110 (c)	−180 (c)	−221 (c)	−216 (c)	−230 (s)
Orbital period	88 days	225 days	1 year	1.9 years	11.9 years	29.5 years	84 years	165 years	248 years
Average Orbital Speed (km/sec.)	47.9	35.0	29.8	24.1	13.0	9.6	6.8	5.4	4.7
Rotational period	58.7 days	243 days retrograde	24 hours	24.6 hours	9.8 hours	10.2 hours	17.3 hours retrograde	16.1 hours	6 days 9.4 hours retrograde
Number of satellites‡	0	0	1 moon	2 moons	4 moons 12 minor 1 ring	9 moons 8 minor 1,000+ rings	5 moons 10 minor 10 rings	2 moons 6 minor 4 rings	1 moon
Atmospheric content	helium, hydrogen, trace of carbon dioxide	90% carbon dioxide	80% nitrogen, 20% oxygen	80% carbon dioxide	hydrogen, helium, methane, ammonia	methane, helium, hydrogen	90% hydrogen, helium, methane	85% hydrogen, 15% helium	trace of methane to none
Gravity, compared to Earth's	0.38	0.90	1.00	0.38	2.54	1.16	0.92	1.19	0.06
Inclination of equator to orbit (°)	0	177	23.5	23.6	3.1	26.4	98.9	28.8	90 to 110
Albedo	0.06	0.70	0.39	0.16	0.51	0.61	0.57	0.31	0.55

† Some of these values may vary, depending on the reference source.
‡ "Minor" means minor moons.

4C-10 *Saturn and six of its satellites; the planet and its rings were overexposed to gather enough light to see the moons (top). The brightly colored bands of clouds and rings are visible in this photograph of Saturn (bottom)* taken by *Voyager 2.*

that there are over one thousand. Even areas that appear to be empty when viewed with telescopes on earth have been found to have many tiny rings. One such area, called **Cassini's** (kuh SEE nee) **Division,** appears completely empty from earth, but *Voyager 1* and *2* photos showed hundreds of thin rings in this area.

Uranus

Uranus was discovered in 1781 by the English astronomer William Herschel (1738–1822). The planet is named after the Roman god of the heavens. Under favorable conditions and with some planning, you can see Uranus without a telescope. You must have excellent viewing conditions and an accurate star chart showing just where to look. Using a telescope, however, you can observe, as did Herschel, that Uranus appears to be a disk rather than a point of light. You also may be able to detect a faint greenish color. *Voyager 2* photographs, however, indicate that Uranus is a pale blue color.

Like several other planets, Uranus gets its bright appearance from a cloud layer that surrounds it and reflects sunlight. Hydrogen, helium, and methane have been identified in Uranus's atmosphere.

Uranus has fifteen known moons. Surprisingly, these orbit almost perpendicular to the planet's orbit. Uranus spins at this same strange angle. The planet and its entire moon system give the appearance of being tilted 98° from vertical. Like Jupiter and Saturn, it is a fast-rotating planet.

In 1977 five faint rings were discovered around Uranus. Because none of the rings are bright enough for direct observation from

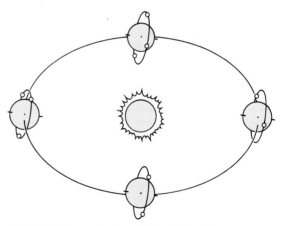

4C-11 *Both Uranus's axis and the orbits of its moons are tilted at an unusual angle compared to other planets and moons.*

earth, astronomers detected them by the dimming they cause when they **occult**† a star. Further observations in 1978 showed four new rings for a total of nine, and *Voyager 2* detected a tenth on its 1986 flyby of the planet.

4C-12 *Uranus's atmosphere obscures any observation of the planet's surface. This photograph was taken by* Voyager 2 *as it flew by the planet in 1986.*

Section Review Questions 4C-3

1. What is the feature of Saturn that makes it stand out from the other planets?
2. List three ways in which Saturn is similar to Jupiter.
3. What is the space that appears to exist in the rings of Saturn when viewed through earth-based telescopes called?
4. When was Uranus discovered? By whom?
5. What color is Uranus as seen in *Voyager 2* photographs?
6. What is unusual about the way in which Uranus rotates?

Neptune

During the years following Uranus's discovery, astronomers watched it closely through their telescopes. They knew its orbit and made predictions about where it should be at any given time. By the early 1800s, though, astronomers began to realize that something was wrong. Uranus was not quite in its calculated place in the sky. Because no other planet has been observed to misbehave in this way, astronomers were puzzled. A few of the more adventuresome thinkers began to speculate that there might be another planet beyond Uranus. Perhaps its gravitational pull was pulling Uranus away from its calculated path.

Two mathematicians, John Couch Adams (1819–92) and Urbain Jean Joseph Leverrier (1811–77), made independent calculations about where the new planet would have to be to affect Uranus's orbit. Johann Gottfried Galle (1812–1910) of the Berlin Observatory searched for and found the new planet in 1846, less than 1° from the position that Leverrier had calculated. The correctness of this prediction was a major victory for Newton's law of gravitation, which had been the basis for the calculation. The new planet was named Neptune, for the Roman god of the sea.

Neptune is slightly smaller than Uranus. It looks similar to Uranus through a telescope, although Neptune is smaller and fainter because it is farther away. It has a beautiful blue color with a banded, cloudy atmosphere

† *Occult* means to hide or eclipse.

containing the chemicals hydrogen and helium and a Great Dark Spot similar to Jupiter's Great Red Spot. Neptune has at least eight moons, but only two are observable with earth telescopes. Triton is somewhat larger than our moon and has a retrograde orbit; that is, it orbits Neptune in a direction opposite the planet's rotation. While Nereid does not have a retrograde orbit, it is traveling in the most eccentric orbit of any known moon in the solar system. The 1989 flyby of *Voyager 2* added much data about Neptune, including the discovery of six additional moons and several faint rings.

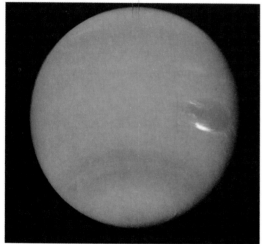

4C-13 *Neptune has a Great Dark Spot similar to Jupiter's Great Red Spot.*

Pluto

The chances of finding another planet beyond Neptune seemed remote to most astronomers. The great distance would make the planet exceedingly dim. Spotting such an object among the many millions of stars would be almost impossible, but one man was certain that a ninth planet existed. That man was Percival Lowell (1855–1916), a wealthy American astronomer who owned his own observatory, Lowell Observatory. By 1915

he had calculated where another planet should be. His observations were fruitless, however, and he died without finding the planet.

Other workers at Lowell Observatory continued the search. In 1929 a young astronomer named Clyde Tombaugh (1906–) joined the observatory staff. One year later, after much painstaking work, he found the elusive planet. It was much fainter than Lowell had predicted and hard to distinguish from the stars. Tombaugh was certain from its motion among the stars, however, that the object was a planet. Just to be sure, he watched it carefully for more than a month. Finally, on March 13, 1930, Tombaugh announced his discovery to the world. The new planet was named Pluto, after the Roman god of the underworld. The first two letters of the name are in honor of Percival Lowell, the man who had begun the search for the planet.

Unlike the other outer planets, Pluto is only about 2,294 km (1,425 mi.) in diameter. It is the smallest planet; in fact, it is smaller than the earth's moon. Pluto's moon, Charon, was discovered in 1978. Like the moons of Uranus, Charon orbits the planet almost perpendicular to Pluto's orbital plane. This indicates that the planet rotates on its axis with a tilt of over 90° (some estimates as large as 118°). Charon's diameter is about half Plu-

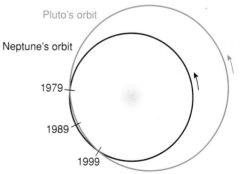

4C-14 *Orbits of Neptune and Pluto—for about 20 years Neptune is the farthest planet from the sun.*

to's, making it the largest moon in proportion to its planet in the solar system.

Beginning in 1985, astronomers began observing the eclipses that occurred as Pluto and its moon crossed in front of each other. This happens only a few years out of every 124 as the earth passes through the plane of Charon's orbit. These eclipses have allowed astronomers to calculate many facts regarding Pluto's features, size, mass, and density. Using supercomputers, astronomers have constructed a map of Pluto based on the variations in brightness during the eclipses. The map shows bright polar caps, a large dark spot near the equator, and a somewhat lighter equatorial band. Calculations of density have led astronomers to suggest that Pluto is more than half rock with a mixture of gases.

Pluto's orbit is also unusual. Since its average orbital speed is only a sluggish 4.7 km/s (2.9 mi./s), Pluto spends 248 years making its long trek around the sun. It has the most eccentric orbit for a planet, and its orbit is tipped at the greatest angle to the earth's orbit. Furthermore, Pluto's perihelion is closer to the sun than Neptune's orbit. For this reason about 20 years out of every 248, Neptune, rather than Pluto, is the outermost planet. Pluto's perihelion was closer to the sun than Neptune's in 1989.

Section Review Questions 4C-4

1. What caused some astronomers to expect that there was another planet beyond Uranus?
2. Which two men made mathematical calculations about the location of Neptune? Who discovered it?
3. What is different about Neptune's moon called Triton?
4. During what year was Pluto discovered? By whom?
5. What is the name of the moon that orbits Pluto?
6. What is unusual about the orbit of Pluto?

4D–Origin of the Planets

Those who deny the truth of the Bible have been unable to explain how the planets were formed or how they were placed in orbit around the sun at their proper speeds. Since the 1700s evolutionists have believed that the solar system condensed by itself from a large cloud without the need of a Creator.

The most obvious difficulty with the theory, of course, is the question of where the cloud came from. Another difficulty is that the particles in the cloud would not stick together to form planets. Gravity is far too weak a force to draw the specks of dust in the cloud together and make them stick. Only in bodies of a kilometer (0.6 mile) or so in diameter does gravity play a significant role by drawing chunks of material together. No one has figured out how these large bodies could form.

Certain things about the planets spell trouble for the evolutionary theories. If the solar system indeed condensed from a cloud, everything in the system should have inherited the same spin that the cloud had. This would mean that everything in the solar system would be turning the same way. But at

FACETS OF ASTRONOMY

4D-1

SETI: Is Anyone Out There?

Are we alone in the universe? Scientists scoff at popular accounts of flying saucers and aliens. Yet they are spending billions of dollars in their own Search for ExtraTerrestrial Intelligence, known as SETI. In fact, SETI is one of the driving forces behind astronomy and space exploration.

The search for aliens began in our own solar system. Early astronomers focused their telescopes on Mars, the most earth-like planet in our solar system. Imaginative writers proposed that lines on Mars were a network of irrigation canals constructed by intelligent beings trying to survive on a dying world. They also proposed that seasonal changes in the color of the Martian surface resulted from the growth of plants during the summer. Modern probes have proved these theories wrong. As with probes to the moon, Mars probes have been greeted by a bleak, dead planet.

Scientists are also looking beyond our solar system for alien life. If evolution is correct, then extraterrestrial life should abound. There are about 200 billion stars in our galaxy alone, and over 10 billion galaxies fill the universe. According to popular estimates—

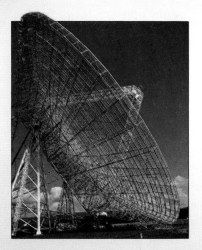

A radio telescope at
Green Bank, West Virginia

1. half of our galaxy's 200 billion stars have inhabitable planets;
2. 1 million of these planets contain advanced civilizations;
3. the closest civilization must be approximately 300 light-years away.

The estimates sound convincing, until you realize that we do not have solid proof for the very first requirement of extraterrestrial life—planets outside our solar system.

Unable to see distant planets, astronomers hope to find the by-products of intelligent aliens —radio transmissions. If a civilization is 300 light-years away, its messages must be 300 years old by the time they reach the earth. The first efforts to find these interstellar communications occurred in 1960. An American observatory listened for signals from two nearby stars over the "quiet" interstellar radio channel of 1,420 megahertz. Since then, American and Soviet radio observatories have made around fifty SETI efforts, using increasingly sophisticated equipment. In SETI's heyday, NASA prepared a radical plan—called Project Cyclops—a $10 billion, 40-km-wide network of huge radio antennas to detect signals from outer space. But each successive effort has concluded, "Searched, found nothing."

Sinners fear what it means to be alone in the universe. Having rejected the existence of a Creator, they are clutching to the theory of evolution for security. They want to believe that they are just one of many "accidents" in the universe. The last thing they want to admit is that an extraterrestrial intelligence made them in His unique image and holds them responsible for their sins. Yet in rejecting the unique Creator of the earth, they have rejected the unique work of the Saviour, who became man and died for man's sins so that "in the ages to come he might shew the exceeding riches of his grace in his kindness toward us through Christ Jesus" (Eph. 2:7).

least two of the planets, Venus and Uranus, spin ''backwards,'' and about one-third of the moons in the solar system revolve ''backwards'' around their planets. Evolutionists have put forth several explanations of the problem. The most popular of these is the idea that originally everything turned the same way, but various accidents happened to change some rotations. It is difficult, if not impossible, even to imagine an accident that would reverse the spin of a planet or the orbital direction of a moon without shattering it. These explanations are fantasy, not science.

The various theories of the origin of the solar system are continually being changed. As new findings reveal more defects in a theory, it becomes so obviously useless that evolutionists scrap it and replace it with a new one. Many different theories have been popular during the last three centuries, but most astronomers agree that no evolutionary theory of the origin of the solar system is satisfactory. These facts would surprise a reader of the popular writings about astronomy, whose writers talk as though the evolution of the solar system were an established fact.

The most important thing to remember is that all theories are based upon faith. ''In the beginning something . . . .'' Whether that something is a cloud of gas, cloud of dust, proton, mass of energy, or whatever, is irrelevant. It is by faith that the unbeliever accepts the substance that was ''in the beginning.'' The Scripture contends, ''In the beginning God created the heaven and the earth.'' In what will you choose to place your faith?

The only way we can know for certain how the planets came into existence is to learn from the one who made them. Thus the only statements on the subject of origins that will endure are those set down by ''holy men of God [who] spake as they were moved by the Holy Ghost'' (II Pet. 1:21).

4D-1

... AND SO THE ''COSMIC FLY SWATTER THEORY OF ORIGINS'' WAS BORN.

Section Review Questions 4D

1. What kind of material do some evolutionary theories hold that the solar system was formed from?
2. What characteristic of Venus and Uranus is a difficulty for the condensation theory?
3. What signs of intelligent alien life do astronomers hope to find?
4. Which planet has occasionally been identified as a UFO?

Terms

albedo
aphelion
astronomical unit
Cassini's Division
density
ellipse
focus

Galilean moons
gas giants
Great Red Spot
inferior planet
Jovian
mass
occult

perihelion
planet
retrograde motion
superior planet
surface gravity
terrestrial planet
transit

What Did You Learn?

1. Why would the fact that some planets spin "backwards" and some moons revolve "backwards" present problems for evolutionary theories?
2. In what ways can planets be distinguished from stars?
3. From what you have learned in this chapter, is it likely that life exists on other planets in our solar system? Explain your answer.
4. Is it possible that other planets exist within our solar system? What problems would astronomers encounter in finding them?
5. How are all the planets' orbits similar?
6. How do terrestrial planets and gas giants (Jovian planets) differ?
7. List the planets in correct order from the sun, and give a unique characteristic of each planet.

What Do You Think?

1. Imagine that we lived on another planet and were trying to determine the surface temperature and atmospheric composition of the earth. How would we determine these? What wrong conclusions might be made? What else might we learn about the earth from our home planet?
2. Suppose a small sample of Venus's atmosphere was collected and returned to earth for study. Do you think its composition would be the same as it is now believed to be? What would be some reasons its composition would differ from our current understanding?
3. If a human colony settled on Mars, how might they solve the problems of extreme cold, dust storms, and lack of oxygen?

ASTEROIDS, COMETS, AND METEORS

FIVE

5A–Minor Planets

Besides the sun and the planets, there are also many smaller objects in the solar system. These other celestial bodies are so small that even if we could gather them together, they would not make one good-sized planet. Yet, in spite of their unimpressive size, these lightweights sometimes put on a spectacular display. If you have ever seen a comet or meteor, you have experienced one of the marvels of God's handiwork. These smaller members of the solar system generally fit into three groups: minor planets, comets, and meteors.

The largest of the three types of objects is the minor planets; yet you are more likely to see comets and meteors, which are smaller. You would not be able to see the comets and meteors, however, if they did not glow or

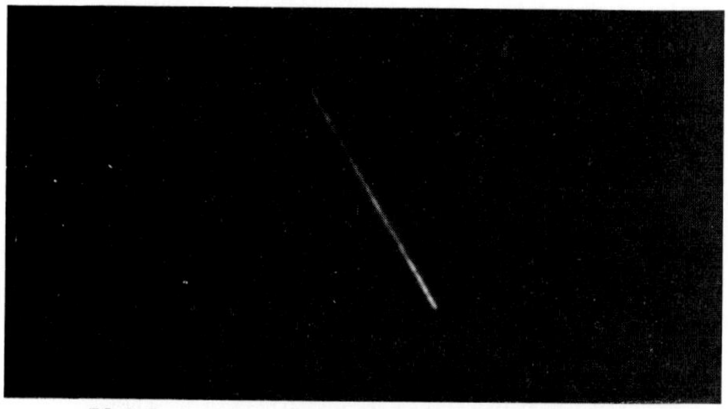

5A-1 *Trail of the minor planet Eros; with long exposure times a photo of a minor planet will appear as a streak.*

burn. Though the minor planets are larger, they are still too small to be seen without a telescope, and since they do not glow, the unaided eye cannot see them.

Discovery of the Minor Planets†

In the late 1700s astronomers noticed that the distance between Mars and Jupiter was unusually large. Could there be a "missing" planet? Astronomers turned their most powerful telescopes toward the gap to find out. In 1801 the Italian astronomer Giuseppi Piazzi (1746–1826) announced that he had found a planet. This planet was surprisingly small; its diameter is roughly 1,000 km (620 mi.). Piazzi chose to call it Ceres, after the Roman goddess of grain and agriculture.

The next year, Heinrich Olbers (1758–1840), a German astronomer, found a second planet in the gap. He called it Pallas, for the Greek goddess of wisdom. Pallas is just over half the diameter of Ceres. Soon astronomers had found two more **minor planets,** Juno in 1804 and Vesta in 1807. Vesta is about the same size as Pallas, while Juno is considerably smaller. Although Vesta is smaller than Ceres, Vesta's surface reflects light so well that it is the brightest of the minor planets. Vesta is sometimes bright enough for us to see without a telescope when viewing conditions are exceptionally good.

After these four minor planets were discovered, a long period followed when none were found. We now know that Ceres, Vesta, and Pallas are the largest of the minor planets and thus the easiest to find. Finally, in 1845 Karl Hencke (1793–1866), a German astronomer, found Astraea. This much fainter planet has a diameter of about 80 km (50 mi.). When astronomers realized that other minor planets also would be small, they began finding them in great numbers. By 1890 more than three hundred minor planets were known.

After 1890, astronomers developed a new technique for finding minor planets. By using timed exposures made with a telescope that follows the stars, astronomers could simply take pictures and study the plate for objects that move. In such photographs stars appear as points and minor planets as short streaks. There are more than three thousand minor

5A-2 Notable Minor Planets

Number†	Name	Interesting Facts
1	Ceres	largest asteroid; first asteroid discovered
4	Vesta	brightest asteroid
14	Irene	has a halo like a comet
323	Brucia	first asteroid discovered photographically
433	Eros	oblong shape; rotates by tumbling end over end
944	Hildalgo	travels farthest from the sun
1000	Piazzia	named in honor of first asteroid discoverer
1566	Icarus	comes closest to the sun; most eccentric asteroid orbit
	Hermes	closest to the Earth

† Numbers indicate order of discovery. No number was ever assigned to Hermes, which disappeared after it was first sighted.

† Minor planets and asteroids are the same thing.

5A-3 *Trails of two minor planets. The brighter trail is Bellona.*

planets known today, and most of them were discovered by astronomers using photographs.

Description of the Minor Planets

The minor planets resemble the nine major planets but are much smaller. Ceres, the largest minor planet, has a diameter less than one-half the diameter of Pluto, the smallest major planet. Because minor planets are so small, through a telescope they look like stars rather than planets. Thus, they are sometimes called **asteroids,** meaning ''starlike.'' Most stay between the orbits of Mars and Jupiter, but some have orbits outside this region.

Minor planets have such small masses that a single minor planet's gravity is negligible. One asteroid cannot noticeably change the orbit of a major planet, although a large group can have a measurable effect. A minor planet's surface gravity is also too weak to hold an atmosphere. On a minor planet a person could not say that what goes up must come down. A baseball hit from any minor planet would escape into space.

Each minor planet is given a name and a number when its orbit is known. The catalogue number shows the order of the planet's discovery; for example, Ceres is number 1.

The names of the first asteroids were those of Greek and Roman goddesses. When astronomers had exhausted these, they began to use the names of famous persons (Piazzia, Hooveria, Rockefellia), cities (Chicago, Pittsburghia), flowers (Arnica), and even friends, relatives, and pets of the discoverers. These names are usually changed to sound feminine. The minor planet's full identification, then, is a number, usually circled, followed by a name: ①   Ceres, ⑦   Iris, ⑩⑩⑩   Piazzia.

Families of Minor Planets

Most minor planets have orbits between those of Mars and Jupiter, but some do not. When several minor planets have similar orbits, especially if the orbits are not between Mars and Jupiter, these minor planets are said to be a *family.*

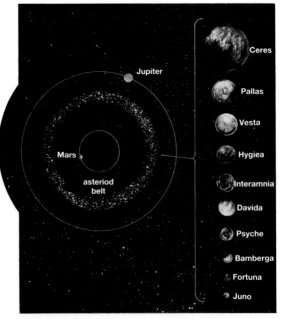

5A-4 *The relative sizes and brightnesses of the larger asteroids*

The Trojan asteroids are a family of minor planets with nearly the same orbit as Jupiter. They are all named after heroes of the Trojan War, such as Achilles, Hector, and Odysseus. The family is divided into two groups, one that precedes Jupiter and one that follows it. All Trojan asteroids are about the same distance from Jupiter as they are from the sun.

The Apollo asteroids are a family of minor planets that come nearer the earth than any major planet. Eros, the first to be discovered, comes within 21 million km (13 million mi.) of the earth. This unusual minor planet is an oblong chunk of rock about 24 km (15 mi.) long and about 6 km (4 mi.) wide. It rotates by tumbling end over end. Several smaller minor planets, about 1.6 km (1 mi.) in diameter, come even closer to the earth. For example, Amor approaches within 16 million km (10 million mi.), and Icarus, within 6.4 million km (4 million mi.). Hermes came

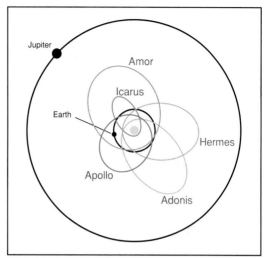

5A-6 *Orbits of five of the thirty-one known Apollo asteroids in relation to the orbits of Earth and Jupiter. Asteroids whose orbits are not between the orbits of Jupiter and Mars and that have similar orbits are called a family.*

closer to the earth than any other minor planet we have seen when it passed within 780,000 km (480,000 mi.) in 1937. These minor planets have eccentric orbits. Some go closer to the sun than the earth does. Icarus holds the record for closest approach to the sun, 30 million km (19 million mi.).

On March 23, 1989, a previously undiscovered asteroid, several hundred meters across, passed the earth 800,000 km (500,000 mi.) away. This is only twice the distance to the moon. The asteroid was not seen until after it had passed by on April 6 because its approach was from the direction of the sun. Now known as 1989 FC, it has been determined to have an orbital period of just slightly over one year; so it will pass close to the earth about every twenty-five to thirty years.

Are we in danger of being struck by an errant asteroid? No one knows for sure, but those who know most about the subject think that it is extremely unlikely. The known

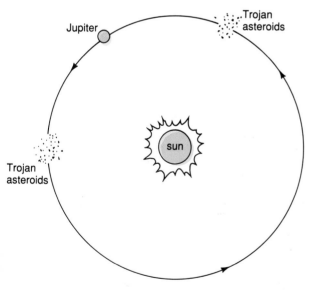

5A-5 *The Trojan asteroids have nearly the same orbit as Jupiter.*

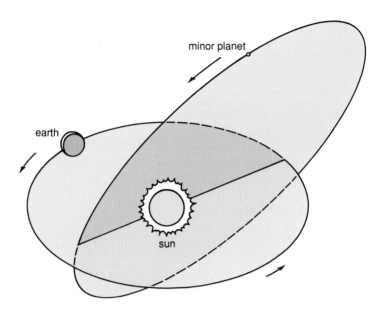

5A-7 *Apollo asteroid orbits do not presently intersect the earth's orbit.*

Apollo asteroids are not in the same plane as the earth's orbit. However, the strong gravitational influence of Jupiter appears to cause the plane of their orbit to precess (wobble like a top). Thus the orbits could overlap sometime in the future. However, there does not seem to be any immediate danger from these asteroids.

How damaging would a direct hit from such an object be? It could be more destructive than the combined force of many hydrogen bombs. Even a small body in solar orbit carries a great deal of kinetic energy (energy of motion) because of its tremendous speed. Although it would not destroy the earth, it could cause devastation over a wide area. All such events are controlled by the Lord, and this is reassuring for the Christian. "But whoso hearkeneth unto me shall dwell safely, and shall be quiet from fear of evil" (Prov. 1:33).

Section Review Questions 5A

1. Between what two major planets are most minor planets or asteroids located?
2. Name the three largest minor planets in the order of their discovery.
3. How many minor planets are there?
4. How are minor planets named?
5. What family of minor planets have nearly the same orbit as Jupiter?
6. Explain why it is unlikely that an Apollo asteroid would strike the earth even though it orbits inside the earth's orbit.

5B–Comets

Unlike minor planets, **comets** are often visible without a telescope. Many comets become more brilliant than the planets, and some even outshine the moon for a short time. When a bright comet is visible, millions of people watch it and perhaps wonder if it has some special meaning.

Theories About Comets

Since ancient times there have been fanciful superstitions connected with comets. They have been regarded as forerunners of wars, plagues, crop failures, earthquakes, and all manner of evils. However, while the heathen nations were fretting about what the future held, God's people, the Israelites, had peace of mind. God had instructed them not to heed such omens: "Thus saith the Lord, Learn not the way of the heathen, and be not dismayed at the signs of heaven; for the heathen are dismayed at them" (Jer. 10:2). The same is true for the Christian today. Instead of fearing the ill effects of unfavorable stars, planets, or comets, he needs only to fear (reverence) God and heed His Word.

The Greek philosophers decided that comets were merely lights in the atmosphere, like prolonged lightning. This theory persisted until the sixteenth century, when Tycho Brahe proved from his observations that a comet may be at least six times as far away from the earth as the moon. Even then, astronomers believed that comets were not subject to the laws of celestial motion. Kepler himself believed that comets moved in straight lines, rather than the ellipses required by his laws.

The first man to treat comets as ordinary bodies was Edmund Halley (HAL ee) (1656–1742). Using Newton's theory of gravitation, Halley calculated the orbits of several bright

5B-1 *This Babylonian tablet records the appearance of Halley's comet in the year 164 B.C.: "the comet which previously had appeared in the East in the path of Anu in the area of Pleiades and Taurus."*

5B-2 *Comet Arend-Roland as it appeared in 1957*

comets. Three of these, the comets of 1531, 1607, and 1682, had almost identical orbits. The time between the first and second comets and between the second and third comets was

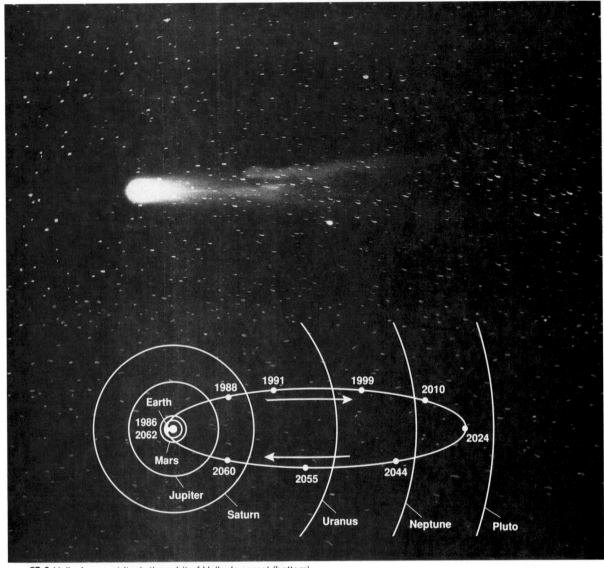

5B-3 *Halley's comet* (top); *the orbit of Halley's comet* (bottom)

about the same, seventy-five to seventy-six years. Halley concluded that these three were all the same comet and that it traveled in an ellipse with a period of seventy-five to seventy-six years. From this conclusion he predicted that the comet would return in 1758.

Although Halley did not live to see his prediction fulfilled, other astronomers watched the comet return as Halley had said. Halley's reasoning was proved right, and the comet was named in his honor. Halley's comet has returned on schedule four times since his death: 1759, 1835, 1910, and 1986. Its next appearance should be in 2062.

FACETS OF ASTRONOMY

5B–1

The Halley Fleet

Halley's comet, which passes the earth once every seventy-six years, provided the world's young space program a once-in-a-lifetime opportunity in March of 1986 to study a comet up close. The leading nations of the world planned years ahead to send a small fleet of space probes to unlock its secrets.

In the 1970s the United States proposed a bold plan for a probe to rendezvous with the comet, to stay with it, and to make continuous observations. But such a probe would need a new "ion drive" propulsion system, and the funds were not granted in time. So, U.S. scientists did the best they could—they organized the International Halley Watch to coordinate earth-based scientific studies.

Three other nations proposed to send probes on quick flyby missions, each with a slightly different, overlapping aim. The Soviets sent *Vega 1* and *2* to within 8,000 km (5,000 mi.) of the comet, three days apart. While still 172 million km (107 million mi.) from the nucleus, they found dust particles from the comet. As the probes entered the coma, the abrasive dust damaged the instruments, but the magnetometer on *Vega 1* and a plasma-wave sensor on *Vega 2* survived.

Two probes from Japan, *Sakigake* and *Suisei*, did not come

very close (within 150,000 km [93,000 mi.]). *Suisei* focused on the solar wind in front of the comet; and *Sakigake,* on the trailing coma. *Suisei* confirmed that the coma stops for a moment every fifty-three hours, apparently while the nucleus rotates.

The European probe *Giotto* was the most exciting. It entered the coma and came to within 600 km (370 mi.) of the nucleus, taking over sixty pictures. About twelve seconds before its closest encounter, a dense stream of dust knocked it into a tumble and shut down its camera, but it survived and continued to transmit data. Anticipating this rough encounter, its makers had stripped the probe of the long, delicate booms used in other probes to detect plasma waves and electric fields. Instead, its sensors studied the plasma's make-up, energy, and concentration.

The *Vega* and *Giotto* probes provided a wealth of information about Halley's core. Dramatic pictures unveiled a peanut-shaped black core, about 16 km (10 mi.) long and 8 km (5 mi.) wide. Expecting it to be like a hard snowball, scientists found a fluffy mass with a density as little as one-tenth that of frozen water. The nucleus's surface was cold, ranging from –27° to –127° C (–17° to –197° F). Ice could be seen vaporizing out of cracks in the hard, protective crust. Many gases appeared in the coma, caused by complex processes that scientists cannot fully explain. The comet dust proved to have silicates, carbon, and organic compounds. Astronomers, armed with many new questions, are eager for more opportunities to study the mystery of comets.

Sakigake and *Suisei* were very similar.

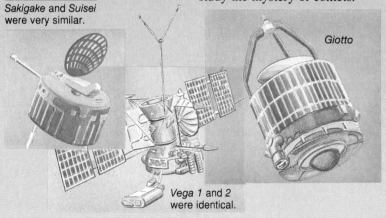

Giotto

Vega 1 and *2* were identical.

Description of Comets

Structure

Comets have two main parts: the **head** and the **tail.** The head, in turn, consists of two parts, the **nucleus** and the **coma.** The nucleus contains most of the comet's material. Its diameter is usually less than 80 km (50 mi.). It consists of rocks, dust, and frozen materials called **ices.** Surrounding the nucleus is the coma, which contains mainly ice particles and gases. The coma reflects light well, especially near its center. It has no sharp edges, but simply becomes less dense farther from the nucleus. The coma may be very large; some comas may appear larger than the sun!

Comets change as they orbit the sun. When a comet is far from the sun, it is difficult to see and its temperature is low. As a comet approaches the sun, its surface ices vaporize and release materials that the sun forces back into a long tail. This tail consists of gas, dust, or a combination of the two. Astronomers have identified two types of tails. The **type I tail** is mainly gas that is pushed away from the sun by the solar wind. This type of tail forms quickly and is almost straight. In contrast, the **type II tail** is mainly dust and is pushed away from the sun by the pressure of sunlight. This type of tail forms more slowly than a type I tail and tends to be curved. A

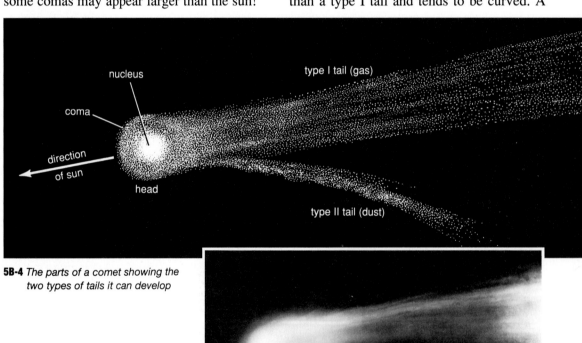

5B-4 *The parts of a comet showing the two types of tails it can develop*

5B-5 *Halley's comet; the head and part of the tail are shown here. The large coma obscures any view of the nucleus.*

5B-6 *This photograph of Comet West was taken three days before its nucleus separated into at least four parts. The tails are not very distinct in this photo.*

comet may have either type of tail, or it may have one or more of each. The Great Comet of 1744 had six tails.

A typical comet does not have a tail when it is far from the sun. A comet may never develop a tail if it is small or if its perihelion (the point in its orbit nearest the sun) is much beyond the orbit of Mars. When a comet does have a tail, it points away from the sun. Although the tail may be bright and millions of miles long, it contains less material than the best vacuum we can make on earth. The tail is longest when the comet is near the sun and quickly shrinks as the comet moves away from the sun. Finally, all the tail material is lost into space, and only the head remains. Nevertheless, material from the head forms a new tail the next time the comet comes near the sun.

One comet that scientists have studied closely is Halley's comet. Although its 1986 return was disappointing for many because it was more difficult to see than expected, Halley's comet did provide a wealth of information when space probes passed near it. Halley's nucleus is a peanut-shaped object about 16 km (10 mi.) long. It emits material

in groups of jets when it is near the sun. The ices in the comet include organic (carbon-containing) compounds. Halley's nucleus is surprisingly dark; it is covered with a crust that is blacker than black ink. An unexpected increase in brightness of the comet in 1991 still has scientists poring over data to determine the cause.

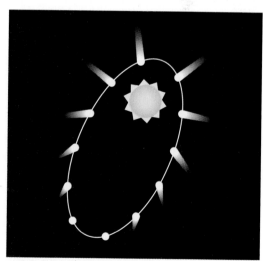

5B-7 *A comet's tail generally points away from the sun. The tail is longest when the comet is nearest the sun.*

Orbits

A comet's orbit may be elliptical or parabolic. If a comet keeps returning, it has an elliptical orbit and is called a **periodic comet.** If it has a parabolic orbit, a comet will pass the sun only once. All periodic comets that astronomers have seen more than once have periods less than 200 years. Comets with longer periods have much longer orbits. We can see a comet only while it is near the sun. From that fragment of an orbit, it is hard to tell whether the orbit is a long ellipse or a parabola. Thus, many comets that astronomers think follow parabolic orbits may actually have elliptical orbits with periods of thousands of years or more.

Some comets have periods of only a few years. Encke's comet has the shortest known period, 3.3 years. Many have periods from 5 to 7 years. These comets' aphelia (farthest distances from the sun) are often near Jupiter's orbit. Astronomers speculate that these comets once had longer orbits but passed close to Jupiter often enough for the giant planet's gravity to disturb their orbits. Some

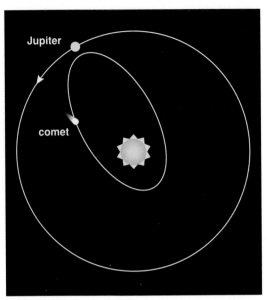

5B-9 *Short-period comets rarely orbit beyond Jupiter.*

comets have been observed to shorten their orbits after one close encounter with Jupiter.

The orientation of comet orbits spells serious trouble for the evolutionary theories of the origin of the solar system. If the solar system did accrete (uh KREET) (accumulate) from a rotating cloud, and the accretion process went on for millions of years, the system should by now be flattened into a disk. But comet orbits do not conform to this picture at all. They are tipped at all different angles to the ecliptic, many of them even at right angles to the orbits of the planets.

Degeneration

Comets are fragile structures. Every time one approaches the sun, it is in danger of disruption. As we have seen, solar energy drives the material of the comet's tail into space. This material is lost from the comet.

In addition, the sun can have more drastic effects. The sun's gravitational pull, acting unevenly on different parts of a comet's nucleus, can tear it apart. Biela's comet divided

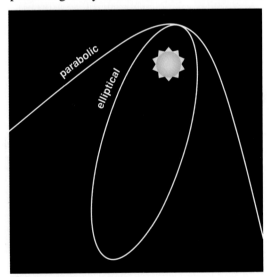

5B-8 *Types of comet orbits*

into two comets in the year 1846. Both returned in 1852, but after that, instead of the two comets there was an impressive display of meteors, especially in the years 1872 and 1885. Apparently the breakup of a comet can be rapid. If comets are so delicate and unable to last for long periods of time, why do we still have comets today? Most astronomers agree that comets can last for only hundreds or thousands of years at the most.

Because they believe that the solar system is billions of years old, evolutionists have trouble explaining the existence of comets. Some evolutionists theorize that the supply of comets is continually being replenished by a comet "storehouse" beyond Pluto's orbit. Some also imagine a belt of comets just beyond Saturn. These unseen storehouses, or some similar fanciful idea, are needed to rescue the evolutionary explanation for the origin of the solar system. The comet storehouse not only is invisible to us but also does not agree well with the evolutionary theory it was designed to save.

Creationism affords the only answer with the theory that the earth is relatively young. Comets, then, furnish a good example of the degeneration spoken of in Hebrews 1:11: "They all shall wax old as doth a garment." The heavens and the earth are waxing old (wearing out) in the same way that a piece of clothing wears out.

5B-11	**Notable Comets**	
Date	**Name**	**Interesting Facts**
240 B.C.	Halley's	only periodic comet visible to the naked eye; only known retrograde comet
1744	De Chéseaux's	had 6 tails
1770	Lexell	closest approach of a comet's head to earth
1772	Biela	broke into meteroids (confirmed in 1872)
1786	Encke	shortest known period, 3.3 years; most frequently observed
1811	Great Comet of 1811	largest recorded coma (larger than the sun)
1843	Great Comet of 1843	longest recorded tail, 320 million km (200 million mi.)
1910	Daylight	brightest comet of 20th century
1925	Schwassmann-Wachmann 1	nearly circular orbit
1957	Arend-Roland	had an "anti-tail"†
1965	Ikeya-Seki	speed of 1.6 million km/hr (1 million mph) at perihelion
1973	Kohoutek	a major disappointment; expected to be "the comet of the century"
1976	West	head broke into 4 parts

† An "anti-tail" points in the opposite direction of the tail.

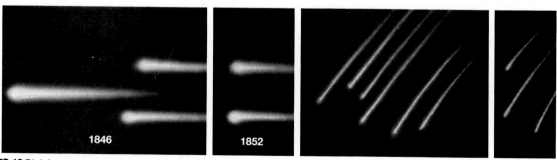

5B-10 *Biela's comet was observed to break into two comets. On successive return dates only meteor showers occurred.*

1846   1852

Section Review Questions 5B

1. List the two main parts of a comet.
2. List the two divisions of a comet's head.
3. (a) Which type of comet tail is composed mostly of dust? (b) Which type of tail forms rapidly as the comet approaches the sun? (c) Which type of tail is more curved?
4. When is Halley's comet expected to return next?
5. Comets that have elliptical orbits are called by what name?
6. Which comet has the shortest known period?
7. Which comet broke into two comets in 1846?
8. What material from Halley's comet damaged probes sent to observe it?

5C–Meteors

Like comets, meteors are visible to the unaided eye. However, meteors last for no longer than an instant. At certain times you may observe hundreds of meteors in a single night. When some people see a meteor, they hope it has some special power to grant wishes. However, we know it is just an inanimate* object with no more power than the idol Baal that Elijah mocked, saying, ''Cry aloud: for he is a god; either he is talking, or he is pursuing, or he is in a journey, or peradventure he sleepeth, and must be awaked'' (I Kings 18:27).

Shooting Stars

The flash of a ''falling star,'' or ''shooting star,'' is a familiar sight in the night sky. This streak of light signals another fulfillment of Hebrews 1:11, the destruction of one more celestial object. One minute a particle orbits the sun as it has probably done for thousands of years; the next minute, it ventures too close to the earth and is pulled in by the earth's gravity. As a particle falls through the atmosphere, friction heats it to a glowing brilliance. Most particles are no larger than a speck of dust and are burned completely in the air. Only one in millions survives its trip

through the atmosphere to land on the earth's surface.

When a particle in space orbits the sun, it is called a **meteoroid.** As it glows coming through the atmosphere, it is a **meteor.** An extraspectacular meteor seen by observers over a wide area is called a **fireball,** or a **bolide** (BOH lide) if it explodes. Sometimes fireballs leave lighted trails, **trains,** behind them. A train can remain visible for as long as half an hour. Some fireballs are bright enough to be seen in broad daylight, and oth-

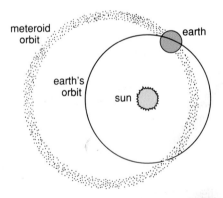

5C-1 The intersection of a meteoroid orbit with the earth's orbit (not to scale). Each year, some of the meteroids in the orbit will enter the earth's atmosphere.

---

inanimate: in- (L. IN-, not, no) + -animate (L. ANIMA, soul, life)

ers light up the night sky so brightly that it is possible to read by their light. Meteoroids large enough to become fireballs often survive the fall through the atmosphere to reach the ground. These are called **meteorites.**

Our chances of seeing meteors are generally better after midnight. This advantage exists because after midnight the observer is on the leading side of the earth as it goes through its orbit. Thus, the earth is approaching meteoroids and often catches up with meteoroids moving away from it. Between noon and midnight, the observer is on the trailing side of the earth. Thus, the earth is moving away from meteoroids, and only those fast enough to overtake the earth become meteors.

When you first see a meteor it is probably between 100 and 130 km (60 and 80 mi.) above the earth's surface. Most meteors have largely spent themselves by the time they reach a height of 80 km (50 mi.). If they are that far away and still seem to be moving rapidly, their speed must be tremendous. In-

deed, meteors have been clocked at speeds up to 72 km/s (45 mi./s)! This maximum speed occurs when the meteor and the earth are moving toward each other; their rate of approach is the combined speed of the two bodies.

Theoretically, you can see meteors any night of the year. Nevertheless, there is an element of chance. On some nights you may not see any, and on other nights you may see several. Success in viewing a meteor depends both on being in the right place at the right time and on looking at the right part of the sky. Most meteors come from random directions and fall at any time. These meteors are called **sporadic meteors.**

During a few times of the year your chance of seeing a meteor increases. Meteoroid orbits cross the earth's orbit at several points. When the earth arrives at such a place in its orbit, some meteoroids in the orbit will fall to the earth. Such meteors are called **shower meteors.** The number of meteors falling in a

5C-2 The likelihood of seeing meteors is better if you are on the leading side of the earth as it travels through its orbit. You are on the leading side after midnight.

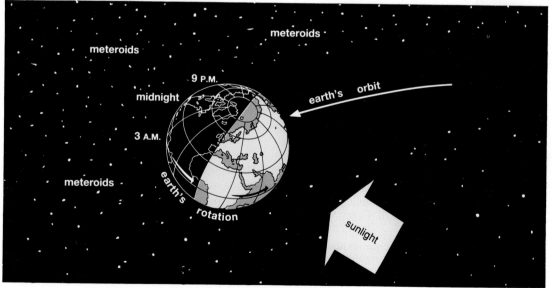

shower depends on the number of meteoroids located in the part of the orbit the earth crosses.

The two best times to see shower meteors are around August 12 and November 17. The August 12 shower meteors are called **Perseids** (PUR see id) because they appear to be coming out of the constellation Perseus. This is just an optical illusion, for the stars are actually hundreds of thousands of times farther away than the source of the meteors. Perseid meteors are debris remaining from Comet 1862 III, a faint comet seen in the year 1862.

The November 17 meteors are called **Leonids** (LEE uh nid) because they appear to be coming out of the constellation Leo. The Leonid meteors represent debris from Comet Temple. In fact, scientists think that all the shower meteors are fragments from the breakup of comets. The connection between most of the meteors and comets is a testimony to the reality of degeneration in the solar system.

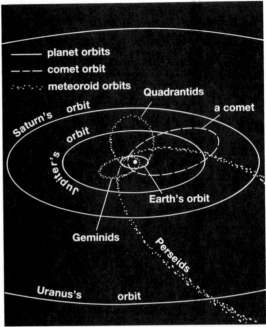

5C-4 *Meteor showers occur on each date that the earth intersects a path of orbiting meteoroids. Many of these meteroid paths are believed to be debris from comets.*

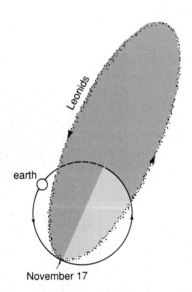

5C-3 *The Leonid meteor shower occurs on November 17 when the orbits of the earth and meteroids intersect.*

Meteorites

Although most meteors are completely consumed in the atmosphere, a few of them, as we have noted, do make it to the ground. Of these, smaller meteorites are much more common than larger ones.

The 60-metric-ton (66-ton) Hoba West is the largest meteorite ever found. Discovered in 1920 near Grootfontein in Namibia, Africa, the meteorite has a volume of about 7 m^3 (9 yd.^{3}).† Because of its great weight, the Hoba West meteorite has not been transported to a museum. The largest meteorite on display in a museum is "Ahnighito," found in 1897 near Cape York, Greenland. Admiral Robert E. Peary, the arctic explorer, brought the meteorite to the United States, and it is now exhibited at the Hayden Planetarium in New York City.

† The abbreviaton m^3 means cubic meters.

The Allende Meteorite Shower

Yes, that's right, meteor*ite* showers (as opposed to meteor showers) occur on rare, spectacular occasions. The most studied shower in history, named for the Mexican village of Pueblito de Allende (ah YANE day), occurred after midnight on February 8, 1969. Villagers witnessed an impressive fireball, seen for hundreds of kilometers around and even in the United States.

As a series of sonic booms hit, the object split in two and then scattered in an explosion of light. An estimated 4 tons of debris fell over an area approximately 50 km (30 mi.) by 10 km (6 mi.). Meteorite hunters from the United States and Mexico scoured the region, collecting thousands of samples weighing a total of 2 tons. The largest sample, 110 kg (240 lb.), marked the farthest boundary of the elongated **strewn field,** with progressively smaller specimens falling behind.

This meteorite from the Allende meteorite shower hit the base of a cactus. The sunglasses were added for scale.

Classes of Meteorites

Using chemical composition, scientists can distinguish three types of meteorites. **Stones,** or **stony meteorites,** contain 85 per cent to 90 per cent stony materials, such as silicate

5C-6	Hits and Near Hits
Indiana, 1991	A meteorite weighing 483 g missed a thirteen-year-old boy by about 5 feet.
California, 1973	A 2-inch meteorite fell through a carport.
Alabama, 1954	An 11-pound meteorite struck and bruised a woman's hip.
Egypt, 1922	A dog was struck and killed by a meteorite.

5C-5
The Ahnighito meteorite on display (top right); the Hoba West meteorite is the largest meteorite ever discovered (bottom right).

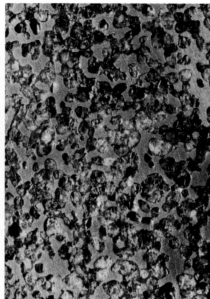
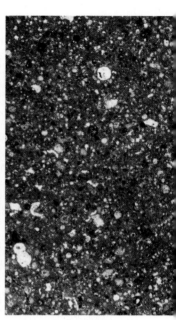

5C-7 *Iron meteorites show a characteristic pattern when polished and treated with acid* (left); *a stony-iron meteorite composed of iron surrounding crystalline silicate material* (middle); *the polished surface of a stony meteorite* (right)

minerals, and 10 per cent to 15 per cent iron and nickel. They are the most common type of meteorite. **Irons** are alloys of metals containing 85 per cent to 90 per cent iron, the rest mostly nickel. Irons are the second most common type. They can be polished to form reflective surfaces. These polished surfaces show a characteristic pattern when treated with acid. **Stony-irons** are about half silicate and half iron. They seem to combine the properties of the other two types. Stony-iron meteorites are rare.†

Meteorite Craters

Meteorite craters have been found in various places on the earth. Probably the most famous crater is the Barringer Meteorite Crater near Winslow, Arizona. It is 1,265 m (4,150 ft.) across and 174 m (570 ft.) deep on the inside. Its rim rises 46 m (150 ft.) above the level of the surrounding terrain. Although scientists have not found the main body of

the meteorite, they have unearthed 30 tons of fragments. Astronomers theorize that the meteorite may have been only 30 m (100 ft.) in diameter. They explain the large size of the crater by the meteorite's exploding on impact. According to the theory, the explosion was caused by the great amount of kinetic energy (energy of motion) suddenly being converted to heat energy. Much of the meteorite was vaporized, and the rapidly expanding vapors forcefully blew material out in all directions.

The Barringer Crater is not the largest crater known on the earth's surface. That honor goes to the Manicouagan Crater in Quebec, which is 75 km (47 mi.) in diameter. Scientists now recognize several dozen craters 3 km (2 mi.) or more in diameter. These large craters, though often considerably eroded, closely resemble the craters on the moon, Mars, and Mercury. Those craters are probably also meteorite craters.

---

† A certain amount of experience is necessary to identify meteorites reliably. Meteorites are black on the outside and gray, brown, or black on the inside. To be certain that a meteorite is genuine, the discoverer can send it to the American Meteorite Laboratory, Box 2090, Denver, Colorado 80201.

5C-8 *Barringer Meteorite Crater near Winslow, Arizona (top); a lake has filled Ungava-Quebec Crater (formerly called Chubb Crater) in Quebec, Canada (bottom left); Manicouagan Crater also in Quebec is the largest known crater on earth (right)*

Meteors and the Age of the Earth

Studying meteorites brings to light a problem about the age of the earth. The problem is the lack of meteorites in the fossil layers of the earth's crust. If the fossil layers did take hundreds of millions of years to form, many meteorites should have accumulated in them. With their extensive excavation of these layers, scientists should have found numerous meteorites. They have not. They are not sure whether they have found any. Again we have strong evidence that the earth is young. The creationist approach, as we have seen in many other instances, is superior.

The Siberian Explosion (June 30, 1908)

At 7:17 A.M. in a remote forest of Siberia, local farmers and herders were startled by an explosion the equivalent of a 12-megaton nuclear bomb. "The sky was split in two, and high above the forest the whole northern part of the sky appeared to be covered by fire," said one frightened witness. "My shirt was almost burned on my body. At that moment there was a bang in the sky and a mighty crash." The force threw him down, knocking him unconscious.

He had witnessed what is known as "the Tunguska (toon GOOS kah) Event." A mysterious fireball blew down an 800,000-acre circle of trees and fried five hundred reindeer in their tracks. Horses fell off their feet 650 km (400 mi.) away. People heard the blast 1,000 km (600 mi.) away. A rush of air pressed around the globe twice. Tremors were felt around the world, and a reddish haze lit the skies for days.

Years later researchers found a circle of flattened trees and tiny diamonds similar to those found in meteors. But they found no crater or meteorite. Many teams have since visited the site. They have offered some wild explanations of what hit the earth: an ex-

Many explanations have been given for the Tunguska Event; one of the more credible ones suggests that it was a comet striking the earth.

ploding spaceship, a piece of antimatter, a black hole. Most scientists accept the conclusion that a million-ton comet or comet fragment, perhaps a football field in width, smashed into the atmosphere at a speed of 120,000 km/hr. (70,000 mph). Modern soil studies support this hypothesis: they uncovered tons of powdery material that could be the remains of the shattered core of a comet. If so, this is the only known case of a comet's ever hitting the earth.

Section Review Questions 5C

1. Distinguish between meteoroids, meteors, and meteorites.
2. Why is it easier to see meteors after midnight?
3. When are the two best times during the year to see meteor showers?
4. List the three types of meteorites.
5. When studying meteorites, what problem comes up concerning the age of the earth?
6. What do most scientists think the Tunguska Event was?

Terms

asteroid
bolide
coma
comet
fireball
head
ices
irons
Leonids

meteor
meteorite
meteoroid
minor planet
nucleus
periodic comet
Perseids
shower meteors
sporadic meteor

stones (stony meteorites)
stony-irons
strewn field
tail
train
type I tail
type II tail

What Did You Learn?

1. Why is Pluto not considered a minor planet?
2. What are the differences between a comet and a meteor?
3. How old will you be when Halley's comet returns?
4. Could the composition of a meteorite be used to determine the composition of comets?
5. Discuss three different evidences from this chapter that the solar system is much younger than evolutionary estimates of its age.

What Do You Think?

1. Do you think an asteroid could be "captured" and used for a space station? Explain your answer.
2. Suppose a space vehicle were able to "hitch a ride" on a comet. What things would you expect scientists to find out?
3. Should Christians fear collisions with comets, asteroids, or meteors? Explain your answer.
4. What should be the attitude of the Christian in regard to the Genesis account of creation even if scientists were to find some evidence that the earth is much older?

THE MOON: TO RULE THE NIGHT

SIX

6A–Description of the Moon

The moon is the closest of all the astronomical bodies we see in the sky; it is a satellite or companion of the earth. As it orbits the earth approximately once each month, it accompanies the earth around the sun. The moon is a dark body like a planet, but we see it by reflected sunlight. Scripture tells us that God created the moon to be "the lesser light to rule the night" (Gen. 1:16).

As a Globe

Size and Shape

The moon is much smaller than the earth. Its diameter is only 3,475 km (2,159 mi.), which is less than the width of the United States. Its surface area is a little more than that of Africa. The moon is only $\frac{1}{81}$ as massive as the earth; it has not only a smaller volume than the earth but also a smaller density.

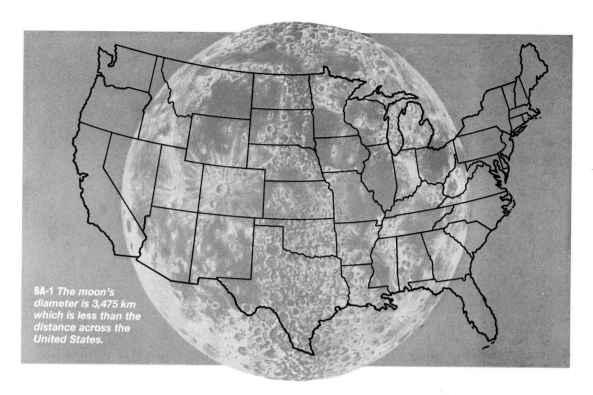

6A-1 *The moon's diameter is 3,475 km which is less than the distance across the United States.*

The moon is almost a perfect sphere; its diameter differs by no more than 1 per cent in any direction. The faster an astronomical body spins, the more it becomes bulged at the equator and flattened at the poles. Because the moon rotates slower than the earth, it is more nearly spherical.

Gravity

Since the moon is only $\frac{1}{81}$ as massive as the earth, the force of gravity at its surface is only about $\frac{1}{6}$ as great as the force of gravity on the earth. A 50-kg (110-lb.) person would weigh only 8.3 kg (18.3 lb.) on the moon. You could throw a ball much higher and farther on the moon than you can on the earth. Also you would notice that the ball would fall to the ground much more slowly.

The moon's **escape velocity** is low because its gravity is weak. Escape velocity is

6A-2 *On the moon, gravity is one-sixth of that on earth. Walking your dog would be quite a challenge.*

FACETS OF ASTRONOMY

Weight vs. Mass

"How much do you weigh?" If you were in outer space, you could honestly say you do not weigh anything. On the earth, you have less *weight* on the top of a mountain than down at the beach. These "weight losses" are not due to less fat. If you are overweight on earth, you will still be overweight in space, even if you do not weigh anything. This confusion arises because the English language does not easily distinguish between weight and mass.

Weight refers to the gravitational pull exerted on an object. The farther you are from the source of gravity—the earth, for example—the less gravitational pull you experience and the less you weigh. That is why you weigh less at high elevations. Scientists report weight in units called newtons (N). The kilogram is actually a unit of mass but in common usage has become a unit of weight. The weight of an object is found by multiplying the mass of the object by the acceleration due to gravity at the location of the object.

mass (kg) × acceleration
$$= weight\ (N)$$

The mass of an object is defined as the amount of matter in an object. Moving an object from the earth to the moon would not change the amount of matter in the object. Therefore an object with a *mass* of 1 kg on the earth also has a *mass* of 1 kg on the moon.

What is acceleration due to gravity? As you probably know, as an object falls its speed increases each second that it falls. On the earth the rate of increase is about 10 m (32 ft.) each second. If an object is falling at a speed of 20 m/s and continues to fall, one second later it will be falling 30 m/s, and two seconds later it will be falling 40 m/s, and so on. This increase in speed as the object falls is called acceleration due to gravity. On the earth the average acceleration is 9.8 (m/s)/s (9.8 meters per second per second).† On the moon, the rate of acceleration is only $\frac{1}{6}$ of that on earth, about $1.6\ m/s^2$. A 1-kg object on the earth would weigh
$$1 \times 9.8 = 9.8\ N.$$

A 1-kg object on the moon would weigh
$$1 \times 1.6 = 1.6\ N.$$

Astronomers are more interested in mass than weight. *Mass* describes the amount of matter an object contains, regardless of where it is in the universe. The standard unit for mass is the kilogram. The moon's mass is 7.4×10^{22} (74 followed by 21 zeros) kg. The sun's mass is 2.0×10^{30} (2 followed by 30 zeros) kg. What is your mass today?

† Instead of writing (m/s)/s, scientists frequently write the units of acceleration as m/s^2 (meters per second squared). Time is not squared in the measurement. This is simply a short way to write the units.

the speed an object must travel to free itself from gravitational pull. For the earth, the escape velocity is 11 km/s (25,000 mph), whereas for the moon it is only 2.4 km/s (5,400 mph). Because of its low escape velocity, the moon's atmosphere is negligible. Even if the gases needed to form an atmosphere appeared around the moon, they would soon escape because the speed of their molecules would be greater than the escape velocity.

Atmosphere

Long before machines and men reached the moon, scientists knew that it lacked an atmosphere. How did they know this? One clue came from the moon's passing in front of, or *occulting,* a star. If the moon had an atmosphere, the star would dim gradually as the moon's atmosphere passed in front of the star. But stars blink out abruptly when the moon occults them. Another evidence of the moon's lack of atmosphere is in the **terminator,** the line dividing the lighted side of the moon from the dark side. If the moon had an atmosphere, it would create a twilight zone in which the light gradually shaded into darkness. Instead, the terminator shows a sudden change from light to dark.

The earth's atmosphere is essential for life. It is the source of oxygen for us to breathe. Its pressure, 100,000 N/m^2 (14.7 lb./in.^{2}) helps our bodies to function efficiently. It serves as a blanket to protect us from the

6A-3 *The abrupt change from light to dark along the moon's edge occurs because the moon has no atmosphere. By comparison, the earth's atmosphere makes the change more gradual.*

extreme heat of the sun and the extreme cold of space at night. It also assists in our communication because sound does not travel in a vacuum. But the moon has no atmosphere. The astronauts* who walked on the moon had to take their own atmosphere with them. The pressure suits they wore provided them with oxygen to breathe, with cooling water to moderate the sun's fierce heat, with proper pressure, and with radios for communication. They did not explore the moon during the night, and so they avoided the need for heating. Radio waves travel in a vacuum, so they had no trouble communicating.

Section Review Questions 6A-1

1. How massive is the moon in comparison to the earth?
2. Why does the moon have such a spherical shape?
3. How does the force of gravity on the moon compare to the force of gravity on the earth?
4. What are the metric units for measuring mass? for weight?
5. The speed that an object must travel to free itself from gravitational pull is known by what name?
6. What term is used to describe one object moving in front of another object?
7. What is the line dividing the lighted side of the moon from the dark side?

---

astronaut: astro- (Gk. ASTER, star)
+ -naut (Gk. NAUTES, sailor)

The Moon's Surface

The Craters

Scattered over the moon's surface are hundreds of thousands of round pits ranging from a few inches to hundreds of kilometers in diameter. These are called **craters,** a name taken from the Greek word for cup. Many craters are surrounded by steep, nearly circular walls that project above the surrounding land.

The most spectacular of the craters is Tycho, located near the moon's south pole. Radiating from Tycho in various directions are many bright streaks called **rays,** some over 1,600 km (1,000 mi.) long. You can see these rays with the naked eye. At full moon they give the appearance of a peeled orange. The rays are thin strips of material probably blown out by an explosion.

After an extensive study of close-up photographs taken by space cameras orbiting the moon, scientists generally believe that most craters were formed by impact, that is, by meteors bombarding the surface. Calculations show that when a chunk of rocklike material such as a meteor strikes the moon's surface at high speed, it should actually explode, producing a crater far larger than the meteor itself.

There are other craters that do not fit this picture. These have low walls or no walls at all. Scientists theorize that such craters were formed by processes similar to volcanism on the earth. Some of these are arranged along fault lines in places where a break in the moon's crust apparently released gases from the interior. Because the moon has no real atmosphere, these gases would expand explosively, blasting away surface material to form a crater.

The Maria

Some people imagine that they see a ''man in the moon.'' Others see both a man and a

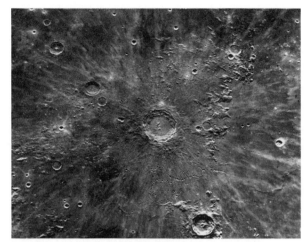

6A-4 *The crater Copernicus showing some of the rays surrounding it.*

6A-5 *The steep, high walls of the crater Tycho indicate that it probably formed by meteor impact.*

6A-6 *This view of Mare Tranquilitatis, as seen from Apollo 8, reveals both large and small craters in the mare.*

woman. Still others claim to see the silhouette of a rabbit, an old woman picking up sticks, or a girl reading. These shapes are formed by the dark areas on the moon, the **maria*** (MAH ree uh) (singular, **mare**). Early astronomers, thinking that these were bodies of water, gave them Latin names appropriate for lunar seas. Some of these are Mare Imbrium (Sea of Rains), Mare Serenitatis (Sea of Serenity), Mare Tranquilitatis (Sea of Tranquillity), and Oceanus Procellarum (Ocean of Storms). The names remain, though we now realize that there is no water on the moon's surface.

The maria cover about half the moon's near side. They are broad lowland plains covered with hardened lava that makes them darker in appearance than the surrounding

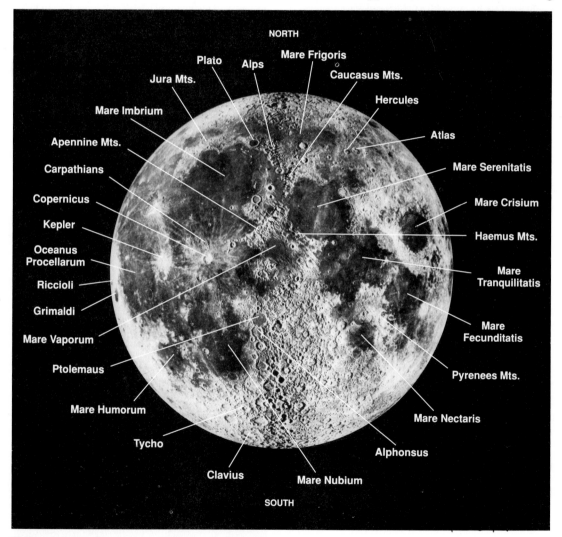

6A-7 *Important surface features of the moon's near side*

mare: (L. MARE, sea)

upland regions. The maria are roughly circular, and some are surrounded by rings of mountains. These features make most lunar scientists think that the maria basins are impact craters formed when huge meteors crashed into the moon. Later the dark-colored lava flooded the giant craters on the moon's near side. The largest of the maria is Mare Imbrium, some 1,100 km (700 mi.) in diameter. The back side of the moon has many large impact craters, but few are covered with dark lava.

The Mountains and Rills

Bordering some of the maria are mountain ranges similar to those on the earth. Several of these have been named after mountain ranges of the earth. For example, the Alps, Apennines, Caucasus, and Carpathian mountains form part of the boundary of Mare Imbrium. These mountains rise abruptly from the plains of the maria to heights up to 8 km (5 mi.). Their steep slopes would be difficult to climb, especially because climbers would need pressure suits.

Another feature of the moon's surface is long, narrow valleys called **rills.** Some rills are fairly straight. These resemble features near faults on the earth. Other rills are wind-

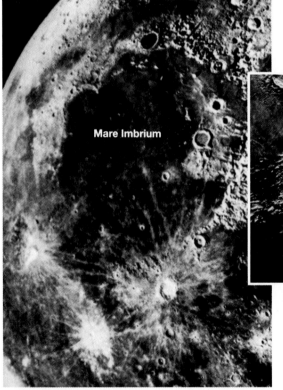

6A-8 *Mare and mountains of the moon; Mare Imbrium* (above), *the Apennines (top right), a mountain range on the edge of Mare Imbrium; foothills of the Appennines (right), the rough surface in the foreground which is part of a relatively fresh crater*

ing. Their general shape resembles that of rivers on earth, but unlike rivers they begin and end abruptly. Scientists believe that the winding rills may have been paths for the molten lava that covered the maria.

6A-9 *Hadley Rill, photographed from lunar orbit (top), was explored by Apollo 15 (bottom).*

Our Moon: Unique in the Solar System

Astronomers recognize that our moon is unusual in many respects. For instance, it is one hundred times larger than the average moon in the solar system. When compared to the size of its planet, our moon is ten times larger than any other moon except Charon. Charon and Pluto are like large asteroids, only about 19,700 km (12,200 mi.) apart, revolving rapidly around one another.

Evolutionists cannot explain such size, but the Bible does. In Genesis 1:16 God said he made a "lesser light to rule the night." We have the only planet with a moon large enough to light up the evening sky. If we had an average-size moon, the night would be twenty times darker than it is.

The Bible also says God specially created the moon "for signs, and for seasons, and for days, and years" (Gen. 1:14). Our moon remains in stable orbit. It does not fall to the earth or spin away. Ever since eclipse records have been taken over the last three thousand years, the moon has moved less than the length of two football fields away from the earth. We can use these predictable eclipse phenomena to date events of the past. The stable moon, "a faithful witness in heaven," reminds us that God is faithful to keep His promises and to provide for our needs (see Ps. 89:37).

Section Review Questions 6A-2

1. What is the name given to the round pits found on the surface of the moon?
2. What are the streaks that sometimes radiate out from a crater?
3. What do scientists believe formed most of the craters on the moon?
4. What is the name given to the dark, lowland plains found on the moon's surface?
5. What are the long, narrow valleys on the moon's surface called?
6. For what purpose does the Bible say that God made the moon?

6B–The Moon's Motion

The earth, you have learned, has two motions. It *revolves* around the sun each year while it *rotates* on its own axis each day. The moon also has two motions. It revolves around the earth while it rotates on its own axis. The moon takes the same amount of time for its revolution and its rotation, about one month. Because the rotation rate equals the revolution rate, the moon always keeps the same face to the earth. Before space travel, no one knew what the back side of the moon looked like. Now we know that it has many craters like the front side, but it has fewer maria.

The back side of the moon (far side) and the dark side of the moon are not the same.

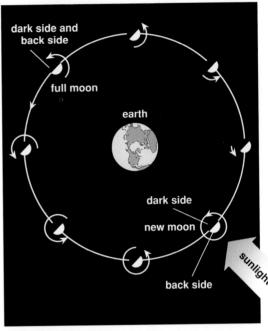

6B-2 *The back side and dark side of the moon are usually not the same.*

6B-1 *The back side has many craters like the front side, but it has fewer maria. You cannot see the back side of the moon from earth. This photograph of the back side of the moon was taken from the Apollo 16 service module.*

The back side is the side away from the *earth,* and the dark side is the side away from the *sun.* The back side and the dark side occupy the same space at full moon; however, during other phases of the moon, the back side and the dark side do not occupy the same space.

The Moon's Orbit

The moon's orbit is shaped like an ellipse, like a slightly squashed circle. Its distance from the earth thus changes. The average distance from the center of the moon to the center of the earth is about 385,000 km (239,000 mi.). The moon's point of closest approach, called the **perigee*** (PER uh jee), is about 356,000 km (221,000 mi.). At the most distant point of orbit, called the **apogee*** (AP uh jee), the moon is about 407,000

perigee: peri- (near) + -gee (Gk. GE, earth)

apogee: apo- (away from) + -gee (earth)

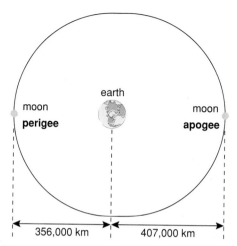

6B-3 *The point in the moon's orbit that is nearest the earth is called perigee; the point that is most distant from the earth is apogee.*

km (253,000 mi.) away. A careful observer can notice that the moon actually looks larger at perigee than at apogee.

Astronomically speaking, the moon is a close neighbor. So far, it is the only body that

manned space expeditions have studied. A trip to the next nearest object, Venus, would be far more difficult. Even at its closest approach, Venus is more than one hundred times as far away as the moon.

The exact length of the moon's **period,** the time it takes to complete one orbit, depends on your vantage point as you observe the moon. If you could somehow watch the moon from a nearby star, you would observe that its period is $27\frac{1}{3}$ days. However, when you watch it from the earth, you find its period to be $29\frac{1}{2}$ days. The reasons for the difference are that the moon and the earth are moving around the sun and that observers in different places choose different references to measure. From a distant star, you would measure the time between two alignments of the moon and a particular spot on the earth. This time is $27\frac{1}{3}$ days. From the earth, you measure the time between two alignments of the moon, a place on earth, and the sun. Because the earth and moon are moving, it takes two extra days to realign with the sun. Thus, the period as measured from earth is $29\frac{1}{2}$ days.

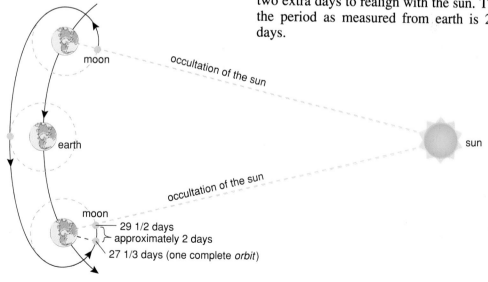

6B-4 *On earth, the period of the moon's revolution is $29\frac{1}{2}$ days; the time from one occultation of the sun to the next.*

waxing crescent (age 4 days)   first quarter (age 7 days)   waxing gibbous (age 10 d

6B-5 *Phases of the moon*

The Moon's Phases

Perhaps the most striking characteristic of the moon that we see from earth is its **phases,** its changes of shape. These phases repeat when the sun, moon, and a particular place on earth realign. Thus the period of the moon's phases is $29\frac{1}{2}$ days. Phases are due to our angle of observing the illuminated part of the moon.

The cycle begins at **new moon,** when the moon is in the same direction as the sun. Because the sun is so bright, we cannot see the moon at all then. If we could see the moon, we would say that it rises at sunrise and sets at sunset. On the second night after the new moon, the moon should be far enough from the sun to be visible. Look for a thin sliver crescent low in the western sky shortly after sunset. This phase, called the **waxing crescent,** continues through the first week of the cycle. The **cusps,** or horns, of a crescent moon always point away from the sun. If the crescent were a bow, the bow would shoot an arrow directly at the sun. During the early part of the lunar cycle, you can often see the dark part of the moon by **earthshine,** sunlight reflected from the earth to the moon and back again.

The crescent grows progressively thicker while the position of the moon changes toward the south. At $7\frac{3}{8}$ days into the cycle, the moon is high in the sky and almost due south at sundown. The moon rises at noon and sets at midnight. Now the western half is lighted while the eastern half is dark. (All directions are given as they appear from the Northern Hemisphere.) The terminator, which usually appears curved, now forms a straight line up and down the middle of the moon's disk. This phase, 90° away from the sun in the sky, is called the **first quarter.**

During the second week of the cycle, the moon gradually works its way to the east. The lighted portion continues to grow until the whole disk is illuminated. This phase, as it increases between first quarter and full moon, is the **waxing gibbous** (GIB us). The moon is on the eastern horizon at sundown.

A **full moon** is exactly 180° away from the sun. For this reason, the rising of the full moon takes place at about the same time as the setting of the sun, and the setting of the full moon takes place at about the same time as the rising of the sun. This fact enables you to know just where the moon is in the daytime or where the sun is at night, even though you cannot see them. The moon is nine times as bright when it is full as when it is only half visible in its first- or third-quarter phase. The angle of the sun's rays that strike the moon affects the moon's brightness. Because the sun is at the observer's back at full moon, he sees almost no shadows on the moon's surface. At a quarter moon, however, an observer can see many shadows that reduce the moon's brightness.

l (age 18 days)

waning gibbous (age 20 days)

last quarter (age 22 days)

waning crescent (age 24 days)

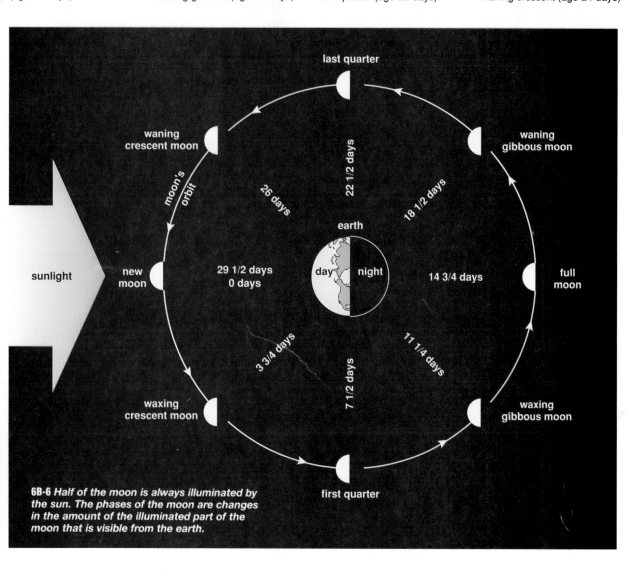

last quarter

waning
crescent moon

22 1/2 days

moon's orbit

waning
gibbous moon

26 days

18 1/2 days

sunlight

new
moon

29 1/2 days
0 days

earth

day   night

14 3/4 days

full
moon

3 3/4 days

7 1/2 days

11 1/4 days

waxing
crescent moon

waxing
gibbous moon

first quarter

6B-6 *Half of the moon is always illuminated by the sun. The phases of the moon are changes in the amount of the illuminated part of the moon that is visible from the earth.*

The **harvest moon** is the full moon that occurs nearest to the time of the autumnal equinox (September 21-23) in the Northern Hemisphere or the vernal equinox (March 21-23) in the Southern Hemisphere. Traditionally it has aided farmers in gathering their crops after sundown. The full moon occurring one month after the harvest moon is called the **hunter's moon** because the fields are clean of vegetation and hunters can easily spot prey at this time.

The full moon marks the halfway point of the lunar cycle. After full moon the phases repeat in reverse order, but with the eastern side lighted rather than the western. The **waning gibbous** phase occurs during the third week. Darkness appears along the moon's western limb (edge) and encroaches over more of the moon's surface each night. By **third quarter** (also called **last quarter**), at $22\frac{1}{8}$ days, the whole western side of the moon is in darkness, and the terminator forms a straight line as it did at first quarter. The lighted area continues to decrease through the last week of the cycle. This

phase, between third quarter and new moon, is the **waning crescent.** About two days before the end of the cycle, the moon goes out of sight, lost in the sun's glare. The new moon occurs at $29\frac{1}{2}$ days, marking the beginning of a new cycle.

6B-7 *Earthshine has illuminated the remainder of this waning crescent moon. Jupiter is seen to the right of the moon.*

Section Review Questions 6B-1

1. What is the most visible difference between the back side of the moon and the front side of the moon?
2. What is the difference between the back side of the moon and the dark side of the moon?
3. When do the dark side of the moon and the back side of the moon occupy the same space?
4. What is the average distance from the center of the earth to the center of the moon?
5. What is the term that relates to the moon's closest approach to the earth? the farthest distance from the earth?
6. What is the name given to the periodic changes in the shape of the moon?
7. Beginning with the new moon, list in order the phases of the moon.
8. In what direction do the cusps of the moon always point?
9. At what phase of the moon would few shadows be seen on the moon's surface?
10. What is the name given to the full moon that appears closest to the autumnal equinox?

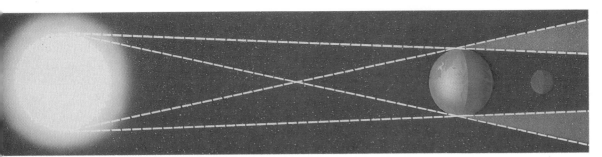

6B-12 *A lunar eclipse: The earth cuts off the sunlight reaching the moon.*

when the earth is directly between the moon and the sun.

Eclipses of the moon are easy to observe. The dates and times of their occurrence are listed well ahead of time in publications about astronomy. If you are on the side of the earth toward the moon during the eclipse, and if your weather is favorable, you can see the eclipse. Your local newspaper should give you more specific directions on when to view it from your particular location.

The moon travels from west to east in its orbit. This orbital motion carries it through the earth's shadow and out again. If it goes through the center of the shadow, the moon will be totally eclipsed; if it skims the edge of the shadow, it will be partially eclipsed. Even during the darkest part of a total eclipse, the moon is visible. It has a dull coppery-red color because of sunlight bent toward it by the earth's atmosphere. The longest period that the moon can be completely in the earth's shadow is one hour and forty minutes. It may be as long as three hours and forty minutes from the time it touches the shadow to the time it leaves completely. The length of time, however, varies from one eclipse to the next.

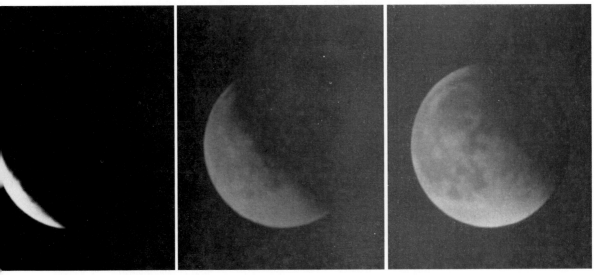

6B-13 *The moon becomes progressively lighter as it emerges from a lunar eclipse.*

In ancient times the heathen usually regarded eclipses as signs of impending evil. God told His people, "Learn not the way of the heathen, and be not dismayed by the signs of heaven" (Jer. 10:2). There is nothing to fear from an eclipse. It is a normal event that occurs according to a definite pattern. To predict eclipses, astronomers simply project the past eclipse pattern into the future. The ability to predict eclipses years, decades, and even centuries ahead of time is striking proof of the mathematical precision that the Creator has designed into the solar system.

Section Review Questions 6B-2

1. What word is used to mean "cutting off the light of one celestial body by another"?
2. At what phase must the moon be for a solar eclipse to take place?
3. When the moon is at its apogee, the solar eclipse is such that light from the sun shines around the edges of the moon. What type of eclipse is this called?
4. What causes the bright pinpoints of light called Baily's beads?
5. What is the term that relates to the moon's passing into the earth's shadow?
6. What direction does the moon travel in its orbit?

6C–The Moon's Origin

When men reject the Word of God on the subject of origins, they cut themselves off from the only true means of gaining any real knowledge of the subject. No man was present when the earth and the moon were created. We must therefore accept the account of the one who was present when these bodies were formed. Man, in his rebellion against God, has put forth various theories to satisfy himself that a moon could have come into existence without the need for a Creator. As we discuss each of these theories, you will begin to understand the inadequacy of man's reasoning when it comes to the question of origins.

The Capture Theory

The idea that the moon was once a planet traveling around the sun in its own orbit is attractive to many. They say that the earth managed to capture the moon. How could the earth capture the moon from the sun, which has a much stronger gravitational pull? There seems to be no reasonable way for this to happen. Some kind of catastrophe, the like of which has never been seen in the solar system, would be necessary. From what we

6C-1 *The capture theory holds that the earth pulled the moon from its own orbit around the sun.*

have observed of the solar system, we understand it to be an orderly arrangement of celestial machinery, not given to "accidents."

Those who have carefully studied the mathematics of lunar capture realize how improbable such an event is. The moon would need to be dislodged from its original orbit around the sun in such a way that it would come near the earth in just the right direction and at just the right speed. If it were traveling too fast and too far from the earth, it would be deflected into a new orbit around the sun rather than being captured.

Another problem is that if the earth succeeded in capturing the moon, the process probably would generate a tremendous amount of heat. Calculations indicate that such intense heat would have melted large portions of the earth's crust and that oceans would have vaporized into a corrosive steam. No evidence for these events occurs anywhere in the earth.

The Fission Theory

Since the late 1800s, people have entertained the idea that the moon spun off from the earth. Some have even said that it was ripped out of the Pacific Ocean, thus explaining the great depth of that ocean. But this theory has not held up under close study. To launch the moon at a speed great enough to go into orbit around the earth, the earth would have to be spinning at a dizzying rate, one complete rotation every two or three hours. If the earth had this much turning speed originally, what could have slowed it down to its present rate of turning? No one has suggested a satisfactory answer to this difficulty.

Another problem is that the process of fission would generate enough heat to increase the earth's temperature to 2,500° C (about 4,500° F). Again, the earth's crust has no

6C-2 *The fission theory holds that the moon was spun off from the earth while the earth was forming.*

record that this ever happened. Most astronomers have discarded this theory as hopeless, especially now that the moon rocks have proved different enough from earth rocks to suggest a separate origin.

The Accretion Theory

The idea that the earth and moon both accreted (accumulated) from the same original cloud of dust and gas is popular. The theory, however, has some serious problems that are often ignored in popular books and magazines.

First, small particles do not stick together to form large particles. Fairly large chunks of material are needed before gravitation can start drawing the pieces together. The same problem exists for the formation of the earth and other planets. There is no way to "glue" the dust particles of the supposed cloud together to form large enough chunks of material.

A second problem is that the moon as a whole seems to consist of lighter materials

6C-3 *The accretion theory holds that the moon and earth both condensed from the same cloud of dust and gas.*

6C-4 *The impact theory holds that a smaller planet struck the earth and that the moon formed from the resulting debris.*

than the earth. Whereas the average density of material in the earth is 5.5 times as dense as water, the moon is only 3.3 times as dense. Two astronomical bodies formed from the same area of the same cloud should have the same or similar composition.

The Impact Theory

A new theory devised after the Apollo explorations is the impact theory. The theory says that a planet the size of Mars struck the earth near its edge. The lighter parts of the earth and the other planet then broke away to form the moon. This theory attempts to explain why the moon rocks are similar to, but not identical with, those on earth.

The major problem with this theory is its unlikeliness. The other planet would need to strike the earth at just the right angle and just the right speed for the broken-off material to form a moon instead of falling back to earth or escaping entirely. From our observations, we know that collisions of any kind between planet-sized bodies are rare, if they ever occur. Our knowledge of the orderly solar system shows this event to be unlikely.

Every theory of the moon's origin has failed. The moon expeditions provided information that exposed the weaknesses of the major theories. Nothing reasonable has come along since to replace them. These theories show man's unwillingness to give God the glory that is rightfully His. Only by recognizing the role of the Creator in the history of the moon and the universe can we hope to develop a true knowledge of origins that will stand the test of time.

Section Review Questions 6C

1. What is the name of the theory that states that the moon was at one time orbiting the sun?
2. What two theories state that the moon at one time was part of the earth?
3. Which theory suggests that the moon accumulated from a cloud of dust or gas?

Terms

annular eclipse	harvest moon	rills
apogee	hunter's moon	solar eclipse
Baily's beads	last quarter	terminator
crater	lunar eclipse	third quarter
cusps	mare	total eclipse
diamond ring effect	new moon	waning crescent
earthshine	partial eclipse	waning gibbous
eclipse	perigee	waxing crescent
escape velocity	period	waxing gibbous
first quarter	phases	weight
full moon	ray	

What Did You Learn?

1. What is your mass in kilograms? What is your weight in newtons on the earth? on the moon?
2. What are two ways which scientists think craters on the moon may have formed?
3. How long is the moon's period as observed from the earth?
4. What is earthshine?
5. Why do lunar eclipses not take place every full moon?
6. Why is it that the moon can be explained only as a specially created object?
7. How would you determine whether a crescent moon was waxing or waning?
8. Unlike the sun and stars, the moon does not produce any of its own light. How then does it obey the command of God in Genesis 1:15 "to give light upon the earth"?

What Do You Think?

1. Suppose the earth had two or three moons instead of just one. How could we tell the difference between them?
2. Where on the moon would you advise NASA to build a permanent moon base? Why?
3. How would life on the earth be different if there were no moon?

EXPLORATION OF SPACE

SEVEN

7A–Rocketry

Millions of people all over the world watched by television as Neil Armstrong stepped off the ladder and onto the moon. For centuries men had dreamed of walking on the moon. The first science fiction story about space travel was written before 1700, but at that time no one knew how to leave the earth. How did men finally travel to the moon?

Here on earth, we usually move by pushing against something outside ourselves. You walk by pushing against the ground. Wheels turn by pushing against the ground. Boat oars and propellers push against water, and airplane propellers push against air. But in space, there is nothing to push against. Thus, we need some other way to move through space.

Early Rockets

Weapons

In the Middle Ages, the Chinese invented a weapon that moves without pushing against an outside surface. A **rocket** is a device that moves by pushing material (usually hot gases) out its end. The Chinese used rockets in 1232 to defend the city of K'ai-Fung-Foo against the Mongols. These early rockets, called "flying fire," consisted of black powder propellant packed into a bamboo tube that was attached to an arrow.

Why does forcing hot gases out of a rocket move it? Sir Isaac Newton explained this mystery when he stated his third law of motion: when an object pushes against another object, the second object pushes back with the same force. Thus, when a rocket pushes hot gases out its end, the hot gases push back against the rocket to propel it forward. The rocket produces hot gases by burning a fuel. The law is often stated "for every action, there is an equal but opposite reaction."

7A-1 *The Chinese are credited with developing the first rockets.*

For centuries, rockets were much like the Chinese rockets. They produced hot gases by burning black powder and were attached to long sticks for stability. Because these primitive rockets were difficult to aim and had short ranges, they were used more often as fireworks than as weapons.

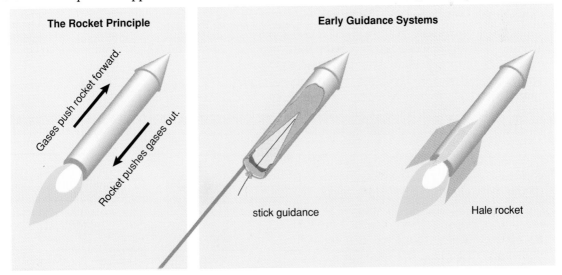

The Rocket Principle

Gases push rocket forward.

Rocket pushes gases out.

Early Guidance Systems

stick guidance

Hale rocket

7A-2 *Development of early rockets*

By the eighteenth century Sir William Congreve (KAHN GREEV), a notable solid-fuel rocket designer of England, developed the **Congreve rocket,** which weighed up to 60 pounds. The British troops fighting in the Napoleonic Wars found that this weapon shot farther than the smooth-bore cannon. The Congreve rocket was noted for its noise and its glare upon ignition. During the War of 1812, Francis Scott Key described the weapon in action with the words "the rocket's red glare" in our National Anthem. Improvements in structure led to greater ranges, but the rockets were difficult to aim because they still used the stick guidance system.

The first change in the rocket's form was proposed by William Hale of England. The Hale rocket replaced the stick stabilizer with three fins at the back of the rocket. The fins allowed more accurate aiming and shorter rockets; thus, the use of the rocket as a weapon increased.

Research

In the early 1900s three men independently came to the same conclusion: rockets could carry people into space. Konstantin E. Tsiolkovsky, a Russian schoolteacher, published a paper about rockets but did not experiment with them. Hermann Oberth of Germany started the German Society for Space Travel to research rockets. Robert H. Goddard (GAHD urd), an American, did many experiments with rockets.

Goddard made significant changes in rocket design. Because black powder was a dangerous fuel, Goddard invented a rocket that burned gasoline and liquid oxygen as fuel. His liquid-fuel rocket was launched in 1926. By 1935 Goddard had rockets that could fly higher and faster than any solid-fuel rockets.

Goddard also introduced a guidance system for the rocket using a rotating wheel. This "gyroscopic" system controlled the an-

7A-3 *Early Goddard rocket* (top); *the smoke trail of a Goddard rocket launch* (above) *shows its course being controlled by the gyroscopic guidance system.*

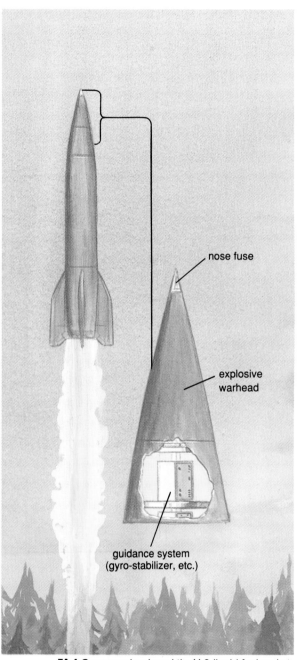

nose fuse

explosive
warhead

guidance system
(gyro-stabilizer, etc.)

7A-4 *Germany developed the V-2 liquid fuel rocket when conventional long-range artillery was banned.*

gle of the fins, which in turn controlled the direction of the hot gases as they left the rocket. Modern steering systems for rockets are often based on Goddard's idea. Goddard's contribution to rocketry was so great that he is called the father of the modern rocket.

World War II Rockets

In the treaty ending World War I, Germany was forced to agree not to use long-range artillery. To replace the forbidden weapons, the Germans established a rocket research center at Peenemünde under the leadership of Wernher von Braun (BRAWN). There they designed large liquid-fuel rockets with long ranges. The V-2, an important weapon in World War II, was their best rocket.

When Germany was defeated in 1945, the Soviet Union took over the Peenemünde research center, with some technicians and many V-2 rockets. Von Braun and the rocket development team, however, surrendered to the United States and took some V-2 rockets with them. Thus, both the United States and the USSR received German rocket knowledge and German V-2 rockets. Both nations used the German rockets to develop their own weapons, such as Intercontinental Ballistic Missiles, **ICBMs.**

Rockets in Space

From July 1, 1957, to December 31, 1958, many nations cooperated in a scientific study of the earth called the International Geophysical Year. To gain a new perspective on the earth, both the United States and the USSR decided to place an object in orbit around the earth. Such an object would be an artificial **satellite** of the earth. The Soviet Union launched the first manmade satellite, *Sputnik 1,* on October 4, 1957. *Sputnik 2,* launched a month later, carried the first living creature into orbit, a dog named Laika. She remained in orbit until her death. The United States launched its first satellite, *Explorer 1*, on January 31, 1958. This satellite contributed to the knowledge of the earth by discovering a band of charged particles trapped by the earth's magnetic field, the Van Allen belt.

Both nations used converted military rockets to launch their satellites. These rockets actually consisted of two or more rockets stacked one on top of another. Each rocket in such a stack is called a **stage;** multistage rockets are important in space exploration. A rocket uses most of its fuel as it takes off. If it had only one stage, it would have to drag a mostly empty fuel tank with it through space. In a multistage rocket, each stage separates from the rocket as its fuel runs out, and the next stage then begins to burn. Thus, a multistage rocket has enough power to reach space and a minimum mass while traveling through space.

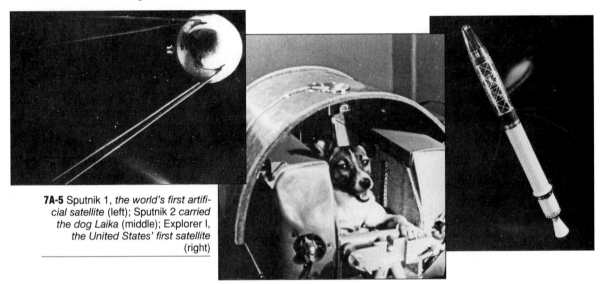

7A-5 Sputnik 1, *the world's first artificial satellite* (left); Sputnik 2 *carried the dog Laika* (middle); Explorer I, *the United States' first satellite* (right)

Section Review Questions 7A

1. What group of people first used rockets for defense?
2. What was the propellant used for most early rockets?
3. State Newton's third law of motion.
4. Because most early rockets were difficult to aim, they were not used extensively as weapons. What were they used for?
5. Who designed the rocket that was referred to in the phrase ''the rockets' red glare'' in the National Anthem?
6. What improvement did the Hale rocket have over earlier rockets?
7. Who is known as the father of the modern rocket?
8. What two improvements did Goddard add to the rocket?
9. What is the name of the large rocket developed by Wernher von Braun that was used so successfully by the Germans during World War II?
10. What was the name of the first U.S. satellite?
11. What development in rockets allowed scientists to send satellites into orbit?

7B–Unmanned Programs

As the name indicates, unmanned programs do not have human passengers. The two main categories of unmanned programs are satellites and probes. Unmanned programs were a necessary step in the development of manned programs due to safety considerations. However, it is not the goal of all unmanned programs to serve as a steppingstone to manned programs. As you shall see, many are designed to provide very useful services and information without any pretense of developing a manned program.

Satellites

Placing a satellite into orbit requires both a powerful rocket and a sophisticated guidance system. The United States and the USSR already had powerful rockets for ICBMs, and they could easily make more powerful rockets by adding stages. Developing a guidance system was more difficult. To orbit the earth, the satellite must have a high speed parallel to the earth's surface. Thus, the satellite must travel up to the desired altitude, turn to the proper angle, then accelerate to the proper speed. If its speed is wrong, the satellite may fall to the earth, speed into outer space, or at best have the wrong orbit. The guidance systems that place the satellite in a proper orbit are so complex that they must be controlled by computers.

The speed needed for a proper orbit depends on the distance of the satellite from the earth. For a lower orbit, a satellite must have higher speed than for a higher orbit. The reason for this is that gravity increases as the satellite orbits closer to the earth. An orbit is a balance between gravity and forward speed; thus, when gravity increases, forward speed must increase.

7B-1 *For a low orbit, a satellite must have a faster speed than for a high orbit.*

Satellites in higher orbits travel more slowly and must travel farther to complete one orbit than satellites in lower orbits. Thus, satellites in higher orbits require more time for each orbit than satellites in lower orbits. For example, a satellite in an orbit 320 km (200 mi.) above the earth circles in ninety minutes, while the moon, at 380,000 km (240,000 mi.) requires more than twenty-nine days to complete one orbit.

The United States and the USSR are no longer the only nations that launch satellites. France, Japan, China, and a group of nations in the European Space Agency now have their own space programs. The United States and the USSR also launch satellites for other countries that do not have their own launch facilities.

Scientific Satellites

Satellites have many different purposes. **Scientific satellites** are used mainly for scientific studies. The first few satellites were designed to help in the International Geophysical Year (IGY), a cooperative effort of many countries to collect data about the earth and the atmosphere for geologic (land studies) and meteorological (weather) purposes. *Explorer I*, the first U.S. satellite, transmitted data about the earth's radiation belts, and *Vanguard 1*, the second U.S. satellite, transmitted data about the shape of the earth. *Sputnik 3* carried instruments to study various characteristics of the earth and its atmosphere. The Soviet satellite *Sputnik 5* showed that animals can survive orbit and return to earth. Other satellites since the IGY have contributed to science.

Satellites have helped scientists study the sun, the stars, the earth, the atmosphere, meteoroids, and many other objects in space. More recent U.S. satellites include the *OSO-1* (Orbiting Solar Observatory), *Solar Max,* *IRAS* (Infrared Astronomical Satellite), and the Hubble Space Telescope. Both the Soviet Union and the United States have programs designed to one day place a permanent space station in orbit. Complications such as the *Challenger* disaster, as well as other problems with the space shuttle, and more recently, flaws with the Hubble Space Telescope, have bogged down government funding for the space station.

Applications Satellites

Applications satellites are used for specific, useful purposes such as weather prediction, communications, navigational references, and survey instruments. Communications satellites allow people on separate continents to communicate quickly and easily. The United States launched the first communications satellite, *SCORE,* in 1958. Today many nations have launched communications satellites, and some satellites are used commercially for telephone and television transmissions.

Communications satellites are especially helpful if they stay over the same spot on the earth's surface. To do this, they must orbit once every twenty-four hours in the plane of the equator. A satellite that is about 35,000 km (22,000 mi.) high will orbit once each day. Such a satellite is in a **synchronous*** (SING kruh nus) **orbit** and is said to be **geostationary*** (not moving with respect to the earth). The first geostationary satellite was *Syncom 2,* launched by the United States in 1963. Today, communication satellites are placed into orbit and used until they malfunction or until a better satellite is developed. The *Telstar* and *Intelsat* series are other communications satellites used by the United States.

The United States also launched the first weather satellite, *TIROS 1,* in 1960. Weather satellites photograph the earth frequently to note changes in the clouds, and they sometimes have temperature sensors to determine the temperature of the area below them. You have probably seen a satellite photograph of the clouds if you have watched a weather report on television. A weather satellite is usually placed in **polar orbit,** passing over

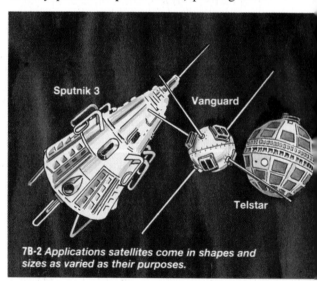

7B-2 Applications satellites come in shapes and sizes as varied as their purposes.

synchronous: syn- (Gk. SUN, together, same) + -chronous (Gk. KHRONOS, time)

geostationary: geo- (earth) + -stationary (L. STATIONARIUS *from* STARE, to stand)

the earth's poles, so that the earth rotates under the satellite once each day. Another way to survey the entire earth frequently is to have several satellites in geostationary orbit. Like the communications satellites, the weather satellites are continually being replaced as the old ones malfunction and as newer, more efficient ones are developed. The *GOES* and *NIMBUS* satellites are other U.S. weather satellites.

Another important group of applications satellites is the navigational satellites. These are important to ships and aircraft. A vessel's exact location can be established using these satellites. Before the navigational satellites, stars were used for navigational purposes. In times of storms it was not uncommon for a ship or airplane to get lost. Radio communication with navigational satellites, however, is not lost during cloudy weather, and the problem of getting lost is now significantly reduced. The *TRANSIT* series is presently being used for this purpose by the United States but is being replaced by the *GPS* system.

Survey satellites are important in the study of the earth. *Seasat, Geosat,* and *Landsat*

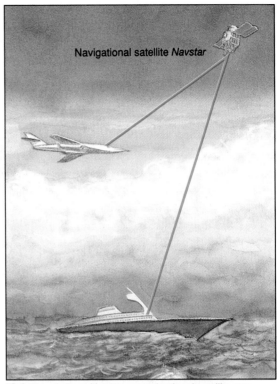

Navigational satellite *Navstar*

7B-3 *Signals from* Navstar, *a navigational satellite, are used to help determine a ship's or airplane's true location.*

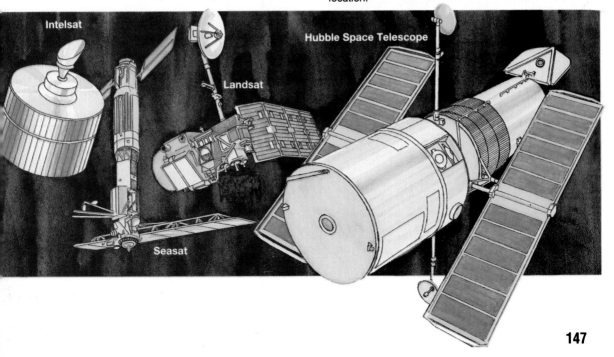

Intelsat

Hubble Space Telescope

Landsat

Seasat

series have mapped earth structures that were previously inaccessible. Even the interior of the earth is being mapped from outer space through the use of scanning devices similar to those used in medical research. These satellites also aid in discovery of oil reserves, alert scientists to areas of pollution, and provide the military with information of interest to our nation's security.

7B-4	Key Earth Satellites	
Name	**Launch Date**	**Notes**
Sputnik 1	1957†	first satellite
Explorer 1	1958	first U.S. satellite
Score	1958	first communications satellite
TIROS 1	1960	weather pictures
OSO 1	1961	orbiting solar observatory
Syncom 2	1962	first geostationary satellite
Explorer 17	1963	first satellite to study the atmosphere
OGO 1	1964	orbiting geophysical observatory
OAO 2	1968	orbiting astronomical observatory
Landsat 1	1972	study of Earth's resources
GOES 1	1975	geostationary weather satellite
Navstar	1978	a system of 18 satellites to aid navigation
HEAO 2	1978	high energy astronomy observatory
Nimbus 7	1978	study of atmosphere and oceans
HEAO 3	1979	observation of gamma rays in deep space
Solar Max	1980	observation of solar flares
IRAS	1983	infrared astronomical satellite
Hubble	1990	space telescope using visible light
UARS	1991	study of ozone layer
† USSR launch		

Probes

While satellites orbit the earth or other heavenly bodies, many space vehicles are not

GPS—Global Positioning System

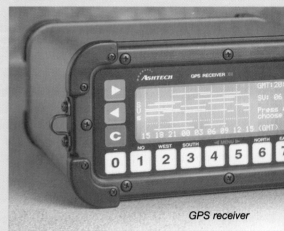

GPS receiver

During the war with Iraq in 1991, a new satellite navigation system received its initiation into the military arsenal and introduction to the public eye. U.S. troops in the nearly featureless landscape used hand-held receivers to receive signals from orbiting GPS satellites. With signals from three satellites, the soldiers could compute their surface location; with four signals, altitude could be determined as well. Ships, missiles, tanks, aircraft, and foot soldiers all used the GPS system to navigate and to fire accurately at targets. Officially, positions can be deter-

placed into orbits. These vehicles fit into a classification known as **probes.** As the name implies, these spacecraft are the explorers of space, ''probing'' into regions that are often inaccessible any other way.

Sounding Rockets

One type of probe was known as the **sounding rocket.** Sounding rockets were used to make a **sounding,** or environmental vertical probe, of the atmosphere. These rockets did not carry payloads into orbit or to other planets. Rockets such as the Scout, V-2, Aerobee,

mined to within 17.8 m with the GPS system, but it is widely believed that the real accuracy is within 5 mm!

The GPS system has peacetime uses as well. However, false information is added to the satellites' signals so that hostile forces cannot make use of the satellites' amazing accuracy. The peacetime accuracy for most uses has been reported to be between 10 and 100 m. Providing navigational information for ships and aircraft is the primary use of GPS. With this kind of information, locations can be pinpointed in all types of weather, day or night, instantly, anywhere on the earth. This type of information has also been used to accurately determine mountain elevations and to measure earth movements prior to earthquakes and volcanic eruptions.

The GPS system consists of twenty-one active satellites and three spare ones. During the war with Iraq, only sixteen satellites were in use. When the full complement of twenty-four is in operation, the entire earth will be provided with accurate navigation information. All that is needed to use the GPS system is a GPS receiver. This hand-held receiver with a built-in computer receives the satellite signals and calculates the receiver's location in latitude, longitude, and altitude if needed.

Viking, and Nike, carried instruments to the upper atmosphere to collect information. The instruments on these missions test radiation, measure temperature and magnetic fields, and count the number of meteors in nearby space.

7B-5 *Sounding rocket—Nike* Ajax

Lunar Probes

After learning how to place satellites in orbit, the Soviet Union and the United States began developing vehicles designed to investigate space and other planets. One target of these early probes was the moon. The Soviet Union called its lunar probes *Lunas;* the American

7B-6 *Mockup of* Luna-9, *the first probe to soft-land on the moon on February 3, 1966*

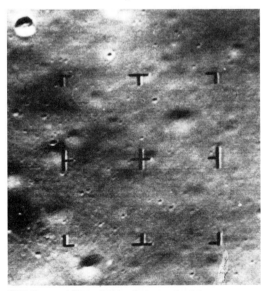

7B-7 Ranger VIII *took this photograph of the moon from an altitude of 8.2 km (5.1 mi.).*

failed, so the U.S. *Mariner 2* was the first probe to send back data from Venus. Several Veneras landed on the surface of Venus, but the tremendous pressures of the Venusian atmosphere crushed them. *Venera 7* survived the pressure and transmitted data from the surface, and later probes transmitted pictures from Venus's surface. Several U.S. probes of the Mariner and Pioneer series also studied Venus. The *Magellan* probe during the early

7B-8 *Lunar landscape photographed by* Surveyor V (top); Lunokhod 1 (above) *was carried to the moon on* Luna 17. *It explored the moon by remote control from earth.*

probes in the Ranger, Surveyor, and Lunar Orbiter series also investigated the moon. The Russian probe *Luna 1,* launched in 1959, was the first to fly by the moon. The Soviet Union followed this with other firsts: the first pictures of the back side of the moon *(Luna 3),* the first soft lunar landing *(Luna 9),* and the first manmade object to orbit the moon *(Luna 10).* The U.S. probes thoroughly investigated possible landing sites for the manned Apollo program. The probes from both nations sent back valuable photographs of the moon and information about its soil.

Planetary Probes

The next target for space probes was Venus, the planet nearest the earth. The Soviet *Venera 1* flew by Venus in 1961. Its transmitter

7B-9 *Photograph of Venus taken by* Pioneer-Venus (top); Pioneer-Venus *released four separate probes into Venus's atmosphere. In the model* (above), *the silver-colored cones are the individual probes. The part of the spacecraft that carried them was called the "bus."*

7B-10 *Surface of Mars near the* Viking Lander 2 *shows a few square meters of the area. The rock in the right foreground is about 25 cm (10 in.) across.*

1990s sent the most complete and accurate maps of the surface of Venus.

The Soviet Union sent its first Mars probe, *Mars 1,* past the planet in 1962. Several U.S. Mariner probes also studied Mars by flying past the planet and by orbiting it. The most detailed information about Mars has come from *Viking 1* and *Viking 2,* U.S. probes launched in 1975. These probes landed instruments on the planet's surface to photograph the terrain and to analyze the soil. The Vikings continued to send back data until the 1980s.

So far, the United States is the only nation to explore the **outer planets,** those beyond Mars. In 1972 the United States launched *Pioneer 10,* which explored the asteroid belt and Jupiter, then continued on a path that will eventually take it out of the sun's gravitational field. It has already passed beyond Neptune. *Pioneer 11,* or *Pioneer-Saturn,* primarily studied Saturn. *Voyager 2* was able to take advantage of a once-in-a-lifetime opportunity to visit all four gas giants: Jupiter (1979), Saturn (1981), Uranus (1986), and Neptune (1989). Each time the probe has encountered a planet, it has sent back data that completely changed our perceptions of the planet. The first probe to orbit a gas giant was *Galileo,* which studied Jupiter and its moons. *Galileo* included a capsule designed to penetrate Jupiter's atmosphere to tell us more about the largest planet.

Mercury, with its small size and forbidden temperatures, because of its closeness to the sun, has had little attention from space probes. Probably the most notable is the *Mariner 10.* Pictures show the planet to be similar in appearance to the earth's moon. Only Pluto remains to be explored by a planetary probe to this date.

Specialized Probes

A smaller object studied by probes from many nations is Halley's comet. The Soviet Union, Japan, and the European Space Agency sent probes to the comet during its 1986 return to the sun. The USSR's probes *Vega 1* and *Vega 2,* after a trip to Venus, were the first to encounter the comet. Other nations refined the paths of their probes, using the data from the *Vega* probes. A Japanese probe, *Sakigake,* next passed by Halley's head, while a second Japanese probe, *Suisei,* studied the comet's interaction with the solar wind. The European probe, *Giotto,* went closest to the comet, within 605 km (376 mi.) of the nucleus. This marked the first close-up study of Halley's comet.

It is important to understand that many space vehicles have more than one purpose and therefore may be classified under more than one category. For example, the Soviet *Vega 1* and *Vega 2* both investigated Venus before their encounter with Halley's comet. Therefore, these could be considered both planetary probes and specialized probes. Had either of the vehicles orbited Venus, they also would be classified as satellites while they were orbiting the planet.

7B-11		Key Space Probes			
Name	**Launch Date**	**Notes**	**Name**	**Launch Date**	**Notes**
Luna 1	1959†	first lunar probe	*Viking 1 & 2*	1975	Mars probe, surface pictures
Mariner 2	1962	Venus probe, temperature data, first interplanetary flight	*Voyager 1*	1977	Jupiter and Saturn probe
Mariner 4	1964	Mars probe, photographs	*Voyager 2*	1977	first Uranus and Neptune probe
Luna 9	1966†	first lunar soft-landing	*International Sun-Earth Explorer*	1978	first comet probe
Luna 10	1967†	first lunar orbit			
Venera 4	1967†	Venus probe, atmospheric data	*Pioneer Venus 1*	1978	Venus probe, surface maps with radar
Zond 5	1968†	first to circle the moon and return to the earth	*Pioneer Venus 2*	1978	Venus probe, atmospheric data
Venera 7	1970†	Venus probe, surface data	*Venera 15 & 16*	1983†	Venus probes, surface maps with radar
Mariner 9	1971	first Mars orbit	*Vega 1 & 2*	1984†	Halley's comet probes
Mars 3	1971†	first Mars soft-landing	*Giotto*	1985‡	encountered the nucleus of Halley's comet
Pioneer 10	1972	first Jupiter probe			
Pioneer 11	1973	first Saturn probe	*Galileo*	1988	in-depth study of Jupiter and its moons
Mariner 10	1973	only Mercury probe	*Phobos 1 & 2*	1988†	Soviet launches to Mars
Venera 9	1975†	Venus probe, surface pictures, first Venus orbit	*Magellan*	1989	Venus probe, improved surface map

† USSR launch
‡ European launch

Section Review Questions 7B

1. Establishing an orbit for a satellite requires a balance between two forces. What are these two forces?
2. What is the difference between a satellite and a probe?
3. Name two types of satellites.
4. List four kinds of applications satellites.
5. What was the first country to have a space vehicle send back data from another planet?
6. Which space vehicle visited all four gas giants?
7. The specialized probe *Giotto* had a close encounter with what kind of celestial object?
8. How accurately can the GPS system determine your location?

7C–Manned Space Programs

Early unmanned space programs served as steppingstones into space for man. First, rockets were developed; then the unmanned programs were begun, and animal passengers were later included. Then the inclusion of a human passenger marked the dawning of a new era.

7C-1

Yuri Gagarin

Alan Shepard

John Glenn

Early Efforts

Man in Orbit

For many, manned space exploration is the most exciting part of the space program. On April 12, 1961, Yuri Gagarin (gah GAHR in) became the first man in space. His capsule, *Vostok 1,* was the first of a series of six one-person spacecraft launched by the Soviet Union. *Vostok 6* carried the first woman, Valentina Tereshkova (teh resh KAW vah), into space in 1963.

America's first manned space flights were called **Project Mercury.** Less than a month after Gagarin's orbit, Alan Shepard in *Freedom 7* became the first American in space. Shepard did not orbit the earth; he simply traveled up above the atmosphere and back down. After a second suborbital flight, John Glenn orbited the earth in *Friendship 7.* Three more orbital flights completed the Mercury project. All Mercury capsules were launched by converted ICBMs.

The Race for the Moon

After putting a man in space, the next goal was to put a man on the moon. Actually, one man could not go to the moon alone, so all plans for reaching the moon required vehicles capable of carrying at least two men. The Soviet Union again led the way with *Voskhod 1,* a three-man capsule launched in 1964. *Voskhod 2,* a two-man mission, took another step forward when Aleksei Leonov became the first man to perform extravehicular (out-of-the-vehicle) activity in space. That is, he left his capsule and floated in space, attached to the capsule by an oxygen tube. For the next two years, the USSR launched no men into space. Then, in 1967 she began the Soyuz program of manned capsules, which continues today.

The next step for the United States was called **Project Gemini** (JEM uh NY), from the Latin word for twins. The two-man Gemini crews tested procedures that would be needed for a safe lunar exploration. They also tested human reaction to the prolonged pe-

7C-2 *Second stage of the Gemini launch vehicle under construction (top); "Walks in space," or extravehicular activities, were performed in the Gemini project (above).*

riod of weightlessness that would be necessary for a trip to the moon. In June 1965 on board the *Gemini 4,* Edward White became the first American to walk in space. He enjoyed his excursion so much that his partner, James McDivitt, had trouble coaxing him to return to the capsule. Most of the later Gemini missions also included extravehicular activity. Another procedure needed for a moon flight was docking, or joining two spacecraft in space. *Gemini 8* was the first mission to dock with another vehicle. The ten Gemini missions showed that America was ready to begin the last leg of the journey to the moon: **Project Apollo.**

The Apollo spacecraft consisted of three parts: the command module, the lunar module, and the service module. These three parts were to be propelled into space with the Saturn V rocket. The Saturn V was a powerful three-stage rocket. The lower (booster) stages of the rocket propelled the vehicle into earth orbit and fell back to the earth once their job was finished. The upper stage provided the thrust for sending the Apollo spacecraft into lunar orbit. It did not return to the earth, but was discarded in space.

The command module was the control center for the trip. It provided living and working space for all three astronauts for most of the eight-day trip. This module never touched the moon's surface, but remained in lunar orbit, piloted by one astronaut. It was the only part of the spacecraft to return to earth. The lunar module was designed to land two astronauts on the moon and return them to lunar orbit. For this job it had two stages, the descent stage and the ascent stage. The descent stage remained on the moon after landing. The ascent stage returned the astronauts to lunar orbit, where they docked with the command module. When the astronauts were safely aboard the command module,

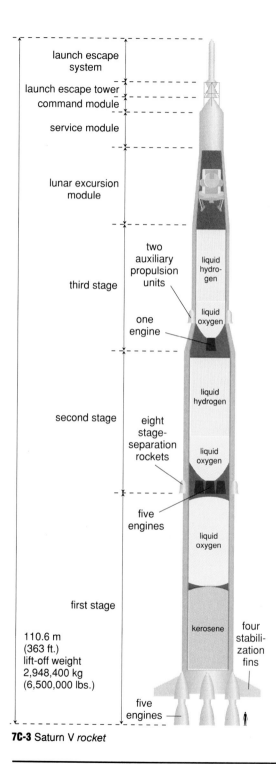

launch escape system

launch escape tower

command module

service module

lunar excursion module

third stage

two auxiliary propulsion units

liquid hydrogen

one engine

liquid oxygen

second stage

eight stage-separation rockets

liquid hydrogen

liquid oxygen

five engines

liquid oxygen

first stage

110.6 m (363 ft.) lift-off weight 2,948,400 kg (6,500,000 lbs.)

kerosene

four stabilization fins

five engines

7C-3 Saturn V *rocket*

they discarded the lunar module. The service module included engines to place the command module in lunar orbit, then send it back to earth. It was discarded just before the spacecraft re-entered the earth's atmosphere on its return trip.

The first few Apollo missions tested the actual equipment and orbit used to place men on the moon. The program's beginning was disastrous. During a prelaunch test, all three astronauts on *Apollo 1* were killed when it caught fire. The next months were spent making the modules as fireproof as possible to protect future astronauts. *Apollos 7-10* successfully tested the launch vehicle, the moon orbit, and the lunar module.

On July 20, 1969, years of feverish activity were rewarded as Neil Armstrong and Edwin Aldrin walked on the moon. The astronauts set up experiments, collected soil and rock samples, and left memorial items for astronauts and cosmonauts* (KAHZ muh NAWT) (Soviet astronauts) who had died. Then they rejoined Michael Collins in lunar orbit and returned safely to earth four days later. Ten other men on five Apollo missions landed on the moon. So far, only these twelve U.S. astronauts have walked on the moon.

7C-4 *Astronaut Edwin Aldrin setting up an experiment next to the* Apollo 11 *lunar module on the moon*

cosmonaut: cosmo- (Gk. KOSMOS, universe) + -naut (sailor)

FACETS OF ASTRONOMY

The First Man on the Moon

"The Soviets Beat Us to Space!" On October 4, 1957, shocked Americans read the newspaper headlines in disbelief. The Soviet Union—the red communists—had launched the first manmade satellite, *Sputnik 1*, into orbit. That beeping metal ball, heard around the world, started the greatest race in history. Two foes—the United States and the Soviet Union—dedicated their vast resources to become the technological leader of the world.

The Soviet Union enjoyed a significant head start. It had a stockpile of big rockets designed to carry nuclear warheads to the United States. Its early successes embarrassed the American scientific community. Americans were again stunned when Soviet cosmonaut Yuri Gagarin became the first man to fly in orbit—for one hour forty-eight minutes. America's flight the next month lasted fifteen minutes and failed to reach orbit. Yet America rose to the challenge. President John F. Kennedy announced to Congress, "I believe that this nation should commit itself to achieving the goal, before this decade is out, of landing a man on the moon and returning him safely to earth."

With these words he launched the greatest undertak-

ing this nation had ever attempted. Some 385,000 km (240,000 mi.) of cold, empty space lay between the earth and its moon. Much of the equipment for the trip did not yet exist, and the difficulties seemed insurmountable. The spacecraft would require millions of components and 99.9999 per cent reliability. Yet by the end of the decade, at a cost of more than $25 billion, America had accomplished the task and left their competitor far behind.

At 4:17 P.M. (EDT) on July 20, 1969, an estimated 600 million people listened in awe to these words: "Houston, Tranquility Base here. The Eagle has landed." Astronaut Neil Armstrong informed headquarters in Houston, Texas, that his lunar module, the *Eagle,* had landed safely on the moon. After donning his space suit, Armstrong made his gentle first step on the moon. He paused to say these historic words, "That's one small step for a man, one giant leap for mankind."

The feat was the culmination of work by over four hundred thousand people connected to the Apollo program. NASA had built a Saturn V rocket, thirty-six stories high and carrying 6 million pounds of propellants, to boost three astronauts to the

moon. All told, Aldrin and Armstrong spent two hours and thirteen minutes walking on the moon, gathering samples and setting up experiments. They left behind a plaque on *Eagle's* descent stage, signed by the mission's three astronauts and President Nixon:

HERE MEN FROM THE PLANET EARTH
FIRST SET FOOT UPON THE MOON
JULY 1969, A.D.
WE CAME IN PEACE
FOR ALL MANKIND

Scanning the beautiful expanse of God's universe, Aldrin began to quote Psalm 8: "When I consider thy heavens, the work of thy fingers, the moon and the stars, which thou hast ordained; What is man that thou art mindful of him?"

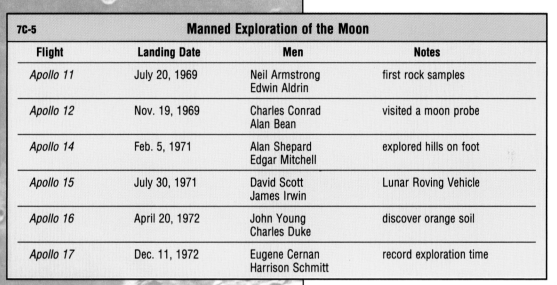

7C-5	Manned Exploration of the Moon		
Flight	**Landing Date**	**Men**	**Notes**
Apollo 11	July 20, 1969	Neil Armstrong Edwin Aldrin	first rock samples
Apollo 12	Nov. 19, 1969	Charles Conrad Alan Bean	visited a moon probe
Apollo 14	Feb. 5, 1971	Alan Shepard Edgar Mitchell	explored hills on foot
Apollo 15	July 30, 1971	David Scott James Irwin	Lunar Roving Vehicle
Apollo 16	April 20, 1972	John Young Charles Duke	discover orange soil
Apollo 17	Dec. 11, 1972	Eugene Cernan Harrison Schmitt	record exploration time

† The Apollo 13 mission failed when an oxygen tank exploded, but the crew returned safely.

Space Stations

After a man walked on the moon, the U.S. and Soviet space programs began to experiment with long-term missions in space stations. While the United States was busy with the Apollo program, the USSR placed in orbit the first space station, *Salyut 1*. Six other Salyut stations have followed. Their time in orbit has varied from a few months to over two years. The later Salyuts had places for two Soyuz spacecraft to dock so that more than one crew of cosmonauts could occupy the station at once.

The United States launched its first space station, *Skylab,* in 1973. The first crew of astronauts had to repair the station because it was damaged in the launch. In all, three crews of three men each occupied *Skylab,* the last staying for eighty-four days. While in the station the astronauts did experiments and

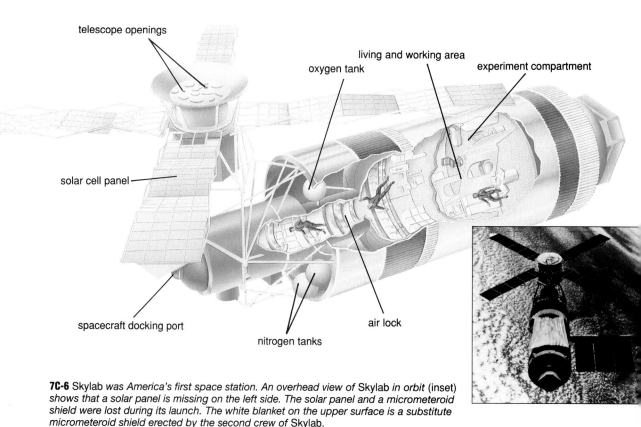

telescope openings

oxygen tank

living and working area

experiment compartment

solar cell panel

spacecraft docking port

nitrogen tanks

air lock

7C-6 Skylab *was America's first space station. An overhead view of* Skylab *in orbit* (inset) *shows that a solar panel is missing on the left side. The solar panel and a micrometeoroid shield were lost during its launch. The white blanket on the upper surface is a substitute micrometeroid shield erected by the second crew of* Skylab.

observed their body's reactions to long-term weightlessness. Almost six years after the last crew left it, *Skylab* fell from orbit into the Indian Ocean and uninhabited portions of Australia.

New Horizons

The former Soviet Union had a strong space program and clearly desired to establish a permanent base in space. She was often the first nation to accomplish a goal in space. However, to achieve these goals, Soviet astronauts sometimes took risks that other countries

would not accept. Of course, U.S. officials have watched these developments with care and concern for some time.

The Soviet Union's commitment to a permanent presence in space showed in her missions. Crews on the Salyut stations set records for mission lengths; one crew on *Salyut 7* stayed 237 days. In 1986 the USSR launched a new space station, *Mir* (peace), with six docking ports. Although it is no larger than the Salyuts, *Mir* is more advanced. It could be used as a part of a space colony or as living quarters for a trip to Mars. The collapse of the

7C-7	**Key Manned Flights**		
Name	**Launch Date**	**Crew**	**Notes**
Vostok 1	1961	Yuri Gagarin	first man in space
Mercury-Redstone 3	1961	Alan Shepard	first American in space
Mercury-Atlas 6	1962	John Glenn	first American in orbit
Vostok 6	1963	Valentina Tereshkova	first woman in space
Voskhod 1	1964	Vladimir Komarov Konstanin Feoktistov Boris Yegorov	first multiple crew
Voskhod 2	1965	Alexei Leonov Pavel Belyayev	first extravehicular activity (space walk)
Gemini 4	1965	James McDivitt Edward White	first controlled space walk
Gemini 8	1966	Neil Armstrong David Scott	first docking in space
Apollo 11	1969	Neil Armstrong Edwin Aldrin Michael Collins	first men on the moon
Salyut 1	1971	multiple crews	first space station
Skylab 1	1973	multiple crews	first U.S. space station
Apollo-Soyuz	1975	Alexei Leonov Valeri Kubasov Donald Slayton Thomas Stafford Vance Brand	only U.S.-Soviet joint mission
Columbia	1981	John Young Robert Crippen	first space shuttle flight
Mir	1986	multiple crews	advanced Soviet space station

Soviet Union caused a setback for its space program. One cosmonaut was compelled to stay in space longer than planned, 313 days, to train cosmonauts from the country that owns the launch facilities. But even if it survives as only a fragment of its former grandeur, the superpower's space program will still be a significant player in space.

The U.S. space program since *Skylab* has concentrated on a reusable orbiter, the **space**

7C-8 *The Soviet* Soyuz *photographed from the* Apollo *command module*

FACETS OF ASTRONOMY

Living in the Space Age

Space exploration has changed the way we live. Compact discs, fireproof fabrics, cordless drills, laser surgery, and nonstick pots and pans are a few of the "spin-offs" from space technology. Three more recent technological spin-offs of the space age will be discussed here.

One spin-off is hydroponically grown crops, or crops grown without soil. At "The Land," sponsored by Kraft General Foods, an education and research facility at Walt Disney World's EPCOT center in Flori-

da, plants are grown on A-frame racks in environmentally controlled greenhouses. A nutrient solution is sprayed on their roots as a substitute for soil. Researchers are testing more than two dozen plant species with the ultimate goal to sustain life in space. Hydroponically grown plants have found their way to some supermarkets. Lettuce and cucumbers account for ninety-five per cent of the commercially grown hydroponic vegetables, but wheat, peppers, spinach, oats, barley, strawberries, and

beans are being investigated as well. Additional research will focus on how fungi and bacteria affect plant growth and on which plants can be grown together hydroponically without interfering with the way each grows.

Another technological spin-off involves the field of medicine. Digital image processing, done by computer and x-rays or radio waves, is used to enhance

images of human organs for diagnostic purposes. Computer-aided tomography, known as CT or CAT scan and Magnetic Resonance Imaging (MRI) are some of the more advanced techniques that have been developed. Image data is collected by exposing a portion or "slice" of the body to a fan-shaped beam of x-rays or radio waves from several directions around the perimeter of the body. An image of the inside of the body is reconstructed by computer from the various views. CT is especially good for viewing bone tissue, while MRI is used for viewing soft tissues.

A third technological spin-off is the use of robotic systems. Originally, robotics was developed for use on the space shuttle. The Robot Manipulator System deposited satellites and other cargo in space or retrieved them from orbit. It is a counterpart to the human arm: it has a shoulder, elbow, wrist joints, and "muscles" (electric motors). The "hand" is a gripping device. A robotics "arm" is now used by Canadian National Railways to paint railway cars inside and out and other maintenance operations such as cleaning and washing. The latter operations employ two robots and are fully automatic without human intervention.

Indeed, space exploration technology has benefited man. Thousands of companies have taken advantage of this technology to develop tens of thousands of products and processes. Can you think of other space-age products?

shuttle. The prototype shuttle *Enterprise* was tested as early as 1977, but the first shuttle orbit, using the space shuttle *Columbia,* was not launched until 1981. Several other shuttles have been built.

Both the shuttle orbiter and its solid-fuel booster rockets are reusable to reduce expenses. The main attraction of the shuttle is its large cargo bay, from which satellites can be launched from orbit. The cargo bay is also used for experiments. *Spacelab,* an orbiting laboratory supported by the United States and the European Space Agency, is designed to be carried in the shuttle's cargo bay.

7C-9 *View of the open cargo bay of* Columbia— *experiments and satellites can be hauled to and from space in the cargo bay.*

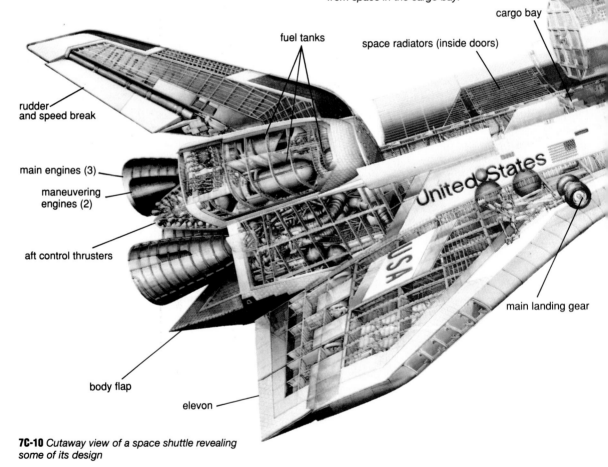

7C-10 *Cutaway view of a space shuttle revealing some of its design*

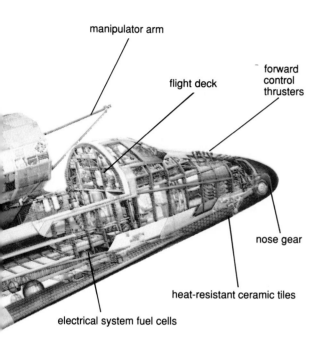

manipulator arm

flight deck

forward control thrusters

nose gear

heat-resistant ceramic tiles

electrical system fuel cells

7C-11 *The space shuttle* Enterprise *is shown mounted atop a 747 during a test flight.*

The shuttle also has living quarters for up to seven astronauts and passengers. The shuttle astronauts include women, for the first time in the U.S. space program. In 1983 Sally Ride became the first American woman in space as an astronaut on *Challenger*. Scientists who are not astronauts have also flown on space shuttle missions, both Americans and those from other countries. Congressmen have ridden on the space shuttle, and the United States has plans to put others such as teachers and journalists in space.

After many successful flights, the shuttle program came to a temporary halt when *Challenger* exploded during liftoff, killing all seven people aboard. Christa McAuliffe, a passenger, was to have been the first teacher in space. The cause of the explosion was apparently a defective seal in one of the boosters. The shuttle fleet was returned to its full complement of five in 1991 by the introduction of a replacement shuttle, the *Endeavour*, for the destroyed *Challenger*.

The disaster intensified a long-standing argument between advocates of manned programs and supporters of unmanned programs. Those who support mainly unmanned programs point out that not only are unmanned programs cheaper, but they are also unlikely to endanger human life. Those who support mainly manned programs point out that there are some times when human judgment is necessary, in spite of the extra cost and danger.

A major reason for exploring space has been to find evidence of life on other planets. Evolutionists thought that on Mars especially life might have begun to evolve. The entire space program has found nothing to support evolution. In spite of some wrong motivations, the space program has increased our knowledge of the solar system and thus our appreciation of God's creation.

Probably the greatest benefit that has resulted from the space program, however, has been the resulting technological advances that were first used in space, or at least developed from space research. Some of these advances have filtered down to the consumer (you and me). Flame-retardant materials used by firefighters and in infant beddings, wash-and-wear clothing, computer technology, communications improvements, and recycling processes, just to name a few, are the indirect result of the space program. Have the benefits been sufficient to justify the cost in both money and life? Only time will ultimately answer the question fully, but few people would answer the question in a negative way if all the technological advances that have resulted from the space program could be listed.

The ultimate future of the space program seems bleak unless the countries involved somehow learn to share costs and technology. There have been some signs that cooperative efforts could develop more and more, but knowing the nature of mankind, selfish ambitions, and the lust for power may prove to be more than those in power can handle.

Without cooperative efforts, however, space exploration seems to be limited severely by cost factors. Perhaps your generation will find a way to overcome these problems.

7C-12 The Discovery *being moved to the Vehicle Assembly Building where it will be fitted with an external fuel tank and booster rockets. The smaller two engines are for maneuvering.*

Section Review Questions 7C
1. Who was the first American in space?
2. Who was the first man in space?
3. What did the Gemini project do?
4. What is the name given to the process of joining two spacecraft in space?
5. What was the name given to the module of the Apollo spacecraft that stayed in lunar orbit while the other module descended to the surface of the moon?
6. Who were the first two men to walk on the moon?
7. What were the Soviets doing while the United States was concentrating on putting a man on the moon?
8. Which space shuttle was lost in an explosion of the boosters in the mid 1980s?
9. List some advantages of the U.S. space program to everyday life in this country.

Terms

applications satellites	Project Mercury
Congreve rocket	rocket
geostationary	satellite
ICBM	scientific satellite
outer planets	sounding
polar orbit	sounding rocket
probe	space shuttle
Project Apollo	stage
Project Gemini	synchronous orbit

What Did You Learn?

1. To stay in orbit at an altitude of 320 km, a certain satellite must travel at least 27,400 km/hr. To orbit at an altitude of 600 km, would the same satellite have a faster or slower minimum speed?
2. Would a satellite used to provide television networks with a communication link be classified as a scientific satellite or an applications satellite?
3. How would you classify a satellite that is designed to map the coastal waters of the United States?
4. Explain the difference between a probe and a satellite.
5. How do sounding rockets differ from other probes?
6. What type of probe would likely be used to examine an asteroid?
7. Why can some probes be classified as satellites?
8. Why would some feel that the efforts to place a man on the moon would have been better spent to develop a space station?
9. Can you think of ways space technology has benefited you?

What Do You Think?

1. What theological implications could you think of in regards to the possibility of life on another planet? (For example: Would men on earth be responsible for evangelization of these people? Would those beings be under the curse of the sin of Adam and Eve?)
2. Is the cost of the space program worth billions of dollars spent and the loss of lives due to accidents? Explain your answer.
3. What kinds of problems would be associated with establishing a permanent settlement on the moon or on another planet?

THE ATMOSPHERE

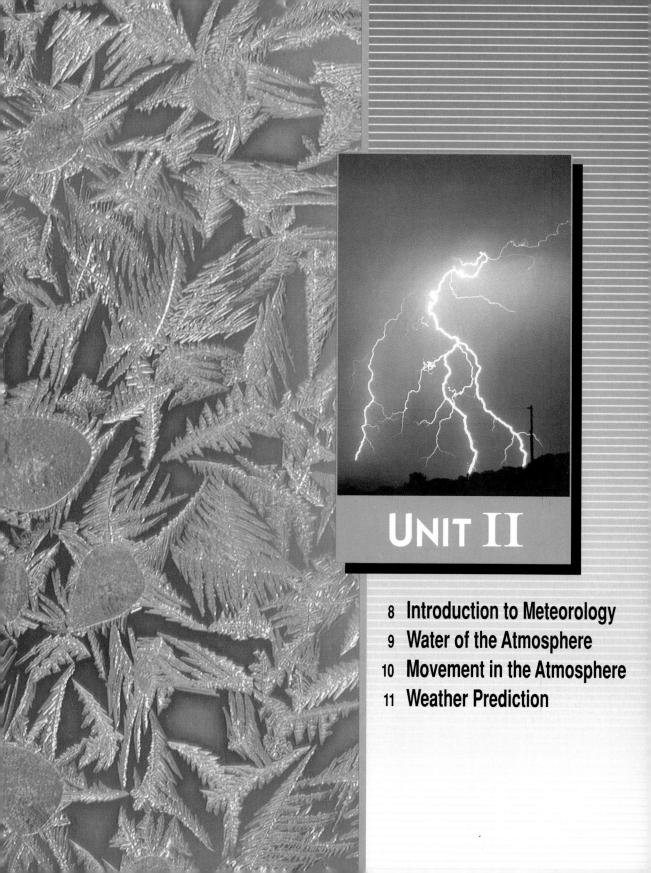

UNIT II

EIGHT

8A–Structure of the Atmosphere

The **atmosphere** is the envelope of gases surrounding our planet. This sea of air is crucial for life on earth. It supplies the oxygen for us to breathe and the pressure for our bodies to work properly. It protects us from meteors and cosmic rays. It helps maintain favorable temperature ranges for living organisms. Planets without an atmosphere like ours cannot support life as we know it.

The Bible describes the creation of the atmosphere as a direct act of God rather than the result of any evolutionary process. According to Genesis 1:6-8, God made the atmosphere on the second day of creation and made the dry land appear on the third day of creation. The Lord divided the water that covered the earth's surface, placing some of it in the atmosphere and leaving the remainder on or below the surface. Some scholars believe the "upper waters" were ordinary clouds, whereas others believe they were a vapor canopy that protected the earth and gave it a worldwide mild climate before the Flood.

Composition Layers

There are several ways to divide the atmosphere into layers for study. One is composition; this divides the atmosphere into two major layers. Another is temperature, which divides the atmosphere into four layers. Also, the atmosphere contains several unique layers that can fit into a broader outline of the atmosphere. We will begin with the atmosphere's composition.

The ancient Greeks believed that all matter was made up of four elements: earth, fire, water, and air. Until the 1600s the universities taught this theory. Then Galileo's work showed the value of experiments, and scientists began to study the "elements." They found that none of them were as simple as the Greeks had thought.

Joseph Priestley (1733–1804), an English clergyman, performed many experiments with air. He believed that air was not just one gas but a mixture of several gases. He was particularly interested in the gas that is consumed by burning and is used in respiration in man and animals. Along with Karl Scheele (SHAY luh) (1742–86) of Sweden, Priestley received credit for the discovery of **oxygen.** Oxygen supports burning, respiration, and oxidation (rusting). If the air were pure oxygen or if there were more than 21 per cent oxygen in the atmosphere, fires would burn out of control.

Shortly after Priestley and Scheele discovered oxygen, Daniel Rutherford (1749–1819), a Scottish physician, discovered **nitrogen.** In the atmosphere the chief function

8A-1 *Early studies by these scientists contributed much to our knowledge of the atmosphere.*

of this gas is to dilute the oxygen. Nitrogen is a relatively inactive gas; we can tell this by its presence as an uncombined element in air. If nitrogen were more reactive, it would combine with the oxygen. Life as we know it would be impossible on the earth if our atmosphere were made up of some oxide of nitrogen rather than oxygen and nitrogen. The fact that nitrogen is uncombined in air is not an evolutionary accident; it is evidence of God's design.

8A-2 *A disadvantage of living in an atmosphere having oxygen is rusting. Rust is a form of corrosion in which iron chemically combines with oxygen and water.*

Today we know that air is a mixture of gases. It consists of about 21 per cent oxygen, 78 per cent nitrogen, and 1 per cent other gases such as radon, argon, hydrogen, and

FACETS OF METEOROLOGY

8A-1

The Greenhouse Scare

Back yard greenhouses work because solar rays enter through the glass and are changed inside the greenhouse to infrared rays (heat) which cannot leave. Our atmosphere acts like a giant greenhouse. The "glass" is made of carbon dioxide and water vapor. Solar rays enter, but the infrared rays which are produced cannot escape.

The thicker the glass in a greenhouse, the more heat it traps. Is the same thing true with our atmosphere? Does more carbon dioxide trap more heat? Common sense says yes. Climatologists fear that the earth is slowly heating from the vast amount of carbon dioxide that pours into the air each year from car exhaust and industry emissions. Even a rise of a few degrees could be catastrophic. The ice caps would begin melting and flood coastal cities, drought and famine would fry the continent interiors, and the world's weather system would be turned upside-down.

The world that God made is more complex than anyone fully understands. It has an amazing ability to wash itself and maintain the delicate balance necessary for life. Alarmists know little about the earth's long-term *natural* weather cycles, the impact of sunspots and volcanic gases, the ability of the ocean to absorb carbon dioxide, or the ability of plants to flourish and absorb carbon dioxide. While we realize our responsibility to properly manage our resources, the alarmists' scare tactics often misrepresent the facts.

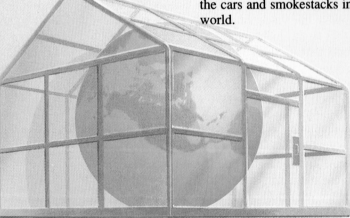

An exhaustive 150-year record of sea temperatures shows no evidence of any catastrophic change in climate. A recent 10-year NASA study of world temperatures from space shows no warming trend during the 1980s. Scientists have found no hard evidence that ice in the Antarctic is melting faster than it is forming or that the rate at which the sea level is rising has increased recently. Alarmists rarely mention that nature produces almost all the carbon dioxide. Termites alone produce more carbon dioxide than all the cars and smokestacks in the world.

helium. These gases have almost constant proportions near the earth. Other gases, especially water vapor and carbon dioxide, appear in varying amounts. Water vapor may be from almost 0 per cent to 5 per cent, depending on the location and the temperature of the air.

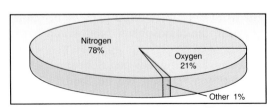

8A-3 Air is mostly nitrogen, which serves to dilute oxygen.

Some environmentalists fear for the future, but for the wrong reasons. They do not want the earth to be destroyed. Yet the earth will be destroyed in a manner more terrible than their worst fears—not by pollution, but by a sudden judgment of God:

> But the day of the Lord will come as a thief in the night; in the which the heavens shall pass away with a great noise, and the elements shall melt with fervent heat, the earth also and the works that are therein shall be burned up. (II Pet. 3:10)

Only a fool will give his life to save the earth. Our fears should impel us, instead, to serve the Lord. "Seeing then that all these things shall be dissolved," Peter asks, "what manner of persons ought ye to be in all holy conversation and godliness?"

All the gases that compose air are mixed together thoroughly; individual gases neither settle to the bottom nor rise to the top of the atmosphere. The percentages of the gases remain about the same up to an altitude of 80 km (50 mi.). This homogeneous mixture of gases is called the **homosphere.***

Beyond the homosphere are several layers of different kinds of gases. A diffuse layer of oxygen molecules exists directly above the homosphere. Above this are layers of helium and hydrogen. These gas layers above the homosphere make up the **heterosphere.*** The homosphere and the heterosphere are divisions of the atmosphere based on gas composition.

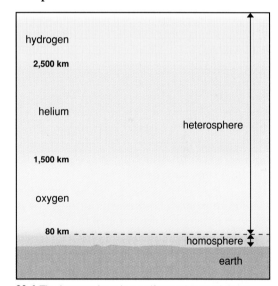

8A-4 *The homosphere is a uniform mixture of gases. The heterosphere, composed of different layers of gases, is above the homosphere.*

Section Review Questions 8A-1
1. What is the name given to the envelope of gases surrounding our planet?
2. The discovery of oxygen is credited to what two men?
3. Who discovered nitrogen?
4. What percentage of the atmosphere is oxygen? nitrogen?
5. What are the names of the two layers of the atmosphere, based upon composition?
6. What gases cause the greenhouse effect?

homosphere: homo- (Gk. HOMOS, same) + -sphere

heterosphere: hetero- (Gk. HETEROS, other, different) + -sphere

Temperature Layers

The layers of the atmosphere may be classified also by temperature. The temperature of the atmosphere changes with altitude. The way the temperature changes is different in each temperature layer. The lowest layer is the **troposphere** (TRAHP uh SFEER), the weather layer. In the troposphere, the temperature decreases with increasing altitude. The temperature drops about 6.4° C for every kilometer (3.5° F for every 1,000 ft.) increase in altitude. This steady drop in temperature is called the **lapse rate.** At an altitude of approximately 11 km (6.8 mi.), the temperature does not decrease any more. At this altitude, the temperature is about –55° C (–67° F).

7 km	–18.4° C
6 km	–12° C
5 km	–5.6° C
4 km	0.8° C
3 km	7.2° C
2 km	13.6° C
1 km	20° C

8A-5 *The steady drop in temperature as altitude increases is called the lapse rate.*

The troposphere is known not only for its change in temperature but also for its change in other factors affecting the weather. The warm air at the bottom of the troposphere is light and tends to rise; the cold air at the top of the troposphere is heavy and tends to sink. Thus the troposphere experiences a continual mixing of air. The rising warm air carries moisture that forms clouds and rain. The sinking cold air, in contrast, brings fair weather. This continual mixing occurs only in the troposphere.

The **stratosphere** (STRAT uh SFEER), the second temperature layer, extends from the top of the troposphere (12 km or 7.4 mi.) to about 50 km (31 mi.). In this layer, the temperature increases from about –55° C (–67° F) at the bottom to about 0° C (32° F) at the top. The stratosphere is free of clouds and dust. Aircraft flying long distances often travel in it to avoid turbulent storms that may prevail in the troposphere. Some winds in the stratosphere travel up to 480 km/hr. (300 mph) in paths called **jet streams.** Aircraft sometimes fly with these jet streams to increase their speed and to save fuel.

The layer above the stratosphere is the **mesosphere** (MES uh SFEER), which extends to about 80 km (50 mi.) above the earth. Its temperature steadily decreases with altitude. The coldest temperature of the atmosphere, –109° C (–164° F), occurs at the top of the mesosphere. Like the troposphere and the stratosphere, the mesosphere consists of a homogeneous mixture of gases. Also like the lower layers, the mesosphere has winds. These winds often have high speeds and a variety of directions.

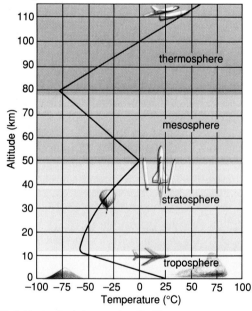

8A-6 *Atmospheric layers classified by temperature*

The uppermost temperature layer of the atmosphere is the **thermosphere** (THUR muh SFEER). Here the widely scattered air molecules are completely exposed to the radiation of the sun. This exposure rapidly raises their temperature thousands of degrees at the highest part of the thermosphere. In spite of the high temperatures, the thermosphere would not warm you. The molecules are so widely separated that too few would contact your body to have a noticeable effect. In the top layer of the atmosphere, you do not need the gas molecules to warm you in the daytime. The sun shines virtually unimpeded. Thus spacecraft traveling through the thermosphere may become hot. An object in the thermosphere at night, however, would be cold. Though the gas particles making up the thermosphere are widely scattered, they block some harmful radiation. They also protect us from meteoroid bombardment by vaporizing the meteoroids into beautiful "shooting stars."

Special Layers

Ozone layer

An important part of the stratosphere is an area containing ozone gas called the **ozone** (OH ZONE) **layer.** This layer extends from about 20 km (12 mi.) to 50 km (31 mi.) above the earth's surface. An ozone molecule has three atoms of oxygen bonded together, while an ordinary oxygen molecule has just two atoms of oxygen bonded together. The ozone layer is vital for living things because it shields them from much of the sun's harmful ultraviolet light. This is an example of the Lord's perfect design of the earth.

Ionosphere

The **ionosphere** (eye AHN uh SFEER) is within the thermosphere. The sun's radiation, as well as radiation from space, breaks the gas molecules into atoms and often causes them to lose electrons and to become electrically charged. These electrically charged atoms are called **ions.** The ionosphere begins at 80 km (50 mi.) and extends to a height of 400 km (250 mi.). The ions of this region reflect short radio waves; therefore broadcasters "bounce" radio waves off the ionosphere to carry their messages around the curve of the earth. Some short-wave signals bounce off the ionosphere and return to earth thousands of miles away from the antenna that transmitted them. Microwaves, the waves used in radar, are not reflected. Instead, they penetrate the ionosphere; thus they are used to communicate with spacecraft.

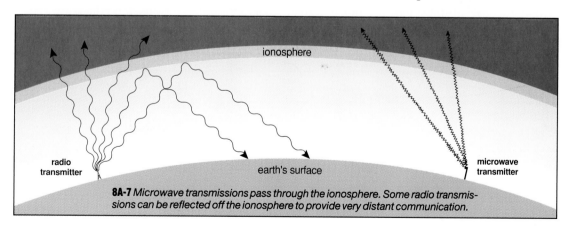

8A-7 *Microwave transmissions pass through the ionosphere. Some radio transmissions can be reflected off the ionosphere to provide very distant communication.*

FACETS OF METEOROLOGY

The Discovery of the Van Allen Belts

Until 1958 scientists believed that space above our earth's atmosphere was essentially empty. The first U.S. satellite, *Explorer 1*, contained a simple radiation counter to measure the small level of radiation striking the atmosphere from the sun and outer space. What was found was unexpected.

As the 31-pound spacecraft moved upward, the radiation level began to increase dramatically. Soon the particles became more intense than the counter could measure. Scientists thought that the measurements were an error caused by a broken counter. But as the satellite descended, the radiation count fell too.

The intensity of particles had increased from 30 particles per second to over 45,000! Dr. James Van Allen, who built the radiation counter, studied the cause. He concluded that the earth's magnetic field loops outward into space and traps a huge concentration of energetic particles. As other satellites went farther into space, they discovered that the radiation level rises, falls back, and then rises again to high intensity before disappearing. With this information Van Allen prepared one of the most astounding maps in modern science. It showed two huge doughnut-shaped belts, one within the other, encircling the earth.

Why was this discovery important? First, it showed that certain regions above the earth are deadly to humans. Even electronic instruments cannot survive long in this region. Second, it showed how the earth, acting like a colossal iron magnet, dominates space around it. In a complex, dynamic process, charged particles from our sun interact with the earth's repelling magnetic force to form these two strange belts. As the solar winds whip around them, particles get trapped within these powerful magnetic fields, bouncing around for as little as a few hours to as much as many years. Some make their way to the earth's atmosphere and others weave back into space.

The search to understand the magnetosphere is still of primary interest to space science. Scientists have sent dozens of instruments into the magnetosphere of our planet and other planets. They have found some interesting things. Only planets with a magnetic field have these belts, and none of them are quite like the earth's. Jupiter's magnetosphere, for example, is one hundred times larger than the earth's, and from the earth Jupiter would appear larger than the moon if its magnetosphere were visible. One fact is clear: God has created a marvelous blanket to protect the earth from the sun's devastating radiation.

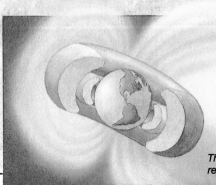

The Van Allen Belts are two doughnut-shaped regions of intense radiation encircling the earth.

8A-8 *The aurora borealis as photographed from NASA's jet aircraft "Galileo" at an altitude of 40,000 ft.*

Magnetosphere

Using information gathered by satellites, James Van Allen discovered the magnetosphere in 1958. The **magnetosphere** (mag NEE toh SFEER) is a zone extending many thousands of kilometers above the earth's surface. It is composed of protons and electrons from the sun that have become trapped in the earth's magnetic field. These particles move back and forth between the poles, following the earth's magnetic lines of force. A sunspot or solar flare increases the movement of charged particles into the magnetosphere.

Some of these particles escape near the poles into the lower regions of the atmosphere. There they collide with particles in the atmosphere and give off beautifully colored light called the **aurora* borealis*** (the "northern lights") near the North Pole and the **aurora australis*** (the "southern lights") near the South Pole.

The magnetosphere, like the ozone layer, protects us from cosmic and solar radiation. It prevents most of the harmful particles from striking the earth directly. This shows the Lord's design in creation.

Section Review Questions 8A-2

1. What is another name for the troposphere?
2. What is the amount of temperature drop in the troposphere per kilometer increase in altitude? What is another name for this temperature drop?
3. What is the name of the layer of the atmosphere that contains the jet stream?
4. Which layer of the atmosphere contains the coldest temperature?
5. Which layer of the atmosphere contains the hottest temperature?
6. Name the four layers of the atmosphere classified by temperature.
7. Name the three special layers of the atmosphere.
8. Which special layer of the atmosphere is important to radio operators?
9. What traps the energetic particles in the Van Allen belts?

aurora: (L. AURORA, dawn)
borealis: (Gk. BOREAS, northern)

australis: (L. AUSTER, southern)

8B–Energy in the Atmosphere

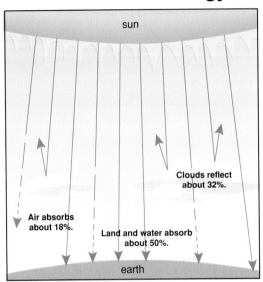

8B-1 *Only about half of the sun's energy that arrives at the earth is absorbed by land and water.*

Almost all the energy on the earth comes from the sun. Although we receive only a tiny portion of the sun's total output, it is enough to sustain all life on the earth. Not all the energy that reaches the earth stays there. The clouds and airborne particles in the atmosphere *reflect* 32 per cent of the radiant energy that reaches the earth. Clouds, dust, and water vapor *absorb* another 18 per cent. Thus, half the incoming radiation is lost through absorption and reflection in the atmosphere.

The sun emits some of its energy as visible light, but sunlight also contains rays with wavelengths both longer and shorter than visible light. The atmosphere absorbs most of the radiation that is not visible light. When the radiation reaches the outer atmosphere, the sparse gas molecules absorb or collide with the sun's most dangerous short-wavelength rays to produce ions. The ozone layer *filters* out most of the ultraviolet rays, the

rays that cause sunburn and other skin damage.

As we have seen, land and water absorb about half the radiation that reaches them. As the earth's surface absorbs this radiation, it becomes warmer and emits infrared radiation (what we feel as heat), which is readily absorbed by the air. Thus the earth warms the air after being warmed by the sun. This indirect warming of the air is called the **greenhouse effect** because a greenhouse uses the same principle in heating air. The sun's direct radiation warms the air only slightly. This arrangement benefits the earth's inhabitants. If the atmosphere were not there, we would be scorched in the daytime by the sun's full radiation, including the deadly ultraviolet and shorter wavelengths. At night the earth's temperature would drop far below freezing. On the other hand, if the atmosphere absorbed all kinds of radiation, the sun's energy would not be able to reach us. Again, the Lord's desire to protect His creatures shows in His design of the atmosphere.

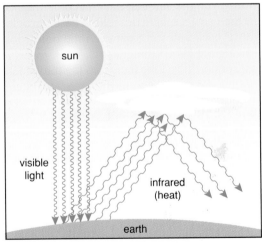

8B-2 *Most heating of the atmosphere comes from the sun-warmed earth.*

Why Is the Sky Blue?

Children often ask questions even scientists cannot explain. Only in the last century did scientists discover the answer to the question "Why is the sky blue?" As sunlight enters the atmosphere, gas molecules scatter some of the sun's white light into its different colors, like a prism. The blue light waves scatter more readily and more intensely than the other colors because blue has a shorter wavelength. Thus the sky appears blue.

"Why is the sky such a deep blue after a rainstorm?" The dust particles in the air have been washed away, leaving a clean atmosphere that scatters pure blue light.

"Why are clouds white?" Water molecules, not gas molecules, make up clouds. Gas molecules scatter light into different colors, but water molecules reflect light as a single white color. The whitest clouds are bright because they reflect light directly from the sun. Clouds with numerous, small water droplets are the best light reflectors.

"Why are many clouds different shades of gray?" Some clouds (or portions of clouds) absorb light rather than reflect it. The more light that is absorbed, the darker the cloud. Clouds before a storm are usually the darkest because their large, sparse droplets are excellent light absorbers. Yet even two similar clouds right next to each other can be completely different colors—one, vivid white, and the other, dark gray. Every cloud is unique, reflecting light differently. Clouds come in an infinite variety of shapes and sizes, with varying sizes of water droplets, ice crystals, and dust.

"Why is the night sky black?" Late at night the only sunlight we see is the feeble rays reflected by the moon. Not enough moonlight scatters to produce colors.

Our blue atmosphere was viewed from above by astronauts. It was an eerie sight. Below them they could see a blue blanket of light wrapped around our planet, but all around them was a perpetual black night. Without our God-given atmosphere, the sky would look like what the astronauts see. Even in the daytime the sky would be black, and the sun would appear as a dot of light in the starry background.

As we discussed in Chapter 1, the sun's energy is most concentrated in its direct rays, which shine on a rather narrow band near the equator. How does this energy reach the higher latitudes? Some energy reaches the higher latitudes directly, but the energy received at the equator also helps to warm the earth's poles. The land and water near the equator absorb the energy and warm the air above them. This air then moves northward and southward to warm the rest of the earth. Warm water also moves north and south from the equator to help spread the sun's energy to the rest of the earth. This distribution of the energy received at the equator makes the equator cooler and the poles warmer than they would be otherwise.

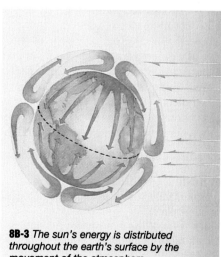

8B-3 *The sun's energy is distributed throughout the earth's surface by the movement of the atmosphere.*

FACETS OF METEOROLOGY

8B–1

Mirages

A delirious traveler, lost in the desert, sees a cool oasis and dives in, only to drink a mouthful of sand. Is he hallucinating? Cartoons make you think so; yet a mirage is not a figment of the imagination. It is a trick that the atmosphere plays on the eyes.†

You can see a mirage while driving down the highway on a hot day. Puddles of water appear in the distance. The "water" is actually light from the sky that slows down in the hot, thick air near the asphalt and bends back upward to the cooler air at your eye level. The blue light of the sky appears to come from the ground.

Other mirages are possible over quiet bodies of water. You may see a boat sailing through the sky above the water! This is the reverse of a desert mirage. The surface air over cold water is *cooler* than the air at eye level, causing the reflected light from the boat to bend downward. Sometimes, when very warm air

A common mirage is the appearance of water on a paved road (top). *A slight change in your position will make the puddle disappear* (above).

is over cold air, the mirage may be inverted and distorted, resulting in weird shapes.

Another spectacular mirage can occur when the sun rises or sets. As the solar fireball rises above the horizon, it often ap-

pears to split into two suns, with the second sun slowly descending back below the horizon. At dusk, the last lip of the descending sun sometimes lingers on the horizon even after the sun has completely set.

Section Review Questions 8B

1. Approximately what percentage of the energy from the sun is absorbed or reflected by the atmosphere?
2. Which layer of the atmosphere protects us from sunburns?
3. What kind of radiation is emitted from the earth's surface as it is warmed by the rays of the sun?
4. What is the name for the indirect warming of the air by warm soil and water?

---

† Even though mirages are physical illusions, they are optically real, which means that mirages can be photographed.

8C–Conditions of the Atmosphere

The lower atmosphere has the most noticeable effect on our daily lives. The study of the atmosphere (especially the troposphere) is called **meteorology*** (MEE tee uh RAHL uh jee). The condition of the atmosphere at any given time is called the **weather.** A description of weather usually includes the temperature, atmospheric pressure, humidity, wind speed and direction, and precipitation.

Temperature

Probably the first thing you notice about the weather on a clear day is the **temperature,** which is defined as the intensity of the heat in the air. If you are wise, you will consider

8C-1 *Atmospheric pressure decreases as altitude increases because the height of the column of air decreases.*

the temperature when you dress so that you do not become too hot or too cold during the day. Humans can tolerate only a small range of temperatures. If the atmosphere is too cold, we must remain inside heated buildings or wear protective clothing. If it is too hot, we must take precautions to avoid heat exhaustion or heat stroke. Thus temperature is an important part of weather.

Atmospheric Pressure

Like other forms of matter, the gases in the atmosphere have weight because of the earth's gravity. The weight of these gases is called **atmospheric pressure.†** If the atmosphere surrounding the earth never changed, the atmospheric pressure would remain constant. However, when air warms, it expands and becomes less dense, thus decreasing the weight of the air over that area. When air cools, it contracts and becomes denser, thus increasing the weight of the air over that area.

Because atmospheric pressure at a given place is dependent on the weight of the air above it, pressure changes with elevation. A mountaintop has less air above it than a valley, and so it has lower atmospheric pressure than a valley. This is why a recipe may have special high-altitude directions. At lower pressures, water boils at lower temperatures and thus food takes longer to cook if it is boiled in water. Bread and cakes rise more because there is less pressure surrounding them. Thus mountain residents may have to boil their food longer and use less leavening.

Atmospheric pressure constantly changes because of the shifting of warm and cold air. Low pressure marks a warm, moist air mass and results in warm, cloudy weather. High pressure occurs with a cooler, drier air mass that produces cool, clear weather.

---

meteorology: meteor- (Gk. METEORON, astronomical phenomenon) + -ology (Gk. LOGOS, word, discussion, subject)

† Job may have realized that air has weight. Job 28:25 refers to "the weight for the winds." This could refer to atmospheric pressure, but Bible scholars are not certain.

Humidity

Another element of meteorology is humidity, the amount of water vapor in the air. Humidity may be reported as absolute or relative. **Absolute humidity** is the exact amount of water a certain volume of air holds. Warmer air can hold more water vapor than cooler air. The ratio of the amount of water the air *does* hold to the amount of water it *can* hold at that temperature is called **relative humidity.** This is expressed as a percentage. If the relative humidity is 67 per cent, then the air holds 67 per cent of the moisture it could hold at that temperature. If the humidity is 100 per cent, the air can hold no more water. If the temperature drops slightly when the humidity is 100 per cent, some water vapor will condense and form droplets of water.

8C-2 Find the air temperature across the top of either chart (Fahrenheit or Celsius), then find the speed of the wind on the side scale. The temperature where the two columns intersect is how cold the wind makes it feel.

The relative humidity affects our comfort. In hot weather we cool off when moisture evaporates from our skin.† If the relative humidity is high, the air is already holding almost all the moisture it can hold, and moisture does not evaporate quickly. Thus we feel hot and sticky. But if the relative humidity is low, the air is dry and readily absorbs moisture. Moisture on our skin evaporates, causing us to feel cooler. In cold weather we do not want to let moisture evaporate rapidly from our skin. Many buildings now have devices for controlling the humidity inside to make people more comfortable.

Wind Speed and Direction

Wind speed and direction also contribute to weather. Wind speed changes the way temperature affects us. A strong wind can make it seem cooler than it is. In hot weather a breeze is a welcome relief from the heat. It helps our cooling mechanism, perspiration,

Wind Chill Tables

Air Temperature (° Fahrenheit)

Wind Speed (mi./hr.)	35	30	25	20	15	10	5	0	-5	-10	-15	-20	-25	-30	-35
0	35	30	25	20	15	10	5	0	-5	-10	-15	-20	-25	-30	-35
5	32	27	22	16	11	6	0	-5	-10	-15	-21	-26	-31	-36	-42
10	22	16	10	3	-3	-9	-15	-22	-27	-34	-40	-46	-52	-58	-64
15	16	9	2	-5	-11	-18	-25	-31	-38	-45	-51	-58	-65	-72	-78
20	12	4	-3	-10	-17	-24	-31	-39	-46	-53	-60	-67	-74	-81	-88
25	8	1	-7	-15	-22	-29	-36	-44	-51	-59	-66	-74	-81	-88	-96
30	6	-2	-10	-18	-25	-33	-41	-49	-56	-64	-71	-79	-86	-93	-101
35	4	-4	-12	-20	-27	-35	-43	-52	-58	-67	-74	-82	-89	-97	-105
40	3	-5	-13	-21	-29	-37	-45	-53	-60	-69	-76	-84	-92	-100	-107
45	2	-6	-14	-22	-30	-38	-46	-54	-62	-70	-78	-85	-93	-102	-109

Air Temperature (° Celsius)

Wind Speed (km/hr.)	8	4	0	-4	-8	-12	-16	-20	-24	-28	-32	-36
0	8	4	0	-4	-8	-12	-16	-20	-24	-28	-32	-36
10	5	0	-4	-8	-13	-17	-22	-26	-31	-35	-40	-44
20	0	-5	-10	-15	-21	-26	-31	-36	-42	-47	-52	-57
30	-3	-8	-14	-20	-25	-31	-37	-43	-48	-54	-60	-65
40	-5	-11	-17	-23	-29	-35	-41	-47	-53	-59	-65	-71
50	-6	-12	-18	-25	-31	-37	-43	-49	-56	-62	-68	-74
60	-7	-13	-19	-26	-32	-39	-45	-51	-58	-64	-70	-77

† Evaporation causes cooling.

8C-3 *The earth's atmosphere has several functions essential to life as we know it.*

(86° F). This is the **wind-chill factor** that you hear weathermen mention.

Wind directions are named by the direction from which the wind is coming. Thus a wind traveling from west to east is a west or westerly wind, and a wind traveling from north to south is a north or northerly wind.

Precipitation

Precipitation is an important characteristic of weather. Rain is the most common form of precipitation; but snow, hail, and sleet also occur frequently. Rain may ruin your plans for outdoor activities, but it is vital for life on earth. Areas where rain is scarce are dry and support less life. Of course, too much rain is also a problem. Heavy, prolonged rains can cause floods and can be destructive. The next chapter discusses precipitation.

Pictures from spacecraft show the earth's atmosphere as a blue blanket swirled with white clouds across the seas and continents. Today we know the atmosphere to be a life-giving blanket containing oxygen for man and animals and carbon dioxide for plants. It is also a protective blanket. A comparison with the craters of the moon is enough to convince a person that the earth's atmosphere protects us from the meteors of space. We are certain that the atmosphere is the work of our almighty God.

to work efficiently. In cold weather a wind is less welcome. A strong wind can lower the apparent temperature by more than 30° C

Section Review Questions 8C

1. What is the study of the atmosphere called?
2. List the five factors used to describe weather.
3. Which of the above factors involves the weight of atmospheric gases?
4. What two things happen to air when it cools?
5. The exact amount of water vapor in a certain volume of air is called by what name? The amount of water in the atmosphere expressed as a ratio to the amount of water that the air can hold is called by what name?
6. How do we feel if the air is very dry? Why?
7. What is the most common form of precipitation? List three other forms.

Terms

absolute humidity
atmosphere
atmospheric pressure
aurora australis
aurora borealis
greenhouse effect
heterosphere
homosphere
ion

ionosphere
jet stream
lapse rate
magnetosphere
mesosphere
meteorology
nitrogen
oxygen
ozone layer

relative humidity
stratosphere
temperature
thermosphere
troposphere
weather
wind-chill factor

What Did You Learn?

1. What is so special about nitrogen in the atmosphere?
2. What is the "greenhouse effect"?
3. Why do some recipes have special high-altitude directions?
4. Why do people wear jackets on windy days even when the temperature is warm?
5. How does God use the atmosphere to protect His organisms from cold?
6. How much of the solar radiation is absorbed, reflected, or otherwise distributed by the the earth's atmosphere?
7. List the atmospheric conditions that compose weather.
8. What is the lapse rate?
9. What is the difference between weather and meteorology?

What Do You Think?

1. Suppose nitrogen gas was gray instead of colorless. How would this affect the weather?
2. Which layer of the atmosphere is most important?

WATER OF THE ATMOSPHERE

NINE

9A–Water Entering the Atmosphere

Most of the water in the atmosphere entered it as water vapor that had evaporated from the ocean. A small percentage of it entered by **evaporation** from lakes, streams, land, plants, and animals. Evaporation is one of two processes by which a liquid changes to a gas or a vapor. The entrance and exit of water from the atmosphere are often associated with changes of state. It is important to understand the processes by which water can change from one state to another.

Water changes from one state to another as it absorbs or releases heat. The change from vapor to liquid is called **condensation.** The reverse, the change from liquid to vapor, is **vaporization** if the water boils or evaporation if it changes to a gas little by little without boiling. As liquid water cools, it

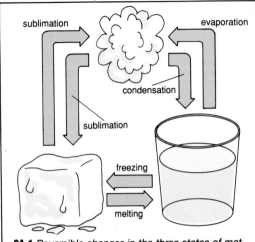

9A-1 *Reversible changes in the three states of matter are illustrated using water.*

changes to the solid state, or **freezes.** When solid water becomes liquid, it **melts.** Snow sometimes disappears into the atmosphere without melting. This change from the solid state directly to the gaseous state is called **sublimation** (SUB luh MAY shun). The reverse of this process, also called sublimation, occurs when water vapor changes directly to a solid in the form of frost or snow crystals.

Molecules of water in the three states are not standing still but are in constant motion. The speed of their movement depends on the amount of heat they hold. When these molecules collide with each other, some of them near the surface of ice or water break loose and fly into the air. By this process, millions of tons of water enter the air each day.

Wind increases the rate of evaporation by blowing away the molecules of water that have escaped into the air. The removal of the evaporated molecules then allows even more water to evaporate. For example, an important feature of hair dryers and clothes dryers is not only the heat they produce but also the air flow from them.

Water molecules absorb heat† when they change into a gas. Because of this heat absorption, evaporation is a cooling process. Liquids, such as water, can cool the skin of a person with a high fever by absorbing his body heat and by evaporating. Each water molecule absorbs a specific amount of heat as it evaporates. When the water vapor condenses to become liquid water again, it releases the same amount of heat that it had absorbed to become vapor. Thus, evaporation absorbs heat while condensation releases it.

9A-2 *Hair dryers add heat energy and moving air to speed up the evaporation process.*

Section Review Questions 9A
1. Where does most of the water in the atmosphere come from?
2. What is the change in state from vapor to liquid called?
3. What is the change in state from liquid to vapor called? (Give two answers.)
4. What is the change in state from solid directly to gas called?
5. What determines the speed of movement of molecules?
6. Does wind increase or decrease the speed of evaporation?
7. Would evaporation be considered a heating process or a cooling process? Does it absorb heat or release heat?

† Technically, this is "thermal energy." Heat is the transfer of thermal energy.

9B–Water in the Atmosphere

Water can exist in the atmosphere in any of its three states. When it is a vapor, it shows up as humidity. When it is liquid or solid suspended in the atmosphere, it appears as clouds.

Humidity

As we saw in the last chapter, temperature affects how much water vapor the atmosphere can hold. At higher temperatures it can hold more water vapor. What happens when the air cools? The temperature at which the relative humidity is 100 per cent is called the **dew point.** For example, suppose the air near the ground has an absolute humidity of 17 g/m^3 at 30° C (86° F). Since air can hold 31 g/m^3 at that temperature, its relative humidity is 55 per cent. If the air temperature drops to 20° C (68° F), it can hold only 17 g/m^3 of water vapor. This is the amount of water vapor it is now holding. Thus, its relative humidity is 100 per cent. If the air cools more, it will not be able to hold the amount of water vapor it now holds. Thus, some of the water must condense or sublimate. The resulting liquid or solid water exists in the air as clouds or mist.

Clouds

Formation of Clouds

A **cloud** is a mass of water droplets or ice crystals suspended in the air. Clouds form when the temperature of a mass of warm, humid air decreases. Air first becomes warm as it contacts the earth's surface which is heated by the sun. At the same time, the humidity tends to increase from the evaporation of water from lakes, streams, and oceans; from the sublimation of snow or ice; or from the evaporation of moisture from the leaves of plants† or from the skin of animals.

As the warm, humid air rises, its temperature eventually decreases below the dew point. Then the water vapor must condense. However, to condense at the dew point, the water vapor needs condensation nuclei. **Condensation nuclei** are small particles of material, such as salt or smoke, around which the tiny water droplets form. Salt spray from seawater and the burning of fuels introduce condensation nuclei into the atmosphere. If the dew point is below 0° C (32° F), the vapor of the humid air cools directly into ice crystals without becoming liquid first. For this freezing to occur, **freezing nuclei,** small particles of clay or dust shaped like an ice crystal, must be present.

The Misery Factor

Why do millions of Americans retire to the deserts of Arizona rather than to the beaches of Florida? One reason is the climate. A 38° C (100° F) day in Tucson, Arizona, is far more comfortable than a 30° C (86° F) day in Orlando, Florida.

The secret to your comfort is not simply temperature. Comfort also depends on the amount of water vapor in the air, called humidity. The body cools off by evaporating water (sweat) into the atmosphere. But when the air is full of water vapor, water cannot evaporate from your skin, and you feel hot and miserable.

Weather reports use the term *relative humidity.* This "misery factor" compares the actual level of water vapor in the air with the maximum level the air can hold. Because hot air can hold more water than cool air, a hotter city has a lower misery factor. The humidity is so low in Tucson, where the average July temperature is 30° C (86° F), that homes rarely need air conditioners. On the other hand, Floridians who face similar temperatures but higher humidity consider air conditioning a necessity.

---

† Water moves from the interior of plants to the air outside by a process called transpiration. In animals the water moves to the surface in a process called perspiration.

9B-1 *Deicing chemicals are used as a safety precaution to keep supercooled water in the atmosphere from clinging to jet and airplane surfaces. Some aircraft have crashed due to excessive icing.*

Sometimes clouds of liquid water exist in the troposphere at temperatures far below the freezing point of water. Some cloud droplets remain liquid even down to temperatures of −40° C (−40° F). This **supercooled water** is a serious problem because it freezes on the wings of airplanes that fly through it. This freezing of supercooled water on airplane wings is called icing. Many planes carry de-icers, special heating units, on the forward edges of their wings to remove the ice.

Cloud Types

As clouds form, the movement of the air determines their shape. Horizontal movement causes the formation of layers, whereas vertical movement forms clumps or billows. Clouds are named by their shapes and their altitudes. The three basic shapes are flat layers or sheets (stratus [STRAY tus]), piles (cumulus [KYOOM yuh lus]), and wispy curls (cirrus [SIHR us]). Another characteristic of clouds is whether they bring rain or not. Nimbus clouds are gray and dark, often bringing rain.

Clouds are classified as one of four basic types, depending upon their altitude: low, medium, high, and vertical development. Vertical development clouds often extend from low all the way through the high altitudes. Low clouds include all clouds up to 2,000 m (about 6,500 ft.). They are identified by the prefix *strato-* in their name. The flat layers of the low-level clouds, however, are simply called stratus rather than stratostratus. If the stratus cloud is so low that it reaches the ground, it is called fog. Sometimes stratus clouds cause **drizzle,** small droplets of rain falling slowly. Very dark stratus clouds that often are associated with long steady rains are called nimbostratus clouds. Another low cloud is the stratocumulus cloud, which is a low (strato-) layer of piled-up (-cumulus) clouds. These are flat on the bottom but billowy on the top. Because their tops do not reach up far, stratocumulus clouds tend to look like they are "rolling" along in the sky.

Middle clouds have the prefix *alto-*. They range from 2,000 m to 6,500 m (about 20,000 ft.) above sea level. Flat, layered clouds between these heights are called altostratus clouds. These are often streaked with gray or a bluish color. If these are thin enough for the sun to shine through, the sun appears to have a corona around it. However, because of the ability of altostratus clouds to scatter light from the sun, objects on the ground do not normally cast a shadow. Altocumulus clouds are usually higher than the altostratus clouds. Like stratocumulus clouds, the altocumulus clouds are white and puffy, but they still appear in layers and appear very small because of their height.

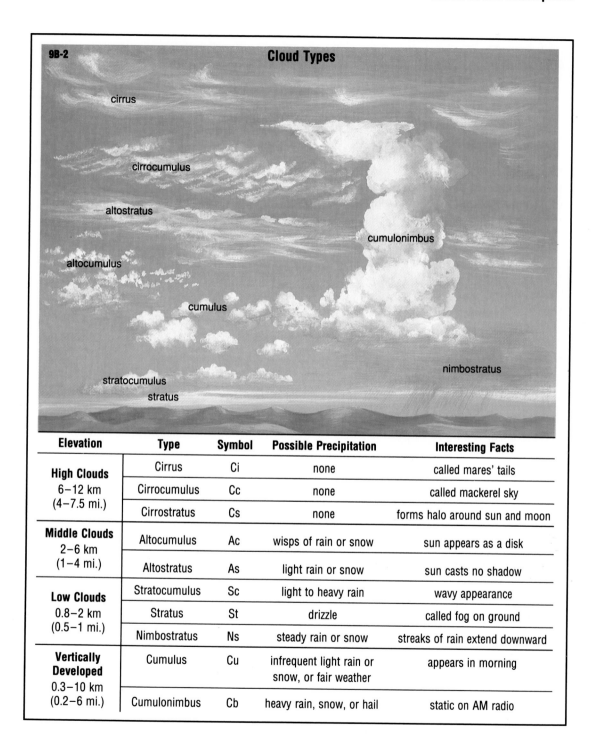

9B-2

Cloud Types

Elevation	Type	Symbol	Possible Precipitation	Interesting Facts
High Clouds 6–12 km (4–7.5 mi.)	Cirrus	Ci	none	called mares' tails
	Cirrocumulus	Cc	none	called mackerel sky
	Cirrostratus	Cs	none	forms halo around sun and moon
Middle Clouds 2–6 km (1–4 mi.)	Altocumulus	Ac	wisps of rain or snow	sun appears as a disk
	Altostratus	As	light rain or snow	sun casts no shadow
Low Clouds 0.8–2 km (0.5–1 mi.)	Stratocumulus	Sc	light to heavy rain	wavy appearance
	Stratus	St	drizzle	called fog on ground
	Nimbostratus	Ns	steady rain or snow	streaks of rain extend downward
Vertically Developed 0.3–10 km (0.2–6 mi.)	Cumulus	Cu	infrequent light rain or snow, or fair weather	appears in morning
	Cumulonimbus	Cb	heavy rain, snow, or hail	static on AM radio

EXPLORING CLOUDS

▼ *Cirrostratus clouds are high, thin sheets of clouds composed of ice crystals. These may refract light to form large circles around the sun or moon.*

▼ *Altocumulus clouds appear as patches or layers of puffy, mid-level clouds. They may form regularly arranged roll shapes. (These may also be called a mackerel sky.)*

◀ *Cirrocumulus clouds appear as small white flakes. They sometimes form a regular pattern called a mackerel sky.*

Altostratus clouds are flat layers of gray ▶ *mid-level clouds.*

◀ Cirrus or mares' tails are high, thin, wispy clouds composed of ice crystals.

▼ Nimbostratus clouds are low, dark clouds that often bring rain.

▼ Stratocumulus clouds are dark and flattened on the bottom but billowy on the top.

▲ Cumulonimbus clouds extend through all three cloud altitudes. These billowy clouds often bring thunderstorms.

189

High clouds, between 6,000 m (about 20,000 ft.) and 12,000 m (about 40,000 ft.) above sea level, are made up of ice crystals.

The prefix *cirro-* is used to identify these clouds. Cirrus clouds are thin, wispy, featherlike clouds. Sometimes they are arranged in bands across the sky called **mares' tails.** Thin, veillike sheets of clouds are called cirrostratus. These clouds sometimes cause a halo to appear around the sun or moon. The halo is usually quite large and easily distinguished as a definite ring rather than the corona found around the sun when altostratus clouds are present. Also, unlike the altostratus clouds, objects on the ground will have shadows when the sun is covered by cirrostratus clouds. Cirrocumulus clouds appear as patches of white flakes or fleecy cottonlike clumps. They may form in groups or lines that resemble the scales of fish so that some people refer to the sky as **mackerel sky** when cirrocumulus clouds are present.

Vertical development clouds consist of the cumulus and cumulonimbus clouds. Cumulonimbus clouds are the billowy clouds that extend from about 300 m (about 1,000 ft.) to about 10,000 m (about 33,000 ft.). They are usually flat on the bottom with dark, gray areas that billow all the way to the top in a long, irregular column. Their tops, made of ice crystals, are often shaped like an anvil.

These thick, towering clouds often bring thunderstorms. Cumulus clouds, on the other hand, are white and puffy. Although they may extend well into upper layers of the atmosphere, they are not nearly as well developed as the cumulonimbus clouds. Small cumulus clouds without a great deal of vertical development are sometimes classified as low-level clouds. They appear individually or in patches rather than in layers, and they are usually signs of fair weather.

▲ Stratus clouds are low layers of gray, sheetlike clouds.

▲ Cumulus clouds are white and puffy.

Section Review Questions 9B

1. In how many states (solid, liquid, gas) can water exist in the atmosphere?
2. What term refers to the temperature at which the relative humidity is 100 per cent?
3. What happens to water vapor if the dew point is below 0° C (32° F) and the water vapor contacts clay or dust particles in the atmosphere?
4. Water in the liquid state that is colder than 0° C (32° F) is called by what name?
5. What are the three basic shapes of clouds?
6. What are the four basic types of clouds?
7. What prefix identifies high-altitude clouds?
8. What is another name for cirrus clouds? for cirrocumulus clouds?
9. What type of cloud is often associated with thunderstorms?

9C–Water Leaving the Atmosphere

9C-1 *Rain (above), hail, sleet, and snow are common forms of precipitation.*

God established physical laws for His creation to operate under. Job recognized that the atmosphere obeys God's direction when he declared that God "made a decree for the rain, and a way for the lightning of the thunder" (Job 28:26). All forms of precipitation, including rain, hail, sleet, and snow occur within the physical constraints decreed by God.

Through years of study, meteorologists have begun to understand the complicated operation of God's laws governing the various forms of precipitation. As a result, meteorologists can predict the amount and form of precipitation with some degree of accuracy. Water leaves the atmosphere in one of two ways. The water vapor may condense or sublimate directly onto cooler objects near the ground, or it may form clouds, which eventually cause precipitation.

Dew and Frost

Condensation of water vapor begins at the dew point. When a cooler surface causes the temperature of a nearby film of air to decrease below this point, **dew** forms. Heavy dews usually form when the air is calm, because moving air cannot be cooled enough to form dew. Dew forms on grass, cars, bi-

9C-2 *The ice crystals of frost can form spectacular patterns. Frost is not a form of precipitation. It is water that has changed directly from vapor to solid.*

cycles, spider webs, or any other object that is cooler than the surrounding air.

In cold weather the air holds less moisture. The dew point for cold air may be below freezing. When this occurs, dew does not form. Instead, water vapor changes directly to ice crystals on cooler surfaces such as windowpanes. Ice formed in this way is called **frost.**

Precipitation

The Bible plainly sets forth God as the one who controls the earth's atmosphere and weather. Weather has been His instrument for both blessing and judgment. In blessing, God has sent bountiful harvests through "the first rain and the latter rain" (Deut. 11:14). In judgment, God sent great destruction when "hail and fire mingled with the hail" rained down on the pharaoh and his people (Exod. 9:24). Weather plays a major role in the world today. But no matter what weather conditions confront us, we can rejoice, knowing that the Lord is in control.

The Gideon Test

You have probably heard the account of Gideon and the wool fleece recorded in Judges 6. As a confirmation of God's instructions, Gideon asked for a twofold miracle. First he asked that a fleece left on the ground outside overnight would be wet with dew in the morning while the ground remained dry. Then he asked that, on a second night, the fleece would be dry while the ground would be wet with dew. God granted Gideon's request exactly as he had stated it. The Bible records that after the first night Gideon wrung "a bowl full of water" out of the fleece, while the ground was dry. After the second night, the fleece was dry and there was dew on all the ground.

By definition, miracles do not have a natural explanation; they are supernatural acts of God. If an event can be explained by natural processes, then it is not a miracle. We know today that dew forms when a cooler surface causes the temperature of a nearby film of air to cool below the dew point. If Gideon had tested God only once with the fleece and dew, the interpretation as a miraculous answer from God would have been in doubt. Scoffers would have said that the fleece and the ground were different temperatures, and that was why dew formed on one and not the other. But Gideon was not content with a questionable answer. He asked for proof. The switched location of dew after the second night could not then nor now be explained by natural events and, hence, was a miracle.

In meteorology the word **precipitation** refers to all forms of water falling from the atmosphere. Whether liquid or solid water particles in the atmosphere fall as precipitation depends on their size. Water droplets that compose a cloud are usually about 0.001 cm (0.0004 in.) in diameter and are supported by the motion of air molecules. However, when the cloud droplets combine, they become larger and the air can no longer support them. The droplets of a fine drizzle are about 0.05 cm (0.02 in.) in diameter and the raindrops in a heavy shower may be as large as 0.6 cm (0.24 in.) in diameter. The smallest raindrop is many thousand times larger than a cloud droplet.

Meteorologists believe that large water droplets develop in two ways. First, water droplets in warm clouds, such as cumulus clouds, form around tiny salt or dust particles in the air called condensation nuclei. If the humidity remains high enough, large cloud droplets form and begin to fall slowly. As these droplets fall, they grow rapidly by colliding with other droplets. The rapid falling of a larger drop also produces a partial vacuum that draws in smaller drops. This building of raindrops by joining many smaller drops is called **coalescence** (KOH uh LEH sence).*

Raindrops also develop in supercooled water clouds. These are clouds that contain liq-

uid water below its freezing point. Supercooled water droplets become ice crystals around freezing nuclei such as clay or dust particles. When the ice crystals become large enough, they fall and continue to grow by coalescence. If the lower atmosphere is warm, the crystals melt and reach the earth as rain. However, if the lower atmosphere is not warm enough to melt them, the crystals fall as snow or ice.

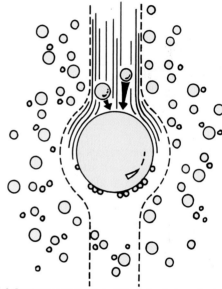

9C-4 *Coalescence is the building of raindrops by joining together many smaller drops.*

How does the process of cloud formation and precipitation occur? There are three basic ways. One way is from **convection.** On a sunny day, the earth warms the air over it. The warmed air rises rapidly and soon cools to its dew point. This produces clouds, and as more warm, moist air rises, the water droplets in the clouds become large enough to fall as precipitation. Most brief showers or thundershowers on hot summer afternoons are caused by convection.

Another process of cloud and precipitation formation is for warm, moist air to *move over*

9C-3 *The size relationship of water droplets helps us understand why cloud droplets do not fall as rain.*

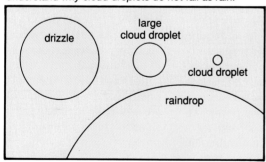

FACETS OF METEOROLOGY

9C-1

"Pure" Rainwater

Few things sound more clean, natural, and healthful than rainwater. You may have heard or read advertisements for products that are "rainwater pure," "rainwater clean," or "fresh as a springtime rain." However, rain is never 100 per cent pure water, since it contains a variety of contaminants.

To begin with, each raindrop has at least one condensation nucleus, which you already know can be a salt or smoke particle, but it could also be a dust, pollen, or clay particle. Carbonic acid is also present in all rain due to atmospheric carbon dioxide dissolved in the water. This makes the rain naturally slightly acidic. Sulfur and nitrogen compounds from sources such as volcanoes, lightning, and living organisms are also naturally found in rain. Most experts agree that the normal pH of rainwater is 5.6–5.7; however, it can be as low as 4.5 due to natural concentrations of carbon dioxide, sulfur dioxide, and nitrogen oxides.

The activities of industrialized nations add even more sulfur and nitrogen compounds to the air, about 90 per cent of the total amount. Sulfur dioxide and nitrogen oxides are the most common pollutants found in rainwater in these areas. These chemicals change to sulfuric acid and nitric acid when

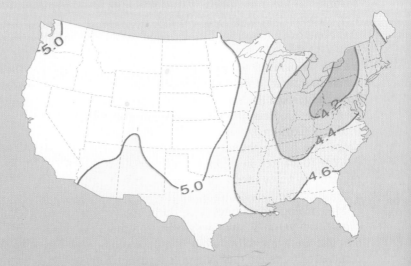

The pH of precipitation is about the same in the areas shaded the same. Notice that the precipitation in the northeastern U.S. is the most acidic.

dissolved in the rainwater. Rain with these additional acids is called **acid rain.** In the northeastern United States, 4.3 is a common rain pH. The pH of acid rain can be as low as 2.0 (lemon juice has a pH of 2.3). Most accounts of acid rain are really about *acid precipitation,* since all forms of precipitation are acidified by the pollutants.

The pollutants that form acid rain come primarily from the burning of coal and oil products which contain sulfur and nitrogen. More than 65 per cent of the sulfur dioxide in the atmosphere over the United States comes from electric power plants that burn coal and oil. The largest source of nitrogen oxides is automobile exhaust.

More than just an atmospheric curiosity, acid rain does have negative effects on the environment. The U.S. government funded a ten-year study of acid rain and found four main effects: (1) Aquatic life has been adversely affected in about 10 per cent of the lakes and streams in the eastern United States. (2) The decline of red spruce trees at high elevations is related to acid rain. (3) Acid rain corrodes buildings, statues, and other materials. (4) Visibility has been reduced because of sulfate particles in the atmosphere. As stewards of the earth, we will have to make decisions to address the acid rain problem.

a mountain. To cross the mountain, the air must rise, and as it rises, it cools. The air usually reaches its dew point and precipitates before it reaches the peak. By the time it reaches the other side of the mountain, it is dry. This is the reason that the side of a mountain facing the prevailing winds usually receives more rain than the other side.

The third way a mass of air reaches its dew point and forms clouds is by *moving over a mass of colder, denser air.* The cold air, like the mountain, forces the warmer air to rise and cool. Soon the warmer air reaches its dew point, forms clouds, and releases its moisture as precipitation.

9C-5 *Causes of precipitation: warm air rising due to convection currents (top); warm air moving over high mountains (middle); warm air moving up over a stationary or slow-moving cold air mass (bottom)*

A castle located in West Germany was adorned with this stone figure. The top photograph shows the figure in 1908. The bottom photograph shows the same figure in 1968. The bulk of the damage occurred during the 20 years preceding 1968.

FACETS OF METEOROLOGY

The Modern Rainmaker

God asked Job, "Canst thou lift up thy voice to the clouds, that abundance of waters may cover thee?" (Job 38:34). In other words, could he command rain to fall? Of course not. The Lord used this question to illustrate that His ways are beyond human understanding and control. Nevertheless, farmers, with so much at stake for their crops, have long tried to "make" rain. Early efforts at rainmaking included the rain dance of the American Indians.

Only in the last century did people begin to discuss "scientific" methods. In 1838 a scientist advocated setting fires in the frontier to end a drought. The heat would rise by convection and theoretically form rain clouds, which would then move to the East. According to another popular belief, cannon blasts "may squeeze the water out of the air like a sponge." To test this theory, the federal government exploded balloons and artillery shells in 1891 and 1892 in west Texas. At the same time "rain companies" proposed another idea to farmers in the West. They claimed the power to make rain by releasing a secret concoction of chemicals into the air, charging as much as $30,000 for their services.

The invention of the airplane created a new possibility for rainmaking. A plane could drop

1 silver iodide released

2 9 min. later

3 19 min. later

4 38 min. later

particles directly into clouds—a process called seeding. Unfortunately, no one knew what particles caused water droplets to coalesce. One man even got the Army to pay for experiments to drop electrically charged sand. But the breakthrough occurred in 1946. A General Electric scientist, inspired by the new ice-crystal theory of rain, dropped 3 pounds of dry ice (frozen carbon dioxide) into a cloud, causing almost instant precipitation.

The modern rainmaker can choose one of two different methods, depending on air temperature. When cloud temperatures are above freezing, he can spray a liquid chemical (ammonium nitrate) under the clouds, either from a plane or from the ground. Rising air currents then carry the chemical into the clouds, where raindrops form around it. If the clouds are below freezing, a plane flies straight into them and releases smoke containing dry ice or silver iodide. These crystals freeze the supercooled water, which then falls and turns into rain.

Yet modern rainmakers are not masters of the weather. In fact, no one can prove that seeding actually produces rain. Seeding works only when clouds are already forming and when circumstances are already favorable to rain. Evidence indicates that seeding increases rainfall by a mere 10 to 20 per cent. Furthermore, the rain covers only a small area. Thus, God's challenge to Job still holds true.

All precipitation of liquid water is called rain, but two forms of rain have other names as well. Drizzle, as we noted before, is small droplets of rain falling slowly. **Freezing rain** is supercooled water that falls as rain and then freezes on the surface it contacts. The weight of the accumulated ice often damages trees and power lines. A freezing rainstorm is often called an ice storm.

Solid precipitation has several forms. When the lower atmosphere is cold, ice crystals formed in the upper atmosphere do not melt, but fall as **snow.** Snowflakes are ice crystals formed when water vapor sublimates to become solid. Most of the crystals are six-sided. Another form of solid precipitation is **sleet,** which occurs when rain falls through a layer of cold air. Sleet consists of small, rounded ice pellets. **Hailstones,** large ice pellets, can greatly damage crops and buildings. Hailstones begin as large raindrops in thunderstorms. These storms have strong updrafts that carry the raindrops to elevations cold enough to freeze them. As they go up, the raindrops collide with other drops and coalesce. Then they freeze, fall, and collide with

more raindrops, which freeze to form the hailstone. This cycle of rising and falling is repeated until the hailstone becomes too heavy for the updraft to keep it in the air. The hailstone then falls from the cloud to the earth. In clouds with strong updrafts, the hailstones may be several centimeters in diameter before they fall to the earth.†

9C-6 *Hail damaged this peach crop in Maryland* (top right); *ice builds up on tree limbs and electric wires, causing widespread damage and power outages* (above); *large hail can damage crops and automobiles and can injure animals and humans* (right).

---

† Grapefruit-sized hailstones were reported in the state of Nebraska in 1928.

Section Review Questions 9C

1. What are two ways in which water vapor leaves the atmosphere?
2. What is the term used for water condensing on a cooler object? sublimating on a cold object?
3. What word refers to all forms of water falling from the atmosphere?
4. What is the name given to the process by which water droplets build up by joining many smaller droplets?
5. List three ways in which cloud formation and precipitation occur.
6. What are two forms of rain other than normal rain?
7. List three forms of solid precipitation.
8. With what form of condensation did Gideon test God?
9. What two acids are found in higher concentrations in acid rain?
10. A breakthrough in rainmaking occurred when what material was dropped into a cloud?

Terms

acid rain	drizzle	mares' tails
cloud	evaporation	melt
coalescence	freeze	precipitation
condensation	freezing nuclei	sleet
condensation nuclei	freezing rain	snow
convection	frost	sublimation
dew	hailstone	supercooled water
dew point	mackerel sky	vaporization

What Did You Learn?

1. Discuss the conditions that are necessary for dew to form on a spider web.
2. If increased temperature makes a day hot, what makes a day muggy? Explain your answer.
3. Explain why you can feel more comfortable in cold winter air if the humidity is high and in the hot summer air if the humidity is low.
4. What name would you give to fluffy mid-level clouds?
5. Explain the difference between sleet and freezing rain.
6. Explain how hailstones increase in size.
7. Explain how mountains can influence the formation of clouds and precipitation.
8. Compare the size of a cloud droplet to the smallest raindrop.

What Do You Think?

1. Could skyscrapers, like mountains, force air to rise and therefore cool and precipitate?
2. How would you prove or disprove the statement "No two snowflakes are exactly alike"?
3. Suppose there were no dust, salt, smoke, etc., in the atmosphere. Would it ever rain?

MOVEMENT IN THE ATMOSPHERE

TEN

10A–Air Masses

Our weather changes because the air is always moving. The composition and movement of air masses is the basis for weather reporting and forecasting. An **air mass** is a huge body of air that has uniform temperature and humidity and covers hundreds or thousands of square kilometers of the earth's surface. An air mass extends not only horizontally but vertically; it can reach heights of several miles. The weather is usually uniform throughout an air mass. Air masses usually do not mix with other air masses, but when air masses meet, the weather changes and often precipitation occurs.

Sources of Air Masses

An air mass forms as air slowly moves over an area of the earth's surface that has uniform temperature and humidity. The air mass takes on the humidity and temperature of this region. Such a **source region** may be over a land mass or a large body of water. The source regions must not be windy areas, because to take on the temperature and humidity of the surface, the air mass must remain in contact with the surface for a period of time. Air masses form only in still air.

Air masses are named after their source regions. Air masses that form over land are called **continental;** those that form over oceans, **maritime** (MAR ih TIME). Air masses from cold areas are **polar,** while air masses from warm areas are **tropical.** Thus there are four general types of air masses: continental polar (cP), continental tropical (cT), maritime polar (mP), and maritime tropical (mT). Air masses affecting the United States form in source regions and then flow over the country. Continental polar air masses form over Canada; maritime polar air masses usually form over the north Atlantic or the north Pacific. The tropical air masses come from the south. Maritime tropical air masses come from the tropical Pacific, the tropical Atlantic, and the Caribbean, while continental tropical air masses come from Mexico.

10A-1 *Air masses affecting the United States form in these source regions and then flow over the country as shown by the arrows.*

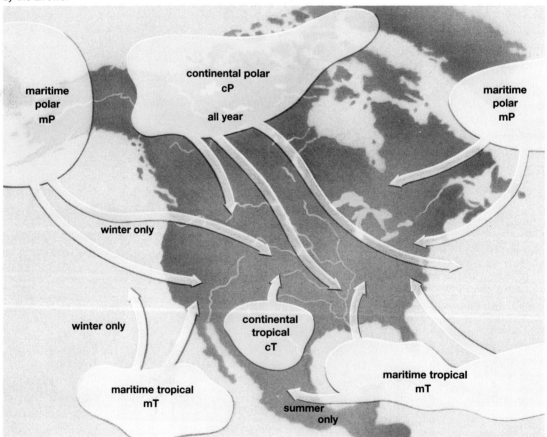

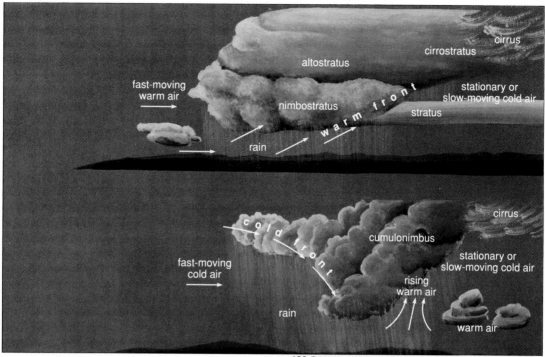

10A-2 *When a fast-moving warm air mass moves up over a slow-moving cold air mass, a warm front is produced* (top). *When a fast-moving cold air mass moves under a slow-moving warm air mass, a cold front is produced* (bottom).

Weather from Air Masses

As air masses move, they carry with them the weather conditions of their source regions. A continental tropical air mass from Mexico brings dry, warm weather; continental polar air masses from Canada bring dry, cold conditions. During the summer, continental polar air masses bring clear, cool conditions. In winter, though, they often bring gripping cold spells that last for weeks. The maritime polar air masses from the oceans often bring in humid and cool or cold air. Maritime tropical air masses bring hot spells to the central and southeastern United States in the summer. Frequent thundershowers and occasional tornadoes are part of the humid, hot air masses. During winter months these air masses often bring mild and cloudy weather.

Meteorologists name an air mass by its temperature compared to the temperature of the ground over which it moves. That is, **warm air masses** are warmer than the surfaces over which they pass, and **cold air masses** are cooler than the surfaces over which they pass. A polar air mass is a cold air mass, and a tropical air mass is a warm air mass.

When two different air masses meet, they do not usually mix unless they have similar temperature and humidity. Instead, they form boundaries called **fronts,** with the colder air mass moving under the warmer air mass like a wedge. The front is a **stationary front** when the boundary is not moving. Usually, however, the boundary moves; one air mass withdraws from the area, and the other re-places it. This action creates a moving front. If warmer air is replacing colder air, the front is a **warm front.** If colder air is replacing warmer air, the front is a **cold front.**

A warm front occurs when a warm air mass overtakes a slower-moving cold air mass. Because of its forward motion, the warm air mass gently rises on the inclined cold air. As this warm air rises, it cools to its dew point. Large systems of clouds develop along the broad frontal surface. These clouds usually bring a long, steady rain over a large area.

Cold fronts often advance faster and have steeper slopes than warm fronts. The slope of the cold front increases when friction with the ground slows the air movement near the surface. When the cold air mass advances at 32 km/hr. (20 mph) or more, it forces the warm air to rise quickly and often brings heavy showers or violent thunderstorms. The scattered heavy showers usually last only a short time. A line of violent thunderstorms, known as a **squall line,** may even occur before the cold front arrives.

Sometimes a cool air mass and a cold air mass trap a warm air mass between them. When that happens, the warm air mass rises over the other air masses and loses all contact with the ground. This arrangement is an **occluded front,** and usually the rising of the warm air causes precipitation. Most interactions among air masses cause precipitation unless the air is dry.

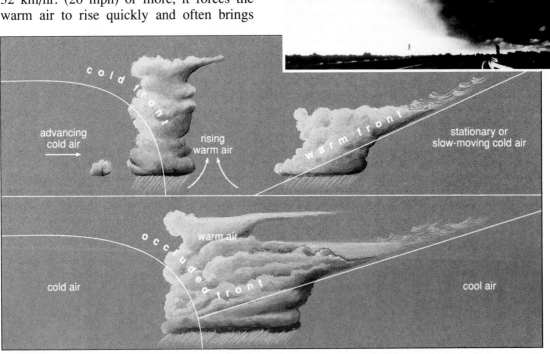

10A-3 *When warm air is trapped between a cold air mass and a cool air mass so that it loses contact with the ground, an occluded front is formed* (above); *an advancing weather front* (inset).

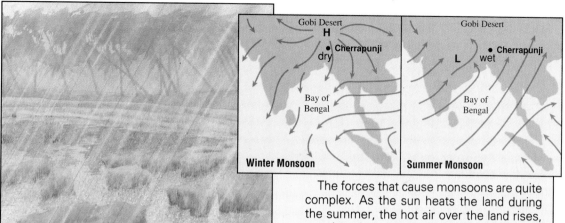

Winter Monsoon   Summer Monsoon

Ninety Feet of Rain

The town of Cherrapunji at the foot of the Himalaya mountains receives an average of 1,143 cm (450 in.) of rain every year. It holds the world's record of 2,646 cm (1,042 in.) of rain in one year—that's almost 90 *feet!*

What causes such heavy rainfall? The **monsoon** (mahn SOON) of southern and Southeast Asia does. Half the world's population depends on this wind for rain. For six months each year the monsoon brings a steady rainy season. Then the winds dramatically shift direction, sometimes in only an hour, and bring a six-month dry season.

The forces that cause monsoons are quite complex. As the sun heats the land during the summer, the hot air over the land rises, creating a low-pressure area. This "vacuum" sucks moist air from the nearby ocean, and then the moisture falls as rain. After six months of heavy rain, winter comes, cooling the dry air of the Gobi desert to the north of the region. A high-pressure system forms and pushes the dry air back out to the ocean. The monsoon's shifting winds make the Bay of Bengal on the southern coast of Asia the mother of cyclones, where millions of people have perished.

Monsoons dump their last drops of water when they hit the mountains. The villages at the foot of these mountains, such as Cherrapunji, receive incredible amounts of rain. Although monsoon winds are most obvious in Asia, they occur on almost every continent. In fact, the name "monsoon" comes from an Arabic word for "season." Arabs used the word *monsoon* to describe the winds that cross the Arabian Sea on a six-month cycle.

Section Review Questions 10A

1. What is a body of air that has uniform temperature and humidity and covers a huge area of the earth's surface?
2. What happens when two air masses meet?
3. What happens when an air mass moves over a source region?
4. List the four general types of air masses.
5. What is the name given to the boundaries between two air masses?
6. What happens when a warm air mass overtakes a slower cold air mass?
7. How does the slope of a warm front differ from the slope of a cold front?
8. What is a line of violent thunderstorms called?
9. How long does the monsoon season of southern and Southeast Asia last?

10B–Winds

Air masses differ not only in temperature and humidity but also in pressure. Cold air masses tend to have higher pressure than warm air masses. These pressure differences are the main cause of winds. Air moves from a region of high pressure to a region of low pressure and from a cold front toward a warm front.

Another phenomenon that affects the direction of wind is the earth's rotation, as we discussed in Chapter 1. The earth's rotation (west to east) causes the north wind to veer to the west of a straight line (drawn from pole to pole) in the Northern Hemisphere, and the south wind to the west of a straight line in the Southern Hemisphere.† This veering contributes to the wind's circling an area of low pressure, an effect called a **cyclone.** In the Northern Hemisphere the wind in a cyclone goes counterclockwise; in the Southern Hemisphere, it goes clockwise.‡

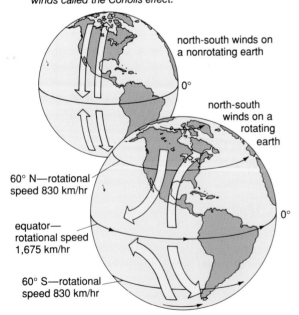

10B-1 *Differences in the speed of the earth's rotation at different latitudes cause the apparent veering of the winds called the Coriolis effect.*

north-south winds on a nonrotating earth

0°

north-south winds on a rotating earth

60° N—rotational speed 830 km/hr

equator—rotational speed 1,675 km/hr

0°

60° S—rotational speed 830 km/hr

Local Winds

Local pressure differences cause local winds. On a sunny day, for example, there may be a breeze from the sea to the shore. Why? The

sea breeze

land breeze

10B-2 *During the day, local winds called sea breezes blow toward land from the ocean (top). At night the winds reverse their flow and land breezes occur (bottom).*

land absorbs energy from the sun more readily than the water does. This warms the air over the land and makes it less dense than the air over the sea. The difference in density means that the air over the sea has a higher pressure than the air over the shore. Therefore, air moves from the sea to the shore, giving a pleasant **sea breeze.** At night the wind reverses. The land cools more rapidly than the water, so the air over the land becomes cooler and more dense than the air over the sea. Thus air moves from the shore to the sea in what is called a **land breeze.**

---

† In the Northern Hemisphere the Coriolis effect causes the wind to veer to the right. In the Southern Hemisphere it causes the wind to move to the left.

‡ Winds in anticyclones (high pressure areas) circle clockwise in the Northern Hemisphere.

FACETS OF METEOROLOGY

10B–1

Jet Streams

High above the earth are rapid currents of wind, called jet streams. Faster, broader, and deeper than water streams on earth, they can reach speeds of 480 km/hr. (300 mph), cover a path 480 km (300 mi.) wide, and plunge 3 km (2 mi.) deep. Some are more than 11,500 km (7,000 mi.) long. Unlike streams of water, jet streams flow uphill as well as downhill and constantly shift their course with the changes in weather.

Jet streams were encountered by B-29 bombers during World War II.

Jet streams are thousands of kilometers long.

Jet streams occur where air masses with different temperatures meet, such as at the head of polar fronts as they push into warmer regions. The contrast in temperature creates a rushing cylinder of wind. The wind blows fastest in the center and slows down toward the edge of the stream. The streams appear to begin and end nowhere. Some appear suddenly and disappear just as suddenly, while others have regular yearly patterns. Most of them flow from east to west.

Jet streams were first discovered in World War II on America's first bombing mission to Japan. A fleet of high-flying B-29 Superfortress bombers, approaching at around 563 km/hr. (350 mph), were suddenly yanked past their targets at even higher speeds. As a result, their mission was almost a complete failure. Puzzled meteorologists later found the cause—the aircraft were caught in a previously unknown stream of pounding winds flowing over Japan.

There are numerous jet streams, some of which have a major impact on weather and climate. In North America the arctic jet stream often loops down deep into the heart of the United States during the winter, bringing bitterly cold air from the Arctic. Subtropical jet streams flowing in from the Pacific through Mexico breed many of the tornadoes for which the Midwest is famous. Although we now know much, we still have more to learn about these mysterious jet streams.

Winds similar to land breezes and sea breezes occur with any local temperature difference. For example, a black parking lot near a wooded park absorbs energy from the sun and causes a breeze to flow from the park to the parking lot. A city absorbs energy more easily than the surrounding fields or woods, and so a breeze blows from the surroundings to the city. Temperature differences also occur at different altitudes. The average temperature of the air decreases as the altitude increases. Thus breezes often flow down from a mountain slope to a nearby valley.

Global Winds

Global pressure differences occur because of the way the sun heats the earth. These pressure differences cause the prevailing winds in each area of the world. The sun heats the equator more than any other area of the earth. Thus the air over the equator tends to have a low pressure. As the air rises, it cools and releases much of its moisture. Then it falls, some to the north and some to the south. This falling air divides, with one portion falling to the earth at about 30° latitude and the other portion continuing on toward the pole. These air movements occur both in the Northern and in the Southern Hemispheres.

Each portion of air that descends will divide again, with part of the air going toward the pole and part going toward the equator. The part going toward the equator moves into the vacuum formed under the rising air at the equator. As it moves toward the equator, this air is deflected toward the west. The winds thus formed are called the **trade winds** because they helped the trade ships sailing from Europe to the New World.

The portion of air that goes toward the pole from 30° latitude is deflected toward the east. These winds are often called the **prevailing westerlies.**† Have you ever noticed that

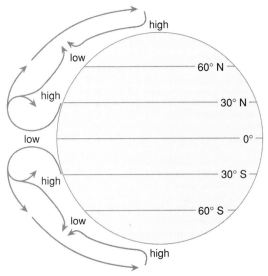

10B-3 *Cross-section of the troposphere showing the generalized circulation of air between the poles*

weather maps of the United States show that weather tends to move eastward? This movement results from our prevailing westerlies. Although occasional winds come from the northwest and sometimes the east, most of our winds are the prevailing westerlies from the west and southwest. The southwest winds bring warm, humid air from the Gulf of Mexico to the United States.

The portion of upper air from the equator that continues toward the pole eventually returns to the surface near the pole. This air then flows toward the equator and is deflected toward the west by the earth's rotation. These winds are named the **polar easterlies.** The polar winds bring cold, dry air over the northern portion of our continent, where they contact the prevailing westerlies. As the cold, dry air from the north meets the warm, humid air from the south, precipitation occurs.

Because of the rising or falling air masses, the earth has permanent high- and low-pressure zones. At the equator are the **doldrums,** a permanent low caused by the rising of

---

† Winds are named according to the direction from which they come. Winds that are blowing toward the east are coming *from* the west and therefore are called westerlies.

warm air. At 30° latitude are the **horse latitudes,** permanent highs caused by the falling air. The doldrums and the horse latitudes were dangerous for wind-powered sailing ships because the air flowing straight up or down provided no wind for the ships to sail in. These areas became traps for the ships. The horse latitudes received their name because ships carrying horses to the New World were forced to dump the animals into the sea when provisions ran short. Sometimes sailors in small rowboats had to tow empty ships from the doldrums or horse latitudes to areas where the winds would fill the sails again.

At 60° latitude the prevailing westerlies meet and rise over the polar easterlies, and the underlying low-pressure area is known as the **subpolar low.** At the poles are the north and south polar highs caused by falling cold air.

The locations of the high- and low-pressure belts shift with the seasons. As the sun's most direct rays move with the seasons, the doldrums and the horse latitudes shift slightly. The shift is about 5° over oceans and much more over large land masses such as Asia. As a result, people living near the equator experience both the trade winds and the calm of the doldrums each year. People living near 30° latitude experience the horse latitudes' calms, the prevailing westerlies, and the trade winds each year.

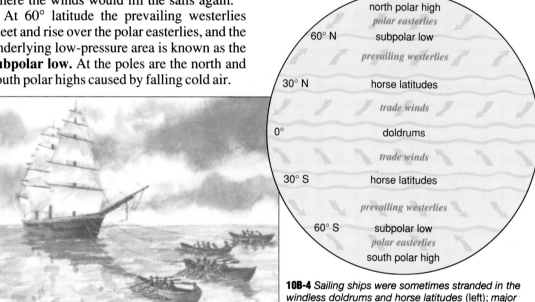

10B-4 *Sailing ships were sometimes stranded in the windless doldrums and horse latitudes* (left); *major global pressure belts and winds* (above).

Section Review Questions 10B

1. What is the main cause of wind?
2. In the Northern Hemisphere, in what direction do cyclones rotate?
3. What type of local breeze occurs near the ocean at night?
4. Why does the air over the equator have low pressure? What is another name for that area?
5. What is the name given to the winds that blow toward the west near the equator?
6. What is the name given to the winds that blow toward the east at 30° latitude?
7. How are winds generally named?
8. Are the winds in jet streams faster in the center or on the edges?

10C-**Storms**

10C-1 *The path of Hurricane Bell as it approaches the East Coast—photographs were taken at 24-hour intervals.*

Although a breeze on a hot day is pleasant, strong winds can be destructive. Most types of storms include precipitation as well as strong winds. There are three types of storms: thunderstorms, tornadoes, and hurricanes.

Thunderstorms

About forty-four thousand thunderstorms occur on the earth each day. They are the most common type of violent storm. Most of these storms are relatively small and rarely more than a few miles in diameter. Thunderstorms usually form on hot summer days because of convection (rising warm air). They may occur in the winter, however, along the edge of cold fronts.

Development of a Thunderstorm

On warm summer days, the hot earth causes the air over it to heat rapidly. This warm air rises with great speed to an altitude of about 7,600 m (25,000 ft.). The air soon reaches its dew point, and water condenses. Condensation forms a cumulonimbus cloud or **thunderhead.** For a time, more warm, moist air replaces the rising air and the precipitation from the upper levels of the cloud falls to the earth as heavy showers. This precipitation carries cool air downward rapidly. As the air strikes the ground, it blows out from the center as gusty winds. Sometimes the rapid upward movement of the warm air continues and carries some water droplets upward, where they often freeze and form hail.

The thunderstorm begins to lose its force when the air that replaces the rising air is no longer warm. Then the rain slackens, and the round, billowing top of the cloud seems to flatten as if it has reached a ceiling. The highest cloud droplets become fine ice crystals that either spill down over the sides like a veil or are blown horizontally to form the anvil-shaped top of the thunderhead.

the cloud becomes positively charged and the bottom of the cloud becomes negatively charged. As the negative area of the cloud gathers more charge and the voltage difference increases, a discharge of lightning occurs. The voltage of lightning is tremendous. For a discharge to jump only 2.5 cm (1 in.) requires about 25,000 volts. Yet lightning bolts are often thousands of meters long.

10C-3 *Time-lapse photograph which includes several lightning strikes from a thunderstorm*

A faint streamer of electricity, a **stepped leader,** heads downward in steps with pauses lasting fifty-millionths of a second. Just before it reaches the ground, the air between the leader and the ground becomes charged. Immediately a vast lightning surge discharges along this path from the cloud to the ground, and a series of flashes, known as **return strokes,** travel up the leader to the cloud. The process repeats itself so quickly that it appears as a single flash of lightning. If a stepped leader branches on the way to the ground, the surges that follow the leader also will travel along the branched paths, forming **forked lightning.**

The temperature within the lightning bolt is estimated to be as high as 28,000° C (50,000° F). This tremendous heat forces the air along the lightning's path to expand with an explosive force, producing the sound we

10C-2 *A severe thunderstorm may produce flash floods, damaging winds, hail, lightning, and tornadoes.*

Lightning

Lightning is an electrical discharge that occurs either between clouds or between a cloud and the ground. Through a process that meteorologists do not understand, the top of

10C-4 *The person who took this photograph heard the thunder after seeing the lightning because light travels faster than sound.*

call thunder. You can determine the distance to the lightning because of the difference in the speeds of sound and light. Light reaches you almost instantaneously, but sound travels only about $\frac{1}{3}$ km ($\frac{1}{5}$ mi.) each second. Thus, if you count the seconds between a lightning flash and the sound of thunder, you can find how far the sound has traveled. For example, if fifteen seconds elapse between a lightning flash and the sound of thunder, the sound has traveled 15 sec. $\times \frac{1}{3}$ km/sec, and the storm is 5 km (3 mi.) away.

Although you can see lightning when it is far away, you usually cannot hear thunder beyond about 16 km (10 mi.). Lightning from distant clouds whose thunder you cannot hear is known as **heat lightning.** In spite of this name, heat lightning is the same as nearby lightning. The fact that we do not hear the thunder does not mean it does not exist.

10C-5 *Forked lightning travels along many branched paths. The brighter, central stroke that has reached the ground is the path of many successive leaders and return strokes.*

Section Review Questions 10C-1

1. List three types of storms.
2. Which of the three storms is the most common?
3. What is a thunderhead?
4. What shape is the top of a thunderhead?
5. Why do the tops of clouds become positively charged?
6. How many volts of electrical discharge are required to make a spark jump 2.5 cm?
7. What is the name of the faint streamer of electricity that heads toward the ground in short steps?
8. What is the name given to the series of flashes that move up toward the cloud after the initial discharge?
9. Lightning that travels in branched paths is called by what name?
10. How far does sound from lightning travel in one second?

10C-6 *An unusual series of photographs demonstrating the increasing size and power of the funnel of a destructive tornado in 1957*

Tornadoes

Each year over two hundred tornadoes hit the United States and cause about one hundred deaths. Although these devastating windstorms occur over all continents, they are most frequent and destructive in the United States. Tornadoes are most common in the central states: Oklahoma, Kansas, Iowa, Nebraska, Arkansas, and eastern Texas. Other areas known for tornadoes are Illinois, Georgia, and Alabama. Tornadoes occurring at sea, called **waterspouts,** are less intense than those occurring over land. A tornado's path of destruction is narrow, sometimes only a few feet, but its whirling wind speeds may be as much as 400 km/hr. (250 mph), higher than in any other storm.

A **tornado** is a narrow funnel cloud extending down from a cumulonimbus cloud. The tornado often looks like a gigantic elephant's trunk or a thin rope dangling from a cloud. The average diameter of a funnel's base is about 400 m (0.25 mi.), but it ranges from 3 m (10 ft.) to 3 km (2 mi.) wide. This base is important because it is the most destructive part of a tornado. Sometimes several funnels extend down from the same cloud and cause great destruction.

Although the tornado may stay in one place, it usually moves, and it may travel at speeds up to 100 km/hr. (62 mph). Its direction is normally from the southwest to the northeast. At the same time, the tornado frequently complicates the efforts of people to dodge it. It may sway from side to side and bounce up and down along its path. Its white or gray color often turns black as it touches the earth, picking up dust and debris. Also, lightning flashing twenty or thirty times per minute may accompany the tornado, and lightning may flash constantly inside the funnel.

10C-7 *Tornados occurring over bodies of water are called waterspouts.*

10C-8	Notable Tornadoes in the United States		
Year	Location	Deaths	Interesting Facts
1884	Southeast	800	deadly cloud system spawned 60 tornadoes
1896	St. Louis	306	a brief tornado hit the city; lowest officially recorded air pressure in a tornado
1925	Missouri, Illinois, and Indiana	689	a mile wide; moving 62 mph, destroyed numerous towns in 3 states
1926	Florida	373	left 40,000 homeless
1932	South	362	tornadoes in 5 states
1936	South	421	tornadoes in 5 states; Tupelo, Mississippi, lost 216 people
1952	Mississippi Valley	238	31 tornadoes in 6 states
1953	Texas	124	tornadoes hit Waco and San Angelo, Texas
1953	Michigan/Ohio	139	numerous tornadoes
1953	Massachusetts	97	rare tornado in the Northeast; $50 million damage
1965	Midwest	271	37 tornadoes cause over $300 million damage
1970	Texas	26	tornadoes cause over $200 million damage; Lubbock hit hard
1974	Mississippi Valley	350	tornadoes in 5 states

10C-9 *Friction at the earth's surface, while the main cloud continues to move, causes a tornado's funnel to bend* (above); *a tornado near Enid, Oklahoma.*

The wind, the low pressure, and the updraft are the three great destructive forces of a tornado. Pressure created by wind increases four times whenever the speed of the wind doubles. For example, winds at 320 km/hr. (200 mph) are four times as destructive as winds at 160 km/hr. (100 mph).

The second destructive force is the low pressure within the funnel of a tornado. Although it has never been measured directly, scientists estimate that the pressure is less than one-tenth the normal pressure at sea level. It was incorrectly believed that buildings explode when hit by a tornado because of the tremendous drop in pressure. However, research has shown that a tornado's winds push the windward walls inward and the tornado's updraft lifts the roof off the building. The other walls fall outward due to the winds.

The updraft within the funnel has amazing strength. It has lifted people, farm animals, automobiles, railroad cars, and even houses into the air. Rarely will a tornado simply move an object some distance and set it down unharmed. Usually it destroys whatever it touches.

10C-10 *The aftermath of a tornado near Fayetteville, North Carolina, demonstrates the tremendous force of destruction bound up in a tornado.*

Section Review Questions 10C-2
1. Approximately how many tornadoes hit the United States each year?
2. What is the name given to tornadoes that form over the sea?
3. What type of cloud is usually associated with tornadoes?
4. What direction do tornadoes usually travel?
5. List the three great destructive forces of a tornado.

Hurricanes

Hurricanes are giant windstorms that form over the tropical oceans near the equator. Unlike tornadoes, these storms are huge, measuring from 160 km (100 mi.) to 1,000 km (600 mi.) in diameter. Some hurricanes can cover nearly 1 million km^2 (0.4 million mi.^{2}) and can continue for three weeks. With winds sometimes exceeding 320 km/hr. (200 mph), they are responsible for widespread destruction to ships and shorelines. Hurricanes bring not only high winds but also high tides and heavy rains. They cause flooding with heavy losses of life and property.

Hurricanes always originate over oceans where there is abundant warm, moist air and little resistance to wind. In the tropical oceans, where the trade winds enter the doldrums, conditions are especially suited for them. Stagnant, overheated, moisture-laden air begins to rise at the beginning of a hurricane, cooling as it rises. When the temperature decreases below the dew point, clouds form and rain begins. Cooler surrounding air rushes toward the low pressure area that is formed at the surface by the rising warm air. Because it is deflected to the right by the earth's rotation, this cool air approaches the center of the low in a counterclockwise spiral in the Northern Hemisphere. This rotation sets up a circuit around the center so that the pressure remains low. The cycle progresses as more winds rush in and rise, and the spiral whirls more vigorously. Eventually the winds attain hurricane speed of 120 km/hr. (75 mph) or more.

Photographs from weather satellites show loose spiral arms at the edges of the storms. These spiral arms become closer together and winds increase in speed as they approach the center. Near the center the winds are strong, and the air rises and cools to produce violent rainfall. In the center of the hurricane, the **eye,** the rain often stops completely and the clouds thin. Sometimes a person can see the sun while in the eye of a hurricane.

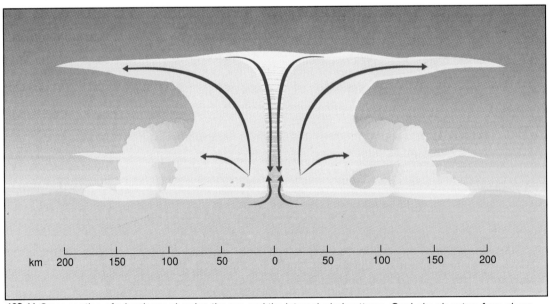

10C-11 *Cross section of a hurricane showing the eye and the internal wind patterns. Cool, dry air enters from above the storm, creating the calm eye of the storm. Warm, moist air spirals in toward the eye near the bottom, upward as it nears the eye, and back out in spiraling fashion as it rises.*

HURRICANE HUGO
15 SEPTEMBER 1989
7:30 AM EDT   120 MPH

VIRGIN ISLANDS
BARBUDA
ANTIQUA
GUADELOUPE
DOMINICA
MARTINIQUE
ST. LUCIA
BARBADOS
GRENADA
TOBAGO

10C-12 *This color-enhanced infrared satellite photo shows Hurricane Hugo over the Atlantic a week before it struck Charleston, South Carolina.*

The eye of a hurricane generally ranges from about 22 km (14 mi.) to about 32 km (20 mi.) across. However, it may be as large as 80 km (50 mi.), or it may not form at all. A slight draft of cool, dry air frequently enters the eye from above the storm. Butterflies or flocks of birds can fly in the eye. Pressures are lower in the eye than in the outer parts of the hurricane.

Because of the friction with uneven land surfaces, a hurricane's winds usually slow down as the hurricane strikes the shoreline and moves inland. The slower wind speed allows some cooler air to reach the center, and the extremely low pressure begins to rise. The storm also loses energy because the land has less moisture than the sea. The wind speed in a hurricane increases when it absorbs the energy that is released from the water vapor as it condenses. Thus, when over land less water vapor gives less energy and slower winds.

The sky covered with a thin haze of cirrus clouds often signals the approach of a hurricane. The air is calm, hot, and humid, and the pressure is high. Then the pressure falls sharply, the cirrus clouds overhead are hidden by cirrostratus and cirrocumulus, and the wind increases. Immediately before the fury begins, blue-black nimbus clouds roll and tumble overhead. The storm also affects the ocean. The high winds produce huge waves far out at sea called the **storm swell.** These waves move at speeds up to 50 km/hr. (31 mph) and break on the shore several hundred kilometers ahead of a hurricane. People who are several miles inland can often hear the waves.

10C-13 *Hurricane Katrina as seen from the camera of an earth satellite*

10C-14			Notable Hurricanes, Cyclones, and Typhoons
Year	Location	Estimated Deaths	Interesting Facts
1737	Bay of Bengal	300,000	deadliest cyclone in history; 20,000 boats sunk
1780	Caribbean	20,000+	"the year of the Great Hurricane," during the American Revolution; 3 to 5 hurricanes developed at the same time; struck fleets from 3 nations (Spain, England, France)
1876	Bay of Bengal	200,000	cyclone and storm wave killed some, and disease killed many others
1881	China	300,000	typhoon and storm wave (figures uncertain)
1882	Bay of Bengal	100,000	cyclone and storm wave wrecked Bombay
1900	U.S.	6,000	deadliest hurricane in U.S. history; destroyed half the homes in Galveston, Texas
1928	Puerto Rico/U.S.	4,000	broke a dike on Lake Okeechobee, Florida, drowning 1,836 people
1935	U.S.	400	the lowest pressure (barometer) reading in the western hemisphere; winds over 200 mph near Tampa, Florida
1938	U.S.	680	first hurricane in New England in 70 years; one of the strongest to hit that far north; $382 million damage
1944	Pacific	790	during World War II winds up to 150 mph hit a U.S. Navy fleet, sinking 3 destroyers, destroying 146 planes, and seriously damaging 18 other ships
1955	U.S.	184	Diane, the first "billion-dollar hurricane"; thought dead, it brought intense floods to the Atlantic coast already soaked by hurricane Connie
1959	Japan	5,041	typhoon Vera caused $1.2 billion damage
1960	Bay of Bengal	45,000	2 cyclones one month apart
1969	U.S.	500	Camille, one of the most powerful hurricanes ever, with average winds of 190 mph; caused over $1 billion damage to Gulf Coast; spawned more than 100 tornadoes
1970	Bay of Bengal	200,000	deadliest cyclone of this century
1974	Honduras	8,000	Fifi destroyed many towns; $1 billion damage
1979	Caribbean/U.S.	2068	David caused $2 billion damage
1988	West Indies/ Mexico	300	Gilbert, the most powerful hurricane recorded in the western hemisphere; the eye was so narrow it looked like a tornado
1989	Caribbean/U.S.	51	Hugo, the most costly hurricane in history (over $10 billion damage), wrecked Charleston, South Carolina
1991	Bangladesh	125,000	20 ft. high wall of water was driven over a dozen islands and on to the mainland, flooding 20,000 sq. mi.

A hurricane destroys with winds and water. During the first half of the storm, strong winds move across an area from one direction. The eye of the storm follows these winds and may bring calm for an hour or more. Then more devastating winds start from the opposite direction, and at the same time, heavy rains cause flooding.

Hurricanes are known by other names in oceans other than the Atlantic. Hurricanes in the Pacific are called **typhoons** (ty FOON), while in the Indian Ocean they are referred to as cyclones. The Australians, on the other hand, call a hurricane a ''willy-willy.''

A single hurricane has claimed as many as three hundred thousand lives. One of the worst struck Galveston, Texas, on September 8, 1900. In that city the hurricane took an estimated six thousand lives and destroyed $20 million worth of property. The storm originated in the West Indies and touched the tip of Florida before it veered westward and came ashore at Galveston.

10C-15 *Fishing trawler driven ashore by hurricane Camille (above); severe damage caused by an extratropical cyclone in Virginia Beach, Virginia (right)*

10C-16 *Hurricanes cause extensive flooding damage; the remnants of Hurricane Agnes caused this flooding in Harrisburg, Pennsylvania.*

An exceptionally destructive hurricane of more recent times was Hurricane Hugo in 1989. The hurricane was responsible for fifty-one deaths and approximately $10 billion in property damage. Advance warning and evacuation procedures helped to keep the death toll to a minimum. It is interesting to note that of the thirty-five deaths attributed to Hurricane Hugo in South Carolina, where the hurricane came ashore, only fifteen happened during the passage of the storm. The rest occurred afterward by electrocution, falls, and tree-clearing accidents.

FACETS OF METEOROLOGY

10C-1

Safety in Storms

Thunderstorms—In the United States, lightning is responsible for about two hundred deaths annually. Many houses are burned each year by fires started by lightning strikes. Conductors called **lightning rods** often protect buildings from lightning. These metal rods are attached to the highest points of a building's roof and are connected with metal conductor cables running down the side of the building to long metal rods driven into the ground near the foundation. Lightning rods may prevent lightning from striking by draining electrical charge from the air. Even if lightning strikes, the rods and the conducting cables carry the current safely to the ground without damaging the structure.

The safest place to be during a thunderstorm is in a building protected by lightning rods or in a car. Avoid water pipes and electrical wiring in a building and stay away from the sides in a car. If you are caught outside a building or car in a thunderstorm, remember that lightning often strikes the highest point in a region. Avoid being near tall trees or other objects that stand alone. Also, avoid being the tallest object in the area. If you are caught in an open field or similar area, crouch down or lie down.

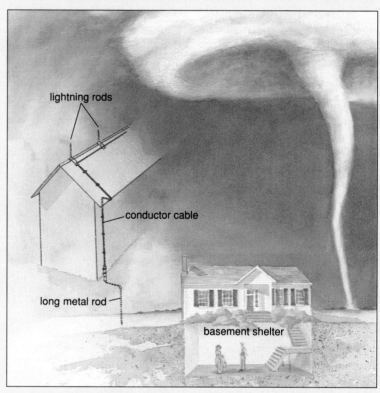

lightning rods

conductor cable

long metal rod

basement shelter

Tornadoes—The best protection from a tornado is a specially constructed storm cellar. These cellars are below ground level and away from structures or trees that might fall on them. If you are in a building and see a tornado, you should position yourself under a strong piece of furniture such as a table or bed along a southwest wall or in a small interior room such as a closet or a bathroom. If you are outside or in a car and see a tornado, go to the lowest level of ground you can reach and lie flat. Do not try to "outrun" the tornado.

Hurricanes—The only real protection against a hurricane is to leave the area. Meteorologists use radar and weather satellites to watch hurricanes so that they can give people plenty of warning before the hurricane reaches their area. In modern America, people usually have time to save themselves and some of their property. Those who refuse to leave risk injury or death.

Section Review Questions 10C-3

1. What is the name given to giant windstorms that form over tropical oceans near the equator?
2. List three things that are forces of destruction associated with hurricanes.
3. What direction do hurricanes normally turn in the Northern Hemisphere?
4. What wind speed must a storm have before it can be classified as a hurricane?
5. What is the name given to the center of the hurricane?
6. What two things cause a hurricane's winds to slow down over landmasses?
7. What name is given to a hurricane in the Pacific Ocean? in the Indian Ocean?
8. What is used to protect tall buildings from lightning?
9. Where is the safest place to be during a thunderstorm?
10. Where is the safest place to be during a tornado?
11. What is the best protection from a hurricane?

Terms

air mass	lightning rod	stepped leader
cold air mass	lightning	storm swell
cold front	maritime air mass	subpolar low
continental air mass	monsoon	thunderhead
cyclone	occluded front	tornado
doldrums	polar air mass	trade winds
eye	polar easterlies	tropical air mass
forked lightning	prevailing westerlies	typhoon
front	return stroke	warm air mass
heat lightning	sea breeze	warm front
horse latitudes	source region	waterspout
hurricane	squall line	
land breeze	stationary front	

What Did You Learn?

1. What would be the characteristics of an air mass moving slowly over the North Atlantic? What type of an air mass would it be?
2. Why are weather predictions, even with sophisticated equipment, somewhat unreliable?
3. What part of the day would you expect winds to be calm at the seashore?
4. If a lightning flash is seen and fifteen seconds later the sound of thunder is heard, how far away was the lightning?
5. Why is it unlikely that storms occur on the moon or on Mercury?
6. What weather conditions are associated with continental polar air masses?

What Do You Think?

1. Will man one day be able to control the weather with any degree of success? Why or why not?
2. Could a lightning bolt be captured and used to provide electricity to electrical appliances?
3. Could energy from a tornado or hurricane be captured to provide electricity or some other form of useful energy? How?

WEATHER PREDICTION

ELEVEN

11A – Gathering Weather Information

Meteorologists have developed many techniques for predicting the weather reliably. The U.S. National Weather Service's weather predictions are about 80 per cent accurate. To achieve this accuracy, meteorologists must first *gather* information about the conditions of the atmosphere. Then they must *report* their information to a central location. The central location must then *analyze* the information and make a *forecast*. The central location is then responsible to *distribute* the data back to the individual stations so that a local forecast can be made after understanding the weather over a large area.

The United States has hundreds of weather stations and thousands of weather substations that contain instruments for measuring the temperature, pressure, humidity, wind, and rainfall. These weather stations are small and often report automatically to a central weather station.

Basic Instruments

Thermometer

The **thermometer*** is a simple instrument that measures temperature. Galileo invented the **thermoscope** in 1592. This instrument consisted of a glass bulb with a long, thin neck inverted over a container of water. Heating or cooling of the glass bulb resulted in expansion or contraction of air in the instrument. The water would fall or rise in the neck with the expansion and contraction of the air. The height of the water in the tube could show a person's temperature.

Modern thermometers are similar to Galileo's. However, now we use a bulb filled with mercury or alcohol and a glass tube sealed at the top. Expansion and contraction of the liquid instead of air is used to indicate temperature. The scale on a thermometer is usually either Fahrenheit or Celsius.

In 1714 Gabriel Daniel Fahrenheit (1686–1736) introduced his temperature scale in Danzig (Gdańsk), Poland. He chose as 0 the lowest temperature he could reach with an ice-water-salt solution. He chose his own body temperature as 100. (Normal body temperature today is 98.6° F.) On the **Fahrenheit scale,** pure water freezes at 32° and boils at 212°. These two tempera-

11A-1 *Galileo's thermoscope*

tures are called the **fiducial** (fih DOO shul) **points** of a temperature scale. By subtracting, you can see that 180 degrees separate the fiducial points on the Fahrenheit scale.

Anders Celsius (1701–44) and Carolus Linnaeus (1707–78) introduced the centigrade or **Celsius scale** at the University of Uppsala in Sweden in 1742. The Celsius scale has the fiducial points at 0 and 100, with 100 degrees between them. That is, on the Celsius scale pure water freezes at 0° and boils at 100°. Comparing the Celsius and Fahrenheit scales, you can see that the Celsius degrees are larger than the Fahrenheit degrees, since it takes 180 Fahrenheit degrees to equal 100 Celsius degrees. The scales not only begin in different places but also have different degrees.

11A-2 *Although better known as a botanist, Carolus Linnaeus (right), along with Anders Celsius, introduced the Celsius scale. Both were professors at the University of Uppsala.*

---

thermometer: thermo- (Gk. THERME, heat) + -meter (Gk. METRON, measure)

Although the Fahrenheit scale is popular in the United States, all scientists use the Celsius scale in their work because it is used with the metric system. Converting from one system to the other is sometimes necessary. To change a Fahrenheit reading to Celsius, use the following formula:

$$C = (F - 32) \div 1.8$$

To change a Celsius reading to Fahrenheit, use the formula below:

$$F = (C \times 1.8) + 32$$

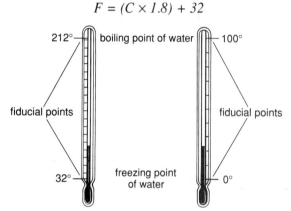

212° boiling point of water 100°

fiducial points   fiducial points

32° freezing point of water 0°

Fahrenheit (180 divisions)   Celsius (100 divisions)

11A-3 *Comparison of Fahrenheit and Celsius*

Weather stations use several types of thermometers. The **maximum** and **minimum thermometers** record the highest and lowest temperature over a certain time, for example, a day. The maximum thermometer is a mercury thermometer with a constriction just above the bulb. As the temperature rises, the mercury expands and forces through the constriction to show the higher temperature. But when the temperature falls, the mercury cannot go back through the constriction. It therefore shows the highest temperature since it was reset. The minimum thermometer is an alcohol thermometer with a thin glass pin inside the stem. As the temperature falls, the alcohol draws the glass pin with it. However,

11A-4 *A maximum and minimum thermometer makes it easy to read the high and low temperatures for a day.*

when the temperature rises, the alcohol cannot push the glass pin ahead of it.

Bourdon (BOOR dn) **tube thermometers** have a sensing bulb outside with a long tube connected to a reading dial inside a building. Some Bourdon tubes connect to a pen arm that traces the temperature on a graph as it revolves. Such instruments are called **thermographs.**

Thermometers in a weather station must have shelter from sunlight and heat radiating from nearby buildings. They also should be located away from rising air currents, which are warmer than the average air temperature. A **thermometer shelter** is a small structure with a top to provide shade from the sun, an airtight bottom to shield from convection currents, and latticed sides to allow the air to circulate freely. In a city, some thermometers are on the roofs of high buildings.

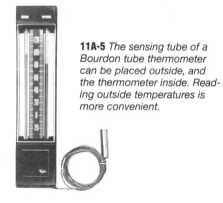

11A-5 *The sensing tube of a Bourdon tube thermometer can be placed outside, and the thermometer inside. Reading outside temperatures is more convenient.*

11A-6 *Thermographs constantly record temperatures, giving a record of all changes during a period of time.*

Barometer

Barometers* measure atmospheric pressure. Evangelista Torricelli (TOR uh CHEL ee) (1608–47), a pupil of Galileo, developed the **mercurial barometer** in 1643. Torricelli's barometer was a closed glass tube extending upward from a reservoir of mercury. Today's mercurial barometer also contains a mercury column enclosed in glass with a reservoir at the bottom. The space between the mercury and the top of the tube is a vacuum. This space is called "Torricelli's vacuum." The atmospheric pressure supports the column of mercury by forcing down on the surface of the mercury in the reservoir.

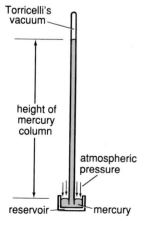

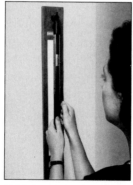

11A-7 *Atmospheric pressure supports a column of mercury in a glass tube (left); reading a barometer (above)*

Atmospheric pressure is about 101,000 newtons per square meter (N/m^2); that is, a column of air that is 1 m^2 reaching from sea level to the top of the atmosphere weighs about 101,000 N. A column of air that is 1 $in.^2$ reaching from sea level to the top of the atmosphere weighs 14.7 pounds; so that the pressure at sea level is about 14.7 $lb./in.^2$ (psi). At this pressure the atmosphere can support a column of mercury that is 760 mm (29.92 in.) high. As atmospheric pressure increases, the mercury rises in the tube; as pressure decreases, it drops. Because the atmospheric pressure is the same indoors and outdoors, barometers are usually inside.

11A-8 *The aneroid barometer is compact and does not contain mercury. In addition to measuring air pressure, it can be used to sense altitude of aircraft.*

Lucien Vidi (1805–66) invented the **aneroid*** (AN uh ROYD) **barometer** in 1844. This barometer includes a round metal vacuum can that collapses slightly under pressure. An increase in pressure collapses the can, and a decrease in pressure allows an enclosed spring to expand the can. A series of levers transmits the minute changes in the can to a dial. Some aneroid barometers, called **barographs,** record changes in atmospheric pressure on graph paper.

The average barometer reading at sea level is 760 mm (29.92 in.) of mercury. Another unit of pressure that the National Weather Service uses is the **millibar** (mb). Originally average sea-level pressure was assumed to be about 1,000 mb, but more precise measurements have determined it to be 1,013 mb. Pressure rarely climbs above 1,050 mb and rarely falls below 982 mb.

---

barometer: baro- (Gk. BAROS, weight) + -meter (measure)

aneroid: a- (Gk. A-, not) + -neroid (Gk. NERON, water)

FACETS OF METEOROLOGY

I Can Feel It in My Bones

The earth is full of signs fore-telling changes in weather, if you know where to find them. Ancient sailors and farmers depended on these signs for their livelihood. Jesus once reminded the Pharisees of a well-known weather indicator when they asked Him for a sign from heaven:

> When it is evening, ye say, It will be fair weather: for the sky is red. And in the morning, It will be foul weather to day: for the sky is red and lowring. O ye hypocrites, ye can discern the face of the sky; but can ye not discern the signs of the times? (Matt. 16:2-3)

Many other sayings have developed to predict weather. Here are some of the more popular sayings and their scientific explanation.

Red sky at night, a sailor's delight.
Red sky in morning, a sailor's warning.

Sunlight turns the sky red (or pink) when the air is dry and filled with dust. The red sky is a good sign if it appears in the west, where the sun sets. It indicates that fair weather is moving into the area, because air circles the globe from west to east. But when the sky is red in the east, where the sun rises, it means that during the night fair weather passed through the area and foul weather is on the way.

A ring around the moon means rain soon.

Cirrus clouds, which form about a day before rain, cause a halo around the moon as the light passes through the clouds at night.

Mares' tails and mackerel scales,
Make lofty ships carry low sails.

Cirrus clouds, which look like mares' tails, herald the coming of a warm-front storm; altocumulus clouds, which look like mackerel-fish scales crossing a clear sky, herald the approach of a cold-front storm.

When a cat frisks like a kitten,
Rain is on the way.

As moisture increases in the air before a rain, the hairs on animals swell, making them uncomfortable.

A coming storm your shooting
corns presage,
And aches will throb, your
hollow tooth will rage.

Low pressure and increased humidity before a storm can increase human aches and pains, such as sore corns, arthritis, and sensitive dental caries.

If a spider works its web in
the morning,
Expect a fair day.

A spider waits until the atmosphere is dry to spin its web, because the web sticks only to a dry wall.

When the snow falls dry, it
means to lie;
But flakes light and soft bring
rain oft.

Dry snow means the atmosphere is relatively cold; so the snow will not melt. But wet snow means that temperatures are on the rise; so the snow will soon melt or turn to rain.

Watching signs is fun and useful, but we cannot depend on signs. We must trust God, who alone knows the future. God wants us to serve in the fields whether the signs look good or bad. Consider the warning of Solomon:

He that observeth the wind shall not sow; and he that regardeth the clouds shall not reap. (Eccles. 11:4)

In the morning sow thy seed, and in the evening withhold not thine hand: for thou knowest not whether shall prosper, either this or that, or whether they both shall be alike good. (Eccles. 11:6)

When the dew is on the grass,
Rain will never come to pass.

Dew forms only when the air cools rapidly. The sky must be clear for this cooling to take place.

Psychrometer and Hygrometer

Two kinds of instruments are used to measure relative humidity. The **psychrometer** (sy KRAHM ih tur) takes advantage of the fact that in high humidity less water evaporates. This instrument contains two thermometers, one ordinary and one with a wet cloth over its bulb. As water evaporates from the cloth on the wet-bulb thermometer, the temperature of the bulb drops. Scientists have compiled tables that give the humidity from the temperature readings on the wet- and dry-bulb thermometers.

11A-9 *A psychrometer measures relative humidity by determining the evaporative cooling on a wet bulb thermometer.*

Stationary psychrometers hang on the wall. The cloth on the wet-bulb thermometer is connected to a wick that draws water from a reservoir below the thermometers. These psychrometers require time to give accurate readings. **Sling psychrometers,** on the other hand, have handles so that they can be twirled through the air. These give accurate readings much more quickly than stationary psychrometers because they pass through more air in less time. Because they work quickly, sling psychrometers do not need a wick and water reservoir.

11A-10 *Sling psychrometer*

11A-11 *A hygrometer measures relative humidity.*

The **hygrometer*** (hy GRAHM ih tur) also measures relative humidity by utilizing human hairs that have had the oils extracted. As the humidity increases, the hair lengthens, and as it decreases, the hair shortens. The hygrometer uses the changes in a hair's length to show the humidity. A recording hygrometer has a pen that records the changes in a hair's length on a revolving drum.

Anemometer and Wind Vane

The **anemometer*** (AN uh MAHM ih tur) measures wind speed. The most common anemometer has small cups attached to a rotating pole. The cups rotate because the pressure of the wind is greater on the concave side. The anemometer converts the rotation to electrical impulses that operate a dial showing wind speed. Anemometers usually include **wind vanes,** instruments that show the direction from which the wind is blowing.

11A-12 *Wind speed can be determined from the cups' speed of rotation on a rotation anemometer.*

hygrometer: hygro- (Gk. HUGROS, moist) + -meter (measure)

anemometer: anemo- (Gk. ANEMOS, wind) + -meter (measure)

11A-13 *Knots, a unit of speed, was first used to report ship speed. A length of line marked with knots was used to determined the distance traveled.*

In the United States, meteorologists report the wind speed on radio and television broadcasts in miles per hour, but weather stations measure the speed in knots (nautical miles per hour; 1 knot equals 1.15 mph). The wind direction is the direction from which the wind blows. Meteorologists say that the wind is "out of" the east, northwest, south-south-east, and so on. The direction is given in one of the sixteen points of the compass or in degrees clockwise from north. If the wind comes from due west, a weather station may report it as a "west wind," as "out of the west," or as "270°." A wind from the northeast may be designated "northeasterly," "out of the northeast," or "45°."

11A-14	Beaufort Wind Scale		

Before the anemometer was invented, people estimated the wind speed from its effect on plants and water. Admiral Francis Beaufort of the English navy devised a system, the **Beaufort Wind Scale,** in 1805. He described the appearance of the sea and the sails of a ship at different wind speeds so that ship captains could record wind speeds accurately in their logs. Today meteorologists occasionally use these terms to describe the wind, but more often they use numbers. Here are some things to look for on the land to show you the wind speed.

Beaufort Number	Designation	Visible Effects	Speed km/hr (mph)	
0	calm	smoke rises vertically	<1	(<0.6)
1	light air	direction shown by smoke	1–5	(0.6–3)
2	light breeze	leaves rustle	6–11	(4–7)
3	gentle breeze	leaves and twigs in motion	12–19	(7–11)
4	moderate breeze	small branches move	20–28	(12–17)
5	fresh breeze	small trees sway	29–38	(17–23)
6	strong breeze	large branches sway	39–49	(23–29)
7	moderate gale	large trees sway	50–61	(30–37)
8	fresh gale	twigs break off trees	62–74	(37–44)
9	strong gale	branches break	75–88	(45–53)
10	whole gale	trees uprooted	89–102	(53–61)
11	storm	widespread damage	103–117	(61–70)
12	hurricane	extreme damage	>117	(>70)

FACETS OF METEOROLOGY

THE HIGHEST WIND EVER OBSERVED BY MAN WAS RECORDED HERE

FROM 1932 TO 1937 THE MT. WASHINGTON OBSERVATORY WAS OPERATED IN THE SUMMIT STAGE OFFICE THEN OCCUPYING THIS SITE. IN A GREAT STORM OF APRIL 12, 1934, THE CREW'S INSTRUMENTS MEASURED A WIND VELOCITY OF

231 MILES PER HOUR

The Windiest Mountain in the World

At a height of only 1,917 m (6,288 ft.), Mount Washington is not much of a mountain. (The highest mountain in the United States, Mount McKinley, is 6,194 m, or 20,320 ft., high.) Yet Mount Washington experiences the fastest surface winds on the earth. One gust recorded in 1934 reached 372 km/hr. (231 mph)! Why is it tormented by such winds?

Though relatively short, Mount Washington towers over the surrounding mountains. It is the highest point in New Hampshire. For that matter, it is the highest point in the entire northeastern United States. Elevation alone does not explain the high winds. The paths of storms originating in the Atlantic, the Gulf of Mexico, and the Great Lakes clash near here. As the storms climb over Mount Washington, they press together and create gusts of wind of hurricane force.

Not surprisingly, this windy mountain is the site of a weather station which has been manned since 1932. Almost every day the weathermen face bitter winds as they make their rounds on "Misery Hill." On the worst days they must tie themselves to ropes so they can get back to base. They also must endure stinging fog formed from warm air rising

over the mountain. The fog freezes on everything it touches. Sleet and hail storms pelt like buckshot in the high winds.

Mount Washington is a little bit of the North Pole in the midst of the United States. Circus entertainer P. T. Barnum once called it the "second greatest show on earth." Tourists may explore the mountain trails *at their own risk.*

Mt. Washington (top), while not impressive as far as height, is impressive in other ways. This photograph of the weather station on Mt. Washington (right), helps explain the name "Misery Hill."

Rain Gauge

The **rain gauge** measures the amount of rainfall on a level surface. In its simplest form the rain gauge is just a vessel for catching rain with a scale to measure the depth. A more complex rain gauge consists of a small bucket divided in half. When one side of the bucket gathers a certain amount of rain, such as 0.25 mm (0.01 in.), it tips. The other side then gathers the same amount of rain and tips. The bucket's tipping affects an electrical gauge that records the number of times the bucket tips and thus the amount of rain that has fallen. Another type of rain gauge weighs the rain as it accumulates to find how much has fallen.

Objects in the path of the rain could block the gauge or deflect extra water into the gauge. To get a true sampling of the rain, meteorologists place the rain gauge 0.9 to 1.8 m (3 to 6 ft.) above the ground in an open space. Wind speed greatly affects the collection of water in rain gauges. A weather station on top of a tall building in a city may have rain-depth readings as much as 10 per cent different from those taken on the ground.

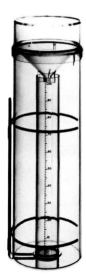

11A-15 *This rain gauge collects falling rain and measures it in a calibrated tube.*

More Elaborate Instruments

Besides the basic equipment, meteorologists use more elaborate instruments to measure the weather. These instruments require human supervision, so only manned stations have them. Also, because they are so expensive, not all stations are equipped with these devices. The instruments are located at enough stations to provide meteorologists with additional information that helps them to forecast the weather accurately.

The conditions above the earth's surface can affect our weather. One way to measure the conditions of higher air is to use balloons to carry instruments aloft. Some balloons carry instruments called **radiosondes*** (RAY dee oh SAHND). Most radiosondes consist of a thermometer, a barometer, a hygrometer, and a radio transmitter for sending the data back to a weather station.

11A-16 *A meteorologist releases a weather balloon with a radiosonde.*

radiosonde: radio- (L. RADIARE, to emit beams) + -sonde (Fr. SONDE, sounding line)

Pilot balloons measure the speed of the wind at various altitudes. In clear weather meteorologists find the wind speed by releasing a pilot balloon and measuring its path with a sighting instrument called a **theodolite** (thee AHD uh LITE). The readings of the theodolite provide the data for calculating the upper wind speeds. When visibility is poor, meteorologists release a larger balloon with a small radio transmitter attached. This arrangement is called a **rawinsonde** (RAY win SAHND). Receivers on the ground pick up the signals and record the path of the transmitter. This recorded path allows meteorologists to calculate the wind speed. The rawinsonde functions in all kinds of weather and can measure wind speeds at greater altitudes than the pilot balloon. Specially designed balloons that can withstand high altitudes stay aloft for several months and are monitored by satellites.

Another tool of the meteorologist is **radar.** This device sends out microwaves that bounce back from clouds of water droplets and ice crystals as well as from precipitation. Ground-based radar sees precipitation. Analysis of these precipitation echoes indicates the presence of thunderstorms, hurricanes, and other heavy precipitation within a radius of 135 km (84 mi.). Some radar units can distinguish between snow and rain and between clouds of water droplets and clouds of ice crystals. A newer technique uses a type of radar called Doppler radar, which can determine wind speed as well as the type of precipitation.

11A-17 *Weather radar tower used to detect storm systems (left); the receiving and transmitting disk of Mile High Radar facility in Denver (above), was exposed before the protective dome was fully installed. Mile High is the forerunner of a material network of Doppler radars called NEXRAD (Next Generation Weather Radar).*

Weather satellites photograph the location and movement of clouds from an altitude of about 800 km (500 mi.). If they are equipped with infrared sensors, the satellites also can determine the temperatures of the earth's surface below them. Some weather satellites revolve around the earth in polar orbits and photograph the entire surface of the earth each day. Others remain positioned over one place on the globe and form a network to show the earth's entire surface. Those in polar orbit are closer to the earth, so they can circle the earth more than once each day. Both kinds of satellites give meteorologists valuable information about the weather, especially about cloud movements.

While it seems almost unnecessary to list the *computer* as an instrument for weather collection, it must be understood that in our modern electronic society, very little data collection is done by an individual meteorologist manually inspecting weather instruments. Most stations have their weather-data-collection devices connected directly to a computer terminal. The terminal reads the device, records the information, and relays the information to weather collecting stations. What previously took hours of time

observing, recording, and transmitting now requires only a matter of seconds. In addition, accuracy has greatly increased. The meteorologist's job today includes checking computer information to insure that the computer is functioning accurately. This is done by doing manual calculations and comparing the data with the computer.

11A-18 *Satellite photograph of cloud patterns superimposed over a map of the United States. A drawing of a Tiros-N type weather satellite, which circles the earth in a polar orbit* (inset).

Section Review Questions 11A

1. List the five steps to successful weather predictions by meteorologists.
2. What are the two common scales used on modern thermometers?
3. What are the two fiducial points on a temperature scale?
4. Who (two people) introduced the Celsius temperature scale?
5. What are thermometers that have sensing bulbs outside with a long tube connected to a reading dial inside a building called?
6. Who developed the first barometer?
7. What kind of barometer did Vidi invent? How was it different form other barometers?
8. What two instruments are used to measure relative humidity?
9. What instrument is used to measure wind speed?
10. What type of weather balloon has a radio that measures temperature, barometric pressure, and humidity?
11. What contains instruments that photograph the locations and movements of clouds from an altitude of about 800 km?

11B–Reporting Weather Information

Weather accompanies air masses as they travel across the earth's surface. A large part of weather forecasting is locating air masses, determining their characteristics, and plotting their movements on a regular schedule so that predictions can be made of future movements of the mass. To do this, meteorologists need to know the weather over a large area. Therefore, more than twelve thousand individual surface weather stations in the United States report their measurements to the National Weather Service. The Weather Service also receives over twenty-five thousand surface aviation reports, fifteen hundred reports from ships at sea, twenty-five hundred aircraft reports, and five hundred radar reports. Satellite reports are also reported to the Weather Service, which then coordinates the reports and makes general forecasts.

To make their reports easy to read, meteorologists report weather data in symbolic form which is translated to a standard format called the **station model.** This format uses symbols and numbers to report the weather.

Figure 11B-1 shows an example of the station model used on weather maps.† The circle in the middle shows the cloud cover at the station. If the circle is clear, less than 10 per cent of the sky is covered with clouds. If the circle is blackened, the sky is completely covered with clouds. Various degrees of blackening show partly covered skies. The line (known as the staff) connected to the circle shows the direction the wind comes from. The lines attached to the staff show the wind speed. Each long line, called a flag, means 10 knots of wind speed. A half-flag means 5 knots. Thus, the $2\frac{1}{2}$ flags in Figure 11B-1 mean that the wind speed is 25 knots.

To the upper left of the circle is the temperature in degrees Fahrenheit. On the lower left is the dew point in degrees Fahrenheit. Directly to the left is a symbol that shows the

11B-1 *To a meteorologist, reading the station model below is a simple task. Each symbol is placed in a specific location. The coded message at the top shows how the model would be transmitted electronically. Computers change the coded message into the station model.*

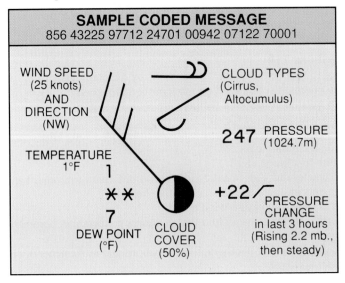

SAMPLE CODED MESSAGE
856 43225 97712 24701 00942 07122 70001

WIND SPEED (25 knots) AND DIRECTION (NW)

CLOUD TYPES (Cirrus, Altocumulus)

247 PRESSURE (1024.7m)

TEMPERATURE 1°F

+22 PRESSURE CHANGE in last 3 hours (Rising 2.2 mb., then steady)

DEW POINT (°F)

CLOUD COVER (50%)

† There is a complete station model in Appendix A.

current form of precipitation. If no symbol is there, no precipitation is falling. To the upper right is the pressure reading in millibars. Actually this number is the last three digits of the reading with the decimal point omitted. Thus, a report of 247 means 1,024.7 mb; a report of 865 means 986.5 mb. Finally, the number and symbol directly to the right of the circle show the change in pressure in the last three hours. The number is the amount the pressure has changed, and the symbol shows how steady the change has been.

The station model is too cumbersome to transmit in the format just described; there-fore, codes have been developed for electronic transmission. These codes are entered into computer terminals and transmitted electronically to a central station. The station model drawings are done by the computer. The numbers at the top of Figure 11B-1 show the coded message that would be sent for the station model shown. Each number in the coded message represents a particular part of the station model. In many cases once the coded message is entered into the computer terminal, it is untouched by human hands until the final forecast is made by a local weatherman.

Section Review Questions 11B

1. Symbolic data that weather stations submit are translated into what type of format?
2. The staff that comes out from the circle in the middle of a station model indicates what type of data?
3. What units do meteorologists use to report barometric pressure?

11C–Analyzing Weather Information

The National Weather Service's computer center, located at the National Meteorological Center at Suitland, Maryland, analyzes the weather-station reports. The center locates high- and low-pressure centers and maps the air masses and fronts. These maps are valuable in predicting the weather. Weather within an air mass is fairly uniform. If a meteorologist knows the direction and speed of a moving air mass, he can predict the weather for the area that the air mass is traveling toward.

Many weather maps point out areas that have similar weather conditions. Some weather maps have lines, called **isotherms,** * connecting stations that have the same temperature. For example, a winter weather map may have a line connecting all stations reporting 3° F, another connecting stations with 2° F, and so on. These isotherms are also used to show differences in climate on a world map. Other weather maps show **isobars,** * lines connecting all stations reporting the same pressure. These maps help meteorologists to locate centers of high and low pressure, which determine much of the weather.

There are four principal weather maps or charts prepared by the National Weather Service daily. Since these charts present a synopsis (general view) of the weather data, they are referred to as **synoptic weather charts.** The *Surface Weather Map* shows station data and the analysis for 7:00 A.M., EST,

---

isotherm: iso- (Gk. ISOS, equal) + -therm (heat)

isobar: iso- (equal) + -bar (weight)

for a particular day. Tracks of well-defined low-pressure areas are indicated by a chain of arrows; areas of precipitation are indicated by shading; fronts are indicated by standard symbols discussed earlier.

The *500-Millibar Height Contours Map* is used to plot the upper-level atmospheric pressures. These are similar to isobars located on the surface map, except the lines represent the altitude (in decameters) at which the barometric pressure is equal to 500 mb (375 mm). Wind speed and direction are indicated by the staff-and-flag system used for the station model. This map also shows the temperatures (isotherms) in dotted lines.

The *Highest and Lowest Temperature Chart* shows the maximum temperature for the twelve-hour period ending 7:00 P.M., EST, of the previous day and the minimum temperature for the twelve-hour period ending 7:00 A.M., EST. The *Precipitation Areas and Amounts Chart* shows the areas (sometimes shaded) that had precipitation during the twenty-four hours ending at 7:00 A.M., EST, with amounts to the nearest hundredth of an inch. The letter T is used for unmeasured amounts to indicate a "trace."

Information from the daily weather maps is used extensively for future reference. These maps, of course, are records of past weather conditions by the time they are printed. However, they play an important part in climatology studies and in prediction of future weather events. Nearly all station models and weather maps are computer generated.

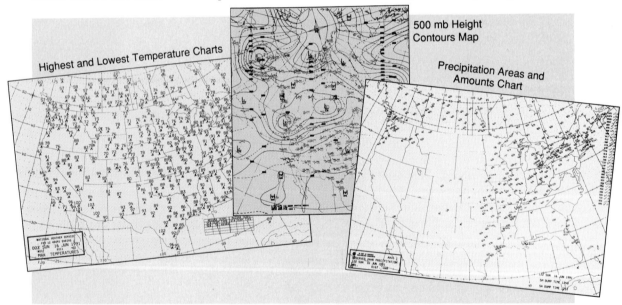

Highest and Lowest Temperature Charts

500 mb Height Contours Map

Precipitation Areas and Amounts Chart

Section Review Questions 11C

1. What are lines on weather maps that connect weather stations having the same temperature?
2. What are isobars?
3. Of what benefit to meteorologists is a map showing isobars?
4. List the four principal weather maps prepared daily by the National Weather Service.

11D–Forecasting the Weather

In the past, weather forecasters predicted the weather mostly by studying maps of air masses and deciding how these air masses would travel. Experienced forecasters can predict weather fairly accurately using this method. They use their intuition guided by experience. However, this method of forecasting is hard to teach to new forecasters. Today, weather forecasters use information about the entire atmosphere in complicated equations, using high-speed computer technology to predict the behavior of air masses.

Making the Forecast

In the United States the National Weather Service issues weather forecasts for the nation. Each day a five-day forecast is issued four times. A six- to ten-day outlook is issued twice a week. Each new prediction takes into account the most up-to-date information. Your local weatherman uses this information in his daily forecasts. The National Weather Service also issues a general thirty-day forecast on the first and fifteenth of each month. This forecast tells, for example, the amount of rainfall expected during the month and the average high and low temperatures for the month.

What is the chance of rain, or rain probability, that we often hear during forecasts? When we hear the weatherman state that there is "a 20 per cent chance of rain," he is telling us that the chance of measurable precipitation (0.01 in. or more) in the forecast period is 20 per cent. He considers information from radar, satellites, computer models, climate, and "gut feeling" in making his prediction. Information from all these sources except "gut feeling" is entered into a mathematical equation on a computer. It calculates the probability of rain for each forecast period and forecast area. Calculating rain probabilities is not as complex when a general rain is predicted (such as when a cold front is approaching). But in the summer when scattered thunderstorms occur, the weathermen also must consider how much of the forecast area will be affected. Since thunderstorms are more isolated events, one section of the forecast area could receive rain while another nearby section does not.

FACETS OF METEOROLOGY

Preparing a Local Weather Report

"Hi, I'm Bill Walker with the latest weather report. . . ."

The job of the weather reporter seems so simple. Why would a news station spend so much money to hire a college graduate (usually in meteorology) to speak only ten or fifteen minutes a day?

Appearances are deceiving. Presenting the weather report is an art that requires hard work and expertise. The broadcast meteorologist must be able to present and communicate abstract facts to a nonscientific audience. He constantly watches developments in national and local weather to make certain that his forecasts are as accurate and up-to-date as possible. It

should be noted that many TV weather people today are *not* trained meteorologists, but rather are broadcasters that professionally present the National Weather Service (NWS) forecast.

The National Weather Service provides four printouts for the United States each day. But local weather can change dramatically in a matter of minutes. The broadcast meteorologist relies on the local NWS office to alert him to any dangerous or severe weather approaching the local area. The NWS office is able to do this because it has installed numerous rain gauges, river gauges, and other automatic equipment all across the area to track the local weather. In addition, it has

dozens of trained volunteers, cooperative observers, and spotters to give information on storms, rainfall, and snow.

In preparing a local weather report, the broadcast meteorologist considers the NWS data and the local weather influences and then produces a precise forecast for the local area. Recall that all weather data is computerized, that is, it is electronically transmitted in code or model form. The broadcast meteorologist will obtain this computerized weather information on his computer at the TV station. At his fingertips is access to weather data from all over the nation and world. From this data he prints surface maps, radar maps, and other technical maps. Using forecast charts pro-

A broadcast meteorologist receives computerized information from the NWS.

Broadcast meteorologists present weather information to the public (above). An easily readable weather map makes weather information more meaningful (right).

duced by the NWS and other companies such as Weather Services International or Accu-Weather, he develops his own forecast. Four forecast maps are produced: 12-hour, 24-hour, 36-hour, and 48-hour. Each map has four panels that show upper-air wind flow, surface maps, relative humidity, and precipitation.† From this information, from information provided by the local NWS office, and from his knowledge of the local influences, the broadcast meteorologist will make his forecast and then report it to the public.

The local broadcast meteorologist also makes special reports during hazardous weather. Rapidly communicating where a violent storm is and where it is going is more important than time-consuming analysis of all the details. These reports which he quickly distributes to the public come directly from the local NWS office. He may make special weather statements for the public, schools, and law enforcement.

As you can see, preparing a local weather report involves teamwork between the media (broadcast meteorologist) and the NWS. The public receives the best weather information possible. Neither the local NWS office nor the local broadcast meteorologist dominates.

The job of the broadcast meteorologist is often thankless. His audience does not take much notice when his forecasts are correct, but he becomes the brunt of jokes when he is wrong. Forecasters have been known to report clear skies during their broadcast, while viewers can see that it is raining outside. Nevertheless, the local TV weatherman is still a much needed commodity in this computerized age. Weather patterns are complex, and there are many factors unique to local areas that computer models do not consider. Human intervention is needed to make correct decisions about the weather forecast.

† Do not confuse these four panels with the four maps provided by the National Weather Service.

Distributing Weather Data

After weather data has been collected and reported to the National Weather Service, the data is analyzed, and weather charts are prepared. The information is then distributed throughout the country. Local meteorologists make their predictions of local weather from these reports. This requires extensive and rapid communication both to and from the local stations.

Computer assistance is used extensively. The AFOS (pronounced A fahs), Automation of Field Operations and Services, data-handling system has done much to speed up the distribution phase of weather forecasting. AFOS transmits data within the National Weather Service. What was once handled by teletype machines and fax systems is now handled by electronic systems and displayed on video screens. No longer is time spent tearing off, sorting, and posting paper messages. Messages arrive at 3,000 words per minute instead of the former rate of 100.

The AFOS system, however, was not designed for the sophisticated Doppler radar; so the newer AWIPS system (Automated Weather Information Processing System) was designed to replace AFOS. Technology is advancing so rapidly in the field of meteorological studies that almost weekly new computer strategies are being developed to gather, report, analyze, and distribute weather data.

Does this mean that a time will come when meteorologists are no longer needed? Probably not. Local weather patterns are so complex, and so many factors need to be considered in forecasting weather that the meteorologist will always be needed to make decisions.

NOAA Weather Radio

NOAA Weather Radio, a service of the National Oceanic and Atmospheric Administration (NOAA), provides *continuous* broadcasts of the latest weather information directly from the local National Weather Service office. The broadcasts are made on high-band FM radio frequencies (between 162.40 and 162.55 megahertz). Special "weather radios" or radios with "weather bands" are required to receive the broadcasts. Taped weather messages are repeated every four to six minutes and revised every one to three hours (or more frequently if needed). NOAA Weather Radio is considered the primary and fastest method of delivering critical, life-saving information directly into the home or office. This is one of the two ways the public can receive the local National Weather Service forecast without interruption by the news media; the other way is by cable weather channels. The cable weather channels scroll the National Weather Service forecast directly as written.

A NOAA broadcast is one of the fastest ways to receive important weather information.

Section Review Questions 11D

1. How many times a day does the National Weather Service issue weather forecasts?
2. What does the weatherman really mean when he states that there is a 20 per cent chance of rain?
3. The latest weather information is broadcast on _____ Weather Radio.
4. What does the abbreviation AFOS mean?
5. What system is designed for Doppler radar?
6. Why is it unlikely that meteorologists will be unnecessary in the future?

Terms

anemometer
aneroid barometer
barograph
barometer
Beaufort wind scale
Bourdon tube thermometer
Celsius scale
Fahrenheit scale
fiducial points
hygrometer
isobar

isotherm
maximum thermometer
mercurial barometer
millibar
minimum thermometer
pilot balloon
psychrometer
radar
radiosonde
rain gauge
rawinsonde

sling psychrometer
station model
synoptic weather chart
theodolite
thermograph
thermometer
thermometer shelter
thermoscope
weather satellite
wind vane

What Did You Learn?

1. On a certain warm spring day the air temperature is 77° F. What temperature is it in Celsius?
2. Why is it necessary to have weather station thermometers in shelters?
3. Why is a one-day forecast more reliable than a five-day forecast?
4. What people should use a thirty-day forecast?
5. Why can a local radio station accurately forecast the weather for the entire nation?
6. What are some of the weather instruments used in *all* weather stations?
7. What is the average atmospheric pressure at sea level?
8. Watch a local weather report. Can you determine which agencies or companies the weathermen in your area consult?

What Do You Think?

1. Suppose you were stranded on an island with no chance of rescue. What instruments could you build to help you forecast your weather?
2. What information would be needed to make thirty-day forecasts as accurate as one-day forecasts are now?

THE LITHOSPHERE

UNIT III

SCIENCE, FAITH AND REASON

TWELVE

12A–The Bible-derived Framework

Science can be defined as the total collection of knowledge gained through man's observations of the physical world. Earth science, then, is what man has observed about the planet earth. Modern scientific research has taught us much about God's creation. Not only has it helped us to appreciate the size and splendor of the earth, but also it has given us knowledge of its make-up and design.

When the scientific knowledge gained about the world is correct, it will fit the Bible-derived framework. You may ask, ''What is the Bible-derived framework?''

The Record of Creation

Three important events make up the framework of the Scriptural teaching regarding the history of the earth and, to a great extent, the processes that still take place today. The first of these is the creation itself as recorded in Genesis 1-2.

It should be noted that the Scriptures in the early chapters of Genesis do not allow for a continuing process of creation. Creation ceased with the end of the first week, and God has rested from His creative works since then. Furthermore, Psalm 33 eliminates the possibility of long periods of time that some have tried to insert in the first week to make the six days of creation fit so-called scientific finds of recent years. Psalm 33:9 states that God ''spoke, and it was done.'' The fact that new matter and energy are not coming into existence today has a scientific name also. It is called the principle of **conservation,** which, simply stated, says energy is not now being created or destroyed but only changed from one form to another. The **first law of thermodynamics** (THUR moh dy NAM iks), the technical name for the principle of conservation, is one of the most basic of scientific principles. According to the Bible, this principle began with the end of the first week and will be in effect until the Lord chooses to destroy the earth by fire sometime in the future (II Pet. 3:7).

Is There Any Room for Disagreement?

In this book the history of the earth is obviously given from a creationist viewpoint. But, did you know that there is more than one creationist viewpoint? The Biblical framework of the earth's history (creation, curse, and Flood) is the foundation on which most creationists build their theories. However, just as different styles of houses can be built on the same kind of foundation, different theories about creation can be built on the Biblical framework of the earth's history. Of course, only one interpretation is totally correct, but which one is it? Has the totally correct one been proposed yet? Only God knows the answer. The Biblical framework leaves room for individuals to believe different interpretations about creation and still not violate the Biblical framework.

The authors of this book chose to interpret various facts, laws, and events with one particular creationist interpretation of the ''Literalist Theory'' in mind. That one interpretation includes the following:

1. six, twenty-four-hour days of creation placed end to end within one week.
2. that the newly created universe looked mature.
3. that the Flood which covered the entire earth produced catastrophic changes in the earth.

Other creationists may disagree with part or all of our chosen *interpretation*. As long as their interpretation does not violate the Biblical framework, they could be correct, and we could be wrong. The most common theories which *attempt* to account for the Biblical framework are listed below.

Major Theories	
Theory	**Explanation**
Literalist	Six, 24-hour, consecutive, end-to-end days of creation
Gap	A great span of time between Genesis 1:1 and 1:2 accounts for geologic formations and most fossils.
Day-Age	Days in Genesis 1 were geologic ages millions of years long.
Theistic Evolution†	God created matter, and then everything else evolved with or without occasional help from God; twists the Biblical account of creation

† As shown on page 245, theistic evolution makes a feeble effort to account for the Biblical framework but ends up denying it.

FACETS OF EARTH SCIENCE

Other Views and Opinions

Three different views of creation are presented below. Each has its own attraction and seeming problems.

The Gap Theory

The word *was* in Genesis 1:2 ("And the earth *was* without form, and void") could also be translated "became" ("And the earth *became* without form and void"). This is an important point because if *became* is the best interpretation, it allows for an earlier time when the earth appeared somewhat like it is now, was destroyed, and then was restored to the way it appears now. This interpretation is a cornerstone to those who believe the gap theory. These creationists believe that there was a great span of time (millions or billions of years) between the events recorded in Genesis 1:1 and 1:2. (Some even propose a similar gap prior to Genesis 1:1.) They hold that during this time the sediments and fossils of the geologic column were deposited. It also allows that evolution could have occurred during that great span of time.

What could have been the reason for destroying an earlier form of the earth? Some gap theorists suppose that the fall of Lucifer somehow brought about the destruction of a previous earth. Most of these creationists

Some creationists propose that the dinosaurs lived millions of years ago, perhaps even in a previous creation. Others suggest that they lived more recently.

believe that after the gap ended with destruction, the "re-creation" events occurred exactly as recorded from Genesis 1:3 to the end of the chapter.

This theory is not without some problems. First, there is no indication that "became" is a better translation of the word in question. In fact, the grammatical construction in the Hebrew language supports the translation of the word as "was." Second, if there was a destruction of a previous earth, it probably was not related to Lucifer's being cast out of heaven. Everything was declared "very good" after the

proposed re-creation (Gen. 1:31); thus, Lucifer probably did not fall prior to or during the proposed destruction. The command given to man in Genesis 1:28 to replenish the earth is sometimes used to imply that there was a previous civilization which was destroyed. However, the word translated "replenish" literally means "fill," which does not imply any previous civilization.

The Day-Age Theory

Suppose the word *day* used in Genesis 1 meant "a period of time" and not a twenty-four-hour day. After all, II Peter 3:8

states that ". . . one day is with the Lord as a thousand years, and a thousand years as one day." A "period of time" could be of any length, one second or a billion years. Creationists who believe the day-age theory hold that the "days" of creation were long periods of time or ages during which God created the universe and all its contents. They try to fit the supposed evolutionary sequence of events and the geologic column to the sequence of events of the creation week. For example, evolutionists would claim there was the "big bang," then star formation; day-age creationists would say the creation of light (day 1) corresponds to the time of the "big bang," and days 2-4 roughly correspond to the eons evolutionists require for star and planet formation.

One problem with the day-age theory is the definition of

day. *Day* is defined in Genesis 1:5 as light bounded by evening and morning. The sun was created during the fourth day (Gen. 1:14) to divide day and night; so until then the length of a day could be questioned. But from the fourth day onward the meaning of *day* was close to twenty-four hours, unless you want to believe that the earth rotated very, very slowly.

Another problem with the day-age theory is that plants, which need light to live, were created on day 3, but the sun wasn't created until day 4. If day 3 was more than a few years long, all the plants would surely have died. However, supporters of the day-age theory would point out that *light* was created on day 1 and the "greater light" on day 4 could have been the development and appearance of the sun as we now know it.

Theistic Evolution

Some people believe a compromise theory between creationism and evolutionism called theistic evolution. These people propose that evolution was the tool God used to create things. Supposedly, God initiated the process of evolution by creating matter and/or life, then allowed it to follow its "natural course." These people twist the entire Biblical account of creation (not just the Genesis account). Many say the literal Biblical account of creation is a fable, a fiction story, or a form of poetry.

This theory's twisting of the Biblical account leads to some very disturbing conclusions. If we can reject one part of the Bible, such as the account of creation, to accommodate our fallible thinking, then we can reject any other part of the Bible which we might happen to dislike. In essence, we end up choosing to believe whatever we want to believe without any real influence from God's Word. By this reasoning we could logically reject everything in the Bible if we wanted to. The Bible is the cornerstone of the Christian faith. As Christians we are supposed to direct our thinking by God's Word, instead of choosing pieces of God's Word to fit our fallible ideas. If the Bible has errors, then our entire faith is in vain.

The Fall and Curse

The second event recorded in Scripture that influences the world in which we live is the fall of man as recorded in Genesis 3. Sin is a concept that many do not like to reckon with. Our nature just does not like to face the fact that we have done wrong. Yet, it is an unmistakable fact that man has sinned, and it is recorded for us to read in Genesis 3. Not only did sin enter the world at this point, but also God cursed the earth. From this point on, God does not refer to His creation as "very good." Now it brings forth thorns and thistles. The New Testament speaks of the earth as waxing "old as doth a garment." This is a process of **degeneration,** or running down. Things left to themselves do not get better and better but rather tend to wear out. Scientifically, this is known as the principle of **entropy** (EN truh pee), which, simply stated, says that things tend toward a state of disorder, not a state of order. Sometimes stated as the **second law of thermodynamics,** it is a basic principle of scientific research as well as a firm part of the skeleton of the Bible-derived framework.

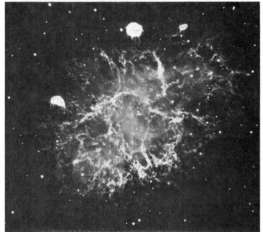

12A-1 *The Crab nebula is the remains of a supernova that was first seen in A.D. 1054. Such observations show that the creation is degenerating.*

12A-2 *Comets break up to form meteors, an example of degeneration in nature.*

The Flood

The third event of the Bible-derived framework is also recorded in the early chapters of Genesis. We must recognize this event to clearly interpret observations of our surroundings. That event is the worldwide Flood of Noah's day. God's Word says that a person who cannot see the evidence for it is "willingly ignorant" (II Pet. 3:5). A careful reading of this passage within its context shows that some believe that conditions today are the same as they have always been (called the doctrine of uniformitarianism). This doctrine could not possibly be true if the Flood occurred. The Flood so changed the processes of the earth through the destructive power, the alteration of the earth's atmosphere, and the erosion of the earth's surface as the waters receded that the "old world" would never again return to its original condition. (Compare the atmosphere as described in Gen. 1:6-8 with the atmosphere as it exists today, for example.)

12A-3 *Rock folded to this degree without cracking and crumbling leads creationists to believe it formed this way while still soft or near the time of the Flood.*

Why would a person desire to be ignorant of these events? Why do unregenerate scientists tend to disregard the three events described above? There are, however, definite reasons that unregenerate man seeks for an alternative answer to creation. First, man, by his sinful nature, does not like to face *responsibility*. By admitting that there is a supreme being who created the universe, man also must admit that he is responsible to that being and subject to the rules that He sets forth. If God did indeed create the world as He said, then we are responsible to Him for our actions and beliefs.

Second, mankind does not like to confront the fact of *sin*. The fall of man shows that man, by nature, is sinful and that he is incapable of doing right, even in the most perfect of environments. Man needs someone more powerful than himself to provide a way to overcome the problem of sin. And third, the Flood proves that God does hold man *accountable* for his actions and that He will judge him for his deeds. If man is simply here as a result of accidental happenings, as the evolutionist would teach, then he is simply a product of his environment and is not responsible for his actions. ''It isn't my fault that I did wrong. Society or my peers or my surroundings contributed to it.'' Likewise, he might argue that a particular sinful deed is

not truly wrong in the first place. He would insist that right or wrong depends upon a person's values, and a person's values are determined by his environment. And finally, the unregenerate mind would further theorize that since he is simply a product of his environment, and since there are really no absolute moral standards, then punishment is not something to be feared.

12A-4 *Evolution did not develop from modern science. Evolutionary philosophy can be traced back to the Greeks of the sixth century B.C.*

In spite of all the ways that man has set out to disprove and discredit the Word of God, God's Word still stands the test of all true scientific research. Man is responsible to a superior being, there is such a thing as right and wrong, and there will one day be a day of judgment for the wrongs that a person has done.

FACETS OF EARTH SCIENCE

12A-2

The Big Bang Theory

How did the universe begin? If a person does not believe in an all-powerful God who created the universe, how can he explain how things began? In reality, he cannot. He must put his trust in some theory that sooner or later turns out to be unworkable. One such theory that has become popular is that the universe began in a gigantic explosion billions of years ago. This big bang theory substitutes a mighty explosion for an almighty God.

According to the theory, all the matter in the universe was originally contracting or falling together under the pull of gravity. This phase has been called the "big squeeze." Eventually, after falling inward for many eons, the matter became so densely packed that a violent elastic rebound occurred—the "big bang." Extremely high temperatures generated by the explosion restructured the simple matter that then existed and formed it into chemical elements. Hundreds of millions of years later, debris from the blast came together in just the right way to form stars, galaxies, and planets.

The big bang theory has several scientific problems. (1) The "big squeeze" could not have compressed the matter to anywhere near the necessary density. (2) Even if it could, matter of such density could never expand because of the titanic crush of its own gravity. (3) There is no feasible way that the debris could come together to form stars, galaxies, and planets. The fragments from the explosion would keep moving off into space, moving farther and farther apart. Human observations have confirmed that explosions have a stronger tendency to disorganize matter than to organize it.

It is actually a form of blasphemy to say that the intricate handiwork of God we see all around us is nothing more than fallout from a cosmic blast. This is completely contrary to the Scriptural picture of a Creator "who hath measured the waters in the hollow of his hand, and meted out heaven with the span" (Isa. 40:12). Also the Bible tells us that God created the universe out of nothing. The big bang theory assumes that matter was already present before the explosion. Thus the theory avoids the question of the creation of matter.

Many scientists are dissatisfied with the big bang theory. Other theories such as the steady-state theory, the oscillating universe theory, the ambiplasma hypothesis, and the radical departure hypothesis have been devised to try to improve upon it. But all such theories have serious scientific problems because they attempt to make nature run contrary to its own laws. They are desperate attempts by unregenerate men to explain the universe without a Creator. Christians should be on guard against compromising their understanding of Scripture with some ungodly theory that was devised to avoid the truth.

Section Review Questions 12A

1. What term is used to identify the total collection of knowledge gained through man's observations of the physical world?
2. List the three important events that make up the framework of the Scriptures regarding the history of the earth.
3. What Psalm discredits the idea that the days of Genesis were long periods of time?
4. What is the technical term used for the principle of conservation?
5. List four major theories related to creation.
6. What word and Bible verse is a cornerstone to gap-theory creationists?
7. What scientific principle describes a process of degeneration? What is the technical name for this principle?
8. List three things that unregenerate men seek to avoid.
9. What is the term evolutionists give to the contraction of matter before the Big Bang?

12B–Science and Faith

The ultimate topic of origins must be accepted by faith. Only three possible choices exist: First, a person could accept by faith the statement "In the beginning God . . . ." His faith would be in the God of creation and in the Holy Scriptures that contain the description of the act. On the other hand, a person could accept by faith the statement "In the beginning something other than God . . . ." His faith would be in whatever that something else might be. If he believes in a blob of energy, a proton, or a force, then that is where he has chosen to place his faith. For a third choice, a person might choose to believe that "In the beginning there was nothing." This, of course, presents some real problems, since there is something today. At some point this choice must be modified and restated, "In the beginning nothing became something." This person has chosen to place his faith in "nothing."

There are always those who would like to accept the "best of every world." This group chooses to believe that God started everything off and then let it go about by chance, intervening only when things would start to go the wrong way. Thus, we arrived by a combination of chance and intervention of God to the point where we are today. This, of course, would be an alternative, but unfortunately for so many who choose this route, it is a very poor choice. These people have chosen by faith what to believe, but in addition to this, they have placed themselves in the position of determining what God can and cannot do. There is no basis for the faith. Only God's Word describes who He is and what He has done, and to accept Him but to reject His Word is somewhat like telling your best friend that you accept him as a person, but you do not believe what he is telling you.

Section Review Questions 12B

1. Is the belief in creation of the earth by God accepted by faith or by scientific proof?
2. Is belief in the earth's formation by means of evolutionary processes accepted by faith or by scientific proof?
3. What is the only source for a description of God?

12C–Science and Reason

Does God expect us to accept blindly everything that we are told? He certainly has a right to, but He doesn't. In the Bible, God instructs us to "believe not every spirit, but try the spirits whether they are of God: because many false prophets are gone out into the world" (I John 4:1). Faith does not require rejection of intellect. One of the most important principles for the Christian to grasp is that God's Word will stand the test. Use any scientific method you choose, but God's Word will always withstand accurate research and experimentation.

Did you know that clear thinking is a characteristic of a Christian? Paul also told Timothy to "try the spirits." Peter tells Christians to "be ready always to give an answer." In order to accomplish these Biblical commands, it is necessary to think clearly. We sometimes refer to clear thinking as reasoning.

Faulty Reasoning

A **fallacy** is a mistake in reasoning; it is one type of incorrect argument. Though there are many types of fallacies, we will look at just five in this chapter: the hasty generalization, circular reasoning, the *ad hominem** argument, missing the point, and the appeal to force.

The hasty generalization is an error in reasoning that occurs when a general conclusion is drawn from a small number of cases that are not typical of the whole group. For example, "It rained the first three days of July at this resort. It must rain all summer here." The problem with this argument is that the conclusion was based upon only three days out of the whole summer. This error is often made by poll takers when they use a sample that is too small or a sample that is not representative of the whole. It might sound like this in a science book written by an unbeliever: "In today's technological world all knowledgeable people are evolutionists. In fact, we would not be too far afield if we defined a knowledgeable person as one who does believe in evolution." This is certainly a ridiculous argument, but unfortunately not very uncommon.

Circular reasoning is assuming what you are trying to prove and using it as support for your argument. It is sometimes called "begging the question." The fallacy often involves two statements, each of which depends on the other for its support. "He claims that I am his best friend. It must be true because nobody would lie to his best friend." Geologists often make statements like "Invariably the oldest rock layers are found to contain the most primitive (earliest and simplest) plants and animals. We can actually date the rocks by the types of fossils they contain."

The *ad hominem* argument involves an attack on the person doing the arguing rather

12C-1 *"This fossil, Turritella, is found in Tertiary rock layers; therefore, Turritella can be used to identify some Tertiary rocks." What kind of faulty reasoning does this involve?*

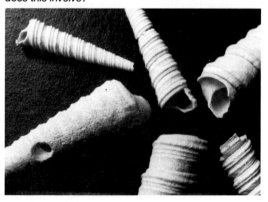

ad hominem: ad (L. AD, to) + hominem (L. HOMINEM, the man)

ELECTRIC FENCE?!! HA!! YOU'RE JUST CHICKEN... AND BESIDES, WHY SHOULD I BELIEVE A THREE-TIME LOSER LIKE YOU?

12C-2 *What type of fallacy does this illustrate?*

than on the argument itself. This action fails in its purpose, for it cannot destroy the argument by showing that the arguer has defects in his character or blots on his record. Even the most disreputable person sometimes makes true statements and offers sound arguments. An example of this type of reasoning would be the following statement: ''Mr. Roberts accused me of cheating on a test, but he is the one who was twice demoted and finally fired from his last teaching posi-

tion.'' The incompetence of the teacher has nothing to do with the question of whether or not the person being accused of cheating was actually cheating. Notice how this ploy attempts to shift the thought to someone else rather than the question actually at hand in this statement from a science article: ''Anyone who questions the fact of evolution simply demonstrates his own ignorance.''

Missing the point is an error in reasoning that is committed when an argument seemingly leading to one conclusion is directed to a different conclusion. ''Crimes of theft and robbery have been increasing at an alarming rate. The conclusion is obvious: we should legalize theft and robbery because the laws against them cannot be enforced.'' Or, there is the old argument presented to teachers by some students, ''On the last two tests I put in a fair amount of study, but I still flunked them both. On this one I am going to try not studying at all.'' It is interesting to read advertisements in magazines or newspapers and find these kinds of errors.

The fifth fallacy is the appeal to force. An arguer commits this fallacy when, rather than offer valid reasons to support his conclusion, he threatens that there will be severe consequences if his conclusion is not accepted. This fallacy's power to persuade rests in the fact that it instills some form of fear in the listener, either directly or indirectly; the threat may be physical, or it may be of a more subtle nature. ''There certainly is a Santa Claus. But he does not bring any presents to children who do not believe in him.'' It is not uncommon to see the argument in science articles in this form: ''It is especially clear that any scientist who fails to uphold the essential correctness of evolution is incompetent and should be denied membership in this organization.''

Be alert to these fallacies as you read scientific articles and test the ideas and thoughts to see whether they are of God. As Christians, then, we should always examine scientific information in the light of God's Word, the Bible. Of course, any information that is contrary to the Bible is wrong. We should also keep in mind that if man cannot observe a thing with one of his five senses, either directly or with the aid of instruments, the thing is outside the realm of science. How the world came into existence, by way of example, is not a question for science to answer.

The Need for Science

God has allowed us to observe and understand only a portion of His vast creation. There is much that man has not yet fathomed. Science, of course, is ongoing rather than static. Many Christian researchers interpret God's command to subdue the earth and have dominion over it (Gen. 1:28) as a continuing charge to study the earth and learn new ways of using it to serve our needs. There is still much to learn.

In addition, the Christian man of science must continue to uphold God's Word. More than a few times in the past, a believing scientist has laid an ungodly theory to rest because he had the proper training and was in the right place at the right time. For example, in the mid-1800s the Christian physicist James Clerk Maxwell demonstrated through higher mathematics that Laplace's nebular hypothesis—which purported to show how

12C-3 *James Clerk Maxwell, the Christian physicist who disproved Laplace's nebular hypothesis*

NEBULAR HYPOTHESIS

the solar system condensed from a cloud by itself without a Creator—could not possibly be true. Not only would the sun have ended up spinning far more rapidly than it does, but the planets could never have formed by this theory. (The materials that were supposed to collect to produce the planets would actually be pulling apart rather than coming together.) The theory that the atheist Laplace had so carefully devised using mathematics had been torn down by the Christian Maxwell using better mathematics. "He disappointeth the devices of the crafty. . . . He taketh the wise in their own craftiness" (Job 5:12-13).

The great Christian leaders of science such as Maxwell and Kepler recognized the Lord's glory in the world. We will study the glory of the earth and the grandeur of the heavens this year. But may we never forget the promise of our Saviour: "I go to prepare a place for you" (John 14:2). Even though the earth gives forth its beauty and the galaxies their splendor, we look forward to far more. The Bible reminds us that "eye hath not seen, nor ear heard, neither have entered into the heart of man, the things which God hath prepared for them that love him" (I Cor. 2:9).

Section Review Questions 12C
1. Does God expect us never to question what we are told?
2. Name five types of faulty reasoning.
3. What fallacy occurs when a general conclusion is drawn from too small a sample?
4. What Christian man of science refuted the nebular hypothesis?

Terms

conservation	entropy	first law of thermodynamics
degeneration	fallacy	second law of thermodynamics

What Did You Learn?
1. Give an example of the second law of thermodynamics.
2. Did the ground bring forth thorns and thistles before or after the Flood?
3. What fallacy is an attack on a person's character rather than the argument presented?
4. The creation was accomplished in a time period of exactly _____.
5. Read Genesis 2-3. Exactly what did Adam do that was sin?
6. Once you admit that there is a God who created the universe, there is a conclusion that follows. What is it?
7. What verse in the Bible is interpreted by many Christian researchers as a command to study the earth? How can that verse mean "study the earth"?

What Do You Think?
1. How would the earth be different if the second law of thermodynamics did not exist?
2. How would the earth be different if the Flood never occurred?
3. Is it ever appropriate to use the *ad hominem* argument?

INTRODUCTION TO GEOLOGY

THIRTEEN

13A–The Design of the Earth

What is geology? The word literally means the study of (*-logy*) the earth (*geo-*). **Geology** is the study of the earth's structures and the processes that affect those structures. A geologist is a scientist who specializes in the study of the earth. Geology is both interesting and practical. Geologists who study rocks and minerals can locate natural resources. They find unusual substances such as oil, uranium, and gold as well as more common substances such as clay, limestone, and gravel. Other geologists study natural forces such as glaciers, earthquakes, and volcanoes.

The planet we live on is a masterpiece of planning. The earth contains 6.6 sextillion tons of the right material for life. Less mass would be unable to hold enough atmosphere; more mass would make atmospheric pressure too great. Since the atmosphere is important in preserving life on earth, the earth's mass is important.

Evolutionists will claim, however, that the environment really is not so critical—that living organisms can learn to adapt to whatever situation they find themselves in, given enough time. This is false. The genes of an organism are totally unaware of environmental problems. The genes would not be able to solve the problems even if they "knew" about them. Furthermore, it makes little sense to talk about long-term adaptation if intolerable conditions would destroy an entire population at the outset.

Another evidence of planning is the speed of the earth's rotation. If the earth turned too slowly, there would be no life. Living creatures on the daylight side of a slow-turning earth would be scorched. Too fast a rotation also would be harmful to life. Certain plants, for example, would fail to reproduce and would soon die out.

13A-1 *Planets, such as Mars (below), were not designed for life. The types of atmospheres, intense radiation, absence of water and oxygen, and extreme temperatures present a stark contrast to the optimal living conditions on earth (right).*

Our atmosphere also contains an optimal amount of oxygen. Nitrogen dilutes the oxygen to the proper concentration for use by living organisms. Interestingly, no appreciable quantities of oxygen have been found in any of the other planetary atmospheres in the solar system. Furthermore, those planets which do have atmospheres contain poisonous gases. Although green plants continually replenish our atmospheric oxygen, they in no way account for its origin. No theory to date has successfully explained the origin of terrestrial oxygen.

Our atmosphere also protects us from meteors. Of the several million small meteors that enter our atmosphere each day, more than 99.99 per cent of them are burned up before they reach the ground. Only a very few—perhaps half a dozen—actually land on the earth's surface as meteorites. At the same time, the ozone layer in the stratosphere protects us from harmful ultraviolet rays. The earth also contains a magnetic field that traps cosmic rays before they reach us.

Probably the most striking evidence of God's design of the earth for life is water. Although astronomers have not found liquid water on the surface of any other planet, 71 per cent of the earth's surface is covered with this vital substance. The physical properties of water are unique and remarkable. They include its transparency, that it expands before freezing, that it dissolves many things, and its surface tension. Whether we realize it or not, we rely heavily upon these properties of water for our survival.

13A-2 *Water, the remarkable compound that is so vital to life, is plentiful on the earth.*

Section Review Questions 13A
1. What is the literal meaning of the word *geology?*
2. How much mass does the earth have?
3. What is the most striking evidence of design on the earth?
4. List four properties of water that we rely heavily upon for our survival.

13B–The Earth's Structure

How is the earth's mass distributed? Is the earth a uniform ball of rock, or a hollow shell, or something else? Is there any way we can find out? Geologists learn about the earth's interior by studying the way earthquakes' waves travel. In this way they have found that the earth has three basic layers: the crust, the mantle, and the core. These layers contain different materials through which earthquakes' waves travel differently.

13B-1 *Much of the knowledge that scientists have discovered about the structure of the earth has been accumulated from studies of earthquakes.*

Crust

The earth's outer layer, the **crust,** is solid rock. This rock's thickness ranges from about 5 km (3 mi.) under the oceans to about 60 km (37 mi.) under the mountain chains. It is usually six times as thick under the continents as it is under the oceans. In 1909 the Yugoslavian seismologist (earthquake scientist) Andrija Mohorovičić (MOH huh ROH vuh chik) (1857–1936) discovered that earthquake waves change speed below the crust. Such a change in speed is called a **discontinuity** and marks the boundary between two layers of the earth. The boundary between the crust and the mantle is called the **Mohorovičić discontinuity** (**Moho** for short).

Mantle

The **mantle** extends from the Moho to a depth of about 2,900 km (1,800 mi.). It occupies about 84 per cent of the earth's volume. Because the mantle is hotter and denser than the crust, earthquake waves travel faster through it. Scientists believe that the material of the mantle is more able to change its shape under pressure than the crust material.

Core

The **core** contains more than 15 per cent of the earth's volume. It occupies all the space below the mantle. Many geologists are unwilling even to guess what the core material is like because it is so different from anything we have experienced. The core must be extremely hot and dense, possibly more than twice as dense as ordinary iron. The core has two parts. The outer core is about 2,200 km (1,400 mi.) thick, and the inner core's radius is about 1,300 km (800 mi.). Because of the earth's magnetic field, scientists believe that the core contains mostly iron. The pressure and temperature at the core are tremendous. Any material under these conditions would be almost unrecognizable.

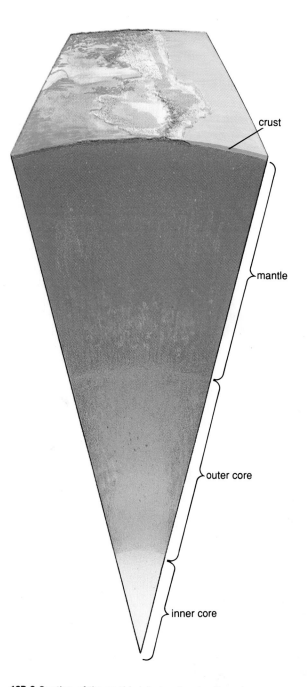

crust

mantle

outer core

inner core

13B-2 *Section of the earth's interior showing the relative size of each part*

FACETS OF GEOLOGY

Journey to the Center of the Earth

Man knows less about the earth beneath his feet than the stars in the heavens. No "telescope" can penetrate the thick crust down to the mantle only a few miles away. Our ignorance has encouraged fantastic accounts of the earth's core, such as Jules Verne's *Journey to the Center of the Earth*. Only recently have modern drills been able to discover some of the earth's deep secrets.

The first effort to break through the crust began in 1961. Maps of the ocean floor indicated that a thin break in the crust really did exist—beneath the Pacific Ocean. The project was named Mohole in honor of the earthquake scientist Andrija Mohorovičić.

Scientists converted a Navy barge into a floating drill rig, called CUSS I. It lowered pipes 3,650 m (12,000 ft.) to the Pacific floor. The drill then pushed through 165 m (550 ft.) of sediment and bit into basalt. Mohole proved that deep-sea drilling was possible, but it barely pierced the crust, coming many kilometers short of reaching the Moho, the border between the crust and the mantle. A bigger rig, more money, and many more tons of pipe would be needed to complete the job. Not willing to bear the cost, Con-

The JOIDES Resolution, *outfitted for ODP, drills deep into the earth's crust.*

gress voted to end the project in 1966. However, in 1991 the Ocean Drilling Program†(ODP), which enlists scientists from around the world, extended one hole drilled in the Pacific to a depth of 2 km.

Highly specialized equipment is required for deep drilling projects.

The greatest surprises have occurred in land digs. Efforts in the United States have been modest. Most deep holes are dug by commercial companies searching for oil and gas. The deepest purely scientific dig in the United States went only 3.5 km (2.2 mi.) in California, stopping far short of the 5-km (3.1-mi.) goal because of high costs and budget cuts. Some shallow digs have practical aims, such as the Energy Department's drilling near the volcanic regions of Yosemite National Park to test whether we can tap magma as an alternative source of energy.

The efforts of the Soviet Union have far exceeded anything else done in the world. They support eleven drilling projects

† For more information on the ODP read "Adventures at Sea," page 392.

designed to exceed 8 km (5 mi.) in depth. The deepest hole on earth was begun in 1970. For over two decades the Soviets have clawed into the crust of the Kola peninsula, above the Arctic Circle. They picked this spot because erosion has washed away as much as 15.3 km (9.5 mi.) of the upper crust. The project's finds are revolutionary, overturning pat theories put forward by evolutionists.

The Kola project has taken samples over 12 km (7.5 mi.) deep. One of their first discoveries was veins of minerals, including copper and nickel, deep in the upper crust. Further down they expected the pressure of the earth to have closed any cracks in the rock, but they were dumbfounded to find channels of superheated water streaming through huge cracks in the granite. As they dug, the temperatures rose 2.5 times faster than they had figured. When they reached the lower crust, where the granite was supposed to be replaced by dense volcanic basalt, they broke into a layer of hard granite. Apparently rock is much more impervious to high pressure than once thought.

High pressures and high temperatures make digs to the mantle too difficult for the near future. (The Soviets never expected to reach the mantle. The only other country now in the deep-dig race—Germany— plans to go 10 km deep.) If these moderate digs have already turned up so many surprises about the crust, can we be sure about our theories of the deeper mantle? Perhaps a more important question is this: If scientists cannot predict basic information about the earth in which they live, how can they be sure about an earth in the past that they have never seen?

earth's surface

German plan
10 km deep

Kola
12 km deep

Ocean Drilling Program
2 km deep (under water 4.5 km deep)

Mohole
170 m deep (under water 3.6 km deep)

California
3.5 km deep

earth's crust
(average, 37 km thick; 5 km under oceans)

Thin slice of an ocean core rock and sediment sample

259

Section Review Questions 13B

1. Which country has drilled the deepest hole in the earth? Did they reach the mantle?
2. List in order, from the surface to the interior, the three layers of the earth.
3. What molten metal do some geologists think the earth's core is made of?
4. Which of the three layers of the earth is thinnest?

13C–The Earth's History

13C-1 *Representation of the sequence of events during the six days of creation*

Some geologists try to study the earth's history as well as its present structure and natural processes. In this **historical geology** creationists and evolutionists disagree.

According to Creationists

As a Christian studies the earth's history, he must remember three major events in the earth's history that the Scripture describes: creation, the curse, and the Flood. These form the framework on which the Christian builds his description of the earth's history.

"In the beginning God created the heaven and the earth" (Gen. 1:1). When God finished creation at the end of the sixth day, He surveyed His handiwork and declared that it was "very good" (Gen. 1:31). We can only imagine the magnificent beauty of the earth in its original state of perfection.

Until a person is willing to face the fact of a supernatural creation—complete, miraculous, and rapidly completed—he will not have a realistic appreciation for the world in which he lives. Although God has not told us all the details about how He created, He has told us how long creation took and how complete it was. "For in six days the Lord made heaven and earth, the sea, and all that in them is, and rested the seventh day: wherefore the Lord blessed the sabbath day, and hallowed it" (Exod. 20:11). The Sabbath was a commemoration of the completed creation. In less than a week's time, God created an entire universe *out of nothing!*

The earth did not remain in its perfect state. Because man sinned, God cursed the earth. "Cursed is the ground for thy sake; in sorrow shalt thou eat of it all the days of thy life; Thorns also and thistles shall it bring forth to thee. . . . In the sweat of thy face shalt thou eat bread, till thou return unto the ground" (Gen. 3:17-19). We do not know all that happened at the curse, but we do know that the earth and living things experienced profound changes.

Later God again judged the world because of man's sin. "And the waters prevailed exceedingly upon the earth; . . . and the mountains were covered" (Gen. 7:19-20). The worldwide Flood of Noah's time greatly changed the face of the earth. It eroded and redeposited vast amounts of **sediment** (loose material that sinks to the bottom of a body of water). The sedimentary layers of the earth's crust, called **strata,** and the fossils they contain are results of this Flood.

13C-2 *Sedimentary rock strata in Paria Canyon, Arizona*

Many creationists believe that the climate after creation was tropical from almost pole to pole. The idea that a worldwide tropical climate changed to a cooler one fits the Biblical framework. The waters above the firmament in Genesis 1:7 may have been a canopy of clouds or water vapor that caused a more significant greenhouse effect than occurs today. Following the Flood, with the canopy removed by precipitation and with the presence of much more surface water, cooling must certainly have occurred.

Most geologists deny that these three important events (creation, curse, and Flood) ever happened. They believe that the Bible is full of errors and exaggerations. The Bible says that such men are willingly ignorant because they have refused to believe God (II Pet. 3:5-6).

The Bible says that God created a mature, fully functioning world full of life. He created Adam and Eve as adults, not as infants who could not take care of themselves. Plants were also fully developed: they had fruit and seeds at creation (Gen. 1:11-12). Some of these trees may have been large enough to appear to be fifty or one hundred or even more years old.

13C-3 *At the time of the original creation, some trees, like the one in the photograph above, would appear old.*

13C-4 *Soil found at the instant of creation would have appeared to be old by methods used to determine age today.*

The soil in which the first plants grew appeared to be even older. Fertile soil contains clay, sand, minerals, and organic materials that plants need to grow well. It must be several inches deep to support many plants. Today this soil forms by the gradual weathering of rocks and the decomposition of plant and animal remains. An inch of soil usually takes about a century to form. If a modern geologist had examined the soil after creation week, he would have concluded from his experience with modern soil formation that it was several centuries old. Yet, it was actually only a few days old.

The original earth was ready for man's use by the time God placed him on it. It was undoubtedly beautiful and complete, with lush vegetation covering the hills, beasts inhabiting the fields, and birds soaring through the air. Likewise, rivers and seas teemed with living creatures. Beneath the surface of the ground, many minerals awaited man's use. In His omniscience (all knowing) God knew exactly what man would need, and in His omnipotence (all powerful) He supplied this need in the miraculous way His Word describes.

Not only the earth but also the celestial bodies were ready to fulfill their purposes. God placed the sun, moon, and stars in their proper locations "to divide the day from the night," and to be "for signs, and for seasons, and for days, and years" (Gen. 1:14). The light from these astronomical bodies was already visible from the earth by the end of the creation week. It did not spend eons traveling to the earth. God created not only the universe but also everything in it, even starlight, in substantially its present form. "Thus the heavens and the earth were finished, and all the host of them" (Gen. 2:1). The creation was complete; it lacked nothing.

13C-5 *Stars were visible at creation.*

The concept of a full-grown creation is important for the Christian student of science. It explains, for example, why some dating methods give large ages for the earth. Unbelievers often deny the possibility of a full-grown creation. Some people object to the idea of a mature creation because they think that making something appear old when it is young is deception. But God does not deceive us; He tells us that He made a mature universe. He shows His great power with such mighty wonders as creation.

Section Review Questions 13C-1
1. What two words did God use after the sixth day of creation to describe his handiwork?
2. Name the three events in the Biblical framework of the earth's history.
3. Was Adam created in the form of a baby or an adult?

According to Evolutionists

Evolutionists deny the truth of God's Word and insist on discovering earth's history from the earth itself. They interpret the earth's history by using the **doctrine of uniformity,** or **uniformitarianism** (YOO nuh FOR mih TAR ee uh NIHZ um). This says that the processes that occur today are the processes that have shaped the earth throughout its history; that is, the present is the key to the past. To an extent, this is true. God has set up certain laws of science that do not change. If this were not so, science would be useless because the laws would change as quickly as scientists formulated them. But evolutionists believe that these laws existed before the earth was formed. If they even believe in God, they do not recognize that He is not bound by these laws. Thus they say that the earth formed according to current scientific laws, and they deny the possibility of miracles.

According to the doctrine of uniformity, features that are not like those forming today should not have formed in the past. However, many of the earth's features are not being formed today. Some kinds of rocks—for example, red sandstone—have never been observed to form. Coal is not being formed today in the vast quantities at which it once was. No one has observed **fossil graveyards** forming, yet these tangled heaps of mixed fossils abound in the earth's rocks. Furthermore, no one has seen a mountain form, except a volcano, and most of the world's mountains are not volcanic. The earth itself should not exist, according to this principle. Neither in the solar system nor anywhere else do we see planets forming today.

Evolutionists contradict their own doctrine of uniformity when they describe the earth's past climate. During one era, the Mesozoic, the climate supposedly was warm and humid from nearly pole to pole. During the next and present era, the Cenozoic, the climate was generally cooler and drier. Thus, evolutionists choose to ignore their own dogma in respect to climate.

13C-6 *The doctrine of uniformitarianism is insufficient to explain fossil graveyards (far left), coal formation (left), or nonvolcanic mountain formation (top). These processes have not been observed taking place.*

Evolutionists claim that the earth began as a mass of "molten rock" that had steam and other gases dissolved in it. The surface solidified into a solid crust that was often pierced by volcanoes. Many evolutionists say that all the water in the oceans came from steam separating from the molten rock emitted by volcanoes. Modern volcanoes do emit steam, but in such great quantities that it would more than supply the earth's oceans over 5 billion years. If the doctrine of uniformity were correct and if the earth were truly 5 billion years old, where has all the water gone?

The Bible warns against the error of uniformitarianism in II Peter 3:3-4. "Knowing this first, that there shall come in the last days scoffers, walking after their own lusts, And saying, Where is the promise of his coming? for since the fathers fell asleep, all things continue as they were from the beginning of the creation." Not all things continue as they were, regardless of how loudly the scoffers of today protest. God has intervened supernaturally many times, and He may do so again at any moment. Our hope of the Lord's soon return is a rejection of the uniformitarian doctrine.

Section Review Questions 13C-2
1. Name the doctrine that states, "The present is the key to the past."
2. What future event is a rejection of the doctrine in question 1?

Dating Methods

One dispute between evolutionists and many creationists is the earth's age. Evolutionists say that the earth is nearly 5 billion years old, but many creationists believe that the earth is only a few thousand years old. How can we decide who is right? Is there a reliable way to date the earth?

Present-day observations are no basis for determining the earth's age. Trying to find the earth's age from present processes is like trying to figure out how long a dripless candle has been burning. Even if you know how fast the candle is burning, you cannot tell how long the candle has been burning unless you know how tall it was when it was lit and whether it has been burning at a constant rate. Similarly, we cannot tell how long the earth has been here by looking at how fast it deposits sediments, for example.

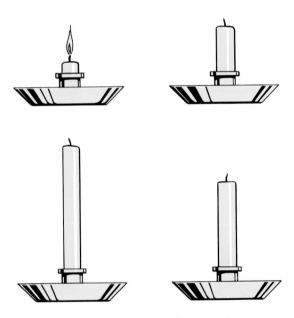

13C-7 *Just as the height of a candle does not prove how long it has been burning, sediments on the earth do not prove how old the earth is.*

One reason that creationists and evolutionists disagree on the earth's age is that they disagree on the earth's initial condition. Creationists believe God's Word when it says that the earth was complete after creation. It had mountains, seas, rocks, plants, animals, and two humans. Evolutionists, on the other hand, believe that the earth began as a molten mass of rock, which later separated into seas and dry land, developed mountains, and started life. Because they start with "candles" of different "heights," creationists and evolutionists calculate different ages. Which idea is more reliable? Creationists base their conception of the early earth on the Bible, but evolutionists have only their own speculations.

Genealogical

Several ways exist to establish dates. One way is to examine historical records. Both creationists and evolutionists use historical records to attempt to date the age of the earth. Thus one way men have tried to date the earth is by studying the genealogical records in the Old Testament. James Ussher (1581–1656) calculated from these records that creation occurred in 4004 B.C. Johannes Kepler undertook the same task and concluded that creation took place in 4977 B.C.—almost a millennium earlier. The difficulty is determining whether God has given us a complete list of names in the genealogies. From what God has said, though, many Bible scholars are confident that the age of the earth is less than ten thousand years, not the millions or billions of years required by the theory of evolution.

Radioactive Dating

Another way to determine a date is to examine a process that occurs at a constant rate. For example, many materials are **radioactive;** they are unstable and break down into

13C-8 One of the original Dead Sea Scrolls was given a date of A.D. 33 by the radiocarbon method.

different elements. Radioactive materials seem to break down at a constant rate. Radioactive dating methods include radiocarbon, uranium-lead, and potassium-argon.

There are some possible discrepancies with radioactive dating in general. An underlying assumption here is that the doctrine of uniformity is true as it applies to rate of formation, accumulation, and decay of radioactive materials. We do not know that these rates were the same in the past as they are now. Also, if the other aspects of the earth were created with the appearance of age, then would radioactive material also be created with the appearance of age?

❑ *Radiocarbon Dating* The bodies of organisms contain small amounts of a form of the element carbon called **carbon-14.** Carbon-14 is formed in the upper atmosphere when neutrons produced by cosmic rays strike nitrogen atoms. Due to its increased density, it settles to the lower atmosphere where it enters the bodies of plants, animals,

FACETS OF GEOLOGY

Dating a Young Earth

Here is an easy math problem that anyone should be able to figure out. If a city currently dumps 1 m of trash into a landfill each year and the trash is now 2 m deep, then how old is the landfill? Two years, right?

Think again! You did not take into account the other circumstances. The landfill was built on an older landfill. The city dumped different amounts of trash in the past. Sometimes construction crews took away soil for projects. There is no way that you could have known about these other factors.

Modern scientists face a similar difficulty in dating the earth. They measure current accumulations of dust, gas, and so on; then they estimate how many years were necessary for the accumulations to occur. However, they do not know all the factors which affect the accumulation:

1. What quantities existed in the beginning?

2. How quickly did these quantities accumulate in the past?
3. What unusual factors altered the accumulations?

If evolution is correct, then the earth's accumulations should reflect an old age of 4 or 5 billion years. But the accumu-

lations do not even come close. Each accumulation is different. Even more embarrassing for evolutionists, most dating techniques indicate that the earth is *young,* not billions of years old.

The evolutionists reject dating methods that indicate a young earth, not because the methods are wrong, but because they do not fit their theory. Evolutionists choose the few dating techniques that happen to support an old earth and an old ocean, which the evolutionary theory demands. Is their method scientific?

Creationists can estimate the age of the earth, not because

Material	Age Based on Accumulation	Explanation
human population	4,000	Starting with one human couple, it is possible to reach the current population of the world in only a few thousand years.
river deltas	5,000	Modern deltas at the end of rivers required a relatively short time to develop.
magnetic field†	10,000	Even though the earth's magnetic field is decaying rapidly, it is still very large today. It must have been much larger 10,000 years ago.
helium in the atmosphere	1,750-175,000	Uranium releases helium into the air each year, but little helium can be found in the atmosphere.
ocean sediment	30,000,000	Ocean sediment now has twice the amount of matter found above sea level. At the current rate, all rock above sea level would be eroded and disappear into the ocean in only 15 million years.

† age based on decay, not accumulation

adapted from *Biblical Basis for Modern Science*, Appendix 6, Morris

Accumulations, such as these rock strata in the South Dakota Badlands, are of limited use in determining the age of the earth.

they rely on dating techniques, but because the Bible contains an eyewitness account of the creation. We can only guess at conditions in the early days, because the Flood destroyed most of the evidence. Modern accumulations of various materials in the earth help us study changes since the Flood, but their value is limited in studying conditions before that time. Any attempt to *date* the earth based on accumulations of different materials is misleading and unscientific. There are almost as many different ages of the earth as there are accumulating materials.

and humans through food and air. Because carbon-14 is radioactive, it breaks down into nitrogen through changes in its nucleus. While an organism is living, the amount of carbon-14 entering its body balances the amount that breaks down, so the organism has a constant amount of carbon-14 in its body. When it dies, however, it no longer eats or breathes; thus no carbon-14 enters its body. The amount of carbon-14 that is present begins to decrease steadily.

To determine the date of an organism's death, a scientist uses a Geiger (GY gur) counter to measure the amount of carbon-14 left in its body. The less carbon-14 present,

13C-9 *A Geiger counter with an attached strip-chart recorder like those used to determine carbon-14 dates*

the longer the time since the organism died. To translate the amount of carbon-14 present to the time since death, the researcher uses a **calibration curve,** a graph made from objects of known ages. That is, scientists date an object by historical clues or a tree by counting its rings and then determine the amount of carbon-14 in it. They plot the amount of carbon-14 on the vertical axis and the age on the horizontal axis. Then they draw a smooth curve through the points. To date an object, they find the age that corresponds to the amount of carbon-14 in it.

Radiocarbon dating has limitations. The most important of these is that the calibration curve goes back only about 5,000 years. No one has been able to find an object that can be reliably dated by history or tree-ring counts as more than 5,000 years old. Thus, a scientist cannot be confident about radiocarbon dates of more than 5,000 years. Another problem is that some radiocarbon dates that can be verified by other means are wrong. These are called **anomalous*** (uh NAHM uh lus) **samples.** Scientists do not always understand why the dates are wrong or how to correct them. Radiocarbon dating is also limited to materials that contain carbon, such as wood, charcoal, shells, and bones. It is useless for dating rocks or metal artifacts.

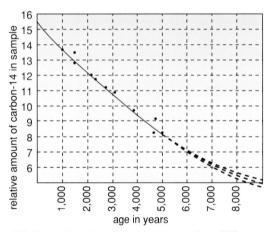

13C-10 *A radiocarbon calibration curve—the solid line reflects samples (dots) of known age. Past these samples the curve becomes increasingly unreliable (dotted lines).*

In spite of these limitations, radiocarbon dating is a worthwhile tool. With proper precautions, it is reasonably accurate. Radiocarbon dating occasionally provides evidence against evolution. Coal and oil samples that evolutionists estimate are millions of years old have been dated by carbon-14 at a few thousand years old. This dating method cannot support the time scale of billions of years required by evolution because it is valid for only thousands of years.

❑ *Uranium-Lead Method* The **uranium-lead method** is based on the natural decay of uranium into lead by a series of slow nuclear changes. Many rocks contain both uranium and lead. The dating method assumes that the ratio of lead to uranium in a rock shows its age. The more lead and less uranium in a rock, the older it is. The problem with this method is that we do not know how much lead was in the original rock.

Because two kinds of uranium decay into two kinds of lead, they give two dates for each rock. Scientists can therefore check these dates to see if they are the same. If they are, the date is confirmed; if they are not, the date is doubtful. Scientists have found that the dates from the uranium decays are rarely the same. In one rock the two uranium decays as well as two other dating methods gave four

13C-11 *The age of rock from near Pikes Pike was determined from two different uranium isotopes. They differed by 80 million years.*

anomalous: an- (Gk. AN-, not) + -omalous (Gk. HOMALOS, even, same)

different results ranging from 100 million years to 10.5 billion years. These results show how unreliable the uranium-lead method is. Another problem with the uranium-lead method is that it sometimes gives results that are clearly wrong. Rocks in Texas gave ages as high as 11 billion years, about twice as old as evolutionists believe the earth is. The rocks cannot be older than the earth.

❏ *Potassium-Argon Method* The **potassium-argon method** is similar to the uranium-lead method. Potassium-40 decays into argon-40, a gas. The method uses the ratio of argon to potassium to find the age of a rock. Again, to use this method to date a rock, scientists must decide how much argon the rock had originally. They usually assume that it had none. This assumption lacks any observation to support it.

The potassium-argon dating method has been tested and found wanting. Some volcanic rocks in Hawaii were observed as they formed in 1800 and 1801. About 170 years later, scientists dated these rocks using the potassium-argon method. They found ages ranging from 160 million to 3 billion years. Other volcanic rocks known to be less than 200 years old gave potassium-argon ages ranging from 12 million to 22 million years. Such results prove conclusively that the potassium-argon method is unreliable.

What conclusions can we reach about attempts to date the earth? For one thing, some so-called scientific dating methods are thoroughly unreliable. Science, by its nature, cannot give us a true age for the earth because no human being made scientific observations of the earth at its beginning.

13C-12 *Lava rocks such as these were seen forming during a volcanic eruption. About 170 years later, they were given potassium-argon dates of millions to billions of years. The potassium-argon dating method is unreliable.*

Section Review Questions 13C-3
1. What two men calculated creation dates based on Biblical genealogies? What were the dates?
2. Does the amount of carbon-14 in a dead object increase or decrease with time?
3. Name the instrument used to measure the amount of carbon-14 in an object.
4. Name two radioactive dating methods other than the radiocarbon method.

Terms

anomalous sample	fossil graveyard	radioactive
calibration curve	geology	sediment
carbon-14	historical geology	strata
core	mantle	uniformitarianism
crust	Mohorovičić discontinuity	uranium-lead method
discontinuity	(Moho)	
doctrine of uniformity	potassium-argon method	

What Did You Learn?

1. List several examples of the earth's design that show God's care for living organisms.
2. Name two things that were changed about the earth as a result of the curse.
3. What verses in Genesis 1 support the conclusion that the earth was created with the appearance of age?
4. How does the evidence for a globally tropical climate refute uniformitarianism and support the Biblical framework of the earth's history?
5. Give an example in which the doctrine of uniformity is incorrect.
6. How does the amount of carbon-14 in a piece of charcoal change as time goes on?
7. In what ways are long-term dating methods unscientific?
8. Why is having two kinds of uranium and two kinds of lead in one rock sample sometimes a problem for uranium-lead dating?

What Do You Think?

1. Seasons were mentioned during the fourth day of creation, but the first mention of cold and winter in the Bible occurs immediately after the Flood (Gen. 8:22). How does this affect your opinion that the pre-Flood climate was or was not tropical worldwide?
2. If you were a geologist, which area would you like to specialize in? Why?

Minerals and Ores

FOURTEEN

14A – **Components of Minerals**

What exactly are minerals? A **mineral** is a naturally occurring, inorganic, crystalline solid. The definition excludes items such as steel and artificial gems because they are manmade. It excludes coal and pearls because they are **organic;** that is, they contain carbon atoms. It excludes air and water be-cause they are not solid. It excludes glasses because they do not have the definite arrangement of their atoms that crystals have. Minerals include substances like gold, natural gems, asbestos, quartz, and metal ores (minerals that contain metals).

EXPLORING MINERALS

▽ Staurolite often appears as six-sided crystals that intersect at either 60° or 90° angles.

△ Impurities can make quartz any color. This specimen is called smoky quartz.

▽ Bornite, also called peacock ore, is an important copper ore.

The blue color of chrysocolla comes from the presence of copper.
▽

Tourmaline is usually black; however, multicolor crystals are used as gems. If heated, tourmaline will develop electrical charges.

◁ Pyrite, also known as fool's gold, is composed of iron and sulfur.

▽ Cinnabar, or mercury sulfide, is the ore of mercury.

△ Orpiment, or arsenic trisulfide, is very poisonous. It was once used to make a yellow dye.

◁ Native lead has a silvery color and is rare.

Elements

Minerals, like all other matter, are made up of atoms. About three thousand different minerals exist, as well as many other kinds of matter that are not minerals. Does each kind of matter contain a different kind of atom? No, scientists have found only about one hundred different kinds of atoms. Each kind of atom is called an **element.** A **native mineral** contains only one kind of atom and is therefore a pure element. Gold, silver, and diamond are examples of native minerals.

14A-1 *This mass of pure gold was found uncombined with any other element and thus is a native mineral.*

Compounds

Atoms of several elements can combine to form a **compound.** A compound contains elements in a fixed ratio. For example, the mineral quartz is a compound of silicon and oxygen. Quartz always contains twice as many oxygen atoms as silicon atoms. If the ratio changed, the compound would not be quartz. Most minerals are compounds.

14A-2 *The mineral quartz is a compound since it has a fixed ratio of silicon and oxygen.*

Mixtures

Some forms of matter contain several elements in proportions that vary. Salt water, for example, may contain various amounts of salt and still be salt water. This form of matter is called a **mixture.** Minerals are never mixtures, although they may contain small amounts of impurities. Most rocks are mixtures of minerals.

14A-3 *This rock contains several minerals in no particular ratio and is therefore a mixture.*

Section Review Questions 14A

1. What are materials that contain carbon atoms called?
2. What is a mineral composed of a single kind of element called?
3. What are minerals that are composed of two or more different kinds of atoms called?
4. What are substances that are made up of elements in varying proportions called?

14B–Identifying Minerals

Although some minerals have distinctive characteristics that make identification easy, many minerals resemble other minerals or contain impurities that make identification difficult. Geologists have the task of identifying minerals.

To accomplish their task, geologists observe and test specimens carefully. They observe the specimen's appearance and physical characteristics. Sometimes they also use chemical tests to determine the elements present in the specimen and the percentage of each element. Such tests might be used to determine whether a mine would be profitable. To be sure of their results, geologists use not just one test, but a battery of tests.

14B-1 *Small amounts of impurities give this quartz its rose color.*

Properties of All Minerals

Color

Geologists begin to identify a specimen by observing its color. Only rarely does the task stop here because many minerals have the same color. Moreover, minerals sometimes change color when they are exposed to air because their surfaces oxidize or tarnish. Often the same mineral has different colors because of tiny amounts of impurities. Quartz, for example, may be green, pink, blue, violet, milky, or smoky. A small amount of manganese as an impurity changes clear quartz to the violet gem amethyst. Corundum, another example, is usually colorless. Yet with traces of chromium, corundum becomes ruby, and with traces of iron and titanium, it becomes sapphire.

14B-2 *Amethyst is quartz with a small amount of manganese.*

Streak

More reliable than the apparent color is the mineral's **streak,** the color of its powder. Rubbing a specimen across a **streak plate,** a piece of unglazed porcelain, makes its streak evident. As the specimen rubs across the plate, it leaves a trail of fine powder that has a characteristic color. Even though a specimen may vary in color because of impurities, its streak remains the same. Iron pyrite, one type of fool's gold, is a good example of a mineral whose streak is different from its outward color. This brass yellow mineral has a greenish black streak, while gold's streak is the same as its color.

14B-3 *Even though impurities change the color of a mineral, its streak remains the same.*

Luster

Another characteristic of a mineral is its luster. **Luster** is the quality and intensity of the light reflected from a mineral's surface. The mineral copper, for example, has a metallic luster. Quartz shines like glass, and therefore mineralogists say that it has a glassy luster. The luster of gypsum is pearly. The brilliant luster of a diamond is called adamantine* (AD uh MAN TEEN). Asbestos, with a fibrous texture, has a silky luster. Other common lusters include greasy, dull, and resinous.

Crystal Shape

Crystals come in assorted shapes and have always been a curiosity of creation. Their sizes range from the small microscopic crystals of kaolin (KAY uh lin) (clay) to the giant crystals of beryl or feldspar that sometimes weigh several tons. Crystals take their shape from the the arrangement of the atoms in the mineral. Each mineral has a characteristic crystal shape. For example, quartz crystals are hexagonal, and halite (common salt) crystals are cubic.

Crystals enlarge by adding additional particles to their structure, a process called **accretion** (uh KREE shun). During accretion, particles arrange themselves in a definite pattern. Crystals also may form when molten rock cools. When molten rock cools slowly, the molecules have time to arrange themselves and form large crystals. When the molten rock cools rapidly, the molecules have little time to arrange themselves; thus, the crystals are small if they exist at all. Glasses, solids that do not contain crystals, often form when molten rock cools rapidly.

14B-5 *Shapes of crystals vary from the long needle-like crystals of arogonite* (left) *to the cubic crystals of halite* (below).

14B-4 *Asbestos has a silky luster* (above) *while gypsum has a pearly luster* (left).

adamantine: (Gk. ADAMAS, a hard stone from Greek mythology considered unbreakable)

Cleavage

Cleavage is the characteristic of some minerals to break into flat sheets or along certain planes. This splitting of a mineral happens because the bonds between the atoms in the crystals are not equally strong in all directions. Though the bond in one direction of a crystal may be strong so that cleaving is difficult, the bond in another direction may be weak enough to allow cleaving. Mineralogists have established five ratings for mineral cleavage: perfect, good, fair, poor, and none. At one end of the scale are minerals such as mica, which separate easily; these have perfect cleavage. At the other end of the scale are minerals such as quartz, which do not break along flat surfaces. Along with ease of breakage, cleavage deals with the number of directions or planes that a mineral will cleave. Mica cleaves in only one direction, halite cleaves in three directions, and sphalerite (blackjack) cleaves in six directions.

14B-7 *Obsidian's characteristic of breaking along smooth, curved surfaces is called conchoidal fracture.*

14B-6 *Mica is easily identified by its ease of cleavage into thin sheets.*

Minerals that do not break along cleavage lines but seem to have some pattern in their breaking have **fracture.** The different types of fracture include conchoidal (kahng KOID l), fibrous, uneven, and hackly. Conchoidal fracture, as in flint, is breaking along curved, smooth surfaces. The chips or pieces have the shape of a shell. Fibrous fracture is breaking that produces surfaces having splinters or fibers as with asbestos. Uneven fracture produces surfaces that are irregular and rough as in chalcocite (another kind of fool's gold). Hackly fracture is breaking along ragged surfaces.

Hardness

A simple procedure in identifying a mineral is the **hardness test,** which determines the ability of a mineral to withstand scratching and abrasion. Some minerals are so soft that they can be scratched with a fingernail; others are so hard that virtually nothing can scratch them. In 1822 a German mineralogist named Friedrich Mohs (1773–1839) devised a method for determining the hardness of a mineral and a hardness scale. On the **Mohs scale,** minerals range from 1, very soft, to 10, very

14B-8 *Mineral set used to test the hardness of other mineral specimens*

hard. Mohs assigned a hardness of 1 to talc and 10 to diamond. The test for a mineral's hardness is whether it can scratch or be scratched by certain minerals that Mohs assigned to each number in his hardness scale. For example, if a mineral scratches gypsum (number 2) but is scratched by calcite (number 3), its hardness is between 2 and 3.

14B-9	Mohs Hardness Scale
Diamond	10
Corundum	9
Topaz	8
Quartz	7
Feldspar	6
Apatite	5
Fluorite	4
Calcite	3
Gypsum	2
Talc	1

Specific Gravity

Another characteristic used for identifying minerals is their **specific gravity.** Specific gravity is the ratio of the mass of a substance to the mass of an equal volume of water at 4° C (39° F). If a mineral with a volume of 1 cm^3 has a mass of 5 g, and the mass of 1 cm^3 of water is 1 g, then the mineral's specific gravity is

$$\frac{5\,g}{1\,g} = 5.$$

Sometimes a geologist can estimate the specific gravity of a mineral by lifting or handling a chunk of each of two different minerals. If the chunks are about the same volume, the geologist can compare their specific gravities. Some minerals such as pumice are light; others such as gold are heavy. With practice in lifting minerals, a person can become proficient in estimating whether a specific gravity is low, average, or high.

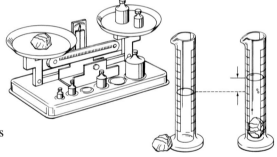

14B-10 *The mass of a rock is measured on a balance, while its volume can be measured by the amount of water it displaces.*

Section Review Questions 14B-1

1. What color test used in identification of minerals is more reliable than simply observing the apparent color of the mineral?
2. What mineral has adamantine luster?
3. What is the name given to the process of enlarging crystals by adding particles?
4. Name the characteristic that is determined by the differences in bonding strength between atoms within a mineral.

Properties of Some Minerals

Most minerals are identified by their color, streak, luster, crystal shape, cleavage, hardness, and specific gravity. A few minerals, however, have other properties that make them easy to identify.

Flame Test

Some minerals produce characteristic colors of flame or residue when they burn. The **flame test** identifies these minerals. For example, when a small sample of table salt is held in a flame, the flame becomes yellow. The yellow color is due to the presence of sodium in table salt (sodium chloride). Potassium produces a violet flame, and calcium gives an orange-red flame. Other minerals produce other colors of flame.

14B-11 *Minerals can be identified by the color of flame they produce.*

Acid Test

Carbonates, sulfides, and sulfites can be identified by the **acid test.** If an acid, usually hydrochloric acid, is applied to these miner-

14B-12 *The reaction of some minerals with acid is another method of identification.*

als, it fizzes, giving off bubbles of carbon dioxide, hydrogen sulfide, or sulfur dioxide, respectively. Calcite, dolomite, and galena are minerals that react with acids. For dolomite to react, the acid must be slightly heated.

Magnetism

Some minerals display **magnetism.** Not only can a magnet pick up these minerals, but some of them are strong enough to pick up small pieces of iron. The best example of a magnetic mineral is magnetite. According to one legend, a shepherd discovered this mineral when he noticed that pieces of a black rock stuck to the iron point of his staff. During the twelfth century A.D., mariners in China and Europe apparently independently developed the magnetic compass. This compass always pointed north and south to guide a

14B-13 *Magnetite is a natural magnet. It will pick up iron objects just as magnets do.*

ship. Because magnetite could be used in a compass, it was called **lodestone.***

Radioactivity

Geologists locate uranium-containing minerals, such as pitchblende, using Geiger counters because these minerals are radioactive. Although uranium is more abundant in the earth's crust than silver, mercury, or

---

lodestone: lode- (Old Eng. LOAD, way) + -stone (Old Eng. STAN, stone)

14B-14 *Torbernite is a green mineral that is radioactive. It contains both uranium and copper.*

iodine, its concentration in any area is so slight that mining operations are expensive. Geologists are, therefore, continually prospecting for high concentration deposits of pitchblende and other radioactive minerals.

Glow

Some minerals glow when they are placed under ultraviolet light. Minerals produce this glow by absorbing the invisible ultraviolet light and giving off visible light. Minerals that emit light while absorbing radiation from another source are **fluorescent** (fl*oo* RES unt). Some minerals emit light not only when

they are illuminated but also after the light source is removed. Such minerals are **phosphorescent** (FAHS fuh RES unt).

Refraction

Some transparent minerals can be identified by the way they bend light rays. All minerals bend light as it passes through them. This bending is called **refraction.** The index of refraction of a mineral tells how much it bends light. Diamond has a high index of refraction; this is the reason for its brilliance.

14B-16 *Calcite has double refraction.*

A few transparent minerals show **double refraction;** that is, they produce a double image as light passes through them. Calcite is a good example of a doubly refracting mineral.

14B-15 *This may look like an ordinary rock (above), but it contains two fluorescent minerals (right); willemite (green) and calcite (red).*

Section Review Questions 14B-2

1. What mineral was the development of the compass dependent on?
2. What two terms might be used to describe minerals that emit light?
3. What term is defined as "the bending of light"?

14C–Minerals in Nature

Native Minerals

From the beginning to the end, the Bible speaks of the minerals of the earth. Genesis 2:11-12 links gold and onyx indirectly with the Garden of Eden. In the New Testament, Revelation 21:19-20 speaks of twelve minerals within the New Jerusalem. The Scriptures also depict the uses of various minerals. For example, the Israelites used precious stones in jewelry (Exod. 35:22), hewn stone in houses (II Chron. 34:11), and uncut stones in altars (Exod. 20:25). In the beauty of crystals, the radiance of gold, or the usefulness of iron, minerals testify to the wisdom and glory of God.

Minerals are a solid testimony to the wisdom and nature of God. God has created on this earth not just stone, but diamond and ruby, gold and silver, iron and copper, silicates and carbonates. Through His creation, God has revealed Himself. Not only is the creation of infinite variety, beauty, and usefulness, but also it has been satisfying to man by providing him with a challenge for his intellect and energy. One of these challenges is locating, identifying, and utilizing minerals.

Gold

Gold is one of the heaviest minerals, with a specific gravity of about 19. Gold deposits nearly always contain about 10 to 15 per cent silver. In most gold veins the mineral is so finely distributed in quartz sand that it is invisible. As gold-bearing rock erodes away, the metal washes into nearby streams and sifts through the sand until it is deposited in crevices, in river sand bars, or along beaches. These stream deposits where eroded gold or other minerals are found are called **placer deposits.**

14C-1 *The Israelites were directed by God to use specific minerals in the high priest's breastplate to represent the twelve tribes.*

Gold in placer deposits can be separated from the sand and gravel in a number of ways. **Panning** washes away the lighter material and exposes the nuggets, the larger pieces of gold. **Sluicing** (SLOOS ing) involves washing a specimen so that its flecks of gold collect behind crossbars in a trough called a sluice. The crossbars are often coated with mercury because it holds the gold better. **Dredging** can separate the metal from thousands of cubic yards of sand and gravel each day.

FACETS OF MINERALOGY

Worth Its Weight in Gold?

You may never hold a gold or silver coin in your hand. Most of the coins in your pocket, including the dime, are primarily made of copper. The penny is almost pure zinc (97.6%) with a thin copper coating, the five-cent piece is a mixture of copper (75%) and nickel (25%), and dimes and quarters are solid copper covered by a mixture of copper and nickel. The metal in each coin, including the half dollar, is worth less than a penny. The paper in our bills is worth even less.

Coins and currency were once worth their face value. The $10 gold eagle, issued in 1795, was worth its weight in gold until the U.S. government stopped minting gold coins in 1933. Silver dollars were worth $1 until their minting ended in 1935. The government also issued certificates that you could exchange for gold or silver. But gold certificates ceased in 1933; silver certificates ceased in 1963.

Modern coins have almost no value in themselves. They are *tokens,* designed for durability and difficulty to counterfeit. Paper currency does not even have the advantage of durability. Few bills last more than a few years in circulation. Banks routinely send worn-out bills to the Federal Reserve Bank, where they are shredded and replaced with crisp, new bills.

Currency was not always worthless. Early coins had *intrinsic* value. They could be converted into something of value—swords, jewelry, bells, and so on. Ancient people found three soft metals that they could extract from ores and shape into coins or jewelry: copper, silver, and gold. The first coins, as we know them, appeared in Asia Minor about the seventh century B.C. They were made of a natural mixture of gold and silver, known as electrum. The mixture varied from one coin to the next, and thus the relative value of each coin was never certain.

Only with time did countries develop pure gold, silver, and copper coins. These metals seemed almost the ideal medium of trade around the world. They had a number of benefits: they were easy to carry, easy to

20-dollar gold coin

silver coin

Modern coins have almost no value in themselves.

Gold bullion

Uses of gold—each of these items has gold in or on it.

measure and divide, and difficult to counterfeit. Also, they were common in most places of the earth.

God has placed different amounts of each of these three metals in the earth. Gold, which is rare, is more valuable than an equal amount of silver, and silver is likewise more valuable than copper. These metals have maintained their value relative to each other through history. The relative value of gold, silver, and copper is evident in the Bible. Solomon's temple was made from 100,000 talents of gold, 1,000,000 talents of silver, and brass (containing copper) "without weight" (I Chron. 22:14). These talents were lumps of metal, not coins, stamped with different values. For years the relative value of the metals was reflected in

America's coins: the ten-dollar gold piece, the silver dollar, and the copper penny (10 : 1 : 0.01).

When a country runs on a metal standard, the value of money fluctuates constantly with the changing value of the metal. During the Great Depression of the 1930s, most countries, including the United States, abandoned the gold standard because they wanted to be able to print and spend money without worrying about how much gold they possessed. Another reason for abandoning gold was that gold mines were not keeping up with the rapid increase in world population. The scarcity of silver coins later led the U.S. treasury to abandon silver certificates. And finally in 1964 most minting of silver ceased.

However, a few silver and gold coins are still being minted. The government mints a limited number of silver "dollars" each year for collectors. (They contain 60 per cent copper and sell for a much higher price than $1.) You can even buy $10 gold coins, but not for $10. Sometimes the government also mints commemorative coins to honor an individual or event, such as the black scientist George Washington Carver. These coins are all legal tender, but you will find them only in the hands of collectors.

Commemorative coins are minted to honor an individual.

14C-2 *Gold nuggets (above) are often found by panning. A gold note from 1928 (right). Our money is no longer backed by gold.*

Gold has many uses. Because it is beautiful and easy to work, it is used in jewelry and dentistry. Because it is valuable, it has been used as a standard for currency or as an investment. In the United States, paper money could be redeemed for gold prior to 1933. In 1976 the practice of determining the value of U.S. money by comparison to gold was abandoned. Its electrical properties and resistance to corrosion make gold an important material for making reliable electrical contacts. A film of gold on glass transmits light but not heat. Thus it is used to make visors for astronauts and others who must see while facing severe heat.

14C-4 *An astronaut's visor coated with a film of gold for protection*

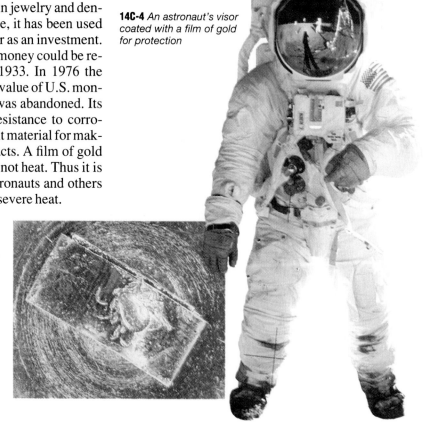

14C-3 *A tick coated with an extremely thin layer of gold for viewing by a scanning electron microscope.*

FACETS OF MINERALOGY

14C-2

Around the World in Search of Gold

The dream of finding a treasure of gold has inspired some of the greatest migrations of men in history. The early conquistadors from Spain crossed the Atlantic to the New World in search of fabled cities of gold. Coronado found nothing but scorching heat and sagebrush in the American Southwest. Pizarro, on the other hand, found his city of gold at Cuzco, the capital of the Inca empire. The Incas filled an entire room with over six tons of gold artifacts to ransom their emperor, whom Pizarro had captured. But the Spaniards killed the emperor and made the Indians work as slaves in the nearby mines, which were eventually emptied of all their wealth.

The first modern "gold rush" occurred in California in 1849. The discovery of two yellow nuggets in a stream near Sumter's mill attracted over a quarter of a million men to California from 1849 to 1852. The rush turned a barren territory of fourteen thousand people into a full-fledged state of one hundred thousand inhabitants in less than two years. Tent camps lined the gold sites as "forty-niners" crossed thousands of miles of ocean, plains, and deserts by foot, mule, and boat. They came from the East, China, and South America, clamoring for a claim in this land.

The early miners looked for gold dust and nuggets that had washed into stream beds and gulleys. They used pans, rocker boxes, and sluices of running water to wash out the lighter sand, gravel, and dirt, leaving the heavy gold. But these supplies were soon exhausted. Other prospectors began digging shallow mines to find the sources of the gold. Most did not make enough to live on, and they eventually left the state or turned to other means of livelihood. Others worked for the big mining companies that had the money and equipment to dig deep mines in the areas where the gold originally came from. In these "mother lodes," as they were called, so-phisticated equipment dug out tons of rock, crushed it, and extracted gold from the ore.

Hope was rekindled with the news of gold in Australia, discovered in 1851 by a forty-niner who had returned home. It drew eager miners from all parts of the world. Half a million men sailed from England alone. Many miners in California, disillusioned by overcrowded, crime-filled, and high-priced mining towns, boarded ship and sailed "down under" halfway around the world. But the disappointment was repeated. A small find in the nearby islands of New Zealand drew more hopefuls. A string of small strikes and false claims continued in the American West throughout the second half of the century. But the next great finds came in South Africa's Transvaal (1886) and the Klondike region of Canada's Yukon Territory (1896). This find near the border of Alaska attracted the last of this hardy collection of men dreaming to get rich quick in this frozen frontier. Many died from cold, starvation, and disease or turned back before they even reached their destination.

By the end of the 1800s, the last of the major gold rushes was over. All that was left in many areas were ghost towns, such as Deadwood Gulch in South Dakota (gold rush of 1876). More gold had been mined in these few years than all the gold mined since Columbus discovered America. Henceforth all major gold excavation was controlled by big businesses using large machines, bulldozers, dump trucks, and processing mills. More than two-thirds of the world's gold now comes from South Africa, where major gold deposits are still going strong. But the days of the lone prospector are over. Recent finds, such as those in the Ural Mountains deep in the heart of Russia, have attracted new mining towns, but they are all carefully surveyed and developed by big companies and supervised by the government. Teams of geologists continue

the search for new deposits, although much is still not understood about the origin of gold deposits. The most important deposits appear as veins of minerals mixed with gold that spread upward from deep in the earth through cracks (Canada and U.S.). Other deposits appear as placers washed out from these veins (Alaska), and still others, a mixture of veins and placers, appear as reefs (South Africa).

Here and there some dreamers, still smitten by gold fever, can be seen poking around the mountains and making claims. Their efforts are an enduring testimony of the appeal of this amazing metal. If men can brave the Arctic cold, desert heat, privation, and shipwreck to find an elusive metal, cannot Christians brave much more in

the service of God and in an effort to study His Word? Consider the life of the Apostle Paul:

> In journeyings often, in perils of waters, in perils of robbers, in perils by mine own countrymen, in perils by the heathen, in perils in the city, in perils in the wilderness, in perils in the sea, in perils among false brethren; in weariness and painfulness, in watchings often, in hunger and thirst, in fastings often, in cold and nakedness. (II Cor. 11:26-27)

Consider the advice of Solomon:

> If thou criest after knowledge, and liftest up thy voice for understanding; if thou seekest her as silver, and searchest for her as for hid treasures; then shalt thou understand the fear of the Lord, and find the knowledge of God. (Prov. 2:3-5)

Panning for gold in 1889 in South Dakota (Dakota Territory at that time).

Silver

Silver has a specific gravity of 10.5 and a color and streak of silver-white. Deposits of this mineral have various shapes: coarse or fine strands, thin sheets, and irregular masses. In the United States, most native silver came from the Keweenaw (KEE wuh NAW) Peninsula of Michigan.

Because silver is more common than gold, it is less valuable. Silver is also used for jewelry and tableware. Because silver conducts electricity better than any other metal, it is an important component in some electrical circuits. Silver is also used in photographic film and in mirrors.

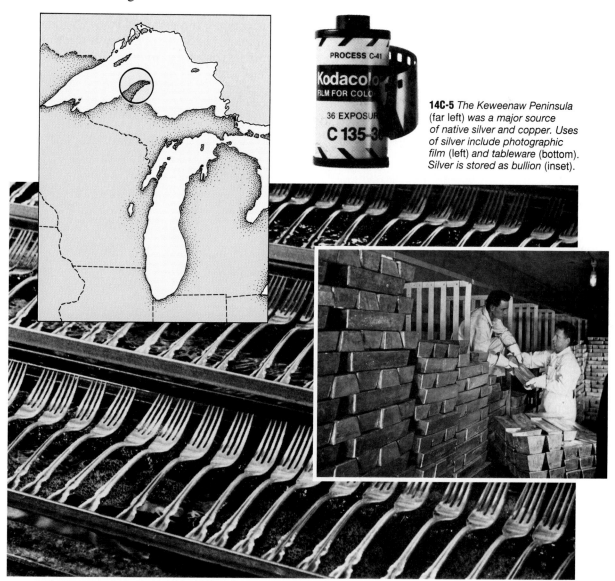

14C-5 *The Keweenaw Peninsula (far left) was a major source of native silver and copper. Uses of silver include photographic film (left) and tableware (bottom). Silver is stored as bullion (inset).*

Copper

Native copper, like silver, occurs in irregular masses, sheets, and twisted strands. The only major deposit of native copper in the U.S. was in the Keweenaw Peninsula of Michigan. Michigan copper was ''discovered'' in 1840, but the American Indians used it much earlier. For the next seventy-five years, men exploited the region for copper. Although most of the copper was in small, irregular pieces, some large masses were found. One mass discovered in 1857 weighed over 420 tons. The United States has exhausted the native copper that was economical to mine and now gets most of its copper from the copper sulfide ores (chalcocite) in New Mexico and Arizona.

Copper, like silver, conducts electricity well. A major use of copper is in electrical wiring. It transmits heat well and so is used in refrigeration pipes and other places where heat conduction is important. Because copper resists corrosion, it is a good material for plumbing pipes. It is also used in jewelry and in sculptures. The Statue of Liberty is made of a copper skin on a frame of iron.

14C-6 *Copper pipe fittings and tubings supply water to many homes because of copper's resistance to corrosion (above); because of its beauty, copper is also used for many decorative elements (top right); copper is also an excellent conductor of heat, which makes it useful for cooking utensils (right).*

Platinum

Platinum exists in a range of sizes, from small particles to nuggets. It has a steel gray color and a bright luster. Platinum has a specific gravity of 21.5, which is heavier than gold. It is also more valuable than gold. The metal was first found in Colombia, South America, in 1735. It was named *platina* from the Spanish word for silver, *plata*. Today most of the world's supply of platinum comes from deposits in the former USSR and South Africa.

Platinum is extremely resistant to corrosion. For this reason the international standard meter bar and kilogram weight were made of platinum alloyed (mixed) with iridium. Platinum also acts as a catalyst for some reactions. A catalyst is a substance that changes the rate of a chemical reaction (usually accelerates) without being consumed itself. Platinum is the catalyst in an automobile's catalytic converter.

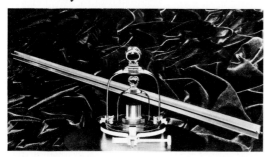

14C-7 *The standard meter bar and kilogram are made of platinum alloy. Platinum was chosen for this because of its resistance to corrosion.*

Diamond

By definition, minerals do not contain carbon, but an exception is made for diamond. Diamond is a native mineral composed of pure carbon. Diamond, the hardest known mineral, has perfect cleavage and a greasy luster before it is cut. The cut gems, however, have a luster so brilliant that it is called the

"Fire of the Diamond." Diamonds are usually pale yellow or colorless, but red, orange, green, blue, and brown diamonds exist. The famous Hope Diamond found in India in 1642 is the largest blue diamond.

14C-8 *Diamonds in the rough are of various sizes and colors. The accompanying rock is kimberlite.*

Diamonds are sometimes found in placer deposits. Usually, however, they are found in **diamond pipes,** round vertical columns of formerly molten rock. The deepest diamond pipe ever mined, named Kimberley, is in South Africa. This pipe grew smaller in diameter with greater depth. Though the pipe continued, mining stopped at about 1,100 m (3,500 ft.). Although Australia produces more diamonds than all other countries, the world's most productive diamond mine, the Premier, is 39 km (24 mi.) west of Pretoria, South Africa. Since 1903 the Premier mine has produced over 30 million carats (6 tons) of diamonds. In 1905 the world's largest diamond, the Cullinan, which weighed 3,106 carats in the rough, was found in this mine. From this diamond over 100 gems were cut which are now part of the British regalia.

Separating diamonds once involved crushing the rocks into coarse chunks and spreading them out on platforms where the sun and rain disintegrated them after a short time. Men then shook the disintegrated chunks through screens that separated the diamonds from the rest of the rock. Today the rock is crushed finely so that the diamonds can be quickly separated. In the final stages of separation, the crushed rock with the diamonds are spread out on tables coated with grease. The diamonds stick to the grease, and the other rock is washed away.

Diamonds are best known for their beauty as gems. The value of gem diamonds depends on their color, purity, size, and the skill with which they are cut. Size is especially important. A one-carat stone is worth only one-fourth or one-third as much as a two-carat stone of equal color, purity, and cut. A **carat** (KAR ut), a unit of mass for gems, is a mass of 0.2 g. Most engagement rings have diamonds, and other jewelry contains them as well.

The hardness of diamonds is 10 on the Mohs scale, and this makes them very useful. Diamonds that cannot be used as gems because of size or flaws are often turned into

powder and used as abrasives. Drill bits and saw blades used for exceptionally hard materials often have diamond tips.

14C-9 *The "Big Hole" at Kimberley* (top), *now filled with water, was a diamond-bearing volcanic pipe. A deep shaft diamond mine also in South Africa* (above). *The mounds of waste are called "tailings." The Hope diamond* (left), *is the largest blue diamond known. It was cut from a 112-carat gemstone.*

Sulfur

Sulfur is identified by its yellow color and conchoidal fracture. Sulfur burns with a characteristic blue flame and produces a poisonous gas, sulfur dioxide. It is often found near the rims of volcanoes and in sedimentary beds deep underground. The United States has an abundant supply of this mineral in Louisiana and Texas. The **Frasch** (FRAHSH) **process** is used to obtain the sulfur from below the surface. In this process, superheated water is pumped down to the sulfur deposit, and compressed air forces the melted sulfur up through another pipe to the surface. Not only is this native sulfur 99.5 per cent pure, but it also is abundant enough to provide half of the world's supply of sulfur.

14C-10 Crystalline form of the mineral sulfur (top left); sulfur crystals at a fumarole vent in Hawaii (left); a collection station for hot, liquefied sulfur mined by the Frasch process at Newgulf, Texas (above).

Section Review Questions 14C-1

1. Where would you find placer deposits?
2. When and where did the first modern gold rush occur?
3. Name the mineral metal that is the best conductor of electricity.
4. What are the columns of rock in which diamonds are found called?
5. What element(s) form diamonds?
6. What units of weight are used to measure gems?

Compound Minerals

Silicates

The most abundant class of minerals is the silicates. Silicates make up about 25 per cent of all known minerals and about 40 per cent of the common ores. More than 90 per cent of the earth's crust consists of silicates. This class of mineral is called silicates because the minerals in it all contain silicon and oxygen. Quartz, the second most common mineral in the earth's crust, contains *only* silicon and oxygen. Feldspar, a type of silicate, is the most common mineral in the crust. Other silicates include chalcedony (a type of quartz), opal, mica, hornblende, olivine, garnet, talc, and kaolin (clay).

Oxides

Mineral oxides are composed of oxygen and some other element, usually a metal. Many mineral oxides are important economically because they are the chief sources of important metals. Significant metal oxides include hematite and magnetite (iron ores), cassiterite (tin ore), and bauxite (aluminum ore).

Sulfides

Mineral sulfides are composed of one or more metals and sulfur. Like oxides, these minerals contain the metals so important for us today. Many sulfides are opaque. Yet they have characteristic colors and often have colored streaks. Galena (lead ore), chalcocite (copper ore), cinnabar (mercury ore), realgar (arsenic ore), stibnite (antimony ore), and pyrite (iron ore and source of sulfuric acid) are all sulfides.

Carbonates

Carbonates are minerals containing a metal ion and the carbonate ion (a carbon-and-oxygen-containing ion that combines with metals easily). When an acid is applied to a carbonate mineral, a salt plus carbon dioxide are always produced. This acid test is commonly used to identify carbonates. Calcite (found in limestone), dolomite (calcium and magnesium), rhodochrosite (manganese ore), and malachite and azurite (copper ores) are some of the minerals in this class.

14C-12 *Galena, lead sulfide, a lustrous, blue-gray mineral that usually crystallizes in cubes, is the principal source of lead.*

14C-11 *Some compound minerals are important metal ores. Calcocite, copper sulfide, is found in this open pit mine in Butte, Montana.*

FACETS OF MINERALOGY

14C-3

Artificial Gems

Most jewels you see in the store are not genuine. They might be imitations, substitutes, or synthetics. The two most common *imitations* come to us from the ancient Egyptians and Romans. They are made of glass and glazed ceramic. Another popular type of imitation is a combination of materials, such as opal and glass.

Many cheap *substitutes* have been produced. One common crystal, made from strontium titanate, disperses light four times better than diamonds. Another common crystal, called cubic zirconia, almost matches the beauty of the true diamond, at a cost of a few dollars. But the imitations lack the durability and fire of true gems; they also have a different atomic structure and chemical make-up.

For many years, scientists have dreamed of inventing *synthetic*, or manmade, gems. The difficulty was not finding the ingredients but imitating how God put them together. We have known for a long time that diamonds are made from the same element as coal and sugar. But not until 1954 were carbon atoms artificially forced into tiny diamonds. It required temperatures exceeding 4,800° F and pressures of over 100,000 kg/cm² (1.5 million lb./in.²).†

To an untrained eye synthetic diamonds look genuine. The artificial green gem (inset) was made from silica-containing volcanic ash.

The components of other gems are also common, but it takes time to form the crystals. Usually the ingredients are melted and allowed to cool into a crystal. Rubies were the first synthetic gems produced this way. They are made from aluminum oxide, with a trace of chromium for color. Unlike most other gems, emeralds are first placed in a solution with a solvent and then heated. The emerald crystals take months to form.

Although synthetics look like natural gems to the naked eye, they are much less valuable. The differences are fairly easy to spot under a microscope. Synthetics are "too perfect" and lack the irregularities and impurities that give natural gems their charm. Most sell for only a few dollars. Even synthetic emeralds, which are almost exact copies of their natural cousins, sell for only a few hundred dollars per carat, as opposed to the thousands of dollars paid for natural emeralds. Synthetic diamonds are the best copy of the original, but they are so small that they are more suitable for industrial uses than jewelry. Man's efforts to synthesize gems are only a weak imitation of God's handiwork.

† Technically, pressure is reported in units of N/cm². However, in common usage kg/cm² or lb./in.² is often substituted.

Section Review Questions 14C-2
1. Name the most abundant class of minerals in the earth's crust.
2. What metal has both oxide and sulfide ores?
3. What artificial gem is a substitute for diamond?

Terms

accretion	fluorescent	native mineral
acid test	fracture	organic
carat	Frasch process	panning
cleavage	hardness test	phosphorescent
compound	lodestone	placer deposit
diamond pipe	luster	refraction
double refraction	magnetism	sluicing
dredging	mineral	specific gravity
element	mixture	streak
flame test	Mohs scale	streak plate

What Did You Learn?
1. List the three distinguishing characteristics of minerals.
2. Why is color alone rarely used as positive identification of a mineral?
3. Explain the difference between cleavage and fracture.
4. What tests can be used to help identify minerals?
5. What two things must be known in order to find the specific gravity of a mineral?
6. How do some minerals become concentrated in placer deposits?
7. Where can native silver and copper be found in the United States?
8. What characteristic of diamond is alluded to in Jeremiah 17:1?
9. What minerals are found in your state?

What Do You Think?
1. What factors make a mineral valuable?
2. Is ice a mineral?
3. Are geologists correct in calling diamond a mineral when it is composed of carbon?

ROCKS AND FOSSILS

FIFTEEN

15A–The Importance of Rocks

Did you ever stop to think of the structure of the earth, of the foundations that must uphold the huge mountains and their towering peaks for miles into the sky? These gigantic supporting masses of rock are solid and sure and may be compared to the foundation of our salvation, Christ Jesus. In I Corinthians 3:11 the Apostle Paul describes Christ as the sure foundation: "For other foundation can no man lay than that is laid, which is Jesus Christ."

Rock is more than a foundation material for the earth; it is important to us in our daily lives. It forms a valuable building material that is both durable and ornamental. Gravel for roadbeds, concrete for sidewalks, marble for monuments, lime for alkalizing the soil, and glass for windows all come from rock.

Coal, a rock that burns, is an important fuel for heating and for generating electricity, as well as a major source of dyes, drugs, and many other chemical products. Some rocks are storage places for petroleum and ground water. Rocks also add to the scenic splendor of the world we live in. All around us we see testimony of the Creator's wisdom in the usefulness and the beauty of rock.

Rock, the solid material in the earth's crust, is a natural combination of one or more minerals or organic materials. Most rocks contain two or more minerals; only a few rocks such as dolomite (DAHL uh MITE) and halite contain only one mineral. In some rocks the different kinds of minerals are easy to see. Others have fine crystals that cannot be seen without a microscope.

15B–Sedimentary Rocks

Geologists recognize three categories of rocks: sedimentary (SED uh MEN tuh ree), igneous (IG nee us), and metamorphic (MET uh MOHR fik). We will begin by studying **sedimentary rocks.** This kind of rock appears to be made of particles bonded together by natural cements or solids that settled from water solutions. They are abundant on the earth's crust, covering about three-fourths of its surface. Many creationists believe that the waters of the Genesis Flood laid down much of this sedimentary rock, especially the layers that contain fossils. Such formations evidence a rapid process that no longer operates today. Sedimentary rocks characteristically form layers called **strata** (STRAY tuh) (singular, stratum). Water-deposited strata begin as horizontal layers, but movements of the earth's crust can tilt them to almost any angle.

15B-1 *Tilted sedimentary rock strata in Glacier National Park, Montana (left). Greenhorn formation near Pueblo Colorado (below).*

Classifying Sedimentary Rocks

Fragmental Sedimentary Rocks

Sedimentary rocks are classified as **fragmental** if they appear to contain fragments eroded from other rocks; they are classified as **chemical** if they appear to come from minerals that were dissolved in water. The fragments in fragmental sedimentary rock formed from the breakup of previously existing rocks. Pressure solidified and various natural minerals bonded the fragments, making different kinds of sedimentary rock. Pebbles and gravel form conglomerate; sand forms sandstone; and silts and clays form mudstone or shale.

15B-2 Conglomerate and breccia are both composed of cemented rock fragments. Conglomerate (left) has incorporated rounded fragments while breccia (right) includes angular fragments.

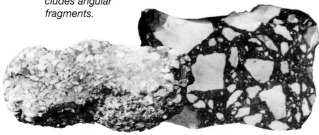

Conglomerate (kun GLAHM ur it), the coarsest grade of fragmental rock, contains gravels, pebbles, cobbles, and even large boulders consolidated by a mass of cemented sand grains. Though almost any kind of rock may appear in the mixture, most of the stones in conglomerate are quartz. Conglomerate is often called nature's concrete. The fragments in conglomerate were rounded by erosion prior to incorporation into sedimentary rock. **Breccia** (BRECH ee uh) is similar to conglomerate except the fragments are sharp and angular. These sharp fragments often appear in a fine-grained matrix such as clay. A **matrix** (MAY triks) is a material in which something is enclosed or embedded.

In sandstone the fragments are smaller. Beds of quartz sand grains consolidate into deposits of sandstone; silica, calcite, or iron oxide cements the grains of sand, which are usually water worn and rounded. The color of the rock results from its cementing material. If silica and calcite bind the rock, it is white, yellow, or buff. If iron oxide is the natural cement, the color is red to reddish brown.

Sandstone always has air spaces between the crystals because the cements never completely fill these spaces. This characteristic gives sandstone **permeability:** fluids can pass through a bed of sandstone. The spaces between the particles of a porous rock often become reservoirs for water or, in some places, for oil.

Mudstone and shale have the smallest particles of any fragmental sedimentary rocks. Shale, unlike sandstone, is so fine-grained that it does not allow water to pass through it. This quality is called **impermeability.** Shale is soft and splits easily into thin sheets. It is usually the color of clay but also may be white, brown, red, green, or black. Mudstone is similar to shale but does not split into thin sheets.

15B-3 A red sandstone cliff in Colorado National Park near Grand Junction, Colorado (left); shale from Montana which easily splits into thin sheets

Chemical Sedimentary Rocks

Chemical sedimentary rocks form from minerals dissolved in water. After the minerals have been dissolved in water, either solids settling to the bottom (precipitation) or evaporation of the water produces the rock. Shells of water animals also can contribute to these rocks.

Limestone, which contains mainly calcite, precipitates directly out of seawater. Limestone deposits on the continents suggest that they were once under water. Limestone is important economically because it is useful for neutralizing acid soils, building roads, and making cement.

15B-4 *Limestone takes many different appearances—nonfossiliferous* (top) *or fossiliferous* (bottom).

God may have created most halite (common or rock salt) as it is now, or the halite may have formed after creation when inland bodies of salt water dried up after the universal Flood of Noah's day. Layers of other material often cover halite. Scientists have found extensive beds of halite ranging from 1 m (3.3 ft.) thick to over 60 m (200 ft.) thick. Halite occasionally exists in nature as vertical pipelike masses called **salt domes.** These seem to have been forced upward from an underlying deposit.

15B-5 *Diagram of a salt dome* (top); *halite (salt) crystals* (right)

Section Review Questions 15B-1

1. List the three categories of rocks.
2. When do some creationists believe much of the sedimentary rock was laid down?
3. What are the layers of sedimentary rocks called?
4. What is the ability of fluids to pass through sandstone called?
5. What kind of sedimentary rocks form from dissolved minerals?

15B-6 *Fish fossil of the genus* Diplomystus *found in shale near Kemmerer, Wyoming*

Fossils in Sedimentary Rocks

A fascinating feature of sedimentary rocks is the fossils they sometimes contain. A **fossil** is any trace or remains of a living organism that has been preserved by natural means. Fossils are most frequently found in limestone, sandstone, and shale. In these rocks, fossils are not necessarily the original remains or trace of an organism. Bone or wood may have been replaced with mineral, and leaves or soft body parts may have left only

15B-7 *A fossilized plant*

an imprint. Some fossils are evidence of land-dwelling organisms, and others sea-dwelling. There are fossils of both plants and animals, ranging in size from bacteria "microfossils" to huge dinosaurs.

Fossils and Evolution

Fossils tell us about the past by giving us a sample of what living things on the earth used to be like. We find many different kinds of creatures in fossils. Some people who reject the Biblical account of creation think that living things went through gradual changes (evolution) from one kind to another. But the fossils do not show gradual changes from one kind to another. They are clearly one kind *or* another, not something in between kinds. For example, fossils of mice exist and fossils of bats exist, but no fossils of a half-mouse or half-bat exist.

Evolutionists believe, for example, that the fins of fish gradually changed into legs so that the resulting creatures could walk around on the land. If such a change took place, we should be able to find many fossils of the

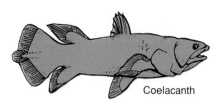

15B-8 *Coelacanths (below) were thought to be an evolutionary link between fish and land animals, but they are still alive today.*

Coelacanth

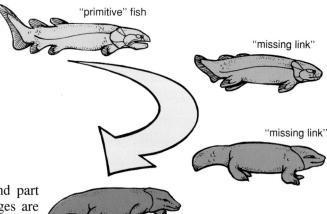

"primitive" fish

"missing link"

"missing link"

"primitive" amphibian

transitional types having part fins and part legs. Yet we do not. Fossil appendages are clearly either fins or legs. The same is true of the imagined change from legs to wings.

The fossils that evolutionists attempt to find, but never do, are sometimes called "missing links." Evolutionists have searched for these missing links for almost a century and a half without finding any. The missing links are a powerful argument for creation and against evolution. Because creationists believe that missing links never

existed and therefore will never be found, creationists prefer to call missing links the "absence of intermediate species."

Many creatures recorded in fossils are the same as those living on the earth today. Many fossilized leaves, for example, match present-day leaves. Fossil seashells, starfish, insects, and many vertebrates (animals with

---

FACETS OF GEOLOGY

15B-1

Fossil "Finds"

The fairy tale "The Emperor's New Clothes" has been enjoyed by generations of children. Two swindlers pretend to weave an expensive set of invisible clothes, which only the wisest men of the realm can see. For fear that he would be considered a fool, the proud emperor praises the fine new clothes—and so do all his attendants and the citizens of the land. The emperor then decides to wear the invisible robes in a grand procession. Only the puz-

zled words of a child bring the crowd to its senses: "But he has nothing on!"

The evolution myth has received almost universal applause in the modern world. Lest they appear foolish, intellectuals pretend to see something that is not there. Evolution demands "missing links," and so—voilà!—scientists find missing links. The missing links between beast and man have proved to be the most farfetched. They have turned out to be a pig's tooth (Nebraska man), human skeletons (Nean-

derthal man, Cro-Magnon man), meaningless chips of bone (Java man), or outright fabrications (Piltdown man).

Some of the latest fossil finds are more interesting. They fall under the classification of *Australopithecus* (aw STRAY loh PITH ih kus), or "southern ape." One in particular, dubbed "Lucy" by its discoverer, apparently was an ape that walked on its hind feet. We now know that a modern chimp, the rare pygmy chimpanzee, apparently can walk on its hind legs, too. Lucy may be one of these or an

backbones) also match those alive today. These counterparts show that no evolutionary change has occurred in that kind of organism between the time the fossil formed and the present. Some fossils do not have living counterparts today. Their absence among the living is due to extinction (dying out).

The occurrence of extinction alone does *not* refute creationism nor evolutionism. Extinction fits the Biblical framework of the earth's history (Chapter 13). Extinction should be expected in a degenerating world following the fall of man and the curse. Also, the Flood of

15B-9 *Fossils can be found for both living and extinct organisms. All three of these fossils can also be found as living organisms today.*

extinct species similar to it. Some evolutionists even speculate that the evidence is too skimpy to be sure that Lucy walked on its hind legs at all. The evidence, even at its best, is far from proving a missing link between ape and man.

Evolutionists are strutting about in invisible clothes. A child who believes the Word of God can see what the most brilliant minds of this day miss. Human beings—*Homo sapiens* (HOH moh • SAY pee unz)— were uniquely created by God in His image to serve Him.

Take heart from the words of the psalmist:

I have more understanding than all my teachers: for thy testimonies are my meditation. I understand more than the ancients, because I keep thy precepts. (Ps. 119:99-100)

Because that, when they knew God, they glorified him not as God, neither were thankful; but became vain in their imaginations, and their foolish heart was darkened. Professing themselves to be wise, they became fools. (Rom. 1:21-22)

Where to Look for Fossils

Some people may have the idea that finding fossils is a difficult task—even for the experts. This is true if you are looking in the wrong places. But really the only hard part about finding fossils is discovering the *right* places to dig.

One of the very best sources of fossil locations is the U.S.G.S. (United States Geological Survey). Most states have a U.S.G.S. office located in the capital city. Simply write that office requesting information about fossil locations in your area. Most likely, what they will send you, will be a list of publications. Decide what you would like to order or subscribe to and then camp by the mailbox until it arrives.

Other sources are rock and gem shops or a university that has a paleontology (PAY lee ahn TAHL uh jee) or geology department.

However, if you cannot find any information about where to find fossils in your area, a few places that might yield some fossils are: along road or railroad cuts, in quarries or mines, on the beach, and in creek or river beds.

Probably your next concern should be securing permission to dig. If the site is on private property, the county courthouse may be able to supply you with the owner's name. Usually, you need to sign an injury disclaimer before searching commercial quarries and mines.

The supplies that you need to take will depend on whether you will be "spoil-sifting" or "slab-splitting." "Spoil-sifting" is often done at mines or quarries where good fossil-bearing

sediment has been moved to huge spoil piles in order to access limestone or gravel layers. Many fossils will be on the surface; however, by sifting through the pile using a claw-shaped hand rake, you can expose many more fossils. The shark's teeth in the photograph above were collected in less than two hours by this method from a quarry in South Carolina.

"Slab-splitting" is most likely to occur at locations with shale rock. Attempt to remove as large as slab as possible. Set the slab on its side and split the rock apart along the bedding planes, using a hammer and a long, flat chisel. In order to get a perfect split, work all the way around the rock before trying to split the rock. Both the fish and the insect shown below were found by this method.

Be sure to take the time to write down as much information as possible about each find. This information will prevent your collection from becoming mere curiosities in the future.

Supply List

insect spray	**For "Spoil-Sifting"**
sunscreen	claw-like hand rake
hat and gloves	small shovel
sunglasses	small bag or
paper and pencils	carpenter's apron
fossil field book	
magnifying glass	**For "Slab-Splitting"**
brush for dusting	long-tapered flat chisel
empty boxes	assorted other chisels
maps	small sledge hammer
masonry hammer	
newspapers (for wrapping)	

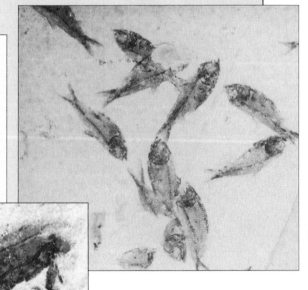

15B-10 *Fossils of extinct organisms: Apatosaurus (Brontosaurus) (above), the largest-ever land animals; claw of a giant ground sloth (far left); a crinoid (left). Some species of sloths and crinoids are alive today.*

Noah's day and climatic changes following it would certainly cause the extinction of some organisms. Part of evolutionary theory, survival of the fittest, also proposes extinction of some organisms.

The fossils that are most interesting to many people are those of the giant reptiles, the dinosaurs.* Many kinds of dinosaurs became extinct long ago, probably during or shortly after the Flood. Dinosaur fossils have been found on every continent, even Antarctica. In most places that dinosaur fossils are found, dozens of them are relatively close together. Fossils of young and old dinosaurs piled in stacks like a log jam give every evidence of having been caught in a violent disaster that deposited sediment and carcasses together in great layers. Later the sediment hardened into rock and the bones fossilized.

To trap and preserve such large creatures, the catastrophe must have been tremendous. The Biblical framework of the earth's history contained such a catastrophe, the Flood, long before these fossil beds were found. Evolutionists have had to change their theories to accommodate the evidence for a worldwide catastrophe. Popular theories suggest that a comet, a huge meteor, or an asteroid hit the earth and caused mass extinction.

Bones of people who lived thousands of years ago have been preserved in the ground. Yet no fossils of "ape-men" have been found. You may have seen artists' drawings of "cave men." The artists are relying on their imagination when they make such drawings. They have no way of telling from the bones that have been found that the faces of early men were any different from ours.

Do human bones in caves prove evolution? The Bible records people living in caves (Gen. 19:30; I Sam. 22:1). People in ancient

---

dinosaur: dino- (Gk. DEINOS, monstrous, terrible) + -saur (Gk. SAUROS, lizard)

times often buried their dead in caves (Gen. 23:17-20; John 11:38). Naturally, then, we find bones in caves. Jumping to the conclusion that bones in caves are subhuman is unscientific.

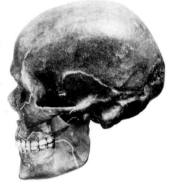

15B-11 *Cro-magnon skull—it is completely human and "modern" in every respect.*

All the fossils that supposedly prove man's animal ancestry fall into one of these four categories:

1. Completely human fossils
2. Misidentified animal fossils
3. Hoaxes
4. Not enough evidence to classify

Scientists have found no transitional fossil between ape and man. Evolutionists disagree about man's ancestry. They cannot even agree about our most recent ancestor. There are almost as many proposed family trees for man as there are scientists who study the fossils.

15B-12 *Fragments of the Piltdown skull, a deliberate hoax*

The table below shows the **geologic time scale,** the history of the earth according to evolutionists. Geologists first proposed it about 1840, when the idea that the earth is millions of years old was becoming popular. The table was not then established by reliable dating methods, nor is it today. Evolutionists usually use fossils to determine the dates. The fossils used to determine the age of rock strata are called **index fossils.** Because they believe that simple creatures evolved before complex ones, they give rocks containing simple fossils older dates than those containing more complex fossils. Furthermore, they assume that rocks containing similar fossils must have similar ages, even if these rocks are far apart.

For example, a common fossil is a trilobite (TRY luh BITE), a group of extinct animals that resembled crustaceans (kruh STAY shun). Evolutionists believe that trilobites were among the first creatures to evolve about 600 million years ago; they then became extinct about 250 million years ago. If evolutionists find a trilobite fossil in a rock, they assign the rock a date of between 250 and 600 million years, depending upon which species of trilobite was found. One problem with dating rocks by index fossils is how the fossils were dated—by the age of the rocks in which they were found! This is a classic example of circular reasoning.

15B-13 *The Nebraska man was constructed from a tooth that later was discovered to have belonged to a peccary—an extinct wild pig.*

15B-14	Evolutionists' Geologic Time Scale			
Era	**Period**	**Epoch**	**Life Form– First Appearance**	**Time (millions of years ago)**
Cenozoic	Quaternary	Recent Pleistocene	man	1
	Tertiary	Pliocene Miocene Oligocene Eocene Paleocene		70
Mesozoic ("age of reptiles")	Cretaceous Jurassic Triassic		birds, mammals dinosaurs	240
Paleozoic	Permian Carboniferous { Devonian Silurian Ordovician Cambrian	Pennsylvanian Mississippian	reptiles insects seed plants amphibians fishes land plants trilobites	600
Precambrian			one-celled organisms	

15B-15 *Shoeprint found in Cambrian shale (below); close-up of the fossil trilobite found in the heel (right)*

Most creationists believe that both the fossils and the rocks are only thousands of years old. They have documented some important finds that contradict the geologic time scale and show that its ages are greatly inflated. For example, in Utah a shoe print was found in ''Cambrian'' shale. Although trilobites supposedly became extinct hundreds of millions of years before humans existed, the shoe print has trilobite fossils in the heel and instep. Evolutionists dated the rocks in which the print was found at 550 million years. This find shows that either man is much older than evolutionists believe (a possibility that even evolutionists reject), or the geologic time scale is utterly unreliable. Thus, the position that the earth is only thousands of years old is reasonable.

In Germany, France, the British Isles, Nova Scotia, California, and several eastern states, fossils that extend through several layers of sedimentary rock have been found. These are called **polystrate*** (PAHL ee STRATE) **fossils.** They are usually tree trunks in an upright or somewhat slanted position. Polystrate fossils furnish clear-cut evidence that sediment was deposited rapidly, as in a flood. If the rock layers surrounding the fossils had formed at the slow rate that evolutionists assumed as they constructed the geologic time scale, the trees would have decayed or fallen rather than fossilized.

One type of polystrate fossil in California is especially interesting. Near Santa Barbara, fish fossils extend through several layers of algae fossils. Evolutionists calculate that each algae layer took hundreds or thousands of years to form. That would mean that the head and tail of the same fish were buried several thousands of years apart! Clearly the beds must have formed rapidly around the fish, not slowly. The most remarkable find was a polystrate whale fossil extending through many layers and many thousand years, in a uniformitarian explanation. These fossils show that strata may form rapidly.

15B-17 *Polystrate tree trunk near Essen-Kupferdreh, Germany; the overall height of the tree trunk is approximately 7.6 m.*

15B-16 *Layers can form very rapidly from water-borne volcanic debris* (right). *This canyon was formed in about a day* (far right).

---

polystrate: poly- (Gk. POLUS, many) + -strate (L. STRATUM, covering, layer)

Spirit Lake's Logs

The aftermath of the 1980 eruption of Mount St. Helens provided striking evidence of how polystrate fossils may have been deposited. Spirit Lake, which is near the base of the volcanic mountain, was heir to volcanic ash, mud flows, and debris produced by the eruption. Much of the material settled out of the water quickly, making sediment deposits up to 183 m (600 ft.) deep in some places. However, some debris, such as thousands of trunks from trees leveled by the blast, washed into the lake and remained floating on the surface.

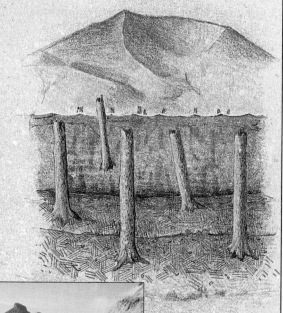

Five years after the catastrophe, some trunks were still floating, but many had become water-logged and sank to the bottom. What is peculiar about this was the way in which they sank. Many trunks which were previously floating prone on the surface had sunk to the bottom in an upright position. The root ends were down, buried in the lake bottom, while the top ends were pointing upward. The bases of some of these upright trunks had been buried in as much as 0.9 m (3 ft.) of sediment, while others appeared to have been just recently sunken.

The significance of these observations is that this could have been how polystrate fossils were deposited and rapidly buried following the Flood. Following the volcanic catastrophe, the logs which ended up in a water environment became rather quickly oriented upright on the bottom and began to be buried in that position by layers of water-borne sediment. In the years following the Flood, similar tree trunks could have been completely buried and fossilized, forming polystrate fossils.

Section Review Questions 15B-2

1. What is the name given to any trace of an organism preserved by natural means?
2. The fossils classified as *Australopithecus* and nicknamed Lucy belonged to what kind of organism?
3. Where could you go to find polystrate fossils?
4. The formation of what kind of fossils may be represented by the logs in Spirit Lake?

Fossil Fuels

Fossil fuels exist as solid, liquid, and gas. **Coal** is the solid fossil fuel. Coal is sedimentary rock which appears to have been laid down by water. However, some geologists consider it to be a metamorphic rock because heat and pressure have changed it. There are three types of coal; lignite (LIG NITE), bituminous (bih TOO muh nus), and anthracite (AN thruh SITE). Each successive type contains more carbon and energy. Coal forms from plant remains. Creationists and evolutionists disagree about how these plants came to be deposited in layers and changed to coal.

Most evolutionists believe that plant debris in swampy areas 286 million to 360 million years ago became covered with sediment whose weight, over long periods of time, caused the chemical and physical changes that converted the plant material to coal. This theory has problems. First, radiocarbon dates show that coal is only thousands of years old. Second, items made by humans have been found embedded in coal. Clearly, man lived on the earth before the coal formed. Third, large boulders have been found in coal. These indicate swift-moving currents, not flat stagnant swamps.

15B-19 *An unusual rock specimen that has both coal and petrified wood*

Most creationists believe that the coal formed as a result of the Flood. The sudden deep burial of pre-Flood plant life during the Flood could generate the heat and pressure needed to change the material to coal. Experiments have shown that little time is needed for coal to form. At high enough temperatures and pressures, coal can form in less than a day.

Oil is the liquid fossil fuel. Creationists and evolutionists agree that oil was formed from ocean-dwelling creatures such as fish and algae. When found, oil is usually associated with sedimentary rocks of marine origin. Again, evolutionists believe that oil formed over millions of years, but creationists believe that it formed quickly during the Flood.

Natural gas, the gaseous fossil fuel, is often found with oil. One theory is that gas is a by-product of the oil-formation process. Gas provides the pressure to force the oil to the surface in the "gusher" sometimes accompanying the discovery of oil. When no gas is with the oil, the oil must be pumped to the surface.

Section Review Questions 15B-3
1. List the three fossil fuels.
2. From what living material was coal formed?
3. With which category of rock is oil found?
4. What was the original source of oil?

15B-18 *The Kuwaiti oil field was set on fire as Iraq retreated at the end of the Gulf War in 1991.*

15C-Igneous Rocks

Rocks that appear to have been molten in the past are called **igneous rocks.** The word *igneous* comes from the Latin word for fire; igneous rocks are "fire rocks." **Magma** (MAG muh) is molten rock beneath the earth's surface. Magma that flows out onto the earth's surface, losing some of its dissolved gases, is **lava.**

Igneous rocks are either **extrusive,** those that solidify above the earth's surface, or **intrusive,** those that solidify beneath the earth's surface. Intrusive igneous rocks may appear at the earth's surface today because of erosion. Magma may force its way between layers of existing rock to form flat sheets called **sills,** or it may fill cracks that cut through existing layers to form **dikes.** Magma also may force the overlaying rock up into huge domes or ridges.

Magma that extrudes onto the earth's surface usually cools quickly. Because crystals have little time to form, they are either microscopic or nonexistent in extrusive igneous rock. Crystals in intrusive rocks, on the other hand, tend to be large. Slow cooling allows time for crystals to form that are large enough for us to see easily.

Intrusive Igneous Rocks

Granite is coarse-grained and is the most common intrusive igneous rock. The word **granite** means "containing grains." Quartz, feldspar, and mica crystals make up most granite. You can usually distinguish these minerals by color: mica, black; feldspar, pink; quartz, white. When granite breaks, the feldspar crystals break along cleavage planes that are smooth enough to reflect light. In contrast, the quartz crystals exhibit a rough fracture. The mica also breaks along smooth planes that reflect light. Because it withstands the forces of weathering for centuries, granite

is an excellent building material and a favorite stone for monuments. Other intrusive igneous rocks include diorite, gabbro, peridotite, and syenite. These all have coarse-grained crystals that are easy to see.

15C-1 *Stone Mountain (Georgia) is solid granite. Confederate personalities have been carved on it.*

Some intrusive igneous rocks contain crystals of different sizes—large crystals embedded in a mass of smaller crystals. Such rock probably formed in two different stages of cooling. In the first stage, the cooling was slow and large crystals formed. The magma then apparently moved to a place where it cooled more rapidly, forming the fine-grained crystals around the large crystals. Rock containing two sizes of crystals is called **porphyry** (POHR fuh ree).

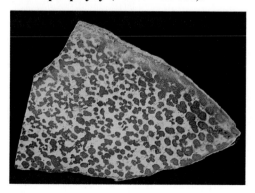

15C-2 *This specimen is called "Leopardite" because of its spots. It is a type of quartz porphory.*

Extrusive Igneous Rocks

Rocks of this group are sometimes called "lava rocks" because they solidify from molten lava. Pumice (PUM is), a porous, light-colored rock, forms from lava that is frothy with dissolved gases. It cools so rapidly that many gas bubbles are trapped inside; as a result, pumice is often light enough to float in water. Scoria (SKOHR ee uh) forms in much the same way, but from lava containing less silica. It is darker than pumice and looks like cinders. Basalt (buh SAWLT), a heavy lava rock that is abundant throughout the world, ranges in color from dark greenish gray to black. Felsite is like basalt, but lighter in color. Obsidian (ahb SID ee un), also called "natural glass," forms when lava cools rapidly. Like glass, obsidian has no crystals. It occurs in several colors, most commonly black, brown, and red, and has conchoidal fracture.

15C-3 *Obsidian, which forms from rapidly cooled lava, is an extrusive igneous rock* (far left). *This columnar basalt was found near Twin Falls, Idaho* (left). *Pumice is a very porous and light-weight rock* (below).

Section Review Questions 15C

1. What does the word *igneous* mean?
2. What is molten rock beneath the earth's surface called?
3. What should you expect to find contained in intrusive igneous rocks but not in extrusive igneous rocks?
4. What does the name *granite* mean?

15D–Metamorphic Rocks

Metamorphic rocks are those that appear to have changed since their creation or formation. *Metamorphic* means "changed in form." Metamorphic rocks were originally sedimentary or igneous rocks but were altered by the heat and pressure in the earth's crust.

Metamorphic rocks are classified as **foliated** (FOH lee ATE ud) ("with leaves") or **nonfoliated** ("without leaves"). Foliated rock contains flattened mineral crystals aligned in parallel layers, often giving a banded appearance. Often the rock breaks easily along these layers. Nonfoliated rocks are not banded or layered and tend to break into sharp, angular pieces.

15D-2 *Schist has a high mica content, making it easily split into thin sheets* (above). *This sample of gneiss has the typical banded appearance of foliated metamorphic rock* (right).

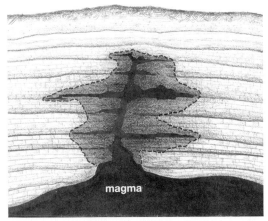

15D-1 *Pressure and heat from magma will change sedimentary rock (shaded area) to metamorphic rock.*

Foliated Metamorphic Rocks

Common foliated rocks are slate, schist (SHIST), and gneiss (NICE). Slate is metamorphosed shale. It has remarkable cleavage and easily separates into broad, thin sheets. In the past, slate was used in roofing tiles and in schoolroom blackboards. Slate comes in various colors including black, gray, purple, red, and green.

The word **schist** means "easily split." Mica schist contains quartz and mica. Using a fingernail, you can easily separate it into thin sheets of mica. Mica schist is one of several types of metamorphic rocks which can be formed from shale. Schist also forms from talc.

Gneiss is a coarsely foliated rock that is obviously banded. The bands result from light-colored minerals such as quartz and feldspar alternating with darker materials such as black mica. A wide variety of sedimentary or igneous rocks can form this metamorphic rock. Granite gneiss, diorite gneiss, and hornblende gneiss are just a few examples.

Nonfoliated Metamorphic Rocks

Common nonfoliated rocks include marble and quartzite. Marble is metamorphosed limestone composed of crystals of calcite and sometimes dolomite. In many specimens the crystals are so small they cannot be seen without a microscope, while in others they may be coarse and show calcite cleavage. Marble, like limestone, will fizz when an acid is applied to it. Pure marble is white, but impurities give it a wide range of colors such as red-brown, green, or black. Because marble takes a high polish, it is used in decorative table tops, gravestones, monuments, and buildings.

Quartzite is metamorphosed quartz sandstone. Intense heat and pressure have restructured the quartz crystals so that they interlock. Silica has filled the pores between the crystals, producing a rock so durable that it has been used to make millstones to grind grain. Quartzite may be red, white, brown, or gray and is usually the same color as the sandstone from which it formed.

Rocks not only are useful but also testify to God's power. After learning about rocks, we can understand more fully why the Lord Jesus is called "The Rock" in Scripture. The person who builds his life on Him is wise. "Therefore whosoever heareth these sayings of mine, and doeth them, I will liken him unto a wise man, which built his house upon a rock: And the rain descended, and the floods came, and the winds blew, and beat upon that house; and it fell not: for it was founded upon a rock" (Matt. 7:24-25).

15D-3 There are several common uses of marble. The term "marbling" comes from the colorful streaks of impurities in marble.

FACETS OF GEOLOGY

15D-1

Rock Hounds

Some people collect stamps; others collect coins or arrowheads. Many people collect rocks. These people are called rock hounds. Rock hounds, with hammers and collecting bags, work on almost any kind of exposed rock. After gathering specimens, they keep some and trade others. Some areas have rock and mineral clubs to make trading easier. Many rock hounds even exchange rocks with people from other states to find the best possible specimens of various rocks.

It is best to learn a little about rock collecting from experienced collectors before you begin collecting. You can join a rock and mineral club to get acquainted with people in your area who know how and where to find good specimens. Rock and mineral clubs hold regular meetings, organize field trips, and often hold exhibits that are open to the public. Some rock hounds polish, cut, and mount gemstones as well as collect rocks and minerals. If there is no such club in your area, you could learn from magazines such as *Lapidary Journal* (which lists rock and mineral clubs once a year), *Rock and Gem,* or *Rocks and Minerals.*

You can begin a rock collection fairly inexpensively. The basic tools you need are some-

thing to dig with, such as a hand shovel, and something to chip off pieces of rock, such as a mason's hammer. You also will need a box to store your specimens. Be careful that your rocks do not roll and bump against each other, since this may damage them. Also a guide book to identifying rocks and minerals may be helpful. When you find a rock, be sure to write down where you found it and later what kind of rock it is.

Eventually you may want to do something with your rocks and minerals other than just making a collection. Cutting, polishing, and mounting your stones require more expensive equipment but can be quite rewarding. You may want to

Specimens collected by a rockhound: copper ore, petrified wood, chrysoprase, agate (top to bottom).

show your finds at a show, trade for other rocks, or even sell them to a rock shop. Rock hounding can be a rewarding and enjoyable hobby.

Section Review Questions 15D
1. What does the word *metamorphic* mean?
2. What forces formed metamorphic rocks?
3. What is metamorphosed sandstone called?
4. What category of rock was marble before it was metamorphosed?
5. What do rock hounds do?

Terms

breccia	granite	oil
chemical sedimentary rock	igneous rock	permeable
coal	impermeable	polystrate fossil
conglomerate	index fossil	porphyry
dike	intrusive igneous rock	rock
extrusive igneous rock	lava	salt dome
foliated metamorphic rock	magma	schist
fossil	matrix	sedimentary rock
fossil fuel	metamorphic rock	sill
fragmental sedimentary rock	natural gas	strata
geologic time scale	nonfoliated metamorphic rock	

What Did You Learn?
1. Describe the main differences between sedimentary, igneous, and metamorphic rocks.
2. Describe how the small grains of sedimentary rocks are held together.
3. What are index fossils?
4. What are polystrate fossils?
5. What is particularly interesting about a fossilized shoe print which contains trilobites?
6. Give some reasons that the Flood model of coal formation is superior to the swamp model.
7. Which type of coal is the best energy source? What substance in coal determines the amount of energy that coal possesses?
8. Where could you go to collect *new* igneous rocks?
9. Why could coal be considered a metamorphic rock?

What Do You Think?
1. Other than body parts, what "traces" of organisms could be fossils?
2. How do you think polystrate fossils formed?
3. Why do you think dinosaur fossils are found in Antarctica?
4. What are some uses of sedimentary rocks, igneous rocks, and metamorphic rocks?

MOUNTAINS AND HIGH HILLS

SIXTEEN

16A–Describing Mountains

You have probably heard the saying "Don't make a mountain out of a molehill" with the intended meaning of "don't make a big problem out of a small problem." The difference between the two seems obvious, but can you accurately describe the difference? Your explanation would probably include your perspective of height.

What Is a Mountain?

We can define a mountain as "a natural elevation of the earth's surface rising more or less abruptly to a summit." This definition applies equally well to a hill. The difference between mountains and hills is mostly in height. What height distinguishes mountains from hills? There is no standard. Usually we think of mountains as landforms with heights of thousands of meters. Yet, in flat terrain even a small rise of land is considered a mountain. A mountain in New Jersey may be a mere foothill in Colorado. The Watchung (WAH chung) Mountains near New York City, for example, are a series of ridges only 90 to 120 m (300 to 400 ft.) high. Since the distinction between a mountain and a hill is strictly local, we must go along with whatever custom has been established in an area.

An important characteristic of a mountain is its height. Where do we begin to measure height? For example, the highest mountain on earth is Mount Everest, at 8,848 m (29,028 ft.). Is that 8,848 m above its base, or above the lowest land on the earth, or above sea level, or above the lowest point under the sea? The height of Mount Everest, and that of other mountains, is usually given in meters or feet above sea level. This measurement is also called the mountain's **elevation.**

Although Mount Everest has the highest elevation on earth, it does not look especially impressive. The mountains around it are nearly as high, and its base is about 5,200 m (17,000 ft.) above sea level. Thus the height of Everest's peak above its base, its **actual height,** is only about 3,600 m (12,000 ft.). The actual height of a mountain is the height of its summit above the surrounding territory. Other mountains have greater actual heights. Mauna Kea (MOW nuh • KAY uh), in Hawaii, has the greatest actual height of any mountain on earth: over 10,000 m (33,000 ft.), nearly three times that of Everest. Mauna Kea's elevation, however, is only 4,200 m (14,000 ft.), less than half Everest's; most of Mauna Kea's height is below the sea.

Other noteworthy mountains are Mount McKinley in Alaska (the highest mountain in North America at 6,193 m [20,320 ft.]), Mount Whitney in California (the highest mountain in the forty-eight adjoining states at 4,418 m [14,494 ft.]), and Mount Mitchell

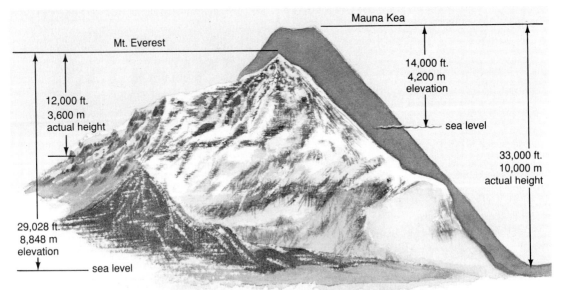

16A-1 *Elevation is measured from sea level while actual height is measured from the base of the mountain. Mauna Kea has a greater actual height than Mt. Everest.*

16A-2 *Mount McKinley, Alaska, is the highest peak in North America.*

in North Carolina (the highest mountain in the eastern United States at 2,037 m [6,684 ft.]).

A measure of elevation differences in a region is **relief,** the difference in height between the region's highest and lowest points. For example, the highest mountain in California, Mount Whitney, is 4,418 m (14,494 ft.) above sea level; the lowest valley, Death Valley, is 86 m (282 ft.) *below* sea level. The relief of the state of California is thus about 4,504 m (14,777 ft.). Mountainous areas have high relief, but plains and plateaus have low relief.

Groups of Mountains

Mountains exist either singly or in groups. A series of mountain peaks is called a **mountain range.** A group of mountain ranges is a **mountain system.** The highest mountain system is the Himalaya-Karakoram, which includes 96 of the 109 peaks of the world that are higher than 7,300 m (24,000 ft.). The most extensive mountain system lies under the Atlantic Ocean. The Mid-Atlantic Ridge

Relief Maps

A map that shows altitude either by a three-dimensional model or by color, shading, or some other device is a **relief map.** One type of relief map uses **contour lines,** lines joining points of equal elevation. The elevation of each line is labeled. Near a mountain the contour lines form closed curves that enclose successively smaller areas toward the summit. Closely spaced contour lines show a steep slope, while widely spaced lines show a gentle slope.

FACETS OF GEOLOGY

Mountaineering

Over sixty people have died attempting to reach the summit of Mount Everest, the highest mountain in the world. The first eight teams to try failed to climb its northern slope. Finally, a British team headed by Edmund Hillary, a beekeeper from New Zealand, and his guide reached the "roof of the world" on May 29, 1953. They chose a route from the south.

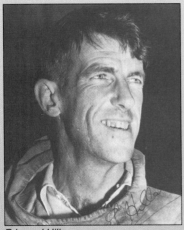

Edmund Hillary

Since then almost two hundred people have reached the summit. The first American team reached it in 1963. Once the peak was scaled, the challenge became to find new, "impossible" routes. For instance, in 1971 an international team scaled the harsh southwest face of Everest, which had previously been assumed unclimbable.

Mountain climbing is an elite sport. There are no more than half a million true mountaineers. Yet their ranks are worldwide, for mountains occur on every continent. Mountaineers usually acquire their interest while hiking on the hills and mountains near their home. Few thrills compare to the sensation of climbing the rocky heights above the timber line. Popular hiking trails crisscross the mountain ranges of the United States. Hiking, an enjoyable sport in itself, is an integral part of all advanced mountain climbing. Even the ascent of Mount Everest begins with long walks at the mountain's base, which take up the greater part of the climb.

A few hundred years ago mountaineering was not a serious sport. In early times people revered the mountains as the home of the gods. (In fact, the climbers of the world's third highest mountain, Kanchenjunga (KUN chun JUNG guh), were not allowed to climb the actual summit because the Sikkimese (SIK uh MEEZ) government considers it sacred.) Moses received the law on top of Mount Sinai, and Jesus was transfigured on top of Mount Hermon. Generals and pioneers explored the mountains to find passes to the lands on the other side.

Rappelling down a mountain

Hannibal's attempt to cross the Alps with a herd of elephants and invade Rome is one of the most famous early attempts at mountain climbing.

Mountaineering became a serious sport about one hundred fifty years ago. Eighteenth-century scientists aroused a new scientific interest in the mountains. European scientists first turned their attention to the Alps on the border of Italy and Switzerland. In rapid succession, skilled mountaineers conquered the high peaks of this range. Mountaineers then looked abroad for new challenges, the last of which was the forbidding Himalayas in Asia. Here on "the roof of the world" were the highest peaks, including the grandfather of them all, Mount Everest.

Why do these sportsmen risk their lives to climb mountains? "Because they are there" is the traditional response. Mountaineering is one of the most demanding sports of all. The mountain is fraught with risks that test the mountaineer's courage, skill, resourcefulness, strength, and stamina. The mountaineer has the pleasure of overcoming some of nature's greatest obstacles and witnessing scenery beheld by few people.

Above all, mountain climbing is a team sport in which leadership is one of the most prized abilities. Only the most experienced climbers take the lead and draw up the rear. The leader must think ahead to find the easiest route, and he must take into account the ever-changing weather conditions. The lead man presses forward, and then the rest of the team, one at a time, catches up with him.

Mountaineers require years to become skillful with their equipment. Each surface—rocks, snow, and ice—demands different skills. The most important "equipment" is the body. The climber always tries to keep three parts of his body in contact with the climbing surface at all times, usually his feet and hands. He almost never jumps. He relies on his legs to push himself upward. His hands are mainly for balance, except when climbing major overhangs. The pitons and ropes are primarily safeguards in case of a fall, not for climbing.

Climbing down a mountain is actually more difficult than climbing up because the mountaineer is blind to the handholds beneath him. However, his descent is much easier if he has ropes. He can then *rappel* (ra PEL). In rappelling, he lets both ends of his rope hang from a piton that is driven into the rock. He then slides down the rope. He retrieves the rope simply by pulling it through the piton. An expert climber has a steady rhythm as he climbs and descends the mountain, inch after inch. An expert in action is an impressive sight.

The United States has many popular mountain ranges. In the winter a short mountain can offer the same challenges as a high one. Major U.S. clubs include the American Alpine Club, the Appalachian Mountain Club, the Colorado Mountain Club, and the Sierra Club.

Mountain climbing is rarely dangerous if you know what you are doing. More deaths occur on hills than on high mountaintops, because the greatest danger is foolhardiness and inexperience. A professional has learned the virtue of patience. The safety of the group is far more important than the success of the climb. The leader must avoid the "point of no return," when supplies are too short, the weather is too bad, or the team is too fatigued. It is not enough to know whether you can make it to the top; you must provide for the descent as well.

Common dangers:
- mountain sickness (caused by little oxygen in the thin air)
- fatigue
- frozen extremities
- bad weather
- avalanche
- falling rocks and ice
- deep crevasses hidden by snow
- fragile snow shelves
- short supplies
- broken equipment

Basic equipment:
- boots
- rope
- pitons (spikes with an eye hole, driven into rock)
- carabiner (ring that clips to the piton and holds the rope)
- crampons (spikes that attach to boots for gripping ice)
- ice ax (for balance, probing, and cutting footholds in ice)

extends for 16,000 km (10,000 mi.) down the middle of the ocean. A few of its peaks are high enough to appear above the surface of the water; the highest of these is Pico (PEE koh) Mountain in the Azores (AY zohrz). Its elevation is 2,351 m (7,713 ft.).

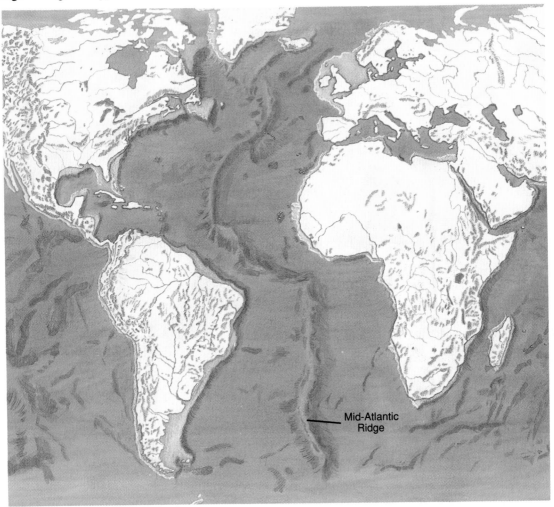

16A-3 *The longest mountain system in the world is the Mid-Atlantic Ridge, which extends almost from pole to pole.*

Section Review Questions 16A

1. What is the difference between a mountain and a hill?
2. What is the altitude of a mountain's summit above sea level called?
3. What is the name of the world's highest mountain? How high is it?
4. What is the highest mountain in North America? Where is it? How high is it?
5. Where is the most extensive mountain system in the world located?
6. What is a map that shows altitude called?

16B–Types of Mountains

Mountains come in many forms. Some are high; others are low. Some are steep; others have gentle slopes. Some are volcanoes; others contain mostly sedimentary rocks. Some have layers that are crumpled; others have flat layers. Geologists have divided mountains into groups based on how they think the mountains formed.

Mountains in the Bible

The Bible refers to mountains more than three hundred times. Noah's ark rested on Mount Ararat. Moses received the Law on Mount Sinai. Abraham offered his son Isaac on Mount Moriah. Elijah retreated to Mount Horeb after a great victory over the prophets of Baal on Mount Carmel. The city of Jerusalem stretches across several mountaintops; its average elevation is 760 m (2,500 ft.) above sea level. Jesus often spoke from a mountainside, as in the Sermon on the Mount. On one occasion the Lord allowed Peter, James, and John to catch a glimpse of His glory on the Mount of Transfiguration. Later, after His resurrection, He left this earth from the Mount of Olives, with a promise that He shall someday return to that mountain when He begins His reign on earth.

Depositional Mountains

Depositional mountains† form by accumulation of rocks on the earth's surface. These materials may be volcanic or carried by wind or glaciers.

Volcanoes accumulate rock by pushing materials out of a central vent. They can form quickly, like Parícutin (puh REE kuh TEEN), which erupted in a farmer's field in Mexico and within a year accumulated a cinder cone over 430 m (1,400 ft.) above the surrounding area. They also can change or destroy themselves quickly. When Mount Ararat in Turkey exploded in 1840, it blew out a large gorge on its northeastern side. The volcano on the island of Krakatoa (KRAH kuh TOH uh) in Indonesia destroyed two-thirds of the island when it erupted in 1883. Molten rock from underground sometimes replaces that which is blown away, but generally the structure of the mountain is considerably different after an explosive eruption.

Sand dunes are wind-deposited hills of sand. Although we tend to think of sand dunes as insignificant hills, those in the Sahara Desert in Algeria may be as high as 430 m (1,400 ft.) and may cover several square kilometers.

16B-1 *Mount Fuji in Japan is a depositional mountain formed from volcanic matter.*

16B-2 *Wind sculptured dunes at Great Sand Dunes National Monument in Colorado rise to 600 feet.*

† These depositional mountains are discussed in more detail in Chapters 17, 18, and 20.

16B-3 *A terminal moraine is a ridge of rock debris that a glacier piled up at its front.*

Glaciers deposit two types of hills: **terminal moraines** (muh RAYN) and **drumlins** (DRUM lin). A terminal moraine is a ridge of rock debris that a glacier pushed at its front. When the glacier melted back, it left the debris at its farthest advance. For the huge continental glaciers, the terminal moraines may be over a hundred meters high and hundreds of kilometers long. Good examples of terminal moraines include the Harbor Hill Moraine and the Ronkonkoma (rahng KAHNG kuh muh) Moraine, which extend the entire length of Long Island.

Drumlins are smooth elliptical hills, 6 to 60 m (20 to 200 ft.) in height and 0.5 to 1 km (0.3 to 0.6 mi.) long, that glaciers deposit as they move along or retreat. They usually occur in groups rather than singly, all parallel

16B-4 *Aerial view of a small drumlin near Sodus, New York.*

to the direction that the glacier traveled. In the United States, drumlins occur from New England to Minnesota, with an unusually high concentration in New York. Bunker Hill of Revolutionary War fame is a drumlin.

Erosional Mountains

Erosional mountains, or **residual mountains,** are mountains that were carved out by extensive erosion, usually from a plateau. A **plateau** (pla TOH) is a region of flat rock structure having a high elevation. Plateaus often consist of sedimentary rock.

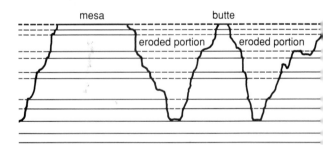

16B-5 *Drawing showing how a plateau becomes dissected to form erosional mountains*

As erosion dissects (cuts apart) a plateau, some parts of it remain intact. These parts apparently contain minerals that strengthen them. Broad, flat-topped hills remaining from the dissection process are called **mesas** (MAY suh); narrow, flat-topped hills are **buttes** (BYOOT). Both mesas and buttes have

16B-6 *Erosional mountains: Monument Valley, Arizona* (top left) *and Fossil Butte National Park, Wyoming* (left). *Severe weathering often leaves just tall spires call pinnacles* (above).

gorges and dissected plateaus to form erosional mountains, riverbeds, and canyons. Shortly after the Flood, the natural cements solidified and the soft material became rock.

Fold Mountains

Rocks can fold or bend if a force is applied to them continuously over a long time. Limestone benches in old gardens, for example, have sagged under the influence of gravity after two or three centuries. This shows how even a weak force can have an effect if applied persistently. Under laboratory conditions, scientists have applied much greater forces to rocks so that they bend much more. As long as the force builds gradually rather than suddenly, the rock usually bends rather than breaks.

Most major mountain ranges contain some folded rocks. The Rockies, the Alps, and the Himalayas all show evidence of folding. In some mountains the folding of the rocks seems to have formed the mountains; these are **fold mountains.** Other mountains contain evidence of other processes working with folding.

steep walls. The Catskills of southeastern New York and the mountains of the Allegheny Plateau of West Virginia are erosional. Sometimes only one area of the higher ground survives to form a single mountain. A **monadnock** (muh NAD NAHK) is an isolated mountain that was resistant to erosion while the area around it was eroded to a flat plain. Mount Monadnock in New Hampshire and Stone Mountain in Georgia are monadnocks.

Places where the Flood deposited extensive sedimentary strata probably experienced much erosion near the end of the Flood and shortly after it. These sedimentary rocks had not yet hardened fully, so the water running off them could easily erode them. There was no shortage of water. It had covered the tops of the mountains and now had to "return from off the earth." Thus, the water cut deep

Because water has deposited most sedimentary rocks, we know that they generally begin as horizontal strata. Where we find slanted or upturned strata, forces under the ground have usually been at work to tilt or bend the rock. These forces may be vertical or horizontal. In some places the bending seems to have happened while the rock was still soft. The concept of rapidly deposited flood strata held by creationists better explains this appearance than do the gradual processes envisioned by uniformitarian geologists.

16B-7 *This folded limestone near Kingston, Tennessee, is an example of an anticline.*

Different types of folds appear above the earth's surface. Erosion has exposed some of them; others are discovered during mining operations, road cuts, and other excavations. Several folds are caused by horizontal forces. Perhaps the simplest is the **monocline*** (MAHN uh KLINE), a double bend that joins strata at two different levels. A monocline resembles a step. An **anticline*** (AN tih KLINE) is an arch of rock layers. A **syncline*** (SIN KLINE) is a trough or downward fold of rock strata. These folds form when horizontal forces press in on the sides of the rocks. Vertical forces form the **dome** and the **basin.** An upward force causes the rocks to curve upward into a dome. A downward force, probably gravity, causes the bowl-shaped basin. These folds have roughly equal length and width.

What forces cause the folds? Can gravity explain them? For basins, the answer is yes. Gravity is a steady downward force like that needed to form basins. However, gravity cannot explain how fold mountains form; their formation requires horizontal or upward forces. How then do fold mountains form? Geologists have suggested some interesting answers to that question.

One popular explanation of fold mountains is the **geosyncline theory.** According to this theory, an elongated syncline, called a **geosyncline,** fills with sediment over thousands or millions of years. As more sediment accumulates, the geosyncline sinks deeper and folds the sediments within it. Finally the geosyncline and its contents are uplifted to form mountains. This theory alone cannot explain how fold mountains came into being. It gives no explanation for the horizontal force that formed the geosyncline. It fails to explain where the sediment to fill the huge trench comes from, why the geosyncline sinks, and what force raises the structure to become a mountain range.

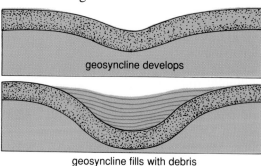

geosyncline develops

geosyncline fills with debris

uplifting forms mountain

16B-8 *Geosyncline theory: one of many unsuccessful attempts to explain how mountain ranges formed.*

monocline: mono- (Gk. MONOS, single, alone) + -cline (Gk. KLINEIN, to lean)

anticline: anti- (Gk. ANTI-, against, opposite) + -cline (to lean)

syncline: syn- (together, same) + -cline (to lean)

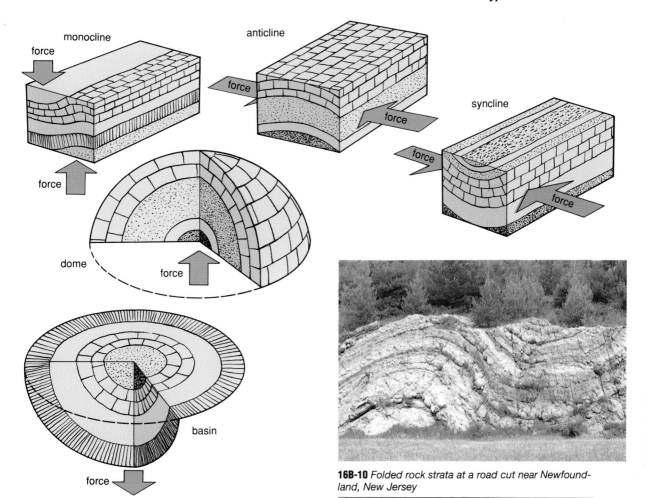

16B-9 *Five major types of folds are diagramed above. Arrows show forces that appear to cause the folds.*

16B-10 *Folded rock strata at a road cut near Newfoundland, New Jersey*

Modern geologists combine the geosyncline theory with the plate tectonics (tek TAHN iks) theory. In this version, the geosyncline is a trench where the edge of one **tectonic plate** (large broken section of the earth's crust) moves under another plate. Sediments are especially plentiful where the plates grind against each other. As the plates move together, the trench becomes deeper, and the sediment strata fold. Eventually, the plates squeeze the sediments up between them to form a mountain range. Thus a fold

mountain range is a wrinkle caused by two colliding plates. This theory has more merit than the unaided geosyncline theory. It provides the necessary forces and material, and it need not take millions of years if the plates move fast enough. Some creationists believe that the plate tectonics view is correct, that the earth's crust broke into sections when "the fountains of the great deep [were] broken up" (Gen. 7:11) during the Flood. This theory may be correct; however, our present understanding of Scripture and science leaves room for more thought and research on this subject.

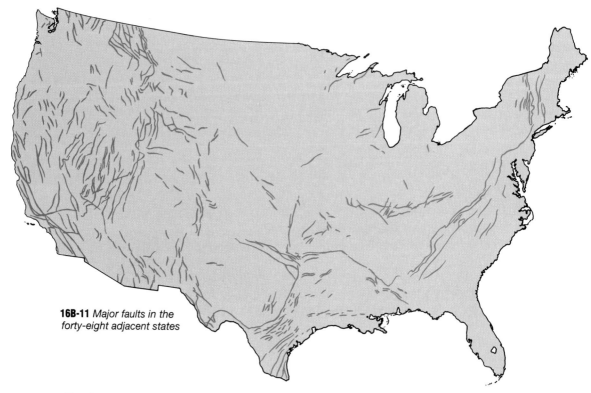

16B-11 *Major faults in the forty-eight adjacent states*

Fault-Block Mountains

A **joint** is a large crack in a rock along which no movement (slippage) has occurred. A crack along which there has been slippage is a **fault.** A fault is caused by a force applied against a rock that cannot relieve the stress by bending; thus it cracks and moves in order to relieve that stress.

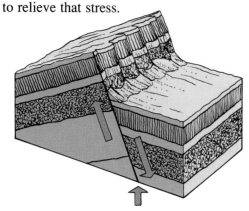

16B-12 *Fault-block mountains are bounded by at least one fault. A land mass on one side of the fault rises above the other (left). Whether they were created this way or whether this was part of the upheaval produced by the Flood is up for speculation. It is by no means necessary to believe that the process took millions of years. The Sierra Nevada mountain range (above) is made of fault-block mountains.*

Faulting plays an important role in the **fault-block mountain,** a mountain bounded by one or more faults. The Sierra Nevada range in California is a classic example of this type. It shows a normal fault in which the surface on one side of the fault has risen above the level of the surrounding country. This raised block of material is enormous, measuring about 120 km (75 mi.) from west to east and about 640 km (400 mi.) from north to south. The eastern end has been pushed upward about 3 km (2 mi.). Various forces have acted to cut the block into separate mountains having gentle western slopes and steep cliffs on the east. California's highest peak, Mount Whitney, is part of this range.

16B-13	Notable Mountains			
Mountain	**Location**	**Height (m)**	**Year Climbed**	**Notes of Interest**
Mt. Everest	Nepal/Tibet	8,848	1953	highest mountain in the world
Aconcagua	Argentina	6,960	1897	tallest mountain in the Western Hemisphere
Huasccarán	Peru	6,768	1908	first ascended by a woman
Mt. McKinley	Alaska	6,194	1913	tallest mountain in North America
Cotopaxi	Ecuador	5,897	1872	highest active volcano
Kilimanjaro	Tanzania	5,895	1889	highest mountain in Africa
Ararat	Turkey	5,165	1829	first major modern climb; site of Noah's ark
Mount Blanc	France/Italy	4,807	1786	first peak to attract mountaineers; highest peak in the Alps
Matterhorn	Switzerland/Italy	4,478	1865	major climb of its sheer cliffs ended the golden age of mountaineering in the Alps
Mt. Whitney	California	4,418	1875	highest mountain in California
Mt. Rainier	Washington	4,392	1870	highest mountain in Washington
Mt. Shasta	California	4,317	1854	famous twin peaks
Pikes Peak	Colorado	4,301	1819	famous landmark in the Rocky mountains for pioneers
Mauna Kea	Hawaii	4,205	early	tallest mountain island in the world
Fuji	Japan	3,776	early	highest mountain in Japan; considered sacred
Olympus	Greece	2,917	early	highest mountain in Greece; legendary home of the Greek gods
Sinai	Sinai Peninsula	2,285	early	Moses received the Law on its peak
Mt. Kosciusko	Australia	2,228	early	highest mountain in Australia

FACETS OF GEOLOGY

16B-1

The Overthrust Controversy

Mountains often form battlegrounds between creationists and evolutionists, since fossils are most easily found on mountain cliffs and rocky slopes. You probably know that evolutionists claim that fossils are one of the best proofs of their theory. Evolutionists say that the fossils in bottom strata obviously formed first and that the fossil record shows that animals and plants became more complex through time. In some places, however, the fossils are in the wrong order—the more complex fossils are on the bottom, and the simpler fossils are on the top. How do evolutionists explain these fossils?

The main assumption of rock dating in evolutionary circles is that more complex fossils are younger than simple fossils. Thus, any layer of rock that contains complex fossils, such as mammals, must be younger than a layer of rock containing simpler fossils, such as trilobites. Regardless of the arrangement of the rocks, the complex fossils are younger. Thus,

where rocks containing simple fossils appear above rocks containing more complex fossils, the upper rocks are older. Evolutionists say that the older rocks somehow moved above the younger rocks.

How can old rocks appear on top of young rocks? The evolutionists' answer is an **overthrust.** This begins with a reverse fault with a slant of less than 45° (called a **thrust fault**).

When the fault is active, rocks on the upper side of the fault are pushed over the rocks on the lower side of the fault. Then the upper layers of the overthrusted rock erode, leaving only the older rocks in the lower part of the overthrusted rock exposed.

Overthrusting has been observed on a small scale, so at first the theory seems reasonable. However, the scale required

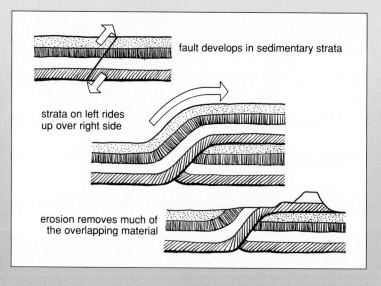

fault develops in sedimentary strata

strata on left rides up over right side

erosion removes much of the overlapping material

16B-14 *This range of mountains near Death Valley, California, is a range of fault-block mountains.*

The Great Basin and Range Province of Nevada and Utah has many fault-block mountains. In this region a complex system of faults has cut the earth's crust into thousands of blocks, forming many basins and ranges. The Wasatch (WAW SACH) Range that borders the Colorado Plateau is well known in this area.

Chief Mountain in Montana, an example of an alleged overthrust

Several other large fossil areas show more simple fossils on top of more complex fossils. The Swiss Alps show a "reversed" sequence of three layers. To account for this order, evolutionists postulate two overthrusts. But no overthrust on this scale is believable. The only alternative is that the rocks were formed in the order that they appear. Most creationists believe that the Flood formed most sedimentary rocks and fossils. The waters of the Flood would have sifted out the dead organisms so that similarly sized organisms would be found together. Thus, all the layers of fossils are about the same age and cannot show evolution.

to explain several "reversed" fossil layers is not small. For example, Chief Mountain in Glacier National Park shows a "reversal." Evolutionary geologists teach that a block of sedimentary rock 25 to 50 km (15 to 30 mi.) wide, 560 km (350 mi.) long, and 3,000 m (10,000 ft.) thick slid over the surface of the ground for about 55 km (35 mi.)! Even if such an immense force were available to move these trillions of tons of rock, the rock would likely shatter long before it had traveled the required distance.

Furthermore, the rocks at Chief Mountain show no signs of motion. The boundary between the "younger" rock and the "older" rock has no rock fragments or powder or grooves that would occur if rock surfaces scraped against each other. In fact, the boundary consists of several layers of "older" rock interspersed with "younger" rock. One mass of rock sliding over another does not produce interleaved layers.

Permian ("oldest")

Jurassic

Tertiary ("youngest")

Two "miraculous," separate overthrusts are suggested to explain this order of strata in the Swiss Alps.

Not all the mountains in the world formed naturally; God created some on the earth. Genesis 7:19 tells about the Flood's great depth: "And the waters prevailed exceedingly upon the earth; and all the high hills [or mountains], that were under the whole heaven, were covered." Many creationists believe that the pre-Flood mountains were lower than the present mountains. The Flood may have begun the processes that formed the highest of our mountains. To discover the truth of the matter, we need Christians who have scientific ability, yet respect the authority of the Word of God. Only when our theories agree with the Bible do we approach the truth of God's creation.

Section Review Questions 16B

1. What are mountains that formed by accumulation of rock called?
2. What type of mountain is Mount Ararat?
3. Name two types of hills deposited by glaciers.
4. Which is larger—a mesa or a butte?
5. Name three types of rock folds.
6. What are the large, broken sections of the earth's crust called?
7. What is a mountain consisting of a raised block of material bounded by one or more faults called?
8. List the four classifications of mountains.

Terms

actual height
anticline
basin
butte
contour lines
depositional mountain
dome
drumlin
elevation
erosional mountain
  (residual mountain)

fault
fault-block mountain
fold mountain
geosyncline
geosyncline theory
joint
mesa
monadnock
monocline
mountain range
mountain system

overthrust
plateau
relief
relief map
sand dune
syncline
tectonic plate
terminal moraine
thrust fault

What Did You Learn?

1. Who was the first to reach the top of Mount Everest? When was this accomplished?
2. The summit of a certain mountain is 3,048 m (10,000 ft.) above sea level. Its actual height is 2,194 m (7,200 ft.). How high is its base above sea level?
3. The highest point in a certain county is 688 m (2,257 ft.) above sea level. The lowest point is 252 m (827 ft.) above sea level. Find the relief of the county.
4. Why does Mount Everest not look as impressive as some lesser mountains?
5. What is the highest mountain in the eastern United States and where is it located?

What Do You Think?

1. Do valleys cause mountains, or are valleys a result of mountains?
2. How would you determine the elevation of an underwater mountain?
3. Why do you think drumlins occur in groups?
4. How did glaciers play a role in the American Revolutionary War?
5. In what ways can mountains be used that flat lands cannot (or not very well)?

EARTHQUAKES AND VOLCANOES

SEVENTEEN

17A-Earthquakes

Earthquakes and volcanism are geological events that occur mostly in the same regions, and both are currently thought to be related to plate tectonics. Both types of events speak of the instability of the earth's structure. People like to think of the earth they stand on as secure and solid. Those who have experienced a severe earthquake or have been near an erupting volcano may have second thoughts about the earth's firmness.

The **plate tectonics theory** states that the earth's crust is made of several large, flat pieces called plates. Most plates are about the size of a continent. The plates move slowly, some carrying the continents with them. The plates collide at their margins, and the edge of one grinds past or slides under the other. The shock waves caused by sections of the plates colliding are **earthquakes.** Fold and fault-block mountains are, in theory, a result of colliding plates (Chapter 16), and a large portion of the earth's volcanoes are found along the margins of the plates as well.

17A-1 *Map showing the major volcano and earthquake belts of the world. Tectonic plates are also drawn in. Larger dots represent epicenters, red peaks indicate volcanoes, and plates are outlined in black.*

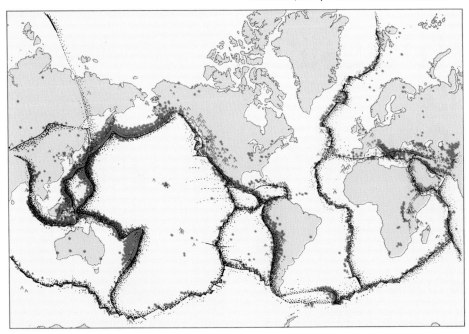

What Is an Earthquake?

An earthquake consists of a series of shock waves traveling through the earth. Some of these waves travel along the surface, and others through the interior of the earth. Most earthquakes are too slight for a person to feel. Still, a few earthquakes each year shake the ground enough to frighten people near them, and occasionally a strong earthquake near a city causes great destruction.

Scientists who study earthquakes, **seismologists*** (size MAHL uh jist), use special instruments to detect and measure earthquake waves. These instruments are called **seismographs.** They usually consist of a large mass attached to a support by a flexible rod. A light attached to the mass traces a line on a rotating drum covered by photographic pa-per. If the earth moves, the drum and support move but the mass does not. The line on the paper thus becomes zigzagged instead of straight. The height of the "zigs" or "zags" shows the strength of the earthquake waves.

Scientists rate an earthquake by the **Richter** (RIK tur) **scale.** This scale is named for Charles F. Richter (1900–1985), an American seismologist who first proposed the system in 1935. The scale is based on the distance that an earthquake displaces a standard seismograph trace. It shows the energy, or **magnitude,** of the earthquake. The Richter scale is not a linear scale; that is, an earthquake of magnitude 4 does not have twice the energy of an earthquake of magnitude 2. Instead, each change of one on the scale multiplies the energy by about 31.6. Thus an

seismologist: seismo- (Gk. SEISMOS, earthquake) + -logist (Gk. LOGISTES, one who calculates)

earthquake of magnitude 3 has 31.6 times as much energy as a magnitude 2 earthquake. An earthquake of magnitude 4 has 31.6 times as much energy as a magnitude 3 earthquake and 31.6 × 31.6, or almost 1,000, times as much energy as a magnitude 2 earthquake.

The Richter scale covers a wide range of earthquakes. An earthquake with magnitude just over 0 barely registers on a sensitive seismograph. People can feel quakes with a rating of 3 or more. A magnitude of 6 or more is potentially destructive; a quake whose magnitude is more than 7 is a "major earthquake." A "great earthquake" has a magnitude of 7.7 or more. The Richter scale is not a 1 to 10

scale but is open-ended. The most destructive quakes usually have had magnitudes between 8 and 9. Calculations show that if an earthquake with a magnitude of 10 occurred anywhere on the earth, people everywhere would feel the shaking.

An earthquake's destructiveness depends not only on its energy but also on its duration and its location. Duration can make a great difference in damage. Some buildings can withstand a few seconds of violent shaking but fall apart after a minute or two. Earthquakes can last anywhere from a few seconds to several minutes, but most earthquakes last less than a minute.

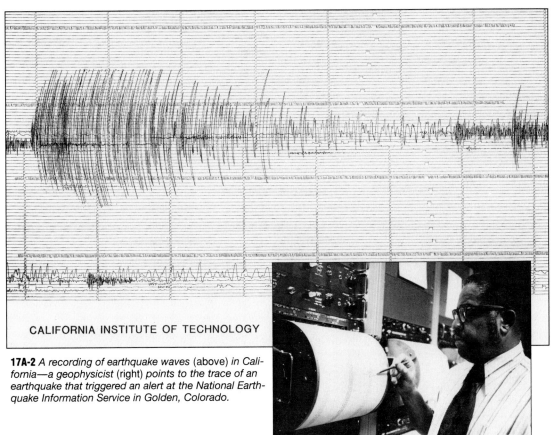

CALIFORNIA INSTITUTE OF TECHNOLOGY

17A-2 *A recording of earthquake waves* (above) *in California—a geophysicist* (right) *points to the trace of an earthquake that triggered an alert at the National Earthquake Information Service in Golden, Colorado.*

17A-3			Notable Earthquakes
Year	Location	Deaths	Interesting Facts
526	Turkey	250,000	destroyed Antioch
856	Greece	45,000	destroyed Corinth
1268	Asia Minor	60,000	shook the province of Silicia
1556	China	830,000	deadliest earthquake in history
1694	Jamaica	1,600	most of Port Royal vanished beneath the sea
1737	India	300,000	devastated Calcutta
1755	Portugal	60,000	destroyed Lisbon; $\frac{1}{4}$ of the city's population died; almost 9.0 magnitude, felt throughout Europe, first systematic scientific study of an earthquake
1783	Sicily/Italy	60-100,000	series of six quakes hit a wide area
1797	Peru/Ecuador	41,000	devastated Cuzco and Quito
1811-12	U.S.	(not reported)	series of earthquakes; hit a sparsely populated area of Missouri; no surface evidence of faults; shook more than $\frac{2}{3}$ of the country
1906	U.S.	503	San Francisco; broken gas and water lines hindered efforts to put out fires; 500 blocks leveled; $350 million in damage
1908	Sicily/Italy	160,000	no foreshocks; worst of many earthquakes in this area; hundreds of convicts escaped jail and terrorized Messina
1920	China	180,000	destroyed 10 cities
1923	Japan	142,802	destroyed $\frac{3}{4}$ of Tokyo; fires and broken gas lines ignited wood-and-paper homes; oil tanks spilled into the harbor, causing an inferno; a rare "fire" tornado, created by rising hot air, swept through the city
1939	Turkey	30,000-45,000	followed by floods and blizzards
1946	Japan	1,088	6 tsunamis; damaged 155,000 sq. km
1960	Morocco	12,000	2 earthquakes, tsunami, and fire; main quake was 15 seconds long
1964	U.S.	131	over $450 million damage to Alaska; deadly tsunami hit at 800 km/hr; world's record for vertical upheaval (15m)
1965	Japan	none	swarm of over 565,000 earthquakes over a 4-month period; caused by movement in a nearby "dormant" volcano
1970	Peru	66,794	most destructive earthquake in the western hemisphere; 800,000+ homeless; a lake high in the mountains burst, washing away 2 towns
1971	U.S.	65	Los Angeles; estimated $1 billion damage
1976	China	242,000	most deadly earthquake in modern times; ruined a city of 1 million
1977	Romania	1,541	strongest quake in Europe in 20th cent.; hit Bucharest; $1 billion damage
1985	Mexico	4,200	hit a large region, including Mexico City
1988	USSR (Armenia)	55,000	extensive damage to shoddy buildings; controversy over USSR's meager aid follcwed the quake
1989	U.S.	64	hit San Francisco during the World Series; $7 billion damage
1991	USSR (Georgia)	80	hit very close to 1988 Armenian earthquake

17A-4 *Earthquake damage in Charleston, S.C., in 1886* (above) *and in San Francisco in 1906* (right)

The location of an earthquake is an important factor in how much damage it causes. The center of an earthquake's activity is called its **focus.** This is usually several miles underground, and it may be as much as 720 km (450 mi.) below the earth's surface. The place on the earth's surface that is directly above the focus is called the **epicenter*** (EP ih SEN tur). Although an earthquake is most severe at its epicenter, a strong earthquake may cause damage hundreds of miles from its epicenter.

Most earthquake deaths occur when the epicenter of a strong earthquake is near a city. Two factors explain this. First, more people are in cities. Second, an earthquake seldom causes deaths directly. Most earthquake deaths result from the failure of things humans have made. For example, a poorly constructed building may collapse, burying its occupants. Broken electrical wires may start a fire that is difficult to extinguish because water pipes are also broken. Thus, if an earthquake strikes a city, especially in a poor country, it causes many deaths because of its effect on the people's surroundings. Properly designed and built structures are not as likely to collapse as poorly constructed ones. Thus, modern cities in earthquake-prone areas try to avoid earthquake deaths by enforcing strict building codes. In December 1988, an earthquake registering 6.9 on the Richter scale struck Soviet Armenia. In well-built cities, the intensity of such a quake would be "potentially destructive." However, the buildings in the towns of Kirovakan and Leninkan were made of stone cemented with clay and mud. The two towns were virtually obliterated, and fifty-five thousand people were killed due to the poor construction.

Earthquakes can be especially hazardous for people who live near water. Earthquakes can trigger devastating waves called **tsunamis*** (tsoo NAH mee) (once called tidal

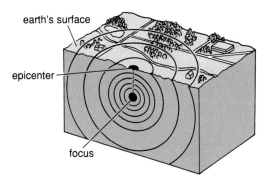

17A-5 *Drawing showing the relationship of the epicenter to the focus*

---

epicenter: epi- (on) + -center (Gk. KENTRON, center)

tsunami: tsu- (Jap. TSU, harbor) + -nami (Jap. NAMI, wave)

17A-6 *Tsunami destruction on the island of Hawaii following an earthquake in Chile*

waves—but they have nothing to do with the tide). Tsunamis can travel as fast as 800 km/hr. (500 mph). In the open sea they are only 2 or 3 feet high, but when they approach the shore they can be much higher. Tsunamis can carry large ships hundreds of feet inland. In earthquakes in or near the ocean, tsunamis often claim more lives than other earthquake hazards. For example, in the 1964 Alaska earthquake, 110 of 114 victims died as a result of the tsunami. Tsunamis also carry devastation far from the epicenter of the earthquake. The tsunamis from the Alaska earthquake killed people as far away as California.

17A-7	Earthquakes in the Bible		
Occasion	**Approximate Date**	**Reference**	**Facts of Interest**
Ten Commandments	1446 B.C.	Exod. 19:18	Mt. Sinai quaked
Judgment of Korah	1426 B.C.	Num. 16:31-33	The earth swallowed the rebel Korah, his followers, and their families; then it closed again.
Battle of Gibeah	1040 B.C.	I Sam. 14:15	A huge Philistine army shook the earth as it fled in panic after hearing rumors of Jonathan's attack.
Elijah	860 B.C.	I Kings 19:11-12	Mt. Horeb trembled as the Lord passed by the prophet
Reign of Uzziah	787 B.C.	Amos 1:1 Zech. 14:5	Israel was hit by an immense earthquake, still famous approximately 300 years later.
Crucifixion	A.D. 30	Matt. 27:51	The veil of the Temple split in two.
Resurrection	A.D. 30	Matt. 28:2	An angel descended from heaven and rolled the stone away from Christ's grave.
Philippian jail	A.D. 53	Acts 16:26	A great earthquake shook the foundation of Paul's prison and loosed his chains.
Tribulation	unknown	Rev. 16:17-21	The greatest earthquake of all time will shake the world.

Section Review Questions 17A-1

1. How large are tectonic plates?
2. Name the instrument used to measure earthquakes.
3. What is the center of an earthquake's activity called?
4. What is the place on the earth's surface that is directly above the focus of an earthquake's activity called?
5. What is the name given to the huge ocean waves caused by earthquakes?

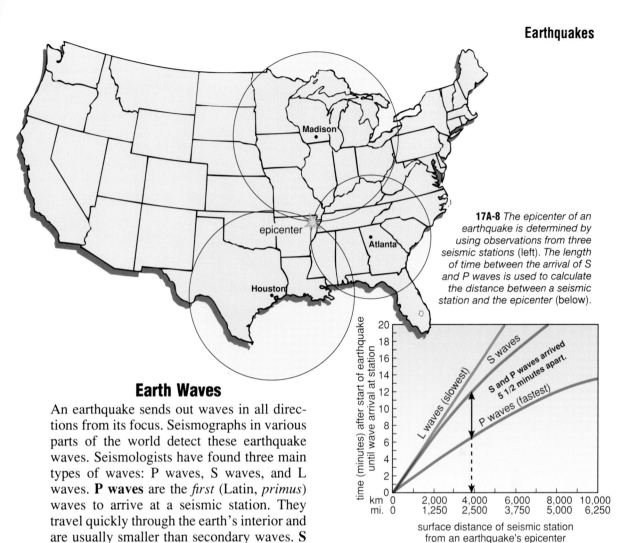

17A-8 *The epicenter of an earthquake is determined by using observations from three seismic stations (left). The length of time between the arrival of S and P waves is used to calculate the distance between a seismic station and the epicenter (below).*

Earth Waves

An earthquake sends out waves in all directions from its focus. Seismographs in various parts of the world detect these earthquake waves. Seismologists have found three main types of waves: P waves, S waves, and L waves. **P waves** are the *first* (Latin, *primus*) waves to arrive at a seismic station. They travel quickly through the earth's interior and are usually smaller than secondary waves. **S**

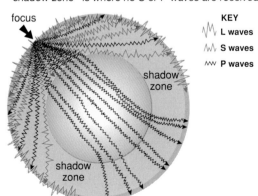

17A-9 *Earthquake waves and the paths they travel; the "shadow zone" is where no S or P waves are received.*

focus

KEY
〰 **L waves**
〰 **S waves**
〰 **P waves**

shadow zone

shadow zone

waves are the *second* waves to arrive at a seismic station. Like P waves, they travel through the earth's interior; however, S waves do not travel through the core. They are also slower and stronger than P waves. **L waves** are the last and largest to arrive at a seismic station. They travel along the earth's surface rather than through it. L waves are the strongest waves of an earthquake.

After studying waves from many earthquakes, seismologists realized that they can find the distance to an earthquake by examining the time between the arrival of P waves and S waves. The farther the station is from the epicenter, the longer the interval between the P and S waves. A single station can tell only the distance, not the location, of the earthquake. Three stations recording the same earthquake can pinpoint its epicenter. A seismologist draws a circle for each station with the center of the circle at the station and the radius being the distance from the earthquake. The point at which the three circles intersect is the epicenter. By studying the arrival times of all three types of waves, seismologists can calculate the depth of the focus.

Faults

Faults are a feature of the earth's surface often associated with earthquakes. A fault, as described in Chapter 16, is a crack in rock where the rock has moved. Some faults are only a few centimeters long; others are hundreds of kilometers. Scientists of the last century thought that faults somehow caused earthquakes. Modern seismologists, however, believe that earthquakes cause faults. Earthquakes begin when large areas of rock under stress break suddenly. This sometimes shows up on the earth's surface as a fault. There may be repeated forces that keep moving the rock along the fault line. These forces often cause repeated earthquakes.

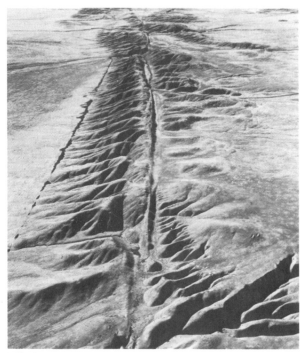

17A-11 *Aerial view of the San Andreas Fault in the Carrizo Plain area of central California*

Movement along a fault may be primarily vertical or horizontal. Faults with mainly vertical motion usually have slanted surfaces when seen in cross section. If the landmass† that is wider at the top of the slanted fault moves down and the landmass that is wider below the slant moves up, it is a **normal fault.** If the wide-topped landmass moves up and the wide-bottomed landmass moves

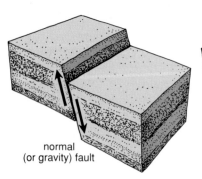

normal
(or gravity) fault

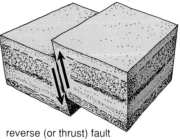

reverse (or thrust) fault

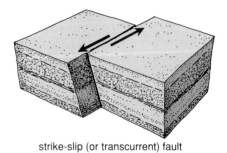

strike-slip (or transcurrent) fault

17A-10 *Faults develop when a mass of rock cracks and then moves. The diagram shows three common types of faults.*

† The landmass that is wider at the top (in cross section) is called the hanging wall; the other landmass is the footwall. These blocks may move in almost any direction relative to each other.

down, it is a **reverse fault.** Horizontal motion causes a **strike-slip fault.** The San Andreas fault in California falls into this category. Movement is not restricted exclusively to vertical or horizontal directions. Many faults have both types of movement.

Attempted Prediction

Seismologists are trying to develop accurate methods for predicting earthquakes. A few days' or hours' notice would do little to save buildings, but it could dramatically reduce the number of fatalities in a major quake. Intensive research throughout the world has gone into reaching this goal. Some success has been reported, but reliable forecasting of earthquakes is probably years away.

An ideal prediction of an earthquake would specify where, when, and with what magnitude an earthquake will occur. Seismologists know what areas are most likely to have earthquakes. Interestingly, almost nine-tenths of all earthquakes occur in the Circum-Pacific and Alpine-Himalayan volcano belts. These two natural disasters seem

17A-12 *Collapsed structure of Interstate 88 in California. A second deck collapsed onto the first deck, trapping many during the rush hour traffic (Loma Prieta Earthquake 1989).*

to be related; in fact, erupting volcanoes often trigger earthquakes. The remaining one-tenth of earthquakes may occur anywhere on earth.

To give crude predictions of earthquakes, seismologists study the history of areas with faults. For example, they have discovered that a major earthquake strikes San Francisco about every 150 years. The city's last major earthquake was in 1906 and had an estimated magnitude of 7.9–8.3. Although there was an earthquake registering at 6.9 in 1989 with an epicenter near San Francisco, it was not strong enough to be the expected major quake. However, this kind of prediction is imprecise and unreliable. Earthquakes do not follow their schedules rigidly; they may be "early" or "late." Furthermore, a city cannot evacuate for an earthquake when the people do not know for sure even what year it will be.

Another way of predicting earthquakes from the history of a fault is to notice what areas have not had an earthquake recently. If major earthquakes have occurred all along a fault except in one area, this "gap" may be due for an earthquake. However, the "gap" may be less earthquake-prone than its surroundings. So, again, prediction is imprecise and unreliable.

The major difficulty in predicting earthquakes is that seismologists do not fully understand their cause. Plate tectonics may help to explain why volcanoes and earthquakes occur and where they are likely, but it does not help to predict when they will occur. Such prediction requires more knowledge of the rocks a few miles down than we currently have. With our current knowledge we cannot even be sure that the theory is correct. Though we cannot predict earthquakes, as Christians we can take comfort, knowing that the Lord controls all natural disasters.

FACETS OF GEOLOGY

17A-1

Is California About to Fall into the Ocean?

California, a rich land of opportunity, is built on what is probably the most earthquake-prone land in America. An ugly fracture over 1,000 km (600 mi.) long, called the San Andreas fault, rips through the state and warns of imminent danger. Ignoring the signs, over 20 million people have built their homes along this fault. Hospitals, schools, dams, highways, bridges, and other structures of modern civilization are located along the fault.

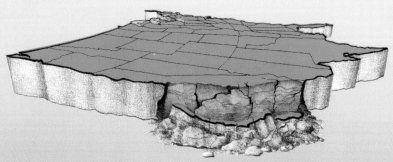

This fault separates a sliver of California from the rest of America. That sliver is moving northward at more than 5 cm a year. The dangers of this earth movement are most apparent along the coast, where unstable cliffs cause landslides. Housing developments have been built right to the edge of these cliffs. A major earthquake would break off huge chunks of these cliffs and send them tumbling into the ocean.

The people on both sides of the fault experience over a thousand tremors each year, but no one knows exactly when a "big one" will strike. Modern efforts to understand and predict earthquakes have a life-and-death urgency to Californians. Hundreds of sensitive instruments operate around the clock in pits, tunnels, and holes near the fault. They attempt to measure surface changes that indicate the build-up of tension—changes in gravity and magnetism or creeping land and tilting earth. Sophisticated lasers measure minute changes in the earth's surface, 2 mm over 16 km. Pressure has been building for decades at the two ends of the fault, near San Francisco (last hit in 1989) and Los Angeles (last major quake in 1857).

Geological excavations indicate that the "big ones" near Los Angeles have occurred on an average of once every 150 years. Yet no one knows when God will send another earthquake. Past major quakes near Los Angeles have occurred as much as 275 years apart. Nor do we have any solid evidence that earthquakes have repeating cycles. Perhaps one will never hit again. Modern instruments have measured the tremendous build-up of tension, only to see that tension suddenly subside without an earthquake.

So, is California about to fall into the ocean? No one knows for sure, but the area is unquestionably prone to major quakes. In the past, disastrous quakes have ripped the state without casting the northward-bound sliver into the sea, but we know so little about earthquakes that anything is possible.

Section Review Questions 17A-2

1. List the types of shock waves that make up an earthquake.
2. Which kind of earthquake wave arrives first at a seismic station?
3. What kind of fault is the San Andreas fault?
4. Why is it difficult to predict earthquakes?

17B–Volcanoes

Almost everyone has heard of volcanoes, the mountains that erupt. Our English word *volcano* comes from Vulcano Island, a dormant volcano in the Mediterranean Sea. This island was named for Vulcan, the Roman god of fire.

What Is a Volcano?

A **volcano** is a land form built up by molten rock that has come to the earth's surface through a vent. Scientists speculate that the source of magma usually extends to a depth of about 50 km (30 mi.). Some magma seeps between layers of sedimentary rock on the way up, but much continues to the earth's surface. A **vent** is a cylindrical opening that connects the surface of the earth with a source of magma far below. The magma travels up through the vent to the earth's surface and is then called **lava** (LAH vuh). Lava,

cinders, and volcanic ash emitted during repeated or lengthy eruptions accumulate around the vent, thus forming the land form known as a volcano.

At the top of this volcanic cone is a depression called a **crater.** In some cases the summit is removed by an explosive eruption, or its walls collapse, either of which forms an enlarged depression called a **caldera** (kal DEHR uh). An especially tall or active volcano may develop a second vent and cone on the slope of the first cone or beside it.

17B-2 *Paricutin at night—glowing projectiles and fragments (bombs, cinders, and ash) outline the conical shape of the volcano.*

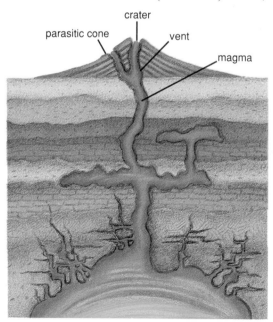

17B-1 *Sectional view of a volcano*

Emissions

While volcanoes are known for their emission of lava, they emit a variety of other materials as well. These materials include solids, liquids, and gases. All these materials come from the magma within the earth.

Gases

Magma contains many gases dissolved in molten rock. These separate from the molten rock as it approaches the surface or emerges from the earth due to the reduction of pressure. Often the first sign of a volcano's eruption is the emission of gases. Sometimes a volcano emits a mixture of hot, solid particles suspended in water vapor or other gases. This hot mixture, called a **glowing avalanche,** is so heavy that it falls down the volcano's slope instead of rising into the air. It suffocates or incinerates everything in its path. This type of eruption from Mount Pelée (puh LAY) in Martinique (MAR tih NEEK) destroyed the city of Saint Pierre in 1902.

Volcanoes often emit steam and water vapor. Although this is usually harmless, it can have tragic consequences on a snow-capped volcano. The 1985 eruption of Nevado del Ruiz in Colombia was mostly steam, but it melted some of the snow. This melted snow caused mudslides, called **lahars** (LAH HAR), that buried thousands of people.

Lava

When most people think of a volcano, they picture red-hot lava flowing down the mountain's side. Most volcanoes emit lava at one time or another. The type of magma that supplies the volcano determines what percentage of its emissions will be lava. A thin, runny magma is more likely to remain fluid enough to flow as lava than a thick magma is. Although lava is frightening, it causes fewer deaths than other types of volcanic emissions. Since lava seldom flows faster than a person can walk, it is easy to avoid.

17B-3 *A lava bubble (above) exploding as it hits seawater, forming black sand; an advancing lava flow, called pahoehoe (top right); lava cascades down the crater walls as Alae erupts (right).*

17B-4	Notable Volcanic Eruptions			
Date	**Name**	**Location**	**Deaths**	**Interesting Facts**
1500 B.C.	Santorini	Aegean Sea	unknown	5 times more powerful than any recorded eruption; possibly destroyed the Minoan civilization on the island of Crete
A.D. 79	Mt. Vesuvius	Italy	unknown	buried the Roman "pleasure cities" of Pompeii and Herculaneum; archeologists found the ancient cities frozen in time
1693	Mt. Etna	Sicily	60,000	caused an earthquake; damaged 40 towns; over 150 major eruptions since ancient times
1783	Mt. Laki	Iceland	10,000	erupted for 7 months; 24-km-long (15 mi.) cracks appeared in the ground; lava covered 580 sq. km (226 sq. mi.); poisonous sulfurous gas killed half the livestock on the island and kept the fishermen from launching their boats; a winter famine killed $\frac{1}{5}$ of the population
1815	Mt. Tamboro	Indonesia	92,000	deadliest volcanic explosion in history; energy of 6 million atomic bombs; ash in the atmosphere turned 1816 into the world's first "year without summer"
1877	Cotopaxi	Ecuador	1,000	one of the highest active volcanoes in the world; melted snow on one slope that caused a deadly mudflow that streamed 241 km (150 mi.)
1873	Mauna Loa	Hawaii	none	world's largest active volcano; eruption lasted 1.5 years; averages one eruption every 3.5 years; noted for beautiful fountains of lava flows
1883	Krakatoa	Indonesia	36,000	blew up itself and $\frac{2}{3}$ of its island; sent ash and smoke over 80 km (50 mi.) high; heard over 4,000 km (2,500 mi.) away; caused a deadly tsunami that hit Java
1902	Mt. Pelée	Martinique, West Indies	38,000	city of St. Pierre ignored warnings of an eruption because it wanted to hold elections and was destroyed by an 800° C (1,450° F) black cloud; two survivors (prisoner in a thick-walled cell and a merchant barricaded in his store)
1943	Parícutin	Mexico	none	within only a year a farmer's cornfield turned into a mountain 430 m (1,400 ft.) high
1963	Surtsey	Atlantic	none	formed a new island within weeks; lagoon, sand beaches, and white cliffs formed within a year
1980	Mt. Saint Helens	Washington	57	North America's greatest recorded eruption; hot ash flew out at 370 km/hr. (230 mph)
1985	Nevado del Ruiz	Colombia	25,000	caused floods and mudslides; covered the city of Armero
1986	Lake Nios	Cameroon	1,734	carbon dioxide gas released from under a crater lake wiped out an entire village by suffocation
1991	Mt. Pinatubo	Philippines	338	explosive eruption 95 km (60 mi.) from Manila; closed two U.S. military bases

Solid Materials

When volcanoes erupt explosively, they emit ash, cinders, and bombs. **Ash** is made up of tiny angular, glassy fragments of solidified magma. It superficially resembles the ashes that come from burning wood. Most of the people who died in the 1980 eruption of Mount St. Helens were suffocated by volcanic ash. The people of Pompeii who died in the A.D. 79 eruption of Vesuvius also suffocated. This is a common cause of death from volcanoes. **Cinders** are like ash but are larger, from 0.5 to 2.5 cm (0.2 to 1 in.) in diameter. **Bombs** are blobs of lava that solidify as they fly through the air.

Explosive volcanoes are more dangerous than volcanoes that allow lava to seep out because their emissions travel faster and are less predictable. They also often destroy the volcano. Mount St. Helens lost nearly 400 m (1,300 ft.) of its height in its 1980 explosion;

volcanic islands often sink beneath the ocean as a result of large explosive eruptions. Volcanic explosions can be very loud. The 1883 eruption of Krakatoa, Indonesia, was heard as far as 4,800 km (3,000 mi.) away.

17B-5 *Shiprock in New Mexico is a dike of volcanic origin* (top). *A flow moving over earlier pahoehoe lava flow* (right)—*note the ropy surface of the pahoehoe flow. Ngauruhoe in New Zealand is a composite volcano; steam and ash are being emitted, and the ash fall has darkened a fresh layer of snow* (far right).

Section Review Questions 17B-1

1. Do volcanoes always explode when they erupt?
2. What is a cylindrical opening that magma travels through to reach the surface of the earth called?
3. What are the two types of depressions that may be found at the top of a volcano? Which one is the larger depression?
4. Besides lava, what else may be emitted by a volcano?

Classification

To study volcanoes, volcanologists (scientists who study volcanoes) group similar volcanoes together. Two major ways to classify volcanoes are by structure and by activity.

By Structure

A volcano's shape and composition depend on the type of material it emits. Some volcanoes emit mostly lava, others emit mostly ash and cinders, and others emit lava and ash in alternating eruptions.

Volcanoes that emit mostly lava are called **shield volcanoes.** They are built up from smooth flows of lava rather than violent explosions of ash. Like a shield, they are dome-shaped and have gentle slopes. The Hawaiian Islands are classic examples of shield volcanoes. Mauna Loa has a greater area than any other volcano in the world. Nearby Mauna

Kea holds the world's record for actual height for any mountain. From its underwater base it stands over 10,000 m (33,000 ft.) high. Surtsey (SURT SAY), a shield volcano located off the coast of Iceland, formed a new island in 1963. Today the island supports plant life, and animals have migrated to the island. This is proof that islands do not take vast spans of time to form. The largest volcano known in the solar system, Olympus Mons on Mars, also has the profile of a shield volcano.

Volcanoes that emit mostly ashes, cinders, and bombs are called **cinder cones.** These have steep slopes and are usually small volcanoes. One famous cinder cone volcano is Parícutin, a Mexican volcano that first erupted in 1943.

Volcanoes that emit lava and solid debris alternately are called **composite volcanoes.** These often have the symmetrical cone shape that most people associate with volcanoes. Most volcanoes are composite volcanoes. Fujiyama (FOO jee YAH mah) in Japan, Mount Etna in Sicily, and Mayon volcano in the Philippines are all composite volcanoes.

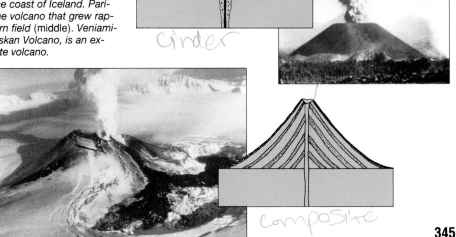

17B-6 *Types of volcanos: Surtsey (top) is a shield volcano off the coast of Iceland. Paricutin is a cinder cone volcano that grew rapidly in a Mexican corn field (middle). Veniaminof (bottom), an Alaskan Volcano, is an example of a composite volcano.*

By Activity

A volcano's activity tells how recently it has erupted. An **active volcano** is one that has erupted within the past fifty years. Examples are Mauna Loa in Hawaii, Vesuvius in Italy, and Mount St. Helens in Washington. A **dormant volcano** has erupted in historical times, but not within the past fifty years. An **extinct volcano** has no historical record of eruption. Mount Shasta in California and Mount Rainier in Washington are both extinct volcanoes.

Although the terms *active, dormant,* and *extinct* help scientists in their study of volcanoes, they can be misleading. The uninformed may believe that dormant or extinct volcanoes are not dangerous. However, occasionally a volcano formerly classed as dormant or extinct erupts disastrously. Mount Vesuvius (vuh SOO vee us) was considered extinct by those who knew that it was a volcano before its eruption in A.D. 79. Two cities

17B-8 *Mount St. Helens, which erupted in 1980, is an active volcano.*

near its base were wiped out because their citizens did not understand the danger. Similarly, Mount St. Helens had not erupted for over a hundred years before its 1980 eruption. Any volcano may erupt at any time. Active volcanoes are simply more likely to erupt based on their recent history.

Locations

More than five hundred active volcanoes exist in the world. Most of them are located in two volcano belts. The **Circum-Pacific belt** is sometimes called the "ring of fire." It includes Japan, the Kamchatka (kam CHAT kuh) Peninsula, the Aleutian (uh LOO shun) Islands, Alaska, the western United States, Mexico, Central America, western South America, New Zealand, New Guinea, the Philippines, and several other Pacific islands. The **Alpine-Himalayan belt** extends from the Mediterranean area eastward to the Indonesian states. It includes Sicily, Italy, the Aegean Sea, Asia Minor, the Indian Ocean, and Indonesia. Other locations of active volcanoes include the middle of the Atlantic Ocean (Iceland and the Azores [AY zorz]) and the middle of the Pacific Ocean (Hawaii).

17B-7 *Oregon's Crater Lake—this lake is set in the crater of an extinct volcano, Mt. Mazama. Wizard Island (center of photograph) was apparently formed from a more recent eruption.*

Section Review Questions 17B-2

1. List the three types of volcano structures.
2. Where is the largest known volcano?
3. What are the areas called where most of the active volcanoes on the earth are found?

17C–Heated Ground Water

Ground water can be heated by either of two sources. If you could descend into the ground and check the temperature as you went, you would find that the earth's temperature increases with depth. The average increase in the areas that scientists have measured is 30° C/km (87° F/mi.). This measurement is the **thermal gradient** of the earth. Water that descends deep into the earth will be heated by the thermal gradient. The other source of heat for ground water is magma. Ground water near magma becomes hot. If a channel exists between the water (heated by either source) and the surface, the hot water will rise to the surface while cooler water sinks to the heat source.

Types of Heated Ground Water

An area where heated water simply rises to the surface is called a **hot spring.** The spring at Warm Springs, Georgia, has a temperature of 31° C (88° F) and is heated by the thermal gradient by descending about 1 km (0.6 mi.) deep. Hot springs in the western United States are heated by magma that has worked its way close to the surface of the earth. A famous hot spring is Mammoth Hot Springs in Yellowstone National Park in Wyoming. Here the water flows out of the ground through a series of fissures in the side of a hill. Terraces have formed on the hillside from **travertine** (TRAV ur TEEN) (a variety of calcium carbonate), which is deposited by the evaporating water. Algae and bacteria which are growing on the travertine color the terraces red, blue, and brown.

Fumaroles* (FYOO muh ROHL) are vents in the ground where steam and other gases escape. Carbon dioxide escaping from fumaroles can be dangerous. A heavy gas (about 1.5 times as heavy as air), carbon

dioxide can collect in depressions in the ground and form a thick layer that shuts out air. Death Gulch in Yellowstone National Park is such a place where carbon dioxide collects. On especially calm days, grizzly bears and other animals have suffocated there.

17C-1 *Travertine terraces* (top), *at Mammoth Hot Springs, Yellowstone National Park; active fumaroles* (bottom), *along the East Rift Zone in Hawaii*

---

fumarole: (L. FUMARIUM, smoke chamber)

A thermal spring that ejects its water from the ground at intervals is a **geyser** (GY zur). Though scientists do not completely understand geysers, they think that nearby magma heats the water in a long, twisting chamber. The twisted chamber prevents the hot water from immediately approaching the surface. When its temperature reaches the boiling point, steam pressure suddenly forces the entire column of water out of the ground. The chamber then refills with ground water, and the heating process begins again.

Geyser openings are often surrounded by a whitish deposit called **geyserite**. This resembles travertine but is not made of calcium

17C-3 *Geyserite around the opening of the Lone Star Geyser in Yellowstone National Park*

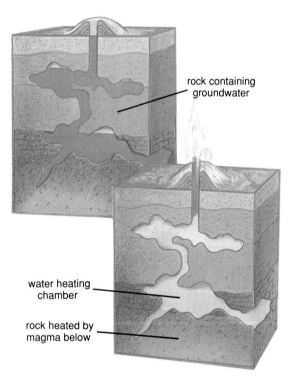

rock containing groundwater

water heating chamber

rock heated by magma below

17C-2 *Geyser "plumbing": Long twisted chambers filled with ground water extend down into areas near hot magma. As steam forms, it develops enough pressure to overcome the weight of the water above and forces some water out the upper chambers. Ground water refills the chambers, and the process starts over.*

carbonate. Instead it consists of silica dissolved from the igneous rock through which the water has passed.

Harnessing Geothermal Energy

In areas with many hot springs, fumaroles, and geysers, the hot water may be a valuable source of energy. This energy is called **geothermal*** energy. Geothermal energy is used both as a heat source and as a force to generate electricity.

The Romans used hot springs as a source of hot bath water. Modern resorts also use hot springs for bathing and swimming. But geothermal energy can heat more than bath water. A hotel near the Kilauea volcano in Hawaii is heated with natural steam that comes through holes drilled in the ground. Natural steam also heats homes, schools, and public buildings in Reykjavik (RAY kyuh

geothermal: geo- (earth) + -thermal (heat)

VEEK), the capital of Iceland, and in other Icelandic towns. Japan is also experimenting with heat from natural steam.

In 1904 engineers at Larderello, Italy, began experimenting with the use of geothermal energy to generate electricity. Their pilot operation has since developed into a plant with a capacity of 370 megawatts. This is enough electricity for over eighteen thousand homes. Although geothermal power plants provide less than one-third the power generated by nuclear power plants being to-day, the danger from radiation in nuclear plants makes the study of geothermal energy an interesting alternative. Japan, Mexico, New Zealand, the former Soviet Union, and the United States have followed suit.

Geothermal energy has been encouraging. Still, not many places have heat close enough to the surface to be accessible. For now at least, geothermal energy is only a minor source of energy. Perhaps in the future we will learn how to tap more deeply into the earth to make more of this energy available.

17C-4 *Waireke Geothermal Project in New Zealand, while not capable of producing as much energy as nuclear plants, provides a considerable amount of the energy needed for the area surrounding it.*

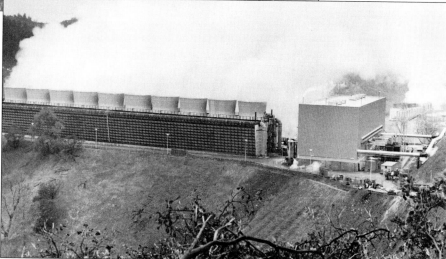

17C-5 *Pacific Gas and Electric Company's geothermal plant, about 90 miles northeast of San Francisco, uses heated ground water to produce electricity.*

Chapter 17C

Section Review Questions 17C
1. Identify the two heat sources by which ground water can be heated.
2. What is the area where heated ground water simply rises to the surface called?
3. What are vents in the ground where steam and other gases escape called?
4. What mineral composes geyserite?

Terms

active volcano
Alpine-Himalayan belt
ash
bomb
caldera
cinder cone
cinders
Circum-Pacific belt
composite volcano
crater
dormant volcano
earthquake
epicenter
extinct volcano

focus
fumarole
geothermal
geyser
geyserite
glowing avalanche
hot spring
lahar
lava
L waves
magnitude
normal fault
plate tectonics theory
P waves

reverse fault
Richter scale
seismograph
seismologist
shield volcano
strike-slip fault
S waves
thermal gradient
travertine
tsunami
vent
volcano

What Did You Learn?
1. Why might a lesser earthquake in one area do more damage than a stronger earthquake in another area?
2. Explain how P and S waves are used to determine how far away an earthquake occurred.
3. Why are three seismic stations needed to determine the location of an earthquake?
4. How much more energy is in an earthquake registering 6 on the Richter scale than in one registering 3?
5. Why do many people think earthquakes and volcanoes are related to plate tectonics?
6. What is the difference between an active volcano and a dormant one?
7. If water on the surface of the earth with a temperature of 4° C descended 2 km into the earth, how hot would the water be?
8. How are travertine and geyserite similar? How are they different?
9. Describe one way in which geothermal energy can be used.

What Do You Think?
1. Do you think Mars has "marsquakes"?
2. Do earthquakes cause faults, or do faults cause earthquakes?
3. Recently a seismologist proposed a theory which stated that earthquakes are triggered by the gravitational pull of the sun and moon in a manner similar to the way tides form. What is your opinion of this theory?
4. Would it be possible to convert the Richter scale to a metric scale?
5. What problems do you think are encountered when harnessing and using geothermal energy?

Weathering, Mass Wasting, and Erosion

EIGHTEEN

18A–Weathering

Hebrews 1:11 says that the heavens and earth "shall wax old as doth a garment." The heavens are indeed wearing out: stars exhaust their fuel and die; comets break up into fragments, some of which burn up in the earth's atmosphere as meteors; and the earth itself rotates more slowly every day. Similarly, the earth's surface shows signs of wear. Three ways that the earth's surface "wears out" are weathering, which disintegrates rocks; mass wasting, which lowers hills; and erosion by streams, which moves tons of soil every year.

Types of Weathering

The two types of weathering are chemical and mechanical. **Chemical weathering** disintegrates rocks by changing their composition.

You may remember from the discussion of minerals that some react with acids. For example, a small piece of limestone will dissolve in a beaker of hydrochloric acid. Natural acids are important agents of chemical weathering. Carbon dioxide combines with water to form carbonic acid, the weak acid present in carbonated beverages. Decayed plants produce a mixture of weak acids called humic acid, and lichens produce acids as well. These acids can dissolve stone. Because the acids are weak, however, they take long periods of time to dissolve the stone. Weathering agents can change some rocks without dissolving them. For example, carbonic acid weathers feldspar to form clay.

Several factors influence the speed at which chemical weathering proceeds. The mineral itself is the most important of these. Whereas calcite (limestone) weathers relatively rapidly, silica (quartz) resists weathering remarkably. Climate is also important. Warmth and moisture promote chemical weathering. Gentle slopes and abundant vegetation, which retain rainwater longer, hasten the process. Another significant factor is the amount of rock surface exposed to the weathering agents. The greater the area, the more chemical weathering takes place. When rocks break apart, new surfaces become exposed to the chemical agents. Similarly, the burrowing of earthworms and other small animals constantly mixes the soil particles and makes them more susceptible to chemical weathering.

Mechanical weathering breaks up rocks into smaller pieces by physical forces. Unlike chemical weathering, mechanical weathering does not affect the composition of the rocks. Plant roots and germinating seeds are effective agents in enlarging cracks in rocks because they exert pressure on anything confining them. Perhaps you have seen a sidewalk heaved or cracked by tree roots. Even small weeds can damage an asphalt driveway or a parking lot by enlarging the small openings into which the seeds originally fell.

Freezing water in cracks and pores of rocks is another forceful mechanical weathering agent. Water expands about 8 per cent when it freezes, and it can exert tremendous pressure against the surfaces it touches. Each

18A-1 *Weather pits formed by naturally acidified water puddles (left); potholes from mechanical weathering by stream sediments (below)*

18A-2 *Water in cracks and pores expands as it freezes, creating enough force to split rock apart* (top and inset). *Boulders raised by frost heaving* (bottom).

time the ice thaws and the water refreezes, it has new opportunities to splinter off small fragments and to extend the cracks farther into the rock.

A second way freezing water causes weathering is by **frost heaving**. Ice below the surface of the ground pushes surface material upward as much as 45 cm (18 in.). This upward push breaks up fine-grained rocks. Because of frost heaving, farmers encounter new rocks in their plowing each spring. Water expands as it freezes and forces the rocks upward. As the ice starts to melt, soil sifts below the rocks and raises them. This freezing and thawing can occur repeatedly, with each cycle pushing the rocks still higher.

Wind erosion is another form of mechanical weathering. It is most obvious in desert regions that have loose sand. Wind-driven sand is an effective abrasive agent that erodes rocks such as sandstone. Its action is like sandblasting, a method used for cleaning stone buildings and rusted metal parts. Many unusual rock formations in the western United States come from wind erosion.

Wind often carries off the loose material from an area, leaving an excavated basin

18A-3 *Spectacular rock formations eroded by wind and water along Peek-A-Boo trail in Bryce Canyon, Utah (left). Desert pavement surrounded by drifting sand in Death Valley, California (below); sand dunes in White Sands National Monument, New Mexico (bottom).*

called a **blowout.** When all the sand and other unconsolidated materials have blown away, only pebbles and cobbles remain. The surface is then a **desert pavement.** Sand that the wind moves from one area is deposited elsewhere in mounds and ridges called **sand dunes.** A dune forms when an obstacle reduces the wind's speed and the wind becomes unable to carry its load. Once estab-

lished, the dune itself becomes an obstacle that slows the wind; this is how the dune grows.

Another method of mechanical weathering is **exfoliation*** (eks FOH lee AY shun), a

---

exfoliation: ex- (L. EX-, off) +
-foliation (L. FOLIUM, leaf)

process that removes thin slabs or flakes of rock from large domes or boulders. It can weather even durable granite. Scientists believe that exfoliation uses both chemical and mechanical weathering. They believe that chemical reactions occur in the joints of the rock (chemical weathering). Because the products of these chemical reactions occupy more space than the original rock, the weathered rock expands outward, pushing away the outer layers (mechanical weathering). Uneven expansion and contraction caused by daily heating and cooling and expansion due to removal of confining outer rock layers also contribute to exfoliation.

A visible result of mechanical weathering is the accumulation of rock debris at the base of a cliff. This debris, **talus** (TAY lus), forms as rock fragments weather and fall from the cliff. Because some of these fragments are angular and large, they often form a steep slope of 34° to 37°.

18A-4 *Talus at the base of cliffs in Glacier National Park, Montana—exfoliation is a type of mechanical weathering that may form talus. This solid rock in Yosemite National Park is undergoing exfoliation* (inset).

Section Review Questions 18A-1

1. List three ways by which the earth is degenerating.
2. What are the two types of weathering?
3. What factors influence the rate of chemical weathering?
4. How much does water expand when it freezes?
5. What is the accumulation of rock debris at the base of a cliff called?

Result of Weathering—Soil

What happens to weathered rock? Large particles form gravel, medium-sized particles form sand, and small particles may become clay or, if they are carried away by water, silt. When sand, silt, and clay mix with organic material, they become **soil.** Not all soil has come from the weathering of rock; the earth must have had some fertile soil at creation to grow plants. This original soil has become depleted by farming and the Flood. God in His providence established weathering to replenish parts of the soil.

Most soils come in three layers, which **pedologists** (pee DAHL uh jist) (soil scientists) call **horizons.** The lowest horizon, the C-horizon, rests on bedrock. It consists of weathered pieces of bedrock fragments. The next layer, the B-horizon or subsoil, contains weathered minerals from the C-horizon as well as minerals that have left the A-horizon. The A-horizon, or topsoil, is the most fertile part of the soil. It contains **humus,** decayed organic material, which provides many nutrients for plants and increases the ability of the soil to hold water. Rainwater carries some of the nutrients down to the B-horizon.

The composition of a soil depends on the kind of rocks in the region, the climate in which it forms, and the vegetation. Soils contain various amounts of sand, silt, and clay. If the region has mostly quartz rocks, its soils may be sandy. If the rocks contain mica, feldspar, or similar materials, they are more likely to form clay. If the soil is near a flooding river or a dried-up lake, it may contain silt. **Loam** (LOME), an especially fertile soil, contains about equal parts of sand and silt and about half as much clay. To be fertile, however, it also must contain humus.

Soils that receive plenty of rain differ from desert soils. Too much rain can remove most of the nutrients from the topsoil. This makes it difficult for plants with shallow roots to grow. Soil in rainy climates also tends to be acidic. Roses and pine trees grow well in acidic soils, but crops such as alfalfa do not. Farmers in rainy climates may add lime (produced by heating limestone) to their soil to neutralize the acid and "sweeten" the soil.

18A-5 Changes in the soil's shade or color mark the soil horizons in this soil profile of a Missouri field (above). A typical soil profile (right) has three main layers (called horizons) above the bedrock.

18A-6 *Furrow irrigation of a cotton farm near Safford, Arizona; water comes from deep wells or the Cila River.*

The eastern United States has mostly acidic soils from rainy climates. Soils in dry climates, on the other hand, tend to have plenty of nutrients in the topsoil. They often need only water to make them productive farmland. Farmers in southern California take advantage of the fertile desert soil by extensive irrigation. Much of the western United States has similar dry, but otherwise fertile, soil.

Organic matter is necessary for a fertile soil. Plants need the nutrients in humus to grow. Areas that are not disturbed by man keep a steady supply of humus as plants die and decay. In farmed areas, on the other hand, farmers often remove all their crops so that only small amounts of plant matter enter the soil. Thus, soils that have been farmed for several years may become infertile. To avoid this, farmers fertilize their fields. They may add chemical fertilizers to replace the missing nutrients, or they may use a kind of organic fertilizer. For example, farmers whose main crops are pasture and grain crops for their animals may use manure as a fertilizer. Another way to replace the nutrients is to grow a crop that will be plowed under. This is called green manure. If the soil is to continue to be fertile, the nutrients that are removed by plants and erosion must be replaced.

Rates of soil formation vary enormously, depending on a variety of factors. On some exposed rock surfaces, soil has not formed; in other places, soil formation has apparently taken thousands of years. In some places, however, weathering and soil formation are more rapid. Volcanic debris often can support plant growth only a few years after erupting. For example, Krakatoa formed about 35 cm (14 in.) of soil from volcanic ash within forty-five years after its eruption.

18A-7 *Just a few years after Mount St. Helens erupted, plants returned to areas covered by volcanic debris.*

Soil has also developed rapidly along the edge of a retreating glacier. About 35 cm (14 in.) of soil formed in Glacier Bay National Park in about two hundred fifty years following a glacier's retreat. Thus, under favorable conditions, soil can form rapidly.

Section Review Questions 18A-2
1. List the components of soil.
2. What is another name for a soil scientist?
3. Which layer of soil has the most humus?

18B–Mass Wasting

Mass wasting is the downhill movement of large masses of soil or rocks under the influence of gravity. It may be either slow or rapid. The occurrence and speed of mass wasting depends on the slope, the vegetation, and the amount of water in a piece of ground. Steep slopes are more likely to experience mass wasting than are gentle slopes, because gravity acts more directly on a steep slope. Plant roots tend to stabilize the soil; thus, land with heavy vegetation is less likely to experience mass wasting than land with sparse or no vegetation. Excessive water acts as a lubricant for mass wasting. Therefore, mass wasting is likely to occur after a heavy rainstorm.

Slow Mass Wasting

One type of slow mass wasting is **creep,** the almost imperceptible downhill motion of soil. It occurs at a rate of a few centimeters each year—so slowly that it does not break the cover of vegetation. Although we cannot see creep happening, we can see its accumulated results. Evidences of creep include tilted fence posts, stone walls, and telephone poles.

Building contractors know that creep can be a serious problem. A house built on soil only, not anchored to bedrock, can be carried downhill along with the soil. Seldom does a house stay level as it moves. Floors and walls often become noticeably crooked a few years after the process of creep has begun. On the other hand, a house anchored to bedrock will collect soil against its upper side. Contractors may dig a level yard above the house and build a retaining wall to keep back the advancing soil.

Rock glaciers furnish another example of slow mass wasting. These are ridges of rocks found extending down the valleys in certain mountainous regions of Alaska, Colorado, and other places where the mountainsides are steep and the ground remains frozen most of the year. Because spaces between the rocks are filled with ice, rock glaciers move slowly.

18B-1 *Some evidences of creep are tilted telephone poles and fence posts, and trees with roots that point uphill* (left). *Effect of soil creep on railroad tracks in the Yukon Territory* (right).

18B-2 *A rock glacier near San Juan, Colorado—the mountain peak on the left is Emery Peak.*

The ice moves much as it does in an ordinary glacier, carrying the rocks with it down the valley.

Rapid Mass Wasting

A far more dramatic type of downhill motion is the **landslide.** This general term describes any rapid mass movement. If the mass includes detached bedrock, its specific name is **rock slide.** If it includes only loose material, the movement is a **debris slide.**

18B-3 *This landslide in Renaz, Italy was caused by events similar to those at Gros Ventre.*

A rock slide is a sudden catastrophic slippage caused by weakness between layers of bedrock. A famous rock slide occurred in Wyoming in 1925. An estimated 37 million m^3 (48 million yd.^{3}) of rock and soil slid down the side of Sheep Mountain, across the Gros Ventre (GROH • VAHNT) River, and 110 m (360 ft.) up the other side of the river valley. This slide created a dam that backed up the water for 8 km (5 mi.). The dam held for two years. Then, during the spring flooding of 1927, the dam broke, and several people downstream drowned.

18B-4 *The Gros Ventre rock slide in Wyoming*

Weak materials—a layer of sandstone resting on a layer of clay—caused the Gros Ventre rock slide. The steep slope was another factor. Melting winter snow and heavy spring rains weakened the adhesion between the sandstone and the clay, and the rock was pulled down by gravity. Human intervention did not cause this slide, because the slide occurred in an undeveloped area. On the other hand, human intervention probably could not have prevented it. Rock slides are the most devastating kind of landslide. They are uncontrollable and seldom give any warning.

Earthquakes sometimes trigger rock slides. In 1959 Madison Canyon in Montana was near the epicenter of an earthquake. Millions of tons of rock slid into the Madison River, creating a lake nearly as large as the one formed by the Gros Ventre slide. So violent was the slide that the winds it created could be felt miles away. Other earthquake-triggered landslides—at least seventy-eight of them—occurred during and after the 1964 Alaska earthquake.

Debris slides include earthflows, mudflows, and avalanches. In an earthflow, a portion of earth slides away from its original location and moves downhill as a flexible solid. In a mudflow a mixture of earth, water, and rocks flows down a slope as a semiliquid; its consistency is similar to that of newly mixed concrete. An avalanche usually includes ice or snow.

18B-5 *Aerial view of a debris slide in Alaska that was triggered by the Alaskan earthquake of 1964*

Section Review Questions 18B

1. What is the downhill movement of large masses of soil or rock under the influence of gravity called?
2. What type of mass wasting would be indicated by tilted telephone poles?
3. What is rapid mass wasting which includes bedrock called?
4. List three kinds of debris slides.

18C–Stream Erosion

A significant force in the wearing down of the earth's surface is running water. Water can **erode*** (ih ROHD) soil and rocks. The most consistent water erosion comes from streams.

Definition of Stream

A **stream** is a body of water that flows either continuously or seasonally on the surface or underground. The term can also be applied correctly to the smallest creek or the mightiest river. The highest point of a stream is its **headwaters** or **source.** The Jordan River, for example, has several sources in high mountainous regions. Near its source, a stream may be merely a trickle. Characteristically, the headwaters of a stream have a high **gradient,** or angle of slope.

---

erode: e- (off) + -rode (L. RODERE, to gnaw)

18C-1			Notable Rivers
Name	**Length (km)†**	**Location**	**Interesting Facts**
Nile	6,650	Africa	world's longest river; passes through desert; waters used for extensive irrigation; birthplace of ancient Egypt
Amazon	6,400	South America	world's largest river basin; $\frac{1}{5}$ of the world's discharge of water; over 1,000 tributaries; floods 65,000 sq. km. (25,000 sq. mi.) of forest each year; "man-eating" piranha
Yangtze	6,300	Asia	irrigates the "rice bowl" of China
Mississippi-Missouri	6,020	North America	although the Mississippi River flows from northern Minnesota to the Gulf of Mexico, the Missouri River (a tributary) is longer
Hwang Ho	5,464	Asia	muddiest river in the world; has changed its course 26 times; birthplace of China; flooding has drowned millions
Ob-Irtysh	5,410	Asia	flows into the Arctic Ocean; world's greatest estuary (where fresh and salt water mix), 800 × 80 km (500 × 50 mi.); passes through semi-desert, swamp, and frozen tundra; frozen about half the year
Congo	4,700	Africa	third largest river basin; rapids and waterfall near its mouth
Lena	4,400	Asia	flows into Arctic Ocean; its mouth is frozen $\frac{3}{4}$ of the year; may freeze solid to the bottom
Mackenzie	4,241	North America	flows into the Arctic Ocean; frozen $\frac{2}{3}$ of the year; ice bridges for truck traffic are built across it in the winter at Fort Providence
Niger	4,200	Africa	source is only 240 km (150 mi.) from the coast; flows inland and northeast from its source and southeast at its mouth
Mekong	4,000	Asia	a major international border in Southeast Asia
St. Lawrence-Great Lakes	4,000	North America	world's largest freshwater lake system; $\frac{1}{5}$ of the world's surface fresh water
Paraná	3,998	South America	basin extends from southern Brazil to northern Argentina
Murray-Darling	3,780	Australia	only major river on the continent
Volga	3,530	Europe	Europe's longest river; birthplace of Moscow, Russia's capital
Zambezi	3,500	Africa	Victoria Falls, a natural wonder of the world
Indus	2,900	Asia	gave India its name; elevation at source is 4,900 m (16,000 ft.) in the Himalayan Mountains
Ganges-Brahmaputra	2,897	Asia	one of the dirtiest rivers in the world; holy river to the Hindus
Danube	2,850	Europe	flows through 80 countries; birthplace of Vienna, Austria's capital; empties into the Black Sea
Tigris-Euphrates	2,800	Near East	"the cradle of civilization"; birthplace of Babylon and Assyria; watered Abraham's homeland, Ur of the Chaldees
Colorado	2,320	North America	deep trenches of which the Grand Canyon is the largest; cities compete for use of its water; empties into the Gulf of California

† Estimates of lengths vary, depending on what is chosen as the river's source.

The lowest point to which a stream extends is its **mouth.** The mouth may be in an ocean, a lake, or another river. The mouth of the Amazon is in the Atlantic Ocean. The mouth of the Jordan is in the Dead Sea. The mouth of the Missouri River, in contrast, is in the Mississippi River.

The lowest level to which a stream can erode is called its **base level.** For many streams this is the level of the lakes into which they flow. If the Lord permits the present processes of erosion to continue long

18C-2 *Profile of a typical stream*

FACETS OF GEOLOGY

18C-1

Controlling Erosion

Experts believe that before the settlement of Jamestown, the United States had an average of about 20 cm (8 in.) of topsoil. Today that depth is only 15 cm (5.9 in.). Scientists still do not know of any economical way to make more topsoil. Therefore, we must learn to conserve what we have.

Several methods can help control soil erosion. A simple way is to plant vegetation in eroded areas. Plant roots hold

Soil erosion damage (left two); *strip-cropping* (below) *and terracing* (right) *can control erosion.*

soil in place well. Because worn-out soil produces only scattered, weak plants that are sometimes unable to hold back erosion, crop rotation is also important. Through contour plowing and planting, farmers arrange crops at right angles to the direction that the water flows. This arrangement forms many small dams that check the flow of water. No-till agriculture limits erosion by planting without plowing or cultivating

the soil; thus, it is not as open to erosion. Strip-cropping, the practice of interspersing strips of row crops such as corn with strips of cover crops such as

enough, most present-day lakes will erode away. Thus, lakes are considered only temporary base levels for streams. For most streams the ultimate base level is sea level. Exceptions occur, however; the Jordan River has a base level 390 m (1,280 ft.) *below* sea level.

Streams are fed by smaller streams called **tributaries** (TRIB yuh TEHR ee). Tributaries flow into the main stream. A stream and its tributaries are a stream system. Seen from above, a river system often resembles the veins in a leaf. The land drained by a system is the main stream's **drainage basin.** The

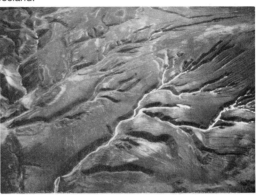

18C-3 *Many tributaries make up this drainage basin in Iceland.*

grass and alfalfa, also helps to prevent erosion. Cover crops are plants that have many small roots close to the surface of the soil. To further slow erosion, property owners may terrace a slope by grading it into level areas with walls around their steep sides.

Flooding is a major problem in some parts of the United States. Not only do floods cause the loss of life and property, but they also rapidly displace large amounts of valuable soil. Although this soil may settle downstream in a useful position, it is more likely to settle in the bottom of a river or lake.

Artificial levees, or walls, on either side of the river are one solution to this problem. These work reasonably well in some areas but prove inadequate in others. Their flaw is that they confine the sediment that normally spreads out over the river's entire flood plain. After the river has deposited sediment inside the walls, the water has less room available. Therefore, the water may rise higher the next year and the levees must be built progressively higher or moved out farther from the river, or both. Though dredging the sediment inside the levees is possible, it is costly.

Another approach to the problem of flooding is to build temporary reservoirs along the course of a river. At flood stage these reservoirs take much of the overflow and store it until the river recedes. The reservoirs then discharge the water back into the river.

Soil is one of our most valuable resources. We need soil to raise crops to feed ourselves and our livestock, to grow trees that we can use for lumber and paper products, and to support plants so that they can perform their vital function of manufacturing oxygen. Without soil the earth would be a desolate wasteland. A good citizen will do his part to help his community in the effort to conserve soil. A Christian has the additional responsibility of being a good steward of what the Lord has entrusted to him (Gen. 2:15).

18C-4 *The North American continental divide is found in the Rocky Mountains. The eastern continental divide separates drainage basins but technically is not a "continental" divide.*

WESTERN CONTINENTAL DIVIDE
GANNETT PEAK
ELEV. 13,785 FT.

size of the drainage basin differs for different streams. For a small stream, it may be only a few hundred square kilometers; for the Amazon, it is 6.5 million km² (2.5 million mi.²), a third of South America. A ridge separating one stream's drainage basin from another's is called a **divide.** The Rocky Mountains form the Continental Divide of the United States. The land east of the Rockies is drained largely by the Mississippi River system and others whose waters flow into the Gulf of Mexico and Atlantic Ocean. The land west of the Rockies is drained by several river systems whose waters flow into the Pacific Ocean.

Types of Streams

High-Gradient Streams
The stream gradient determines its appearance. High-gradient streams tend to be energetic. Such streams, found in mountainous or hilly regions, are characterized by steep sides and deep channels of water that occupy almost all the lower parts of the narrow valleys. These streams often have waterfalls and rapids. High-gradient streams also tend to vigorously erode their beds downward. Their steep-sided valleys tend to experience mass wasting.

Waterfalls form in several ways: by faulting, by the bulldozing action of glaciers, and by the unequal erosion of rocks. A classic example of the last method is Niagara Falls, where the water erodes the underlying shale more rapidly than the upper dolomite. The rate of erosion here is as much as 1.5 m (5 ft.) per year on the Canadian side of the falls.

18C-5 *View of a high-gradient stream in Yosemite National Park*

Rapids are places where the slope is steep and the rocks in the streambed are irregular. The flow of the water is turbulent, with many small eddy currents. The rockiness and the shallowness of most rapids make them dangerous or unnavigable with even a small boat. Rapids can form from a waterfall that has degenerated by extensive erosion.

Lakes frequently form connecting links between high-gradient streams. A lake usually has a stream that feeds its upper end and another stream that drains its lower end. Because the water flows from the upper to the lower end, the lake does not stagnate. The continuous drainage at the lower end keeps dissolved minerals from accumulating in the water; the lake stays fresh instead of becoming salty. The hand of the Creator is obvious in this arrangement, which keeps water pure and fresh for the living creatures that depend on it.

Low-Gradient Streams

Low-gradient streams have less energy than high-gradient streams because gravity supplies less driving force. These streams wind back and forth on a rather flat area known as a **flood plain,** which is covered when the stream floods. Falls and rapids are rare on flood plains, and stream erosion occurs mostly sideways against the stream banks. Ridges of soil, called **levees** (LEV ee), are often present on both sides of these streams. These are the deposits formed when the stream floods.

A typical low-gradient stream comprises many loops called **meanders** (mee AN dur). The water erodes soil from the outside of each meander and deposits it on the inside. During a flood the stream water frequently cuts across the neck of a meander and establishes a new route called a **neck cutoff.** The meander that is by-passed may dry up, or it may retain some water to become an **oxbow lake.**

18C-7 *Characteristic features of a low-gradient stream*

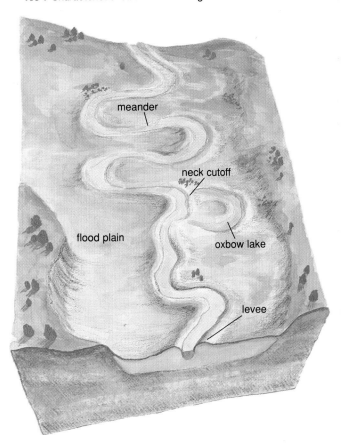

18C-6 *Oxbow Lake on the White River near Newport, Arizona*

FACETS OF GEOLOGY

The Grand Canyon

Most people in the United States at one time or another hear evolutionary propaganda about the Grand Canyon. It may be in the classroom, on television, or in newspapers, books, or magazines. It may come from the lips of a tour guide speaking to a group of awe-struck viewers.

The Grand Canyon is a colossal scenic wonder; it is 350 km (217 mi.) long and 1.5 km (1 mi.) deep. To a Christian it declares the power of God, but evolutionists see it differently. They say that the exposed sedimentary strata in the canyon represent hundreds of millions of years of deposition followed by millions of years of erosion.

The fossils in the strata, they say, tell the story of how life developed on the earth. This differs in every respect from what God's Word tells us.

One creationist explanation of the Grand Canyon is that most of the exposed strata of the canyon represent sediment deposited during the Genesis Flood. Much of the erosion may have happened shortly after the Flood, when the material was still soft and unconsolidated, and large amounts of water were moving from the continents to the oceans. Rivers undoubtedly carried much more water soon after the Flood than they do now. As the strata of

★ denotes pollen find

one type of pollen found

Triassic

Permian

Carboniferous

Cambrian

Colorado River

Precambrian

Precambrian

Cutaway view of the Grand Canyon showing where fossil pollen has been found—evolutionists claim the pollen should not be found below the stratum marked with the arrow.

the canyon hardened and the volume of water in the river decreased, erosion became slower and less extensive. Photographs show that the most recent erosion, at the bottom of the canyon, has been confined to a narrow region on either side of the river.

Creationists are carrying on several research projects to gain additional insight into the history of the Grand Canyon. One of these is investigating the discovery of pollen grains of gymnosperm and angiosperm plants in the lowest strata of the canyon. According to evolutionists, those plants did not exist until several million years after these strata formed. Although evolutionists will almost certainly reject their findings, creationists look confidently to the ultimate victory of God's truth.

A creationist group studying the Grand Canyon

Effects of Streams

Stream erosion moves topsoil from the continents and deposits it in the oceans. The amount of material transported by this process is staggering: an estimated 24 million metric tons of material flow into the oceans each year, never to be recovered. This amounts to a topsoil loss of about 6 cm (2.4 in.) per thousand years in the United States.

The story of erosion begins on mountain slopes and hillsides as rain falls. Raindrops striking the ground splash soil particles in all directions. The particles move more easily downhill than uphill; hence, the overall motion is downward. At the same time, rainwater moving downhill carries soil with it.

18C-8 *A flooding stream can carry a large amount of eroded soil.*

During another process of erosion on hillsides, called **solution,** moving water dissolves minerals from the soil and carries them away. The rainwater from the slopes flows into small streams, which in turn join larger streams. Most stream water eventually reaches an ocean.

Most erosion occurs when a stream is at flood stage. It usually reaches flood stage in the spring, when the stream is moving a large amount of water rapidly.

Stream water carries two kinds of eroded materials: suspended particles, which are carried along by the water's motion, and dissolved particles. The amount of suspended material a stream can carry depends on the speed of the stream. A fast-moving stream can carry more and larger particles than a slow-moving stream. Eventually, however, the water in a fast stream slows down. When it does, the stream deposits some of its suspended load. Deposition, the depositing of transported materials, occurs in an orderly fashion, with larger particles falling out first as the stream slows. The progression continues as smaller and smaller particles settle out. The finest particles—silt—do not settle until the water becomes almost stationary.

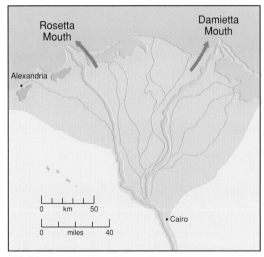

18C-9 *Delta of the Nile River in Egypt—the branching channels in a delta are called distributaries.*

What do stream deposits look like? You have probably seen such deposits, although you may not have recognized them. Flood plains form from stream sediment deposited during floods. Another type of stream deposit is the **delta.** A delta forms where a stream enters a lake, an ocean, a gulf, or other stationary body of water. Where a high-gradient stream flows out from a mountain valley onto a level plain, its speed is suddenly reduced, and an **alluvial** (uh LOO vee ul) **fan** may form. The alluvial fan looks like a delta but is on land, usually in arid climates, instead of at the stream's mouth. Flood plains and deltas are built from topsoil eroded farther upstream and thus contain some of the most fertile soils and are among the most agriculturally productive areas on the earth.

18C-10 *The Cedar Creek alluvial fan near Ennis, Montana* (top); *the contour map* (bottom) *shows the fanlike distribution of the stream sediment.*

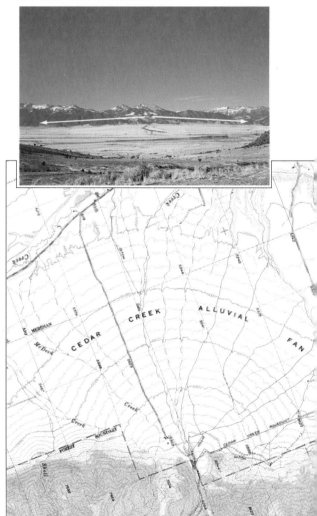

Section Review Questions 18C
1. What is the angle of a stream's slope called?
2. What is the ultimate base level for most streams?
3. What are smaller streams that flow into larger streams called?
4. Which flows faster, a high-gradient or a low-gradient stream?
5. What is a loop in the path of a low-gradient stream called?
6. What kind of erosion occurs when water dissolves minerals and removes them from the soil?
7. Which kind of alluvial deposit occurs where a stream enters a stationary body of water? where it flows onto a level plain?

Terms
alluvial fan	frost heaving	oxbow lake
base level	gradient	pedologist
blowout	headwaters	rock glacier
chemical weathering	horizon	rock slide
creep	humus	sand dune
debris slide	landslide	soil
delta	levee	solution
desert pavement	loam	source
divide	mass wasting	stream
drainage basin	meander	talus
erode	mechanical weathering	tributary
exfoliation	mouth	
flood plain	neck cutoff	

What Did You Learn?
1. How do plants weather rocks?
2. Into which ocean, sea, lake, or gulf does the stream nearest to your school eventually empty?
3. Why might a boat on a low-gradient stream have to travel 2 or 3 miles to make 1 mile of forward progress?
4. List six methods for controlling soil erosion.
5. Which soil horizon is most fertile? Why?

What Do You Think?
1. What problems might be encountered in manufacturing artificial topsoil for eroded farmland?
2. Is soil dirt?
3. Two building sites are offered to you. One is on a hillside next to a lovely row of old, tilted fence posts covered with beautiful rose bushes. The other is on a hillside as well, but it is bordered by unsightly erect telephone poles covered with poison ivy. On which site would you choose to build your house? Why?
4. Should soil from deltas or dredged rivers be transported back to eroded farmland?
5. Should people be allowed to live on flood plains?

THE HYDROSPHERE

UNIT IV

THE OCEANS AND SEAS

NINETEEN

19A–Composition of Seawater

The importance of the oceans cannot be over-emphasized. The oceans cover about 71 per cent of the earth's surface. The Pacific Ocean alone covers more area than all the land masses put together. The oceans represent almost all of the earth's water—more than 97 per cent. If the earth's crust were level, this immense quantity of water would cover it to a depth of 2.7 km (1.7 mi.).

Oceanographers include scientists from almost every field who are striving to gain new information about the ocean. Marine biologists investigate the plant and animal life at different depths. Meteorologists are learning more about the influence of the oceans on weather and climate. Chemists are studying new methods of recovering minerals from the oceans and are trying to find an economical way to produce drinking water from seawater. Physicists and engineers are finding ways to harness the energy of the ocean to generate electricity. Studying the oceans will improve our understanding of the earth. It will also have practical benefits as we improve weather forecasts; find new sources of food, minerals, and energy; and discover safer means of transportation and recreation on the oceans.

Dissolved Minerals

Seawater is a complex solution of water, dissolved minerals, and dissolved gases. Its exact composition varies with local conditions. Most of the dissolved mineral content is table salt, but seawater includes other compounds and elements.

Where do the ocean's dissolved minerals come from? Did God create the sea salty or fresh? We do not know the original composition of the ocean, but we do know that it gains and loses minerals every day. The streams that enter the ocean carry large amounts of dissolved minerals with them. Much of the ocean's salt (mineral) concentration could have accumulated in a few

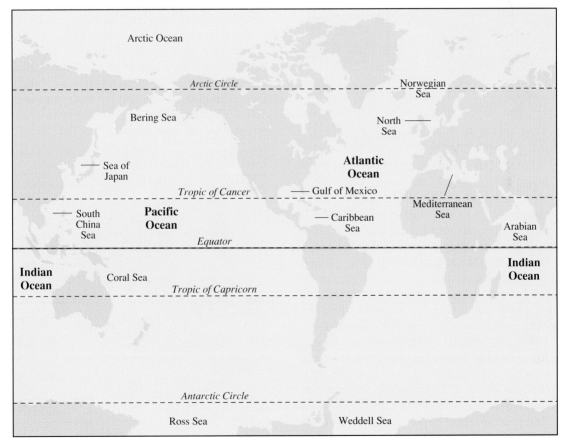

19A-1 *Major oceans and seas of the earth—is the surface of the earth mostly land or mostly water?*

thousand years from the streams. Perhaps the salty concentration of minerals in the ocean was a result of the Flood, when rivers and run-off carried much more sediment than they do now. Perhaps God created the oceans salty. We know that many of the ocean's creatures today can live in salty water but not fresh water.

19A-2

OF COURSE, THEY'RE SAFE! CONFIDENTIALLY, THEY'RE NOTHING MORE THAN SUGAR.

If the ocean's water is replenished by fresh stream water, why is the ocean salty while the streams are fresh? When water evaporates, it leaves its dissolved minerals behind. Thus, the ocean gains minerals and water daily but loses only water to evaporation. A net gain of minerals occurs if only stream flow and evaporation are considered. Lakes that have no outlets, such as the Dead Sea and Great Salt Lake, become salty like the ocean as the water continually evaporates.

How do minerals leave the ocean's water? One way is through the activities of living organisms. For example, the animals that form sea shells and coral reefs remove calcium from the seawater when they build their skeletons. Microscopic diatoms (DY uh TAHM) similarly remove silicon from ocean water by forming skeletons of silica. Miner-

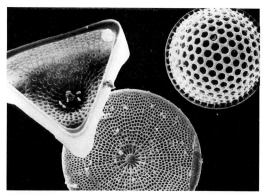

19A-3 *Microscopic diatom skeletons are made of silica.*

als are removed also through seafloor sediments. Clay particles, which are covered with negative electrical charges, bind positively charged substances and then settle to the ocean floor. The elements bound to the clay particles are thus removed from the water. The average time between an atom's entering the ocean and its removal by some means is called **residence time.** Residence time is different for each type of atom.

19A-4 *Magnesium salt is removed from sea water* (below). *The metal is then produced in electrolytic cells* (right).

The amount of dissolved solids in seawater varies throughout the earth. In areas of high rainfall or large rivers, the sea tends to have less salt because the fresh water dilutes it. Also, the ocean near the poles tends to be less salty because it seldom evaporates, and melting icebergs dilute it. In hot areas like the Mediterranean Sea, however, the ocean contains a large proportion of salt. Evaporation is high, rainfall is low, and few rivers flow into the Mediterranean Sea.

The oceans contain vast amounts of commercially valuable dissolved minerals. For example, seawater contains magnesium, bromine, phosphorous, and tin. It even contains gold! Altogether, some fifty-five elements have been identified in seawater. Unfortunately, most are too dilute to be recovered efficiently. For example, 170,000 metric tons (about 160 km^3) of seawater contain only a single gram of gold. A few compounds are concentrated enough to be obtained from seawater. On the average, if 1,000 g of seawater is evaporated, 35 g of various minerals will remain. About three-fourths of this is

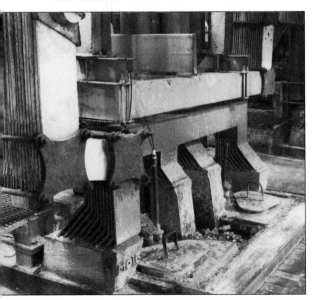

table salt (sodium chloride). Only table salt, magnesium, and bromine are commercially extracted. A potentially usable mineral resource in the ocean is manganese nodules. These nodules are composed mostly of manganese and iron oxides, but they also contain nickel, copper, cobalt, titanium, and zirconium. Nodules can be found on the seafloor in several places. Scientists disagree about whether they are formed by a chemical reaction or are deposited by bacteria.

Although many dissolved minerals in seawater are valuable, its most valuable constit-

19A-5 *A reverse osmosis plant uses a sophisticated filtering process to remove salt from ocean water.*

uent may be fresh water. In many places near the sea, fresh water is scarce. Thus, the people try to **desalinate** (dee SAL uh NATE), or remove the salt from, seawater. The most straightforward way to desalinate water is distillation. This process boils the water and then condenses its vapor. The minerals do not enter the vapor; so the condensed water is fresh. This method is expensive because it requires much fuel to boil the water. Scientists are studying other, possibly cheaper, ways to desalinate water. Experts also think that recovering and selling minerals from the salt removed from the seawater may reduce the price of the fresh water produced.

Dissolved Gases

Besides dissolved minerals, seawater contains dissolved nitrogen, oxygen, carbon dioxide, and other gases. Because the gases do not dissolve in water and the atmosphere at the same rate, their proportions are different from those in the atmosphere. Nitrogen is not as soluble in water as oxygen and carbon dioxide; so it makes up only 64 per cent of the dissolved gases in the ocean, compared to 78 per cent in the atmosphere. Surface water is usually richer in oxygen than deeper water because of the nearness of the oxygen in the atmosphere and the presence of marine plants and microorganisms which produce oxygen. The oceans easily absorb carbon dioxide from the air and thus help to regulate the amount of carbon dioxide in the atmosphere.

Section Review Questions 19A

1. What percentage of the earth's surface do the oceans cover?
2. What percentage of the earth's water do the oceans contain?
3. Name the most abundant dissolved mineral in seawater.
4. What factors may cause the concentration of dissolved minerals in seawater to vary?
5. What is the average weight of the dissolved minerals in 1,000 g of seawater?
6. List the three elements or minerals that are commercially extracted from seawater.
7. Why does surface water have a higher concentration of oxygen than deeper water?

19B–Ocean Motions

The ocean is never motionless. Even when it appears calm, it is moving in currents or is rising or falling because of the tide. The wind causes most of the ocean's surface activity, but gravity and even earthquakes contribute to the motion. There is activity deep beneath the surface caused by other forces as well.

Tides

Tides are caused mostly by the moon's gravity, with some influence from the sun's gravity and centrifugal force. The gravity of the moon directly causes a bulge of ocean water on the side of the earth toward the moon.

The bulge on the opposite side is due primarily to the centrifugal force of the combined earth-moon rotating system. You might think that the centrifugal force generated by the earth rotating on its axis would be the same around the earth; it is. But the centrifugal force causing the bulge on the side opposite the moon does not come from the rotation of the earth on its axis. Rather, this centrifugal force is caused by the rotation of the earth *and* moon around a common point. Since this point is not at the center of the earth, the centrifugal force is not equal across the earth. It is strongest at the far side of the moon and the far side of the earth. The bulge caused by the centrifugal force is somewhat smaller than the bulge caused by the moon's gravity.

A bulge of water is called a high tide. When the bulge is farthest from the coast, the low tide occurs. Along most coasts there are two high tides and two low tides each day. It takes twenty-four hours and fifty minutes for one bulge to travel completely around the

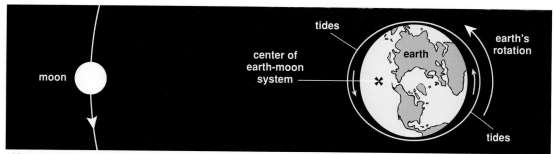

19B-1 *High tides are caused on opposite sides of the earth because of the gravity of the moon and the centrifugal force exerted by rotation of the earth-moon system around a common point.*

earth (twelve hours and twenty-five minutes to go from one high tide bulge to the next.) The tides are not exactly twelve hours apart because as the earth has been rotating, the moon has moved forward in its orbit. It takes fifty minutes more each day for a location on the earth to catch up with its previous position relative to the moon.

The sun's gravity causes tides as well, but in most areas they are much smaller than those caused by the moon. These smaller bulges travel completely around the earth in exactly twenty-four hours and thus eventually catch up with the slower-traveling lunar tides. Twice each month, at the new moon and full moon, the sun, moon, and earth are in a straight line. At these times the sun's gravity works with the moon's to form a higher-than-usual tide called a **spring tide.** When the sun, the earth, and the moon form a right angle, the effects of the sun's gravity work against the moon's to form a lower-

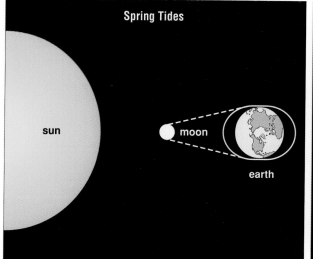
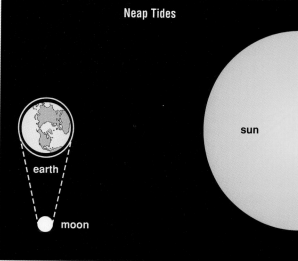

19B-2 *When the sun and the moon are in line, very high tides called spring tides occur (left). When the sun and the moon are at right angles to the earth, lower tides called neap tides occur.*

than-usual tide called a **neap** (NEEP) **tide.** This also happens twice each month, at the first and third quarters (phases of the moon).

The shapes of the coast and ocean basin also affect the height and time of tides. In the Mediterranean Sea, the tide seldom rises more than 30 cm (1 ft.). But at the Bay of Fundy, in Canada, the tide may rise over 15 m (50 ft.). This bay is a V-shaped inlet with its narrowest part away from the sea. It acts as a funnel to bring a large amount of seawater into a small space. During high tide some of the bay's rivers run backward. Most parts of the Gulf of Mexico experience only one high tide per day because of the semi-enclosed nature of its basin.

19B-4 *Bay of Fundy at high* (top) *and low* (above) *tides*

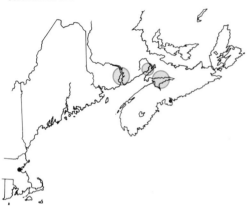

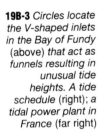

19B-3 *Circles locate the V-shaped inlets in the Bay of Fundy* (above) *that act as funnels resulting in unusual tide heights. A tide schedule* (right)*; a tidal power plant in France* (far right)

What Is Sea Level?

What is sea level? Does it change with each tide and wave, or is it strictly set and unchanging? **Sea level** changes with every tide, but **mean sea level,** which is commonly referred to as sea level, is more steady. Mean sea level is halfway between high tide and low tide. Since the heights of high and low tides vary, they are measured over several years and then averaged to determine mean sea level.

You might expect that since all the oceans are connected, there would be only one mean sea level. Actually, mean sea level varies from place to place. Mean sea level on the Pacific coast of the United States is about 50 cm higher than on the Atlantic coast. Florida's Gulf coast mean sea level is about 19 cm higher than on its Atlantic coast, and mean sea level on the New Jersey coast is about 20 cm higher than at the Florida coast. These differences are caused by many factors, including currents, ocean depth, water density, temperature, and prevailing winds.

In most places mean sea level is rising about 1 mm each year. This average rate was computed from yearly measurements of mean sea level at 193 locations around the world for over one hundred years. Some locations had even greater increases, and a few reported decreases in mean sea level. Most scientists attribute this increase in mean sea level to global warming, and some attribute global warming to the burning of fossil fuels since the 1800s. However, not all the global warming can be attributed to man's industrial activities, because glaciers

were retreating well before the 1800s. Most of the increase in mean sea level is due to expansion of a warming ocean, while the increase from melting glaciers or continental movements is negligible.

Section Review Questions 19B-1

1. Tides are caused mostly by the gravity of what object?
2. What force of the earth-moon system causes the water bulge on the side of the earth farthest from the moon?
3. What is the name given to the higher-than-usual tide formed when the sun's and moon's gravitational pulls work together?
4. In most locations, is mean sea level rising, falling, or staying the same?

Waves

Wave Generation

The most obvious motion of the sea is its waves. Most waves are generated by wind. As the wind blows along the surface of the ocean, it drags the surface water along with it a short distance. Then as the water falls back, it forces the water behind it to move back. Waves move great distances, but the waves do not transport water great distances. Individual drops of water circle up and down as the waves pass, but they move very little horizontally. This action is similar to how individual spectators in a stadium participate in a "wave." Each person stands up and sits down, and the "wave" moves along rapidly; but no single person moves horizontally with the "wave."

Waves have several measurable characteristics. The vertical distance from the **crest** (peak) to the **trough** (lowest part) of a wave is the **wave height.** The **wavelength** is the horizontal distance from one crest to the next. Waves of the sea are usually called surface waves because they disturb only a relatively shallow layer of the water. The **wave base,** the depth to which the wave reaches below the surface of the water, is equal to half the wavelength. A typical wave in the open sea may have a wave height of 1 m, a wavelength of 50 m, and a wave base of 25 m.

Coming Ashore

As a wave approaches the shore, it moves through shallower water. When the water's depth is less than the wave base, the wave begins to change. The bottom part of the wave slows due to friction with the seafloor. Because its motion is hindered below, the water begins to go higher above the surface; the wave height increases. Soon the wave is so high that it becomes unstable. The water at the top peaks sharply, then falls over on

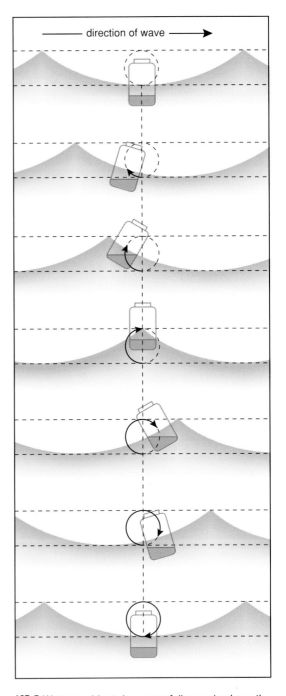

— direction of wave →

19B-5 *Water or objects in a wave follow a circular path.*

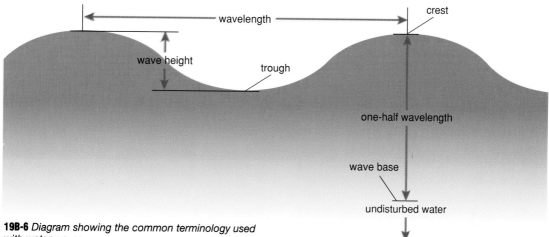

19B-6 *Diagram showing the common terminology used with water waves*

the forward side of the wave. Such a wave is called a **breaker.**

Waves usually approach the shore at an angle. The nearest end of the wave slows down due to friction with the shallow bottom. The other end of the wave continues to travel at its original speed until it too reaches the shallow water. As a result, the direction of the wave becomes nearly parallel to the shoreline.

Waves are rarely exactly parallel to the shoreline. Instead, they strike the shore somewhat diagonally, moving sand, shells, and other materials onto the beach. Gravity then pulls the water and some of the shore material back into the ocean. The repeated

19B-7 *Breakers coming ashore near Big Sur, California*

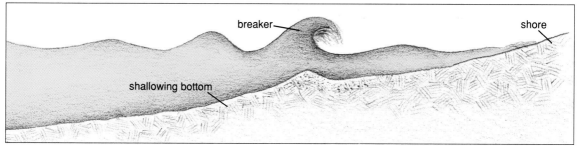

19B-8 *Breakers form as waves pass over shallow areas, such as near the shore. Friction with the bottom causes the wave to slow and go higher. The unstable wave that falls over is called a breaker.*

up-and-back motion of numerous waves usually moves the sand and other debris onto the shore. Waves that approach the shore at an angle also produce a current that flows parallel to the shore, called a **longshore current.**

Water that flows onto a beach will quickly return down the slope of the beach to the ocean. Occasionally water flows back from the shore in a **rip current,** a strong surface current that flows through a gap in the breakers. Rip currents occur when the breakers are large and a large amount of water must return to the ocean. A person who finds himself caught in a rip current can be carried out to deep water and may quickly fatigue by trying to swim against the current. Because rip currents are narrow, the best action for a person caught in one is to swim at a right angle to it. When he is safely out of it, he can swim to shore.

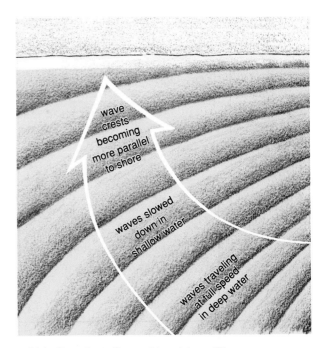

19B-9 The leading end of a wave slows down in shallow water, which allows the trailing end to catch up. Waves become nearly parallel near the shore (above). Longshore currents (below) develop when water near the shore is deep. Little slowing of the waves occurs as they approach the shore. Longshore currents can cause a beach to drift (inset).

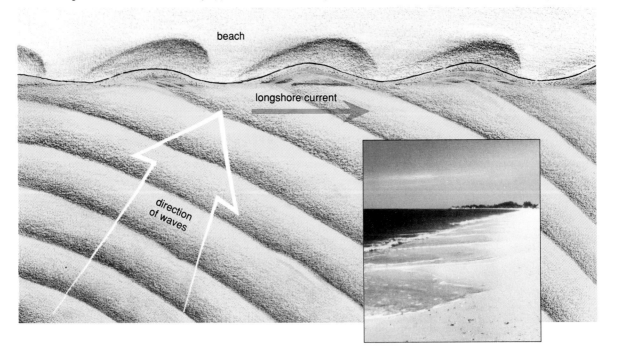

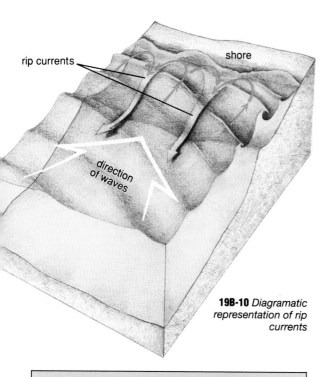

rip currents

shore

direction of waves

19B-10 *Diagramatic representation of rip currents*

Ocean Erosion

Beaches are built from eroded materials deposited by waves. Waves, especially during storms, also can remove or erode the loosely deposited materials. Beach erosion is an expensive danger for people who build homes close to the seashore. At most locations along the mid-Atlantic coast of the United States, beach erosion is occurring at a rate of 0.5 to 1.4 m (18 to 54 in.) per year. In some areas, such as the outer banks of Virginia, beaches are being eroded as much as 7.6 m (25 ft.) per year.

19B-11 *Inlets reopened by a hurricane in Texas* (top); *problems associated with beach erosion* (below)

Rip Currents: Swimmers Beware!

Many beachside deaths are caused by a phenomenon called "rip currents." These swift currents can knock a swimmer off his feet and carry him rapidly out to sea. Panicked swimmers exhaust themselves by fighting against the current and drown.

Rip currents occur when high waves dump large amounts of water on the beach. As the water builds up, it rushes back out into the ocean along narrow paths. These currents usually form in low points in the breakers. They can rip at 1 m/s (3.3 ft./s) for several minutes, racing 760 m (2,500 ft.) into the sea before dying out.

You can easily locate a rip current. Look for strips of water where sand is being carried out by the current, or look for slight changes in the wave patterns as they meet a rip current. If you are ever caught in a rip current, remember that they are narrow. You simply need to swim *parallel* to the shore until you are free of the current. Then you can head back to shore.

Beaches are not the only type of shore that the waves erode. Many coasts are bounded by cliffs. As the waves erode the cliffs, they create beaches in front of the cliffs. Occasionally a weaker part of the rock erodes away, leaving a **sea cave.** If the sides of the cave erode, they may leave a **sea arch,** which resembles a natural bridge. A **stack** is a mass of rock that wave erosion has isolated from the shore.

When the waves erode material, they must eventually redeposit it. When water laden with sand encounters an obstacle, it slows down and deposits some sand. This often happens near the edges of a bay. If the deposited sand forms a straight line from the shore across part of a bay, it forms a **spit.** The spit may eventually extend across the bay's mouth, closing it to the sea. This is a **bay barrier.** A spit with a sharp bend is called a **hook.** When the waves deposit sand across the mouth of a bay but the island of sand has no connection with the mainland, the deposit is called a **barrier island.** Many of the islands of the southeast coast of the United States are barrier islands. Another wave deposit called a **tombolo** (TOME buh LOH) often connects islands with each other or the mainland.

19B-12 *Landforms that are produced by incomplete beach erosion: a sea arch and stack near Quebec, Canada (above); a stack on the coast of New Brunswick (right).*

19B-13 *Debris deposited inside a coastal sea cave*

19B-14 Land forms which are built from eroded material deposited by water: *barrier island* (top left), *spit* (bottom left), *bay barrier* (top right), *tombolo* (bottom right)

Section Review Questions 19B-2

1. What causes most waves?
2. As a wave approaches the shore, does the wave height increase, decrease, or remain unchanged?
3. What two kinds of currents are related to the interaction of waves with the shore?
4. What is the name given to a mass of rock that has been cut off from the mainland by erosion?

Currents

As described previously, longshore currents and rip currents occur only near land because they are produced by waves approaching the shore or by water returning from off a beach. There are other currents in the ocean caused by other forces, which move more water and move it greater distances.

Surface Currents

Surface currents, like waves, are caused by winds. However, surface currents last longer than wave patterns, and they transport water long distances. The surface currents of the ocean tend to follow the prevailing winds. Like the winds, the currents are affected by the rotation of the earth (Coriolis effect). Thus, in the Northern Hemisphere the currents tend to flow clockwise, but in the Southern Hemisphere they tend to flow counterclockwise.

Ocean currents affect the weather by carrying cold or warm water far from its source. For example, the Gulf Stream and the Japan (or Kuroshio) Current are warm currents that flow north from warm areas. The Gulf Stream flows from the Gulf of Mexico toward Europe, and the Japan Current flows along the east coast of Asia toward North America. Winds blowing from the west (the prevailing westerlies) across these warm currents bring warm weather to northern Europe and western Canada. Because of the winds across the Gulf Stream, England is warmer than New York, even though it is farther north than New York. Similarly, western Canada is warmer than eastern Siberia as a result of the Japan Current.

Cold currents flow from the polar regions toward the equator. These also affect the weather of the nearby land. Land near cold currents tends to be dry because cold air can hold less rainwater. For example, a cold current off the coast of Baja California keeps that Mexican state's climate dry. Both the Atacama (AT uh KAM uh) Desert in South America, where rain falls only a few times each century, and the Namib (NAH MIB) Desert in Southern Africa are coastal regions near a cold current.

Subsurface Currents

Because subsurface currents are harder to detect than surface currents, they are not as well known. Several different types have been discovered. One kind is the **countercurrent,** a slow current that flows beneath most major surface currents. The surface currents and countercurrents flow in opposite directions. Countercurrents are much slower than surface currents. The Gulf Stream flows northward at about 6-8 km/hr. (4-5 mph); the Gulf Stream countercurrent flows southward at about 13 km (8 mi.) *per day.*

Gravity produces some deep currents. In some places water with different amounts of dissolved salts meet. The amount of dissolved salts affects the density of the water. Thus, the more saline (salty) water tends to sink, and the less saline water tends to rise. This action produces a current called a **density current.** The Mediterranean Sea is mixed with the Atlantic Ocean by a density current. The floor of the Mediterranean Sea is separated from the Atlantic floor by an underwater ledge where the two meet. Because the Mediterranean water is saltier, it tends to sink. The less-saline water from the Atlantic flows into the Mediterranean Sea at the surface. This flow forces some of the dense Mediterranean water over the ledge and into the Atlantic. Other seas separated from the ocean by a ledge have similar circulation patterns.

Another cause of density differences is temperature. Cold water is more dense than warm water. Thus, water from the poles tends

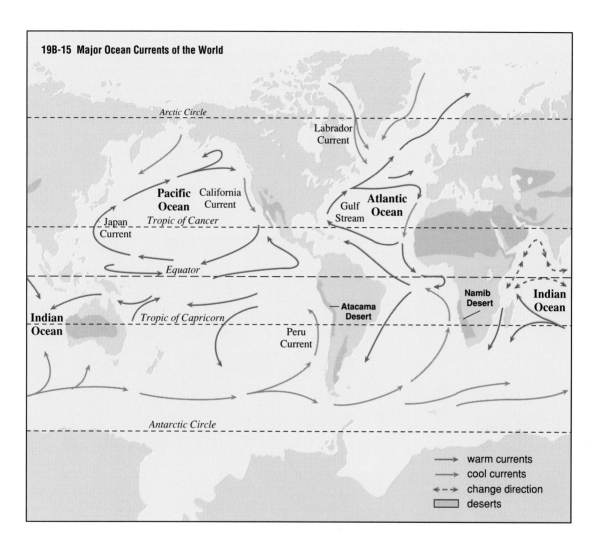

19B-15 Major Ocean Currents of the World

Arctic Circle

Labrador
Current

**Pacific
Ocean** California
Current

Gulf
Stream **Atlantic
Ocean**

Japan
Current *Tropic of Cancer*

Equator

**Indian
Ocean**

**Indian
Ocean** *Tropic of Capricorn*

Peru
Current — Atacama
Desert

Namib
Desert

Antarctic Circle

→ warm currents
→ cool currents
◄- -► change direction
▭ deserts

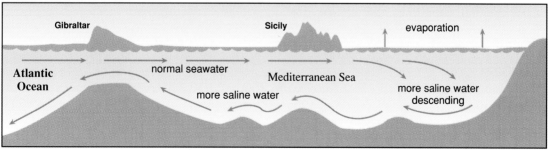

Gibraltar   Sicily   evaporation

**Atlantic
Ocean**   normal seawater   Mediterranean Sea

more saline water   more saline water
descending

A density current mixes the Atlantic Ocean and Mediterranean Sea.

to sink to the bottom when it encounters warmer water. The cold, dense water from Antarctica travels north toward the equator along the bottom of the ocean. The cold water from the Arctic similarly travels southward toward the equator.

Where water is more dense because it carries sediment, another type of density current, called a **turbidity** (tur BID ih tee) **current,** is formed. The sediment-laden water travels along the ocean floor, eroding it as it goes. Some of the underwater canyons in the continental slopes may have been eroded by turbidity currents.

On the western coasts of some continents, especially South America, the trade winds blow from the east strongly and persistently enough to move the top, warm layer of the ocean to the west. Cold water from the bottom moves up to fill the space left in a process called **upwelling** (UP WEL ing). The water from the bottom is rich in nutrients and forms the base of a food chain that includes one of the world's greatest fisheries.

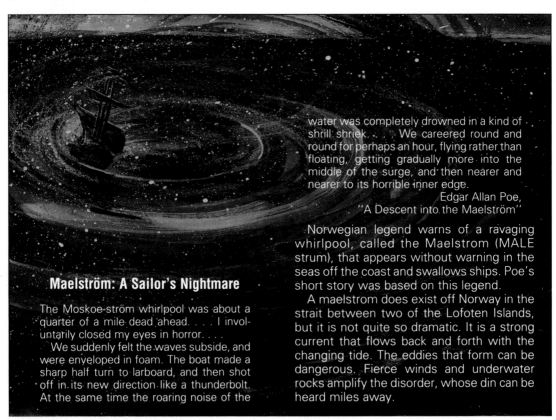

water was completely drowned in a kind of shrill shriek. . . . We careered round and round for perhaps an hour, flying rather than floating, getting gradually more into the middle of the surge, and then nearer and nearer to its horrible inner edge.

Edgar Allan Poe,
"A Descent into the Maelström"

Norwegian legend warns of a ravaging whirlpool, called the Maelstrom (MALE strum), that appears without warning in the seas off the coast and swallows ships. Poe's short story was based on this legend.

A maelstrom does exist off Norway in the strait between two of the Lofoten Islands, but it is not quite so dramatic. It is a strong current that flows back and forth with the changing tide. The eddies that form can be dangerous. Fierce winds and underwater rocks amplify the disorder, whose din can be heard miles away.

Maelström: A Sailor's Nightmare

The Moskoe-ström whirlpool was about a quarter of a mile dead ahead. . . . I involuntarily closed my eyes in horror. . . .

We suddenly felt the waves subside, and were enveloped in foam. The boat made a sharp half turn to larboard, and then shot off in its new direction like a thunderbolt. At the same time the roaring noise of the

Section Review Questions 19B-3
1. Which is faster, a surface current or a countercurrent?
2. What kind of density current is caused by sinking, muddy water?
3. What is cold, nutrient-rich water rising from the ocean bottom called?

19C–Topography† of the Seafloor

The oceans of the earth completely surround the land. Because all oceans are connected, scientists sometimes say that the earth has only one ocean. For convenience, however, they usually divide the world ocean into three major parts: the Atlantic, the Indian, and the Pacific oceans. Parts of these oceans are more or less surrounded by land and are called **seas.** For example, the Mediterranean Sea is a branch of the Atlantic Ocean. Because the arrangement of these oceans and seas was important for international trade, explorers studied and mapped the oceans as they mapped the land. Thus, the surface of the ocean is its best-known part.

Compared to land, the surface of the ocean is flat and featureless. Perhaps that is why scientists of the past mostly ignored the ocean. Modern scientists have found that the ocean is far from featureless and that it has many interesting aspects to study. Its basin and its composition are among the topics that oceanographers study.

Ocean Basins

Until the late nineteenth century, most scientists assumed that the ocean's basin was as flat as its surface. Because they had no way to study the deep ocean floor, they could not test their assumptions. Then, in 1872, the British ship *Challenger* began a three-year voyage to study the ocean. One of its tasks was to determine the ocean's depth in various places. As the scientists measured the depths, they realized that the ocean floor has no fewer features than the land. The ocean floor has deeper valleys, taller mountains, and broader plains than the land.

The *Challenger* used a long rope weighted with lead to measure the depths of the oceans. Modern oceanographic vessels use **echo**

sounding to measure ocean depths. In this technique, the ship sends sound waves to the ocean floor and records the time it takes them to return. Ships using echo sounding have now mapped much of the ocean floor.

Although surface ships have discovered valuable information about the ocean floor, the best way to study a region is to visit it.

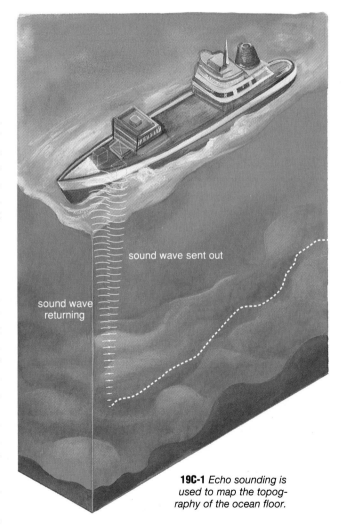

sound wave sent out

sound wave returning

19C-1 *Echo sounding is used to map the topography of the ocean floor.*

---

† Topography is the detailed description of the surface of an area.

The biggest obstacle to visiting the ocean floor is the great pressure of the water. Not until the last few decades have scientists had a vehicle capable of withstanding the pressures of great depths. In 1960 the bathyscaph* (BATH ih SKAF) *Trieste* encountered the greatest pressure known to exist in the ocean—about 1,200 kg/cm^2 (17,000 lb./in.^{2}), more than one thousand times the pressure at sea level. This is the pressure at the bottom of the Marianas (MEHR ee AHN us) Trench, about 11,000 m (36,000 ft.) below sea level. Bathyscaphs and other underwater vehicles allow scientists to travel or send cameras to the ocean floor so that they can see the area that they are studying. The oceans are so vast and the number of vehicles so small that only a fraction of the ocean floor has been studied. Much of the recent mapping of the ocean floor has been done using satellites.

The earliest oceanographers discovered that the ocean is comparatively shallow along the continents. The land slopes out gently from the continents in most places, forming a **continental shelf.** Continental shelves are submerged edges of continents and as such have geologic formations characteristic of continents, such as sedimentary rocks, oil, and gas. A typical continental shelf extends 65 km (40 mi.) from the mainland to a depth of 200 m (654 ft.). Some continents have no such submerged shelf; however, others have a continental shelf extending more than 1,200 km (745 mi.).

At the edge of each continental shelf is a steep **continental slope.** Often the slopes have **submarine canyons** running down them and deltas at their mouths. These canyons are most common near large rivers and often appear to be extensions of river valleys from the land. Christian men of science who have studied the question of how the canyons formed suggest three possibilities for their origin. Some explain the canyons as drowned river valleys produced at a time before the Flood. The sea level was perhaps much lower before the Flood than it is now, leaving the continental slopes and shelves as dry land with large river valleys. Others agree that the submarine canyons are drowned river valleys but suggest that they were formed during a period of glaciation after the Flood. Most scientists agree that sea level was at least 100 m (328 ft.) lower during the ice age than it is today. Some propose that the canyons were carved out immediately after the Flood as large quantities of water were flowing from the continents into the ocean basins.

19C-2 *Topography of the ocean floor*

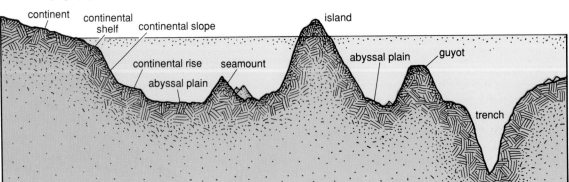

bathyscaph: bathy- (Gk. BATHUS, deep) + -scaph (Gk. SCAPHE, boat)

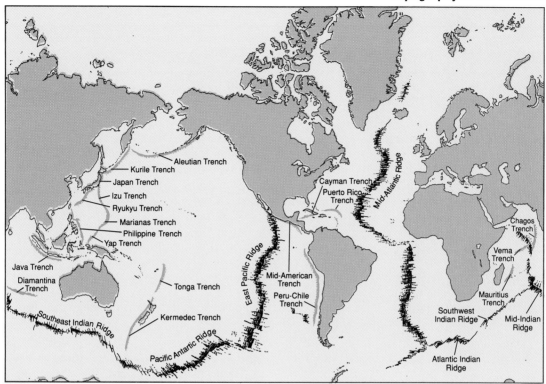

19C-3 *Outstanding ocean ridges and trenches.*

Beyond the continental slope is usually a gentle **continental rise.** The continental rise is built largely from sediments that have washed off the continental shelf. This rise levels off and meets the ocean floor, which has an average depth of more than 3 km (2 mi.). The flat, deep seafloors are called **abyssal** (uh BIS ul) **plains.** These plains are the part of the ocean basin that appear closest to the old idea of a flat, featureless, ocean bottom. The ocean floors are covered by sediments which vary in depth. Scientists study the floor sediments by drilling cylindrical samples from them. Even where the abyssal plains are covered with deep sediments, they are not featureless. Ridges and mountains rise from the plains to give the ocean floor at least as much variety as the land.

Seamounts and Trenches

Each ocean has a **mid-ocean ridge** rising from its depths. These ridges are submerged mountain ranges. The best-known ridge is the Mid-Atlantic Ridge, the longest mountain range on earth. Each ridge is jagged and fractured, indicating instability. Earthquakes often occur near the ridges, and the seafloor appears to be spreading in these areas.

Submerged islands, or **seamounts,** protrude from abyssal plains. Scientists believe that all seamounts are volcanic in origin. Some seamounts have flat tops and are called **guyots** (GEE oh). Perhaps these seamounts were once above sea level and were eroded by waves. Their tops are now an average of 1.5 km (1 mi.) below sea level. Some scientists interpret this evidence of erosion to mean that the seas were once much lower.

Trenches, which are deep valleys in the ocean floor, are another of the interesting features of the ocean floor. The deepest depths

FACETS OF OCEANOGRAPHY

19C-1

Adventures in the Sea

The ocean, as you have learned by now, is more than a featureless expanse of water. It is an exciting world much different from that on the land. Only recently have scientists begun to explore this strange world. Beginning with H.M.S. *Challenger,* research vessels have diligently explored the deep, taking water and seafloor samples, temperature and current readings, and depth soundings. A major new tool has also been added to the research vessels—submersibles.

Two of the most sophisticated research vessels in the world have served the Ocean Drilling Program, which began taking core samples from the ocean floor in 1968. The first drilling rig, *Glomar Challenger,* remained in service for many years. A unique computer regulated its propellers to keep the rig motionless above the drill site, even in the fiercest storms. The rig extracted over 50 miles of core samples from over five hundred sites in the Atlantic, Pacific, and Indian oceans. The samples have provided new insights into the history and make-up of the ocean floors. The *Glomar Challenger's* successor, *JOIDES Resolution,* has continued this drilling.

Another major research vessel, which studies the ocean surface and currents, is called FLIP (FLoating Instrument Platform). It sails to a site on its own power, and then it literally flips up into a vertical position by filling one end of the sleek vessel with water. FLIP is so well designed that it sits almost motionless in all extremes of weather.

The dream of oceanologists has long been to study the ocean floor firsthand. Scuba diving was invented for that purpose. But since the length of stay was so limited, scientists developed underwater laboratories and submersible vehicles.

Scuba divers are limited in depth and duration of their dives.

The laboratories allowed scientists to stay underwater for days without wasting valuable time on the surface. *Tektite I,* launched in 1969, allowed marine scientists to stay just under the surface of the Caribbean Sea for two weeks. The U.S. Navy also commissioned an underwater home called *Sealab.*

As submersibles improve, they enable scientists to go deeper, range wider, and stay in the

Glomar Challenger

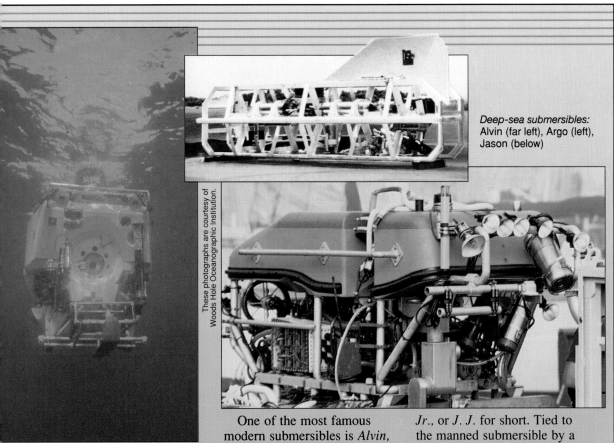

Deep-sea submersibles: Alvin (far left), Argo (left), Jason (below)

These photographs are courtesy of Woods Hole Oceanographic Institution.

ocean longer. The U.S. Navy launched a nuclear-powered research submarine in 1969, *NR-1,* which can remain underwater for twenty days. Although one important task is to locate military equipment lost at sea, *NR-1* emphasizes research. Other submersibles include *Pisces,* which has studied rare deep-sea sharks; *Geo,* which was the first submersible to see a live "fossil," a primitive fish called the coelacanth (SEE luh KANTH); and *Aluminaut,* a submarine made mostly of aluminum.

One of the most famous modern submersibles is *Alvin,* which has made over seventeen hundred dives. Recently improved to withstand depths of up to 43,000 m (13,000 ft.), it has studied volcanic activity and plate movement on the ocean floor. Its most famous expedition was a close-up study of the *Titanic,* nearly 3 miles beneath the ocean surface.

Although the key element in research has always been man, the managers of *Alvin* are proving the great potential of robotics. On its 1986 trip to the *Titanic, Alvin* was aided by a "seeing eyeball" named *Jason*

Jr., or *J. J.* for short. Tied to the manned submersible by a 60-m (200-ft.) line, the 71-cm (28-in.) robot was able to descend the steps leading into the heart of the *Titanic.*

A contemporary of *Alvin* is *Argo* which was used in the discovery of the *Titanic* and another "unsinkable" ship, the Nazi battleship *Bismark. Argo* will become even more advanced when combined with *Jason,* the successor to *Jason Jr.* Like *J. J., Jason* will be a "seeing eyeball" but will also have arms and hands capable of retrieving samples from the seafloor.

in the oceans occur in trenches. Trenches usually appear near Pacific **island arcs** that are near the continents. Arcs are long curved chains of islands such as the Aleutians, West Indies, Philippines, or the Ryukyu (off the southern tip of Japan). Trenches are on the side of the arc that is farthest from the continent. Most trenches have one steep slope near the islands and a gentle slope on the ocean side. These trenches appear to be areas where the edges of tectonic plates are meeting and one is moving downward into the earth's mantle.

Coral Reefs

Another type of feature associated with the ocean is a **coral reef.** Corals are tiny animals which live predominantly in warm tropical and subtropical waters, and most secrete a calcium carbonate shelter. Some corals live together in vast colonies along with other organisms that secrete calcium carbonate. The calcium carbonate accumulates, forming a coral reef. These reefs often emerge above the surface as islands.

Reef-forming corals require light to grow. Thus, coral reefs are found in shallow water near land. The reefs nearest to the mainland are **fringing reefs.** Little water separates the land from the reef. Fringing reefs occur along the Florida coast and the coast of Bermuda.

Barrier reefs are farther from the land, and a lagoon is formed between the reef and the land. The lagoon opens to the sea through passes in the reef. The largest coral reef in the world is the Great Barrier Reef off the northeastern coast of Australia. It extends about 2,000 km (1,250 mi.) and covers more area than many countries.

An **atoll** (AT AWL) is a ring of low coral islands and reefs surrounding a central lagoon. Apparently an atoll began as a barrier or fringing reef around a volcanic island. The volcano, it is believed, formed a caldera

19C-4 *Heron Island* (above) *is surrounded by a barrier reef. The photo confirms the great size of coral reefs. Fiji Island* (right) *in the South Pacific, has a large fringing reef.*

19C-5 *A scuba diver enjoys some of the unusual color and beauty associated with the Great Barrier Reef.*

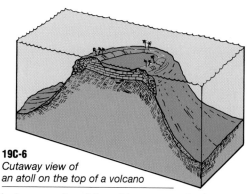

19C-6
*Cutaway view of
an atoll on the top of a volcano*

below sea level by either an explosive eruption or the collapse of its crater. This would leave the ring of coral islands and reefs alone above the sea. Several Pacific island groups are atolls, including Wake, Midway, Bikini, and Eniwetok (EN ih WEE TAHK).

Coral reefs affect people either by forming islands to live on, as in atolls, or by acting as navigation hazards. Shallow seas where coral is common are often difficult for ships to navigate. The coral reefs may not be visible from above the water but are close enough to the surface to damage a passing ship. Many of the first ships that came to the New World wrecked on coral reefs. Coral reefs are also home to colorful communities of sea life, with many species of plants and animals.

Section Review Questions 19C

1. Name the tool that *Challenger* used to measure the ocean depths.
2. What is the name given to the type of vehicle capable of withstanding the pressure of great ocean depths?
3. What is a submerged edge of a continent called?
4. What is the most common type of material that forms a continental rise?
5. What are the flat, deep seafloors called?
6. What is a submerged mountain range rising from the abyssal plains called?
7. What are long, curved chains of islands called?
8. What are deep valleys in the ocean floor near edges of tectonic plates called?
9. Which robotic submersible examined the *Titanic?*
10. Name the type of animal that can ''build'' a kind of island.
11. Where is the largest coral reef in the world located?
12. What is a ring of low coral islands and reefs surrounding a lagoon called?

Terms

abyssal plain	echo sounding	sea level
atoll	fringing reef	seamount
barrier island	guyot	spit
barrier reef	hook	spring tide
bay barrier	island arc	stack
breaker	longshore current	submarine canyon
continental rise	mean sea level	tombolo
continental shelf	mid-ocean ridge	trench
continental slope	neap tide	trough
coral reef	residence time	turbidity current
countercurrent	rip current	upwelling
crest	sea	wave base
density current	sea arch	wave height
desalinate	sea cave	wavelength

What Did You Learn?

1. How does the ocean accumulate dissolved minerals?
2. Can seawater be made simply by dissolving table salt in water?
3. If the one tidal bulge of water was over 80° W longitude (high tide on the eastern U.S. coast), where would the other high tide be?
4. Why are high tides twelve hours and twenty-five minutes apart, not twelve hours exactly?
5. How must the earth, moon, and sun be positioned for a neap tide to occur?
6. Draw two connected ocean waves and label the crest, trough, wave height, and wavelength.
7. Why don't waves transport objects great distances?
8. Explain why waves always approach the shore nearly parallel to the shore.
9. Why do surface currents in the Northern Hemisphere flow clockwise?
10. Explain how warm and cold currents can affect continental climates.
11. Explain how gravity can make density currents.

What Do You Think?

1. Does the earth have one ocean or three oceans?
2. What problems might be encountered when using a weighted rope to measure the depth of the ocean?
3. What problems would have to be overcome to build and live in a self-supporting under-sea city?
4. How do *you* think submarine canyons were formed?

GLACIERS: THE POWER OF ICE

TWENTY

20A–What Is a Glacier?

Having previously studied the effects of liquid water in motion, we now turn to the effects of frozen water in motion. Ice can be a powerful agent of change. A **glacier** (GLAY shur) is a large mass of ice that flows under the influence of gravity.

Formation

Glaciers form in areas where the winter snow fails to melt completely in the summer. These snow-covered areas are called **snowfields.** The lower edge of a snowfield is the **snow line.** Snow below this line melts in the summer, but snow above it does not melt. Near the equator, the snowfields occur only on high mountains. The snow line is often more than 5.5 km (3.4 mi.) above sea level. In the middle latitudes, snowfields occur on lower mountains as well; thus, the snow line is at a lower elevation. Near the poles, snowfields occur at even lower elevations; often the snow line is at sea level.

Over many years the snow in a snowfield may build up to a great thickness. The snow falls as fluffy crystals, but as it accumulates,

20A-1 *The photo below shows an accumulation of new snow on a valley glacier in Alaska.*

the weight of the newer snow compresses the older snow. As the snow is compressed, it slowly melts, refreezes, and compacts into a form of granular ice called **firn** (FIURN). Gradually the weight of the accumulated ice squeezes out the spaces between firn crystals, and the mass becomes **glacier ice.** This is a solid with interlocking crystals. It is usually opaque, with a bluish gray color, and contains fine dirt particles. Glacier ice will start moving as a mass if its weight and the angle of its slope are great enough.

When a glacier accumulates enough snow, it travels even below the snow line. The part of the glacier above the snow line is the **zone of accumulation,** where snow accumulates to increase the glacier. Below the snow line is the **zone of wastage,** where the glacier ice melts and evaporates or flows away. If the glacier accumulates more ice than it loses, it advances; if it loses more than it accumulates, it retreats. Knowing whether a glacier is advancing or retreating can give you information about the climate. If the glacier is retreating, the climate may be warming or

20A-2 *A typical glacier showing the zone of accumulation above the snow line and the zone of wastage below the snow line*

zone of accumulation   snow line

nourishment from snowfall

zone of wastage

melting and evaporation

flow of ice

becoming drier. If the glacier is advancing, the climate may be cooling or becoming more humid. Scientists have discovered that most of the world's glaciers are retreating. They interpret this to mean that the world's climate has been warming since the late 1800s.

Types of Glaciers

When you think about glaciers, you probably picture a long, narrow river of ice in a high valley. This type of glacier is a **valley glacier;** it is also called a **mountain glacier** or **alpine glacier.** A valley glacier begins in a hollow on a mountainside where snow accumulates. When it is large enough, the valley glacier begins to move, usually down a river valley. These glaciers may be only a few hundred meters long, or they may extend over a hundred kilometers. The valley glacier is the most common type of glacier.

At the foot of a mountain, several valley glaciers may merge to form a **piedmont** (PEED MAHNT) **glacier.** Piedmont glaciers usually cover more area than valley glaciers.

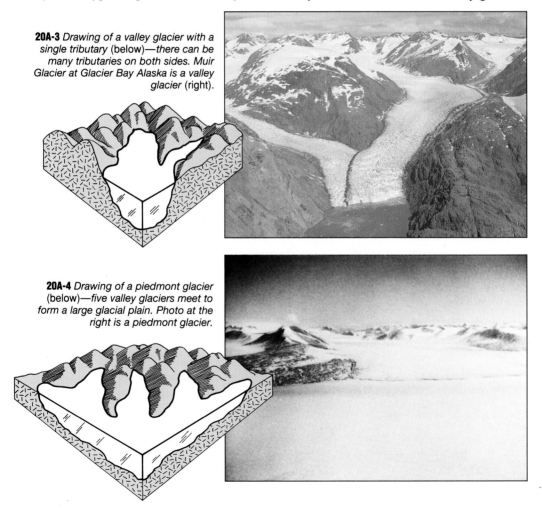

20A-3 *Drawing of a valley glacier with a single tributary (below)—there can be many tributaries on both sides. Muir Glacier at Glacier Bay Alaska is a valley glacier (right).*

20A-4 *Drawing of a piedmont glacier (below)—five valley glaciers meet to form a large glacial plain. Photo at the right is a piedmont glacier.*

FACETS OF GLACIOLOGY

Search for Noah's Ark

The lofty peaks of the mountains of Ararat stand in the background (left). One of the team members explores the Ahora Gorge on the north side of Ararat. The expedition team nears the end of their first day at Ararat (below).

Even in this modern world, "field work" can be filled with adventure. A diary written by John D. Morris describes his amazing expedition in 1972 to locate Noah's ark.

The Bible says the ark came to rest "upon the mountains of Ararat" (Gen. 8:4). Since Noah was not able to see any other mountaintops when he landed, most researchers believe the ark landed on Mt. Ararat Major, the highest mountain in the region. Mt. Ararat is now capped by a permanent ice cover, from which flows at least one glacier. No one has conclusively proved that the ark has survived the last forty-five hundred years, but the variety of reported sightings strongly support this possibility.

Dozens of people claim to have seen the ark, and some say that they have also been inside. These reports indicate that the ark is entombed under the ice; sometimes portions are revealed when unusually warm weather melts large amounts of ice. Perhaps the ark has broken into pieces under the stress of earthquakes, rock slides, and glacial movement. No one has been able to survey the mountain systematically because it is inaccessible at the frontier of Turkey and the Soviet Union. Bands of lawless nomads infest the area, and the Turkish government is reluctant to grant permits. Dangerous snowstorms and rock slides threaten climbers and hide the slopes under a blanket of rock and snow.

In *Adventure on Ararat* John Morris recorded many challenges he had to face. As a part of his preparation, Morris studied the Turkish language and mountaineering. All five members of the expedition spent many weekends hiking and one final week of glacial survival training before departing to Turkey. Upon arrival they discovered that their minibus was not available. They were constantly harassed by local officials. On their climbs around the base of the mountain, they experienced sickness, avalanches, and quarrels among themselves. They narrowly escaped death three times. Once a pack of dogs surrounded them. Another time near the top of the mountain they were struck by a lightning storm, which temporarily caused one of them to lose his memory. The expedition came to an abrupt end when the camp was robbed by armed thieves.

Although Morris did not discover the ark, he limited the number of places where it could be. Perhaps it no longer exists—destroyed by the elements or by survivors soon after the Flood. Yet the hope of finding the ark remains high in many adventurous hearts. They know that such a discovery would strongly support belief in a catastrophic flood, an occurrence which directly conflicts with modern evolutionary theory. Whatever His reason, God has kept the ark's exact location secret so far. Perhaps some day the time will be right.

Ice sheets are broad masses of ice that cover large areas. Instead of following a valley, ice sheets spread out in all directions from their source (snowfield). All ice sheets are close to the poles because they require a large, cold area to form. Two kinds of ice sheets exist, **ice caps** and **continental glaciers.**

Ice caps are the smaller type of ice sheet, usually no more than 160 km (100 mi.) in diameter. Most of them are in northern Canada, but ice caps also exist in Iceland, Ireland, southern Argentina, and Svalbard (a Norwegian island group). The largest ice sheet classified as an ice cap is on Northern Ellesmere Island in Canada; its area is almost 26,000 km^2 (10,000 mi.^{2}).

20A-5 *A U.S. Naval officer stands among large pressure ridges on Antarctica (above). The drawing below is of an ice cap.*

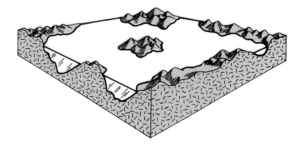

The Titanic *departing on its last voyage*

Jason Junior *photographs an open compartment in the* Titanic.

The Invincible *Titanic*

"God himself could not sink this ship," a crewman reportedly said as the S.S. *Titanic* sailed from the English harbor en route to New York. She was the pride of the world's luxury liners, headed out on her maiden voyage. Her double-plated steel hull could withstand anything nature could send against her. Should a leak somehow develop, the captain could push a button and close down any of sixteen watertight compartments below deck.

Rich and famous Englishmen and Americans made special arrangements to ensure a place on that historic pleasure trip of 1912. The luxury liner boasted crystal chandeliers, Turkish baths, a swimming pool, a live band, and a well-stocked bar. The weather was unusually calm and pleasant for the 2,227 people on board as they celebrated late into the night. Late Sunday night on April 14, few people took notice when the engines suddenly reversed and the swift-moving ship veered sharply left.

A lookout had spotted an iceberg dead ahead in the darkness. The surprised man quickly warned the bridge, "Iceberg right ahead!" The acting officer turned the ship left to avoid it. The boat scraped the edge of the iceberg, spraying ice over the bridge. Soon everyone returned to their games, and the band struck up some lively tunes.

Slowly the captain realized the severity of the damage. Water began to pour into the lower chambers, and the pumps proved useless. Finally the captain sent out a distress signal, but it was too late.

The *Titanic* began to list dangerously. Yet the passengers could not believe that the boat might actually sink. Lifeboats were available for only half of them anyway, because the owners had reasoned that the unsinkable *Titanic* would be the safest place for them to stay in an emergency. The 705 passengers who made it to safety watched in awe as the great ship turned straight up into the air and then slipped beneath the freezing waters of the North Atlantic.

Another hour passed before a rescue boat arrived at the tragic scene. The worldwide shock and outcry that followed led thirteen nations to fund an International Ice Patrol to scout Iceberg Alley along this major shipping route. The U.S. Coast Guard has continued its guard ever since, warning ships of danger and attempting to redirect icebergs that threaten to crash into boats and oil rigs.

A continental glacier, as the name implies, is a vast ice sheet covering most of a continent or large island. Two continental glaciers exist today, one in Greenland and the other in Antarctica. The ice in these glaciers is so thick that only the highest mountain peaks are exposed. As the ice moves outward to the sea, much of it breaks off in large chunks to form icebergs. This process of iceberg formation is called **calving.** Any kind of glacier that reaches the sea may calve, but most icebergs come from the huge continental glaciers.

More than four-fifths of Greenland is covered with ice. The people of Greenland live on the coastal lowlands around the edge of the island. Scientists believe that the ice in the interior is more than 2,400 m (8,000 ft.) thick. Scientists estimate that this glacier loses billions of tons to calving each year. These icebergs are a hazard for navigation in the North Atlantic.

20A-6 *Aerial view of the snowfields of Greenland; diagram showing the vast area of the continent covered by glacial ice.*

Greenland

Unusual rust formations on the ship's bow

The glacier on Antarctica is the world's largest. Its area is about 14.2 million km² (5.5 million mi.²); its maximum thickness is nearly 4,500 m (15,000 ft.). Only the eastern part of Antarctica is solid earth; the rest is a group of islands joined by ice. Research suggests that the weight of the ice has depressed the land as much as 2,400 m (8,000 ft.) below sea level in some places. Huge icebergs have been calved from the Antarctica glacier. One sighted in 1956 was about 333 km (208 mi.) long and almost 100 km (62 mi.) wide. Over 90 per cent of this huge iceberg was below the surface of the ocean.

20A-7 *Antarctica boasts the world's largest glacier and the largest icebergs such as this one at Hallett Station.*

Ross Ice Shelf

The largest ice shelf in the world is located in Antarctica. Fed by eight large glaciers and many smaller ones, a "shelf" of ice floats on the gentle Ross Sea without breaking up. The Ross Ice Shelf, which is the size of California (500,000 km², or 200,000 mi.²),

Three U.S. Naval ships push a huge iceberg from a channel leading to McMurdo Station near the Ross Ice Shelf.

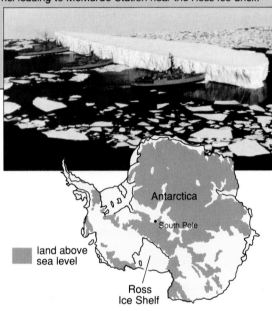

land above sea level

Antarctica

•South Pole

Ross Ice Shelf

20A-8 *Free floating icebergs often create hazards in shipping lanes.*

terminates as a wall of cliffs 45 m (150 ft.) high and 800 km (500 mi.) long. Most of the ice is below sea level, stretching to depths of over 600 m (2,000 ft.).

At the base of the shelf are the Transantarctic Mountains. This mountain range prevents the continent's ice sheet from sliding into the ocean. If you look at a map, you will see that the Ross Ice Shelf cuts deep into the continent, providing the closest "land" route to the South Pole. Understandably, the first explorers started their trek to the South Pole here. After crossing the ice shelf, they climbed the valley glaciers to Antarctica's flat interior.

The Ross Ice Shelf has become a major center of scientific investigation. Drills have taken samples through the entire depth of the shelf. Scientists want to understand the origin and movement of this large crystalline mass. Their knowledge will help them understand more about land movement and glacial movement throughout the world. The Ross Ice Shelf has much to tell us about glaciers, the formation of icebergs, and the interaction of water and ice. Scientists are especially amazed that the ice shelf remains so stable. As snow and glaciers add ice to one end of the shelf, it loses ice at the outer edge from calving.

Section Review Questions 20A

1. What are areas where snow does not melt completely in the summer called?
2. What is the form of granular ice having a composition midway between that of snow and glacier ice called?
3. What is the lowest edge of a snowfield called?
4. What is the part of a glacier that is located below the snow line called?
5. Name the type of glacier sometimes formed where two valley glaciers merge.
6. What is the most common type of glacier?
7. Where is the world's largest glacier? What kind of glacier is it?
8. The term *calving* refers to the formation of what object?

20B–Movement of Glaciers

There are three things to note about the activity of a glacier. The first is its motion, fractures, and zones of movement within the glacier. The second is the erosion of the land beneath the glacier. The third is the land forms produced when the eroded material is deposited.

Motion

A moving glacier has two layers that move differently. The upper layer, the **zone of fracture,** consists of brittle ice that cannot adjust to the glacier's motion. To relieve the stress of the motion, it breaks to form **crevasses** (krih VAS), the deep clefts that are treacherous for explorers. The lower layer, in contrast, can mold itself to new shapes as it passes over changing terrain. This layer is the **zone of flow.** It moves along the ground, often on a film of water, reshaping itself as it moves.

Most glaciers move only a few centimeters or meters each day, but occasionally a glacier moves rapidly in a **surge.** Scientists do not fully understand surge, but they know it happens.

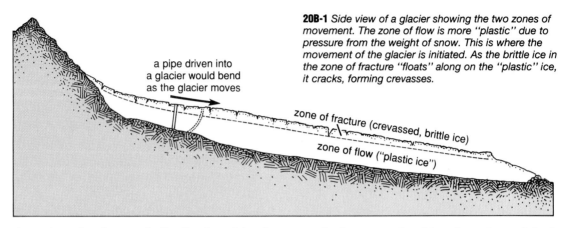

20B-1 *Side view of a glacier showing the two zones of movement. The zone of flow is more "plastic" due to pressure from the weight of snow. This is where the movement of the glacier is initiated. As the brittle ice in the zone of fracture "floats" along on the "plastic" ice, it cracks, forming crevasses.*

a pipe driven into a glacier would bend as the glacier moves

zone of fracture (crevassed, brittle ice)

zone of flow ("plastic ice")

A portion of an ice cap in Svalbard, an island north of Norway, advanced about 20 km (12 mi.) in three years. Its average rate was thus 18 m (60 ft.) per day. The fastest glacier movement recorded is 110 m (360 ft.) per day for the Kutiah glacier in northern India.

Scientists study details of valley glacier motion by placing markers across them. They found that a glacier's speed is greatest in its center and less toward the edges, where friction against the valley walls slows the motion. This unequal motion breaks up the ice in the zone of fracture and forms crevasses.

Observations show that valley glaciers move faster when they add material. Thus, they often travel faster after a winter of heavy snow. Avalanches from the valley sides often add tons of material in a short time and so produce a noticeable acceleration in the glacier's motion.

Glacial Erosion

You have probably heard the question "What happens when an irresistible force meets an immovable object?" The force of an enormous, moving mass of ice is one of the nearest things to "irresistible" that is encountered in the study of geology. Glaciers level almost everything in their path. For example, a valley that once held a glacier is

much deeper and wider than the original stream valley. Glaciated valleys have a U-shaped profile, while stream valleys have a V-shaped profile.

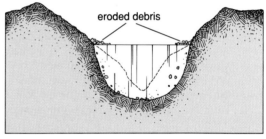

eroded debris

20B-2 *Glaciated valleys* (above) *have been eroded into a U-shaped profile by rock and debris in the glacier. A typical glaciated valley* (below)—*notice the characteristic U shape.*

20B-3 *A waterfall* (left) *emerges from a hanging valley into a heavily glaciated valley in California. A* tarn (below) *and the Matterhorn* (bottom), *the world's most famous example of a horn*

Small valleys often enter a glaciated valley from high on its sides. These **hanging valleys** were formed by tributaries of the stream that occupied the main valley before the glacier formed. The extensive erosion of the main valley left the tributary valleys high above the floor. The tributary valley may be unglaciated, or it may have held only a small glacier. A stream in a hanging valley enters the main valley by waterfalls and steep plunges.

Some mountains show evidence of extensive glacial erosion. The freezing and thawing of the upper ends of valley glaciers break off rocks from valley walls and pull loose rocks from valley floors. This erosive process forms basins called **cirques** (SURK). After the glacier retreats, a cirque often holds a lake called a **tarn** (TARN). If three or more cirques encircle a mountain peak, a slender spire called a **horn** may be all that remains of the peak. The Matterhorn in Switzerland is a famous horn.

As they go along, glaciers pick up rocks and other debris. A glacier can even break up bedrock by a process called **plucking.** As the glacier travels, some of its ice may melt and enter the cracks and pores in the bedrock. Then the water freezes again and adheres to the glacier. The glacier can tear out huge chunks of bedrock by this process.

The rocks and other debris on the underside of a glacier act like sandpaper. Rocks over which a glacier has moved often have parallel scratch marks called **striations** (stry AY shun). Deeper grooves in the rock sometimes extend hundreds of meters along the glacier's

20B-4 *A rock surface polished by a glacier; close up of glacial striations on a highly polished rock surface* (inset).

path. In some places, instead of scratching the rock, the glacier has polished it.

Sometimes glaciers erode their paths to below sea level. When they retreat, the sea enters the glaciated valley, now called a **fiord**

20B-5 *A fiord is a glaciated valley that reaches the sea.*

(FYORD). Some fiords extend inland for over a hundred kilometers. Similar erosion farther inland produces elongated lakes such as the Finger Lakes of New York.

Glacial Deposits

Glaciers deposit their debris in two ways as they melt: the debris simply drops as the ice melts under it, or streams of meltwater deposit the debris. Both kinds of glacial deposits are called **drift.** When ice melts, its debris drops down randomly (unstratified), rather than in layers (stratified). Boulders, pebbles, and soil may be mixed together with no stratification. This unstratified kind of deposit is called **till.**

20B-6 *Erratic boulders left by a glacier in Wyoming*

Transported boulders are an example of till. Boulders that are not like the bedrock under them are called **erratics** (ih RAT iks) because they obviously came from somewhere else. A group of erratics from the same distant bedrock source is called a **boulder train.** These help scientists trace a glacier's path. Sometimes finding the source of erratics has practical value. For example, some erratics in Finland contained copper ore. By tracing the path of the glacier, prospectors found the source of the copper and established a successful copper mine there.

Glaciers often deposit ridges of till called **moraines.** A **terminal moraine** is a pile of debris that the glacier pushed in front of it until it stopped advancing. Thus, terminal moraines mark the glacier's farthest advance.

20B-7 *The terminal moraine, outwash and kettles formed at the end of a glacier*

Debris deposited along the sides of a glacier forms a **lateral moraine.** When two valley glaciers merge, their inside lateral moraines join to form a **medial moraine.** Finally, debris strewn over the whole area that a glacier occupied is **ground moraine.** This moraine forms when the entire glacier melts and drops rock all along its route. Ground moraines tend to smooth out the terrain with a blanket of till that produces a gently rolling surface. The gently rolling countryside in many of our northeastern states was formed by ground moraines.

20B-8 *Several valley glaciers merge. The photo shows the lateral and medial moraines.*

Drumlins are long, streamlined hills composed of till. From the air, drumlins appear roughly parallel to one another and aligned in the direction that the glacier moved. These glacial hills are found from Minnesota to New England as well as in Canada (see Chapter 16, p. 322).

Deposits that are formed by running water are sorted in layers (stratified) according to size. Meltwater along the front of a glacier carries sand and gravel far from the glacier to produce an **outwash plain.** Sometimes outwash plains are pitted with holes called **kettles.** These ''holes'' form when chunks of ice separate from the glacier and then melt, leaving a hole. A kettle may fill with water and become a kettle lake. **Eskers** (ES kur) are long, winding ridges apparently deposited by streams flowing under a glacier. **Kames** (KAME) are steep-sided hills much like eskers, but shorter. Both eskers and kames are stratified deposits.

Lakes that receive streams of glacial meltwater accumulate thin layers of sediment called **varves.** Each varve is a layer with coarser particles at the bottom and finer particles at the top. A varve may be anywhere from a few millimeters to a few centimeters thick. For many years scientists believed that the streams deposited exactly one varve each year. Therefore, they counted varves to date deposits. They have now discovered that more than one varve may form each year.

Storms, floods, and other events can add varves. Thus, varve counting is unreliable as a dating method.

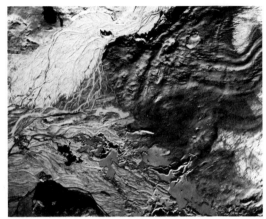

20B-9 *Aerial view of the Casement Glacier, Glacier Bay National Monument, Alaska showing recently formed eskers*

Section Review Questions 20B

1. What is the upper part of a glacier that contains brittle ice called?
2. What are shallow scratch marks in bedrock caused by a glacier called?
3. Name the deep clefts found in the top of a glacier.
4. What term is used to describe very rapid movement by a glacier?
5. What characteristics distinguish a glaciated valley from a stream valley?
6. Name the basins carved into the sides of mountains by valley glaciers.
7. What are glaciated valleys which extend below sea level called?
8. What is the general term used for unstratified material deposited by ice?
9. Which glacial deposits are unstratified?
10. Name the type of moraine formed where two lateral moraines join.
11. What is a flat deposit of sand and gravel extending for many miles from the front of a continental glacier called?
12. What are the sediments deposited in lakes that are fed by glacial meltwater called?

20C–The "Ice Age"

Evidence shows that glaciers were once far more widespread than they are today. Continental glaciers apparently covered northern Europe, Canada, and the northern United States. Many creationists believe that a brief period of glacial action followed Noah's Flood.

Many scientists who are creationists believe that the Flood automatically caused an "ice age." After the Flood, water was abundant on the continents. Lakes were widespread. Such a large surface area of water undoubtedly promoted evaporation. The humidity would have been high, near 100 per cent, so that clouds covered the sky. Thus, it would have rained daily in warm areas, and in cold areas snow would have fallen almost continuously from fall until spring. Snow may have piled up at the rate of 150-300 m (500-1,000 ft.) per year. Because the clouds blocked so much sunlight, summers were short and cool, and little snow melted. What melting did occur only helped compact the snow and eventually form glacier ice.

In the first hundred years after the Flood, as much as 15,000 m (50,000 ft.) of snow could have accumulated. This could have compacted to form about 1,500 m (5,000 ft.) of ice. When the weight of the ice was enough, the glacier would have begun moving outward from the higher snowfields. After a time, a generally southward movement would have predominated. A few hundred years of glaciation at this rate would account for the evidence of widespread glaciation. This "ice age" may have continued throughout much of the Old Testament time period.

The evidence for widespread glaciation includes widespread distribution of glacial till.

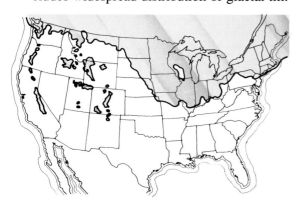

20C-1 *Evidence of extensive glaciation is found in the shaded regions on the map.*

In some areas, a layer of weathered till lies under a layer of less weathered till. Some scientists interpret this to mean that two different glaciers covered these areas and therefore that more than one "ice age" occurred. Other scientists point out that the evidence could equally well have come from a single glacier that advanced, retreated, then advanced again. They believe in a single "ice age." Creationists generally agree with the idea of a single period of widespread glaciation.

Rip Van Winkle from the Ice Age?

Just as in the story of Rip Van Winkle, this man went hunting in the mountains and fell asleep. However, this man lived over 5,000 years ago and never woke up. He set out on a trip, probably unaware that it would be his last. He was a hunter, as evidenced by his belongings—a longbow and quiver of fourteen arrows, a knife, an ax, and enough food for a few days. He was well prepared for the cold weather—insulated jacket, trousers, and boots. His hunt had been successful; he had claimed several small animals. Now resting at his camp high in the Alps, he fell asleep—permanently.

This hunter was born several hundred years before the patriarchs.† Radiocarbon dating and the types of artifacts indicate that he lived around 3500–3000 B.C. The hunter died in the Italian Alps, was naturally preserved (dried in the mountain air, frozen, and covered with snow), and was discovered more than 5,000 years later. Two mountain climbers found him in melting snow in September of 1991. He was an incredible archeological find—a perfectly preserved, Copper Age man with many equally well preserved belongings. He apparently had sufficient food, clothing, and shelter; so how did he die? Perhaps he was stranded in an Ice Age snowstorm following the Flood.

† The patriarchs were Abraham, Isaac, and Jacob.

Section Review Questions 20C

1. According to a creationist view, when did widespread glaciation begin?
2. What areas were apparently covered by continental glaciers during the "ice age" that are not covered today?
3. What is the evidence that glaciers were once widespread?
4. According to a creationist view, how many "ice ages" probably occurred?

Terms

alpine glacier	ground moraine	snowfield
boulder train	hanging valley	snow line
calving	horn	striations
cirque	ice cap	surge
continental glacier	ice sheet	tarn
crevasse	kame	terminal moraine
drift	kettle	till
drumlin	lateral moraine	valley glacier
erratics	medial moraine	varve
esker	moraine	zone of accumulation
fiord	mountain glacier	zone of flow
firn	outwash plain	zone of fracture
glacier	piedmont glacier	zone of wastage
glacier ice	plucking	

What Did You Learn?

1. Why are glaciers more numerous near the poles?
2. What kind of glacier would you expect to find near the equator? Why?
3. Why is the *weight* of snow needed to make glacier ice?
4. What factors determine whether a glacier will advance or retreat?
5. When a glacier retreats, does it actually *move* backward? Explain.
6. List five kinds of glaciers. How do they differ?
7. When did John D. Morris lead an expedition to locate Noah's ark on Mt. Ararat?
8. What is the function of the International Ice Patrol?
9. What causes glaciers to move?
10. What is the origin of the material in glacial drift?
11. How could a boulder train lead to the discovery of an ore deposit?
12. List four types of moraines. How are they similar?
13. How do creationists explain the widespread evidence of glaciation?

What Do You Think?

1. What obstacles would need to be overcome to use icebergs as a source of fresh water in drought-stricken areas?
2. Do you think ice cubes cut from glacier ice could be a marketable fad item?
3. What do you think would happen to the continental glacier if a volcano erupted in the middle of Antarctica?

THE GROUND WATER SYSTEM

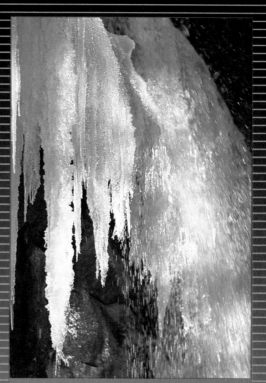

TWENTY-ONE

21A–Underground Reservoir

The earth is the only planet with liquid water on its surface. You have learned from Chapter 19 that over 97 per cent of the water is in the oceans, which cover almost three-fourths of the planet. Ocean water is too salty for humans to drink. Over three-fourths of the earth's fresh water is frozen in the polar ice caps and glaciers, but this ice is difficult to use as a source of fresh water. The second largest reserve of fresh water is **ground water,** which accounts for about 22 per cent of the fresh water. Lakes and streams account for only about 0.33 per cent of the earth's fresh water.

The Water Cycle
Where does ground water come from? To understand that, you must think about the

hydrologic (water) **cycle.** Water continually moves from the continents to the oceans, evaporates into the air, and is carried back to the continents as clouds by the prevailing winds. The cycle is complete when the clouds pour rain back onto the continents.

When rain falls, where does the rainwater go? Some of it runs off the surface of the ground into streams, which eventually carry it into the oceans. Some water forms puddles on the ground, where it evaporates back into the air, and some water soaks into the ground. Plants absorb some of the soaked-in water, and the remainder of it continues to travel downward through pores, cracks, and other spaces between rock particles until it reaches a depth at which all the available spaces are filled by water. The water at this level is called ground water. This water is not on a dead-end path to be permanently locked away underground. It is still an active part of the hydrologic cycle and will eventually return to the surface.

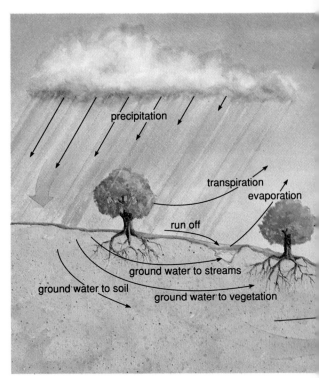

21A-2 *The water cycle is a vast purification process for the earth's fresh water supply.*

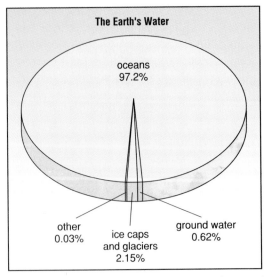

21A-1 *Only a small portion of the earth's water is ground water, but this water is vital to the survival of life.*

The Water Table

The upper surface of the ground water is called the **water table.** Its shape is irregular. Beneath level ground, the water table's depth varies with the type of rock and the ability of rainwater to reach it. Beneath ground that is not level, the general shape of the water table follows the surface. Though it is high under hills and low under valleys, its contour changes less than does the earth's surface. Thus, the top of a hill is farther from the water table than a nearby valley.

In some places the water table is only a few feet below the surface, and in other places it is at a depth of hundreds of feet. In some places, such as springs, the water table is at the surface. A **spring** is a place, usually on a hillside, where water comes from the

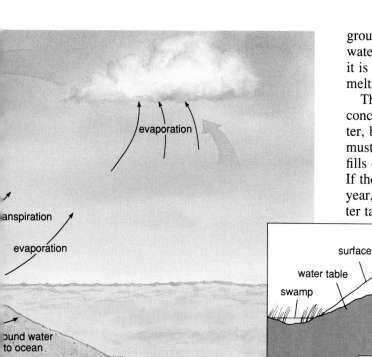

ground, often continuously. The height of the water table also varies seasonally. Generally it is higher in the springtime, when rain and melting snow are plentiful.

The water table is not only a theoretical concept that helps us understand ground water, but it is an actual location of water that must be known before drilling a well. A well fills only if it reaches below the water table. If the well is to produce water for the entire year, it must reach below the dry-season water table.

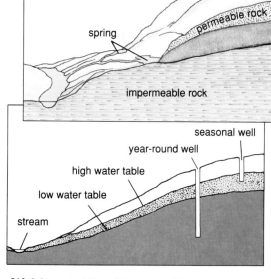

21A-3 *The opening of this spring near the North and South Carolina border has been widened and reinforced.*

21A-4 *Characteristics of the water table: the water table generally follows the contour of the surface (top); typical hillside springs (middle); seasonal variation of water table (bottom).*

To aid in the study of ground water, scientists have divided the ground into several zones. The **zone of aeration*** (ehr AY shun) is the ground above the water table, in which some of the available spaces between rock particles are filled with air instead of water. The **zone of saturation** is the ground below the water table, where every available space is filled with water. Immediately above the zone of saturation is a small region in which water has worked its way upward by capillary action, much as a blotter soaks up ink. This area is called the **capillary fringe.**

21A-5 *The zone of aeration holds some air in its spaces. In the zone of saturation all spaces are filled with water. The water table is the upper boundary of the zone of saturation. Water absorbed upward from the water table by capillary action is called the capillary fringe.*

Storage of Ground Water

A rock that has many open spaces within it is **porous.** For example, pumice contains many bubble holes throughout its interior. To hold ground water, a rock must be porous, but that alone is not enough. Pumice is porous, but its holes are not connected to one another or to the surface of the rock. Thus water cannot easily reach the spaces to fill them.

Another factor in a rock's ability to hold ground water is *permeability,* or how easily it allows water to pass through it. A **permeable** (PUR mee uh bul) material transmits water easily; it contains many open spaces that are connected so that water can flow through them. A material that does not easily permit water to flow through it is **impermeable.** Materials with high permeability include sand, gravel, and sandstone. These materials have many connected spaces. Some types of limestone also transmit water because they contain many small cracks. On the other hand, clay, shale, and most igneous and metamorphic rocks are impermeable.

Because impermeable materials do not allow water to pass through them, they may disrupt the normal flow of ground water. In some places a small sheet of impermeable rock is located above the water table. Since surface water cannot travel through the rock to the main reservoir of ground water, it collects above the rock. The top of this collected

21A-6 *Sandstone (above) is porous and permeable to water, while pumice (right) is porous but not permeable.*

aeration: *(from* Gk. AER, air)

water is called a **perched water table.** Many hillside springs result from a perched water table intersecting the surface.

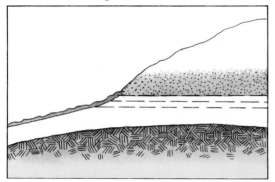

21A-7 *This cross section of a hill shows how there can be two water tables in the same area.*

On some slopes a layer of water-bearing permeable rock is sandwiched between two layers of impermeable rock. If the permeable rock reaches the surface near the top of the hill, it may become filled with water through rainfall. The weight of the water pulls it down the hill. If a well is drilled near the bottom of the hill through the impermeable rock to the water-filled layer, the water will spurt up through the well. This is an **artesian** (ar TEE zhun) **well,** named after the French province of Artois (formerly called Artesium), where Roman soldiers first saw such wells. Artesian wells were an important source of water throughout much of the United States. However, depletion of water in the permeable layer has made pumping necessary in many of the wells.

21A-8 *An artesian well is one in which the water rises under its own pressure above the water table.*

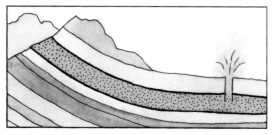

Movement of Ground Water

Ground water tends to move downhill under the influence of gravity, but it moves more slowly than surface water does. Its flow rate varies from 100 m per day to as little as 0.5 m in ten years. Usually subsurface water moves in the same direction as surface water. Ground water moving downhill may come out of the ground as a spring, enter a surface stream or lake, or join an underground stream. Some regions contain several underground streams. Eventually these streams feed into lakes, surface streams, or oceans.

21A-9 *Ground water eventually ends up in lakes or oceans.*

Ground water moves sideways as well as downward. Therefore, pumping water from one place can affect the water table in nearby places. A large pumped well can cause a **cone of depression,** a cone-shaped lowering of the water table that is deepest at the well. If the water table falls too far, nearby wells that were previously dependable may become dry. A cone of depression also may change the direction of ground water flow. The ground water in that area will tend to flow toward the lowest part of the depression, even if it used to flow in the opposite direction. This can be a problem if the well is near the sea or a source of contamination. The bad water

FACETS OF HYDROLOGY

Depleted Aquifers

Ploop! It swallowed a tree. *Plop! Plop!* Now it just swallowed two cars! No, it is not the monster that ate Miami. It is a sinkhole opening at the surface. Sinkholes are underground cavities, dissolved in the rock by ground water, which open at the surface. The accelerated occurrence of sinkholes is just one sign of a lowering water table in Florida.

The level of the water table across the United States varies, depending on how much it rains or snows and how much water is pumped out by man. In times of drought or great demand for water, the depth of the water table can be lowered too much, with disastrous consequences.

One such consequence is the collapse of underground caverns, resulting in sinkholes. Such collapses are more common when the water table is low because the earth is like a giant sponge; when there is not enough water in the sponge, the cavities collapse, forming sinkholes.

Increased occurrence of sinkholes is not the only evidence of lowering water tables, and Florida is not the only state where lowering water tables are a problem. In coastal regions if the ground water is pumped out, salt water will infiltrate from the ocean and make the wells unusable. In Arizona huge cracks appear in the ground where the ground water is depleted. As the water table is lowered, the ground sinks, but it does not sink uniformly. This sinking is called subsidence. Some of the cracks are hundreds of feet long and may extend down to the water table.

These disasters cannot be completely avoided since we cannot control droughts. However, we can control our use of ground water and reduce the demand on the water table. In the United States, farm irrigation uses as much ground water as all the cities use together. One method of irrigation which has reduced water use by up to 50 per cent is ''drip irrigation.'' With drip irrigation, pipes supply water directly to the plant roots and thus eliminate the waste of water. However, the cost of installing such an irrigation system is often prohibitively expensive. Another approach to conserving water is legislation. Laws regulating water use for irrigation or for residential use are already in effect in several cities and states.

Sinkholes like this one in Florida create serious hazards to automobile traffic.

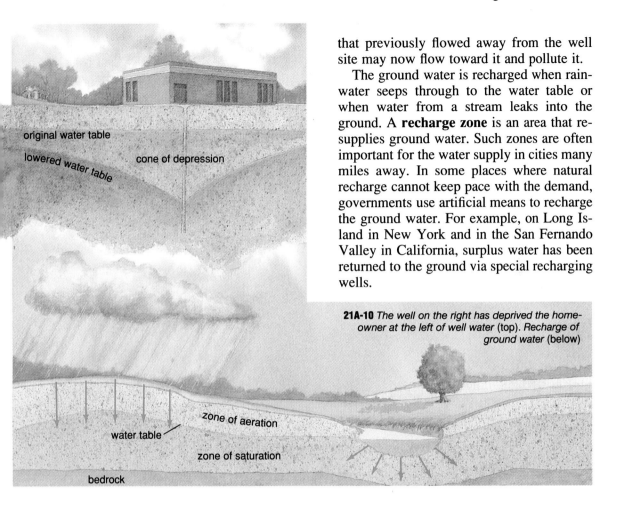

that previously flowed away from the well site may now flow toward it and pollute it.

The ground water is recharged when rainwater seeps through to the water table or when water from a stream leaks into the ground. A **recharge zone** is an area that re-supplies ground water. Such zones are often important for the water supply in cities many miles away. In some places where natural recharge cannot keep pace with the demand, governments use artificial means to recharge the ground water. For example, on Long Island in New York and in the San Fernando Valley in California, surplus water has been returned to the ground via special recharging wells.

21A-10 The well on the right has deprived the home-owner at the left of well water (top). Recharge of ground water (below)

Labels in figure: original water table; lowered water table; cone of depression; zone of aeration; water table; zone of saturation; bedrock

Section Review Questions 21A
1. What percentage of the earth's water is fresh water?
2. What percentage of the earth's fresh water is ground water?
3. What is the continual transfer of water from land to sea to air called?
4. What is an outcropping of the water table from which water flows more or less continuously called?
5. What word describes material that permits water to flow through it easily?
6. List three materials noted for their high permeability.
7. When there are two water tables in an area, what is the name given to the upper one?
8. What is the name given to a well in which the water rises under its own pressure?
9. What water sources normally recharge ground water?
10. What particular problem may occur in coastal regions if the ground water is pumped out?

21B–Ground Water's Dissolving Power

You have probably dissolved sugar or salt in water. Water is known as the "universal solvent." There are two properties of water that make it such a good solvent. One property is the polarity (unevenly distributed electrical charges) of the H_2O molecule; the other is that water is acidic. (Pure water is netural, but upon exposure to the atmosphere or soil, it rapidly becomes acidic.) The acidic nature of water allows it to dissolve various rocks and minerals, especially limestone.

Dissolved Minerals

Although it may look like pure water, ground water always contains various dissolved minerals. In fact, pure water is rare anywhere on the earth. Even rainwater contains dissolved gases, smoke, and dust particles. Water that stays in the ground for a while picks up minerals as it passes through soil and rock. Dissolved minerals are usually harmless. In fact, many resort areas advertise that their mineral waters are especially healthful.

Hard water contains a high concentration of dissolved calcium or magnesium compounds. Lathering soap in such water is difficult because a chemical reaction makes the soap less active. A sticky scum forms instead of lather. This scum is what causes bathtub rings. It can also collect on clothing as it is washed.

Soft water, on the other hand, is naturally low in calcium and magnesium compounds. Any process that removes these undesirable minerals from hard water is called water softening. If the calcium and magnesium compounds are bicarbonates, boiling can soften the water. Heat changes the dissolved bicarbonates to undissolved carbonates that settle to the bottom. In places that have this kind of water, carbonate deposits may form in tea-kettles and hot water pipes. If carbonate deposition continues long enough, the build-up can clog and damage pipes.

Hard water that contains compounds such as chlorides and sulfates, rather than bicarbonates, does not soften with heat. However, borax or washing soda can remove the minerals from the water. Water demineralizers or ion-exchange columns are now available for home use. These devices can soften any type of hard water.

21B-1 *Carbonate deposits from hard water can clog plumbing pipes. Water flow through such pipes would be severely restricted.*

Section Review Questions 21B-1
1. What dissolved elements does hard water usually contain?
2. List three ways of softening hard water.

Caves

Scientists do not agree about how caves†
form. Water containing carbon dioxide,
which makes it acidic, can dissolve limestone. This dissolving may be what begins
the formation of caves. Many caves contain
underground streams that may have helped
to form them. Although we may never see a
new cave form, present caves are being enlarged by ground water.

Some creationists link cave formation to
the Flood. After the Flood, water was abundant on the earth. Rapid cave formation
would have been possible because of the water's seeping through recently deposited
limestone.

When ground water dissolves limestone, it
must eventually redeposit it. Under proper
conditions the redeposited minerals may
form structures in caves. Structures formed
by deposits precipitated from dripping water
in caves are given the general name **dripstone.** Stalactites* (stuh LAK TYT), stalagmites* (stuh LAG MYT), and columns are
types of dripstones. **Stalactites** are iciclelike
projections that hang downward from the
ceiling of a cave, and **stalagmites** are formations that project upward from the floor of
the cave. In some places a stalactite meets a
stalagmite and forms a **column.** Other cave
formations are formed from deposits precipitated from a thin film of water flowing over
the sides and floors of the caves rather than
dripping from the ceilings. These structures
are called **flowstones.** Thin sheets of flowstone hanging from the ceiling are called **curtains;** flat, rounded flowstones attached to
cave ceilings are called **shields.** Flowstones
also form on the sides and floors of caves.

Most scientists agree that dripstone and
flowstone deposits form above the water table. Also, a cave must have a supply of moving air to promote evaporation so that the

stalactite

column

stalagmite

curtain

21B-2 *Stalactites, stalagmites, curtains, and columns
are visible in these two photographs of Luray Caverns,
Virginia.*

---

† A cavern is a large cave.

stalactite: (Gk. STALAKTOS, dripping)

stalagmite: (Gk. STALAGMA, a drop)

21B-3	Notable Caves	
Name	Location	Facts of Interest
Altamira Cave	Spain	cave paintings by prehistoric man first discovered in 1879 by a five-year-old girl
Anemone Cave	Maine	carved by the sea; at low tide tourists can find exotic sea creatures, such as the flowerlike anemone
Berger	France	1,248 m (4,094 ft.) deep, one of the deepest caves in the world
Blue Grotto	Italy	sea cave that turns blue when sunlight filters in
Carlsbad Caverns	New Mexico	largest known cave chamber, the Big Room, could hold an aircraft carrier; Indian wall paintings
Craters of the Moon	Idaho	caves formed by volcanic action; evidence of lava flows and cinder cones
Dead Sea Caves	Israel	desert caves near the shore of the Dead Sea where ancient leather and papyrus manuscripts were found, some are books of the Bible
Eisreisenwelt Cave	Austria	spectacular underground ice formations and very strong winds
Grotto de Lascaux	France	cave paintings by prehistoric man; famous *Hall of Bulls* painting
Jean Bernard	France	reportedly the world's deepest cave, 1,535 m (5,036 ft.)
Lava Beds National Monument	California	world's largest collection of volcanic caves; some are over a mile long
Luray Caverns	Virginia	highly decorated with spectacular formations; contains a stalacpipe organ which creates musical notes by striking hollow stalactites
Mammoth Cave	Kentucky	most extensive known cave in the world, perhaps 800 km (500 mi.) long; sinkholes over 1.6 km (1 mi.) in diameter
Perpetual Ice Cave	New Mexico	perpetual cold air causes ice stalactites and stalagmites in a volcanic mountain cave
Pinnacles National Monument	California	lava rocks have fallen from the canyon pinnacles and are strewn along the narrow floor
Waitomo Cave	New Zealand	glow worms cling to the ceiling, giving the appearance of stars in a night sky
Wind Cave National Park	South Dakota	winds flow in and out of the cave as the air pressure changes; cave walls are covered by a unique boxwork, which looks like honeycomb

deposits will form. When these conditions occur, ground water containing dissolved limestone may form stalactites, stalagmites, and similar structures. As water drips or flows from the ceiling onto the floor of a cave, a chemical reaction may occur at either or both of these places. The calcium bicarbonate that was dissolved in the water now precipitates as calcium carbonate. This compound is chemically the same as the main constituent of limestone (calcite) that was originally dissolved by the ground water. This deposited material is sometimes called "secondary limestone."

All cave formations consist of mainly calcium carbonate. Pure calcium carbonate is

21B-4 *The bizarre shapes and varied colors of cave formations produce a picturesque underground spectacle as evidenced by Carlsbad Caverns, New Mexico (above), and Mammoth Cave, Kentucky (left). Notice the heavy flowstone formations at the left.*

flowstone

flowstone

white, but impurities give it different colors. For example, iron oxide produces the reddish brown color that many cave formations have. The bizarre shapes and varied colors of the formations produce a picturesque underground spectacle.

Although evolutionists have said that the formation of stalactites and stalagmites is evidence that the earth is very old, creationists have demonstrated that these cave deposits (or formations) can form rapidly. In caves that have dried up, the growth rate of these structures is slow. However, stalactites and stalagmites grow rapidly in moist, active caves. For example, Crystal Spring Dome in Carlsbad Caverns is adding material at the rate of 41 cm^3 (2.5 in.^{3}) per year. A typical

FACETS OF HYDROLOGY

21B–1

Spelunking

The hope of discovering vast underground caverns and rock formations of breath-taking beauty lures many spelunkers to the caves. Others simply enjoy the challenge of pushing into a world of darkness and silence unlike any other on earth. The spelunker feels alone and hidden from the world above, much like a child who hides in a dark closet and pretends no one can see him.

Spelunkers are virtually mountaineers in reverse. They carry some of the same equipment, they require many of the same skills, and they face a few of the same dangers. However, other aspects of spelunking are unique. One of the most obvious differences is that spelunkers must be prepared to get dirty. They crawl around on their hands and knees in sticky mud and slime from bacterial deposits. The basic equipment of a spelunker is the following:

- loose-fitting clothes without zippers (preferably overalls)
- a hard hat with a carbide lamp to protect the head from low stalactites
- a jacket or sweater
- a first-aid kit in case of falls or cuts on jagged rocks
- spare carbide cans, plumbers' candles, and a flashlight
- a compass and map of the cave (if available)

- a canteen and high-energy snacks, such as chocolate, raisins, or nuts
- a rope, if needed

If you want to be a successful spelunker, you must follow some common-sense procedures. First, you should become accustomed to cave terrain by visiting caves that offer guided tours and lighted paths. In addition to getting some experience in underground terrain, you can confirm whether you really want to become a spelunker! Next, you can join a local club of experienced spelunkers, located through either a local museum or the National Speleological Society.

Follow the basic rules of spelunking:

1. Go in a group so that someone can help you if you have any difficulties.
2. Inform someone on the surface about your adventure and your expected time of return.
3. Turn back immediately if you become fatigued.
4. Don't panic if you get lost; wait patiently until help arrives.

As you become experienced in simple caves, you can enter more difficult caves that require rappelling down deep holes, crossing "bottomless pits" with

ladders, wading through underground streams, or inching on your belly through tiny cracks. You might even have to take up scuba diving to get through underwater passageways. Some people buy special gear and devote their lives to speleology—the study of caves.

No matter how serious you become, your main duty as a spelunker is to show proper respect for others. Ask permission before you go spelunking on private land. Make sure that you leave the cave exactly as it was before you entered so that future spelunkers can enjoy it too. Take a camera and record your unique and rewarding experiences.

1. Take out all the materials and equipment that you bring in.
2. Leave all rock formations and cave dwellers undisturbed.
3. Do not make markings (such as your initials) on the walls.
4. Do not take souvenirs.

growth rate cited by evolutionists for cave formations in general is 16 cm^3 (1 in.^{3}) in 150 years. Bats are sometimes found encased in stalagmites at Carlsbad Caverns. If their rate of formation had not been fast, the bats would have decayed. Most of Carlsbad Caverns is inactive today; rapid deposition occurs in only about 5 per cent of the cave.

Scientists at Bob Jones University, using simulated cave conditions, have studied the growth of stalactites in the laboratory. In one experiment a 50-cm (20-in.) stalactite weighing about 1.8 kg (4 lb.) added 35 g (1.2 oz.) of calcium carbonate in eighty days. This rate of deposition corresponds to an increase of 0.45 kg (1 lb.) every three years. At this rate the entire stalactite could have formed in only twelve years. At the same time, 17.5 g (0.6 oz.) of stalagmite accumulated beneath the stalactite. The cumulative dripstone formation rate was 0.45 kg (1 lb.) every two years.

Caves and their concealed formations are tempting tourist attractions. A person who explores caves is a **spelunker** (spih LUNG kur). Because spelunking is a dangerous pastime, only people who thoroughly know what they are doing and have all the necessary equipment should engage in it. Some caves require elaborate ropes and other gear. Spelunkers may be faced with a flooding cave stream, a lack of air, a rock fall, a loss of sense of direction, or a dangerously steep slope. Beginners should enter only those caves that are open to the public.

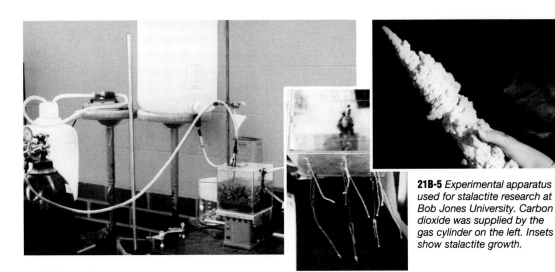

21B-5 *Experimental apparatus used for stalactite research at Bob Jones University. Carbon dioxide was supplied by the gas cylinder on the left. Insets show stalactite growth.*

Section Review Questions 21B-2

1. What term is used to describe limestone that has been dissolved by ground water and then redeposited?
2. What are the iciclelike projections that hang from a cave ceiling called?
3. Name the structure that is formed when a stalactite and a stalagmite join together.
4. What is a cave explorer called?
5. What should a spelunker do if he becomes lost?

Karst Topography

A region where extensive chemical weathering of soluble rock such as limestone has occurred, both on the surface and under the ground, has **karst topography.** The name comes from the Karst Plateau in Yugoslavia,

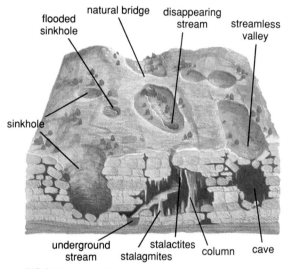

21B-6 *Diagram of karst topography*

flooded sinkhole

natural bridge

disappearing stream

streamless valley

sinkhole

underground stream

stalactites stalagmites

column

cave

21B-7 *A sink hole pond and a sink hole* (inset) *are surface features of karst regions.*

where this type of landscape is strikingly evident. The landscape features caves, sinkholes (collapsed cave ceilings), natural bridges, streamless valleys, and streams that disappear under the ground. It need not have all these features, but only a fair representation of them, to be a karst region. In the United States Florida, Indiana, Kentucky, Tennessee, and Virginia have areas with notable karst topography.

A **sinkhole** develops when a cave ceiling becomes so thin that it can no longer support its own weight. Periodically the news media report that a homeowner, often in Florida, woke up one morning and found a large sinkhole in his yard. He may not even have known that he had a cave under his property. Unfortunately, because he lacks a way to fill .in the hole, it often keeps growing. Sinkholes

have destroyed vehicles and buildings. In many places sinkholes fill with water to form sinkhole ponds.

A **natural bridge** is a stone arch formed by erosion. It may be the remains of a cave whose ceiling collapsed except for the bridge.

21B-8 *Natural bridge near Lexington, Virginia*

Streamless valleys and disappearing streams occur because of extensive weathering. A newly formed opening in the bed of a stream can divert the water underground.

The stream may stay beneath the surface, or it may emerge again downstream. The bed that the stream abandoned is a **streamless valley.**

Section Review Questions 21B-3

1. What is a collapsed cave ceiling called?
2. What is the name given to a stone arch that is left standing after the cave ceiling on both sides of it has collapsed?
3. What special kind of topography is a region that has caves, sinkholes, and streamless valleys said to have?

Terms

artesian well
capillary fringe
column
cone of depression
curtain
dripstone
flowstone
ground water
hydrologic cycle

impermeable
karst topography
natural bridge
perched water table
permeable
porous
recharge zone
shield
sinkhole

spelunker
spring
stalactite
stalagmite
streamless valley
water table
zone of aeration
zone of saturation

What Did You Learn?

1. Why is ground water an important topic, even though it accounts for only 22 per cent of the earth's water?
2. What is the advantage of drilling wells during a dry season instead of a wet season?
3. What is the benefit of having an artesian well?
4. Why do laundry companies prefer soft water rather than hard water?
5. Would you expect a well in an area with karst topography to produce hard or soft water? Why?
6. Cave formations consist mainly of what chemical?
7. Why are stalagmites often found directly under stalactites?
8. What are some dangers commonly faced by spelunkers?

What Do You Think?

1. How would civilization be different if no rocks were permeable?
2. Could hard water prevent leaks in plumbing pipes?
3. How could you tell for sure that a disappearing stream in one area is the same one that resurfaces in another area?

Appendix A–Station Model

SYMBOLIC FORM OF MESSAGE

iii Nddff VVwwW PPPTT N$_h$C$_L$hC$_M$C$_H$ T$_d$T$_d$app 7RRR$_t$s **1**

Note: This abridged code shows only data normally plotted on printed maps.

SAMPLE CODED MESSAGE

405 83220 12716 24731 67292 30228 74542

SYMBOLIC STATION MODEL	SAMPLE PLOTTED REPORT
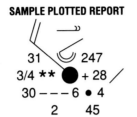	

Weather maps showing the development and movement of weather systems are among the principal tools used by the weather forecaster. To prepare the surface map and present the information quickly and pictorially, two actions are necessary: (1) Weather observers at many places must go to their posts at regular times each day to observe the weather and send the information by computer terminals to the offices where the maps are drawn; and (2) the information must be quickly transcribed to the maps. In order that the necessary speed and economy of space and transmission time may be realized, codes have been devised for sending the information and for plotting it on the maps. A great deal of information is contained in a brief coded weather message. If each item were named and described in plain language, a very lengthy message would be required, and it would be confusing to read and difficult to transfer to a map. Use of a code permits the message to be condensed to a few five-figure numeral groups, each figure of which has a meaning depending on its position in the message. Persons trained in the use of the code can read the message as easily as plain language. Both the code and the station model are based on international agreements. Through such standardized use of numerals and symbols, a meteorologist of one country can use the weather reports and weather maps of another country even though he does not understand the language. Weather codes are, in effect, an international language making possible complete interchange and use of worldwide weather reports so essential in present-day activities.

EXPLANATION OF SYMBOLS AND MAP ENTRIES   **2**

Symbols	Explanation of symbols and decode of example	Remarks on coding and plotting
iii	Station number 405 = Washington	Usually printed on manuscript maps below station circle. Omitted on Daily Weather Map in favor of printed station names.
N	Total amount of cloud 8 = completely covered	Observed in tenths of cloud cover and coded in Oktas (eighths) according to code table in block **6**. Plotted in symbols shown in same table.
dd	True direction from which wind is blowing 32 = 320° = NW	Coded in tens of degrees and plotted as the shaft of an arrow extending from the station circle toward the direction from which the wind is blowing.
ff	Wind speed in knots 20 = 20 knots	Coded in knots (nautical miles per hour) and plotted as feathers and half-feathers representing 10 and 5 knots, respectively, on the shaft of the wind direction arrow. See block **9**.
VV	Visibility in miles and fractions 12 = 12/16 or 3/4 miles	Decoded and plotted in miles and fractions up to 3 1/8 miles. Visibilities above 3 1/8 miles but less than 10 miles are plotted to the nearest whole mile. Values higher than 10 miles are omitted from the map.
ww	Present weather 71 = continuous slight snow	Coded in figures taken from the "ww" table (block **8**) and plotted in the corresponding symbol's same block. Entries for code figures 00, 01, 02, and 03 are omitted from this map.
W	Past weather 6 = rain	Coded in figures taken from the "W" table (block **11**) and plotted in the corresponding symbol's same block. No entry made for code figures 0, 1, or 2.
PPP	Barometric Pressure (in millibars) reduced to sea level 247 = 1024.7 mb	Coded and plotted in tens, units, and tenths of millibars. The initial 9 or 10 and the decimal point are omitted. See Barometric Pressure Conversion Scale in block **3**.
TT	Current air temperature 31 = 31° F	Coded and plotted in actual value in whole degrees F.
N$_h$	Fraction of sky covered by low or middle cloud 6 = 7 or 8 tenths	Observed and coded in tenths of cloud cover. Plotted on map as code figure in message. See block **7**.
C$_L$	Cloud type 7 = Fractostratus and/or Fractocumulus of bad weather (scud)	Predominating clouds of types in C$_L$ table (block **3**) are coded from that table and plotted in corresponding symbols.
h	Height of base of cloud 2 = 300 to 599 feet	Observed in feet and coded and plotted as code figures according to code table in block **5**.
C$_M$	Cloud type 9 = Altocumulus of chaotic sky	See C$_M$ table in block **3**.
C$_H$	Cloud type 2 = Dense cirrus in patches	See C$_H$ table in block **3**.
T$_d$T$_d$	Temperature of dew point 30 = 30° F	Coded and plotted in actual value in whole degrees F.
a	Characteristic of barograph trace 2 = rising steadily or unsteadily	Coded according to table in block **10** and plotted in corresponding symbols.
pp	Pressure change in 3 hours preceding observation 28 = 2.8 millibars	Coded and plotted in units and tenths of millibars.
7	Indicator figure	Not plotted.
RR	Amount of precipitation 45 = 0.45 inches	Coded and plotted in inches to the nearest hundredth of an inch.
R$_t$	Time precipitation began or ended 4 = 3 to 4 hours ago	Coded and plotted in figures from table in block **4**.
s	Depth of snow on ground	Not plotted.

Appendix

3 CLOUD TYPES

Low C_L

Code No.	Symbol	
1	⌒	Cu of fair weather, little vertical development and seemingly flattened
2	⌂	Cu of considerable development, generally towering, with or without other Cu or Sc bases all at same level
3	⌂	Cb with tops lacking clear-cut outlines, but distinctly not cirriform or anvil-shaped; with or without Cu, Sc, or St
4	⊶	Sc formed by spreading out of Cu; Cu often present also
5	⌣	Sc not formed by spreading out of Cu
6	—	St or Fs or both but no Fs of bad weather
7	- - -	Fs and/or Fc of bad weather (scud)
8	⌣	Cu and Sc (not formed by spreading out of Cu) with bases at different levels
9	⬨	Cb having a clearly fibrous (cirriform) top, often anvil-shaped, with or without Cu, Sc, St, or scud

Middle C_M

Code No.	Symbol	
1	∠	Thin As, most of cloud layer semitransparent
2	⫫	Thick As, greater part sufficiently dense to hide sun (or moon), or Ns
3	∽	Thin Ac, mostly semitransparent; cloud elements not changing much and at a single level
4	⌒	Thin Ac in patches; cloud elements continually changing and/or occurring at more than one level
5	⫍	Thin Ac in bands or in a layer gradually spreading over sky and usually thickening as a whole
6	⋈	Ac formed by the spreading out of Cu
7	⍓	Double-layered Ac, or a thick layer of Ac, not increasing; or Ac with As and/or Ns
8	⋔	Ac in the form of Cu-shaped tufts or Ac with turrets
9	⌇	Ac of a chaotic sky, usually at different levels; patches of dense Ci are usually present also

High C_H

Code No.	Symbol	
1	⌐	Filaments of Ci, or "mares' tails," scattered and not increasing
2	⌐	Dense Ci in patches or twisted sheaves, usually not increasing, sometimes like remains of Cb; or towers or tufts
3	⌐	Dense Ci, often anvil-shaped, derived from or associated with Cb
4	∕	Ci, often hook-shaped, gradually spreading over the sky and usually thickening as a whole
5	∠	Ci or Cs, often in converging bands, or Cs alone; generally overspreading and growing denser; the continuous layer not reaching 45° altitude
6	∠	Ci and Cs, often in converging bands, or Cs alone; generally overspreading and growing denser; the continuous layer exceeding 45° altitude
7	⟨⟩	Veil of Cs covering the entire sky
8	⌐	Cs not increasing and not covering entire sky
9	⌇	Cc alone or Cc with some Ci or Cs, but the Cc being the main cirriform cloud

Cloud Abbreviations

St or Fs–Stratus or Fractostratus

Cs–Cirrostratus

Ac–Altocumulus

Sc–Stratocumulus

Cu or Fc–Cumulus or Fractocumulus

Ci –Cirrus

Cc–Cirrocumulus

As–Altostratus

Ns–Nimbostratus

Cb–Cumulonimbus

BAROMETRIC PRESSURE CONVERSION SCALE

MILLIBARS → 956 960 964 968 972 976 980 984 988 992 996 1000

INCHES → 28.2 28.3 28.4 28.5 28.6 28.7 28.8 28.9 29.0 29.1 29.2 29.3 29.4 29.5 29.6

1004 1008 1012 1016 1020 1024 1028 1032 1036 1040 1044 1048 1052 1056

29.6 29.7 29.8 29.9 30.0 30.1 30.2 30.3 30.4 30.5 30.6 30.7 30.8 30.9 31.0 31.1 31.2

4 TIME OF PRECIPITATION R_t

Code No.	Description
0	No precipitation
1	Less than 1 hour ago
2	1 to 2 hours ago
3	2 to 3 hours ago
4	3 to 4 hours ago
5	4 to 5 hours ago
6	5 to 6 hours ago
7	6 to 12 hours ago
8	More than 12 hours ago
9	Unknown

5 HEIGHT OF CLOUD BASE h

Code No.	Height in Feet (Rounded Off)	Height in Meters (Approximate)
0	0 – 149	0 – 49
1	150 – 299	50 – 99
2	300 – 599	100 – 199
3	600 – 999	200 – 299
4	1,000 – 1,999	300 – 599
5	2,000 – 3,499	600 – 999
6	3,500 – 4,999	1,000 – 1,499
7	5,000 – 6,499	1,500 – 1,999
8	6,500 – 7,999	2,000 – 2,499
9	At or above 8,000, or no clouds	At or above 2,500, or no clouds

6 SKY COVERAGE N (Total Amount)

Code No.	Symbol	Description
0		No clouds
1		Less than one-tenth or one-tenth
2		Two-tenths or three-tenths
3		Four-tenths
4		Five-tenths
5		Six-tenths
6		Seven-tenths or eight-tenths
7		Nine-tenths or overcast with openings
8		Completely overcast
9		Sky obscured

7 SKY COVERAGE N_h (Low and/or Middle Clouds)

Code No.	Description
0	No clouds
1	Less than one-tenth or one-tenth
2	Two-tenths or three-tenths
3	Four-tenths
4	Five-tenths
5	Six-tenths
6	Seven-tenths or eight-tenths
7	Nine-tenths or overcast with openings
8	Completely overcast
9	Sky obscured

Appendix

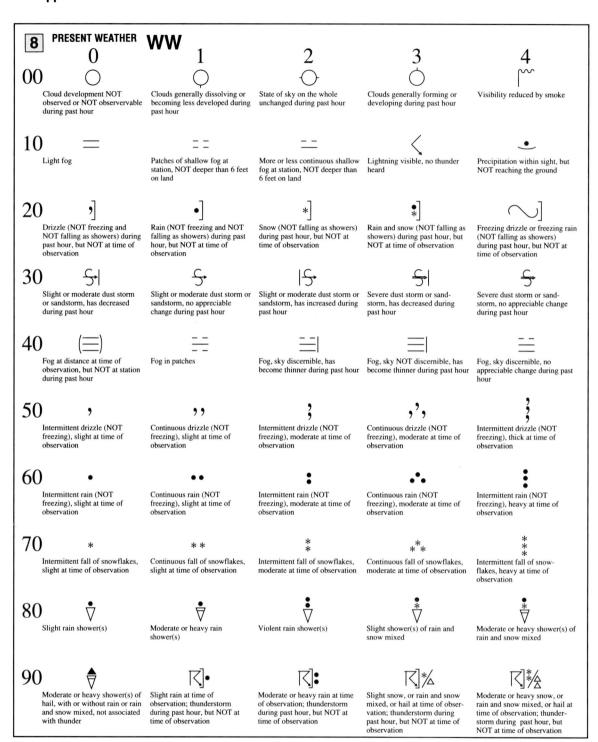

8 PRESENT WEATHER WW	0	1	2	3	4
00	Cloud development NOT observed or NOT observervable during past hour	Clouds generally dissolving or becoming less developed during past hour	State of sky on the whole unchanged during past hour	Clouds generally forming or developing during past hour	Visibility reduced by smoke
10	Light fog	Patches of shallow fog at station, NOT deeper than 6 feet on land	More or less continuous shallow fog at station, NOT deeper than 6 feet on land	Lightning visible, no thunder heard	Precipitation within sight, but NOT reaching the ground
20	Drizzle (NOT freezing and NOT falling as showers) during past hour, but NOT at time of observation	Rain (NOT freezing and NOT falling as showers) during past hour, but NOT at time of observation	Snow (NOT falling as showers) during past hour, but NOT at time of observation	Rain and snow (NOT falling as showers) during past hour, but NOT at time of observation	Freezing drizzle or freezing rain (NOT falling as showers) during past hour, but NOT at time of observation
30	Slight or moderate dust storm or sandstorm, has decreased during past hour	Slight or moderate dust storm or sandstorm, no appreciable change during past hour	Slight or moderate dust storm or sandstorm, has increased during past hour	Severe dust storm or sandstorm, has decreased during past hour	Severe dust storm or sandstorm, no appreciable change during past hour
40	Fog at distance at time of observation, but NOT at station during past hour	Fog in patches	Fog, sky discernible, has become thinner during past hour	Fog, sky NOT discernible, has become thinner during past hour	Fog, sky discernible, no appreciable change during past hour
50	Intermittent drizzle (NOT freezing), slight at time of observation	Continuous drizzle (NOT freezing), slight at time of observation	Intermittent drizzle (NOT freezing), moderate at time of observation	Continuous drizzle (NOT freezing), moderate at time of observation	Intermittent drizzle (NOT freezing), thick at time of observation
60	Intermittent rain (NOT freezing), slight at time of observation	Continuous rain (NOT freezing), slight at time of observation	Intermittent rain (NOT freezing), moderate at time of observation	Continuous rain (NOT freezing), moderate at time of observation	Intermittent rain (NOT freezing), heavy at time of observation
70	Intermittent fall of snowflakes, slight at time of observation	Continuous fall of snowflakes, slight at time of observation	Intermittent fall of snowflakes, moderate at time of observation	Continuous fall of snowflakes, moderate at time of observation	Intermittent fall of snowflakes, heavy at time of observation
80	Slight rain shower(s)	Moderate or heavy rain shower(s)	Violent rain shower(s)	Slight shower(s) of rain and snow mixed	Moderate or heavy shower(s) of rain and snow mixed
90	Moderate or heavy shower(s) of hail, with or without rain or rain and snow mixed, not associated with thunder	Slight rain at time of observation; thunderstorm during past hour, but NOT at time of observation	Moderate or heavy rain at time of observation; thunderstorm during past hour, but NOT at time of observation	Slight snow, or rain and snow mixed, or hail at time of observation; thunderstorm during past hour, but NOT at time of observation	Moderate or heavy snow, or rain and snow mixed, or hail at time of observation; thunderstorm during past hour, but NOT at time of observation

5

∞

Haze

6

S

Widespread dust in suspension in the air, NOT raised by wind, at time of observation

7

$

Dust or sand raised by wind, at time of observation

8

Well developed dust devil(s) within past hour

9

(S→)

Dust storm or sand storm within sight of or at station during past hour

00

)•(

Precipitation within sight, reaching the ground, but distant from station

(•)

Precipitation within sight, reaching the ground, near to but NOT at station

Thunder heard, but no precipitation at the station

∀

Squall(s) within sight during past hour

][

Funnel cloud(s) within sight during past hour

10

Showers of rain during past hour, but NOT at time of observation

Showers of snow, or of rain and snow, during past hour, but NOT at time of observation

Showers of hail, or of hail and rain, during past hour, but NOT at time of observation

Fog during past hour, but NOT at time of observation

Thunderstorm (with or without precipitation) during past hour, but NOT at time of observation

20

Severe dust storm or sand-storm, has increased during past hour

Slight or moderate drifting snow, generally low

Heavy drifting snow, generally low

Slight or moderate drifting snow, generally high

Heavy drifting snow, generally high

30

Fog, sky NOT discernible, no appreciable change during past hour

Fog, sky discernible, has begun or become thicker during past hour

Fog, sky NOT discernible, has begun or become thinner during past hour

Fog, depositing rime, sky discernible

Fog, depositing rime, sky NOT discernible

40

Continuous drizzle (NOT freezing), thick at time of observation

Slight freezing drizzle

Moderate or thick freezing drizzle

Drizzle and rain, slight

Drizzle and rain, moderate or heavy

50

Continuous rain (NOT freezing), heavy at time of observation

Slight freezing rain

Moderate or heavy freezing rain

Rain or drizzle and snow, slight

Rain or drizzle and snow, moderate or heavy

60

Continuous fall of snowflakes, heavy at time of observation

Ice needles (with or without fog)

Granular snow (with or without fog)

Isolated starlike snow crystals (with or without fog)

Ice pellets (sleet, U.S. definition)

70

Slight snow shower(s)

Moderate or heavy snow shower(s)

Slight shower(s) of soft or small hail with or without rain, or rain and snow mixed

Moderate or heavy shower(s) of soft or small hail with or without rain, or rain and snow mixed

Slight shower(s) of hail with or without rain, or rain and snow mixed, not associated with thunder

80

Slight or moderate thunderstorm without hail, but with rain and/or snow at time of observation

Slight or moderate thunder-storm, with hail at time of observation

Heavy thunderstorm, without hail, but with rain and/or snow at time of observation

Thunderstorm combined with dust storm or sand storm at time of observation

Heavy thunderstorm with hail at time of observation

90

9 WIND SPEED ff

Symbol	Miles (Statute) Per Hour	Knots
◎	Calm	Calm
—	1–2	1–2
(symbol)	3–8	3–7
(symbol)	9–14	8–12
(symbol)	15–20	13–17

Symbol	Miles (Statute) Per Hour	Knots
(symbol)	21–25	18–22
(symbol)	26–31	23–27
(symbol)	32–37	28–32
(symbol)	38–43	33–37
(symbol)	44–49	38–42
(symbol)	50–54	43–47
(symbol)	55–60	48–52

Symbol	Miles (Statute) Per Hour	Knots
(symbol)	61–66	53–57
(symbol)	67–71	58–62
(symbol)	72–77	63–67
(symbol)	78–83	68–72
(symbol)	84–89	73–77
(symbol)	119–123	103–107

10 BAROMETRIC TENDENCY a

Code No.	Symbol	Description
0	(symbol)	Rising, then falling; barometer same or higher than 3 hours ago
1	(symbol)	Rising, then steady; or rising, then rising more slowly; barometer now higher than 3 hours ago
2	/	Rising steadily, or unsteadily; barometer now higher than 3 hours ago
3	(symbol)	Falling or steady, then rising; or rising, then rising more quickly; barometer now higher than 3 hours ago
4	—	Steady; same as 3 hours ago
5	(symbol)	Falling, then rising; barometer same as or lower than 3 hours ago
6	(symbol)	Falling, then steady; or falling, then falling more slowly; barometer now lower than 3 hours ago
7	(symbol)	Falling steadily, or unsteadily; barometer now lower than 3 hours ago
8	(symbol)	Steady or rising, then falling; or falling, then falling more quickly; barometer now lower than 3 hours ago

11 PAST WEATHER W

Code No.	Symbol	Description
0		Clear or few clouds; not plotted
1		Partly cloudy (scattered) or variable sky; not plotted
2		Cloudy (broken) or overcast; not plotted
3	(symbol)	Sandstorm or dust storm, or drifting or blowing snow
4	=	Fog, or smoke, or thick dust haze
5	,	Drizzle
6	•	Rain
7	*	Snow, or rain and snow mixed, or ice pellets (sleet)
8	▽	Shower(s)
9	(symbol)	Thunderstorm, with or without precipitation

Appendix B–**Star Charts**

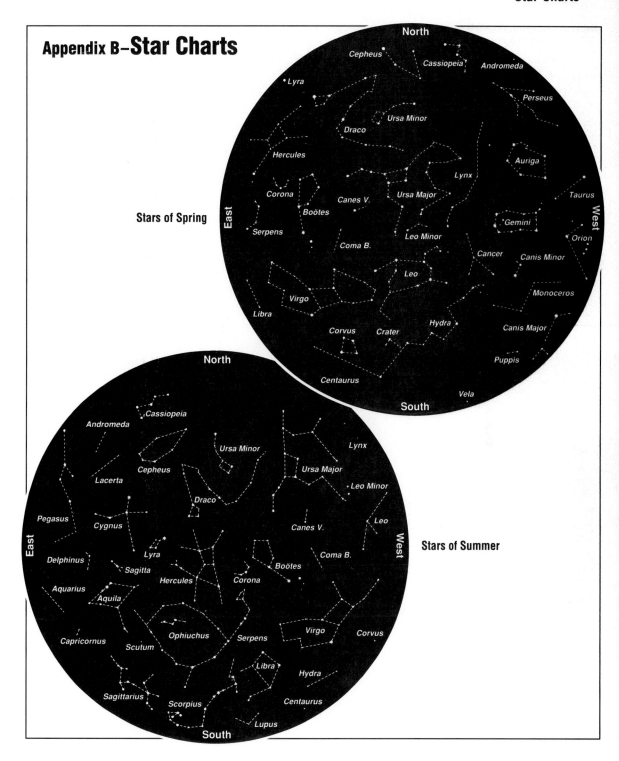

Stars of Spring

Stars of Summer

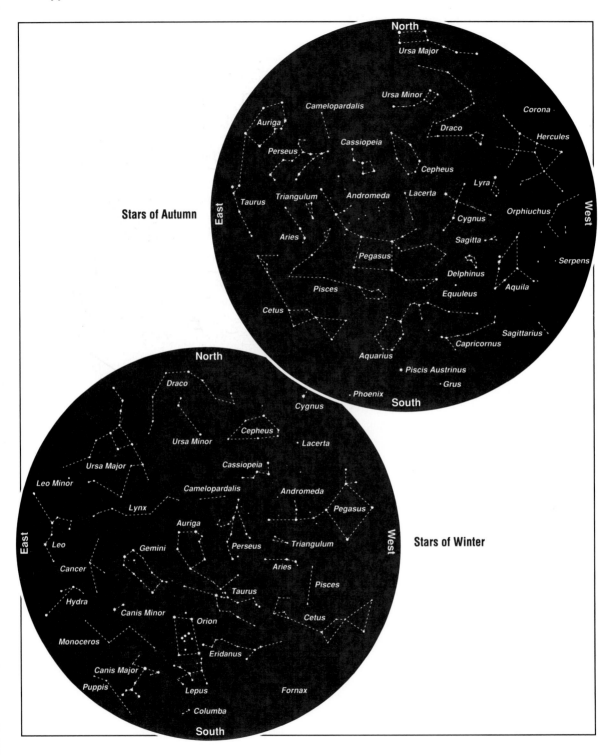

Stars of Autumn

North

Ursa Major

Ursa Minor

Camelopardalis

Corona

Auriga

Draco

Hercules

Perseus

Cassiopeia

Cepheus

East

Lyra

Triangulum

Andromeda

Lacerta

Taurus

Cygnus

Orphiuchus

West

Aries

Pegasus

Sagitta

Serpens

Delphinus

Aquila

Pisces

Equuleus

Cetus

Sagittarius

Capricornus

Aquarius

Piscis Austrinus

Grus

Phoenix

South

Stars of Winter

North

Draco

Cygnus

Cepheus

Ursa Minor

Lacerta

Cassiopeia

Camelopardalis

Andromeda

Ursa Major

Pegasus

Leo Minor

Lynx

Auriga

Perseus

Triangulum

East

Leo

Gemini

Aries

West

Cancer

Taurus

Pisces

Hydra

Canis Minor

Orion

Cetus

Monoceros

Eridanus

Canis Major

Puppis

Lepus

Fornax

Columba

South

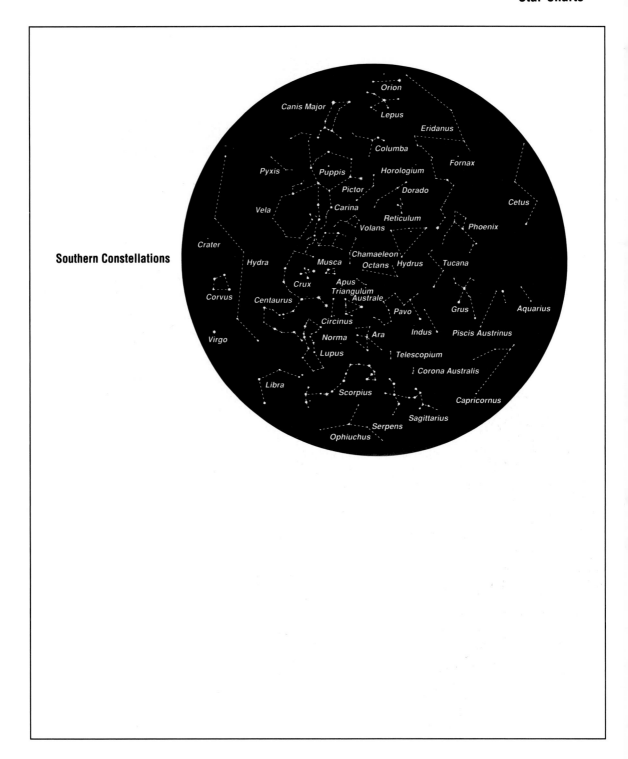

Southern Constellations

Appendix C–**Measurement Conversion Factors**

Units	Metric	Conversion Factor†	English
Length	millimeters	0.039	inches
	centimeters	0.394	inches
	centimeters	0.033	feet
	meters	3.281	feet
	meters	1.094	yards
	kilometers	0.621	miles
Area	square centimeters	0.155	square inches
	square meters	1.196	square yards
	square kilometers	0.386	square miles
	hectares	2.471	acres
Volume	milliliters (cubic centimeters)	0.061	cubic inches
	liters	1.057	quarts
	liters	0.264	gallons
	cubic meters	1.308	cubic yards
Mass	grams	0.035	ounces
	grams	0.002	pounds
	kilograms	2.205	pounds
	metric tons	1.102	tons (short)
Pressure	millibars	0.030	inches of mercury
	grams per square centimeter	0.142	pounds per square inch
Weight	Correct units of weight in the metric system are the dyne and the newton. However, in common American usage the gram, which is actually a unit of mass, is used as a unit of weight.		
Temperature	degrees Celsius	1.8 (add 32 after multiplying or subtract 32 before dividing)	degrees Fahrenheit

† Multiply by factor to convert metric to English; divide by factor to convert English to metric.

Glossary

absolute humidity   The amount of water a certain volume of air holds.

abyssal plain   A flat, deep seafloor.

accretion   The enlargement of a crystal by the additional attachment of particles; the hypothetical combining of particles in space to form planets, satellites, etc.

acid rain   Rain that is more acidic than normal due to higher-than-normal amounts of sulfuric and nitric acids.

acid test   A method for testing the composition of such minerals as carbonates and sulfides by their reaction with dilute acids.

active volcano   A volcano that has erupted within the last fifty years.

actual height   The height of a mountain above the surrounding territory.

air mass   A huge body of air having relatively uniform temperature and humidity and covering hundreds or thousands of square kilometers.

albedo   The ability of an object such as a planet or minor planet to reflect light.

alluvial fan   A fan-shaped deposit of silt or mud formed at the point where a stream emerges from a ravine onto a plain or other relatively flat area.

alpine glacier   A valley glacier.

Alpine-Himalayan belt   The volcano belt extending from the Mediterranean area eastward to the Indonesian states.

altazimuth mount   A mount for holding a telescope that is easily adjusted for altitude and azimuth (compass direction).

anemometer   An instrument for measuring the speed of the wind.

aneroid barometer   A barometer that works by the pressure of the atmosphere on the elastic lid of a metal box containing virtually no air.

annular eclipse   An eclipse of the sun in which a ring of sunlight shows around the moon because the moon is too far from the earth to cover the sun's disk completely.

anomalous sample   A sample tested by the radiocarbon dating method that gives a wrong date.

anticline   A fold or rock stratum that bends downward on both sides from its center.

aphelion   The point farthest from the sun in the orbit of a planet or comet.

apogee   The point farthest from the earth in the orbit of the moon or a manmade satellite.

applications satellite   A satellite that is used for specific, useful purposes such as weather prediction, communications, navigational references, and survey instruments.

artesian well   A well in a formation where water pressure is sufficient to produce a constant supply of water rising to the surface of the ground without pumping.

ash   Glassy volcanic fragments smaller than cinders.

asteroid   Any of the minor planets that orbit the sun, mainly between the orbits of Mars and Jupiter; they are smaller than the major planets and have no atmosphere.

astronomical unit (A.U.)   The average distance between the earth and the sun (150 million km or 93 million mi.).

atmosphere   The layers of air surrounding the earth.

atmospheric pressure   The pressure exerted by the weight of the gases in the atmosphere.

atoll   A ring of low coral islands and reefs enclosing or partly enclosing a lagoon.

aurora australis   The streamers or bands of light which appear in the Southern Hemisphere sky when charged particles escape from the magnetosphere into the lower atmosphere.

aurora borealis   The streamers or bands of light which appear in the Northern Hemisphere sky when charged particles escape from the magnetosphere into the lower atmosphere.

autumnal equinox   About September 22, when the center of the sun crosses the celestial equator, and the day and night are of equal length in all parts of the earth.

axis   An imaginary line about which the earth or other astronomical body rotates.

Glossary

Baily's beads Bright pinpoints of sunlight that appear briefly during a total solar eclipse as sunlight shines through valleys around the moon's edge.

barograph An instrument that automatically records changes in air pressure.

barometer An instrument used to measure the atmospheric pressure.

barrier island A sandy island that has no connection with the mainland.

barrier reef A long line of rocks or a coral reef not far from the mainland.

base level The lowest level to which a stream can erode.

basin A syncline whose length is roughly equal to its breadth.

bay barrier A sandy beach that has been built up across the mouth of a bay.

Beaufort wind scale An internationally used scale of wind speeds, ranging from 0 (calm) to 12 (hurricane).

blowout An excavated basin which resulted from the wind carrying away loose material.

bolide A large meteor, usually one that explodes and falls to the earth as meteorites.

bomb A mass of lava that congeals in midair.

boulder train A group of erratics from the same distant bedrock source.

Bourdon tube thermometer A thermometer consisting of a hollow metal coil filled with a liquid that expands and contracts with temperature change.

breaker A wave in a body of water that peaks sharply, then falls over on the forward side of the wave.

breccia A conglomerate rock composed of angular fragments of various kinds of rocks united by a matrix or cement.

butte A narrow, flat-topped hill.

caldera A large depression at the summit of a volcano formed by the explosion or collapse of the crater.

calibration curve (radiocarbon) A graph that is made by plotting the known ages of various objects and the amounts of carbon-14 isotope in the objects.

calving The process of forming icebergs from a glacier.

capillary fringe The ground region immediately above the zone of saturation where water has worked its way upward from the water table by capillary action.

carat A unit of weight for gems equal to 0.2 g.

carbon-14 A radioactive isotope of carbon used in the radiocarbon dating method for determining the age of organic remains.

Cassini's division The dark region of separation in the ring system of Saturn.

celestial equator The projection of the earth's equator on the celestial sphere.

celestial sphere Space; the environment of the earth.

Celsius scale A temperature scale on which 0° marks the freezing point of water and 100° marks the boiling point of water.

Cepheid variable A type of star that changes in brightness because it expands and contracts regularly.

chemical sedimentary rock Type of rock that either was created in place or was formed from the dissolved minerals carried by water.

chemical weathering The breakdown of rock by the action of carbon dioxide, humic acid, and oxygen dissolved in water; it results in a chemical change in the rocks.

chromatic aberration The distortion of color around the image; it is common with refractor telescopes.

chromosphere The layer of gases that forms the inner part of the sun's atmosphere.

cinder A rough, solidified piece of lava with many small spaces.

cinder cone A mass of volcanic cinders accumulated in the shape of a cone, especially at a vent of a volcano.

Circum-Pacific belt The volcano belt located around the Pacific Ocean.

cirque Steep, hollow excavation in a mountain made by glacial erosion.

cleavage A property of minerals; tendency to

split along certain preferred planes.

cloud A mass of water droplets or ice crystals suspended in the air.

coal A solid form of fossil fuel made from plant material.

coalescence The growing together into a single mass.

cold air mass An air mass that is colder than the surface over which it moves.

cold front The advancing edge of a cold air mass.

column A cave formation formed where a stalactite meets a stalagmite.

coma The spherical region of glowing gas which surrounds the nucleus of a comet.

comet A relatively small, icy body having a very eccentric orbit around the sun. When a comet is near the sun, it produces tails of dust and gas.

composite telescope A telescope that uses both mirrors and objective lenses for gathering light to a focal point.

composite volcano A volcano that is built up by a combination of cinders and lava flows.

compound Atoms of several elements combined in a fixed ratio.

condensation The changing of water vapor into a liquid; it occurs during cloud formation.

condensation nuclei Small particles of material such as salt or smoke around which tiny water droplets form.

cone of depression A cone-shaped lowering of the water table where water has been depleted more rapidly than it has been supplied.

conglomerate Sedimentary rock composed of rounded fragments of various kinds of rocks united by a matrix or cement.

Congreve rocket An early solid fuel rocket designed by Sir William Congreve of England; it made the "rocket's red glare" in the War of 1812.

conservation The principle that energy is not now being created or destroyed but is only transformed from one form to another.

constellation An imagined pattern in a group of stars; for modern astronomers it is an area in the sky, not a pattern.

continental air mass An air mass that forms over land.

continental glacier A vast ice sheet that covers a large portion of a continent or a large island.

continental rise The bottom of the ocean between the continental slopes and the seafloor.

continental shelf The relatively shallow, submerged edge of a continent.

continental slope The slope beyond the continental shelf.

contour lines Lines on a map showing the height above or below sea level; all the points on a contour line have the same elevation.

convection The transfer of heat from one place to another by the circulation of currents of heated particles of gas or liquid.

convective zone The outermost layer of the sun's interior, composed of hot gases.

Copernican theory An accepted theory developed by Nicolaus Copernicus that the earth rotates on its axis and that the planets move around the sun.

coral reef A reef formed from the calcium carbonate shelter of some coral animals and other carbonate-secreting organisms.

core The innermost part of the sun where thermonuclear reactions generate energy; the central portion of the earth lying below the mantle.

corona The extensive outer portion of the solar atmosphere.

coronagraph An instrument used to observe the corona of the sun by making an artificial eclipse.

countercurrent A slow ocean current that flows beneath most major surface currents and in opposite direction to the surface currents.

crater A round depression in the surface of the moon or other astronomical body; a depression at the top of a volcanic cone.

creep Slow movement of disintegrated rock down a slope due to gravity.

crest The peak or apex of a wave.

crevasse A deep fissure in a glacier.

crust The solid outer part of the earth.

curtain A thin sheet of dripstone that hangs from the ceilings of caves.

Glossary

cusps The pointed ends of a crescent moon.

cyclone A hurricane in the region of the Indian Ocean; the effect of wind circling an area of low pressure; general term for any low-pressure area.

debris slide A landslide involving mostly unconsolidated materials (soil, loose rocks).

declination Distance north or south of the celestial equator measured in degrees; celestial latitude.

deferent The earth-centered circle in the Ptolemaic system along which a planet's epicycle traveled.

degeneration The principle that all things tend to become disordered or are running down.

delta A stream deposit that collects at the mouths of some streams.

density The mass of a certain material per volume.

density current An ocean current that is mostly vertical, caused by differences in water density.

depositional mountain A mountain or hill that forms by accumulation or piling up of rock materials.

desalinate To remove salt from water, especially seawater.

desert pavement The desert surface where all the sand and other unconsolidated materials have blown away, leaving only pebbles and cobbles.

dew Water on a surface produced by condensation when the cooler surface cools a nearby film of air to below the dew point.

dew point The temperature at which air, by cooling, becomes saturated with vapor and begins to condense.

diamond pipe Circular bodies of volcanic breccia where diamonds are sometimes found.

diamond ring effect The image of light appearing like a diamond ring, produced by a Baily's bead along the thin remaining solar crescent; it occurs immediately before or after totality in a solar eclipse.

diffraction grating A series of thousands of microscopic lines ruled or molded onto a transparent surface which are tiny enough to interfere with light waves to produce a spectrum.

dike Igneous rock formed by the forcing of magma into cracks that are not parallel to the existing strata.

discontinuity A boundary between two layers of the earth below the crust where earthquake waves change speed.

divide A ridge separating one stream's drainage basin from another's.

doctrine of uniformity The idea that "the present is the key to the past" and that geological change is caused by gradual processes rather than sudden catastrophes; it is not accepted by creationists.

doldrums A permanent low-pressure area along the equator caused by the rising of warm air.

dome An anticline that has roughly the same length as breadth.

dormant volcano A volcano for which there exists a historical record of at least one eruption, but not within the last fifty years.

double refraction The production of a double image as light passes through certain minerals such as calcite.

drainage basin The area that is drained by a river and its tributaries.

dredging A method of underwater mining in which huge volumes of placer deposits are mechanically collected.

drift Any glacial deposit attributable either to ice or meltwater.

dripstone Cave deposits which are formed by precipitation of calcium carbonate from ground water.

drizzle Small droplets of rain falling slowly.

drumlin An elongated, streamlined hill made up of glacial till.

earthquake The shock waves caused by the collision of sections of the tectonic plates.

earthshine Sunlight doubly reflected from the earth to the moon and back to the earth again.

eccentric Off-center; elongated.

echo sounding A method of measuring water depth in which a ship sends sound waves to the ocean floor and records the time it takes them to return.

eclipse The cutting off of the light of one celestial body by another.

eclipsing binary Two stars revolving around each other, one bright and one dim, which appear to vary in brightness from night to night.

ecliptic The apparent path of the sun among the stars; the plane of the earth's orbit.

electromagnetic waves A form of energy which includes visible light, ultraviolet, infrared, x-rays, etc.

element A substance composed entirely of the same kind of atom.

elevation The altitude of a mountain's summit above sea level.

ellipse An oval-shaped figure having both ends alike; the characteristic shape of the orbits of planets, satellites, and periodic comets.

entropy The principle that things tend toward a state of disorder.

epicenter The point from which earthquake waves seem to radiate, situated directly above the true center (focus) of the earthquake.

epicycle A small circle, the center of which moves around on the circumference of a larger circle or deferent; it was formerly used in astronomy to account for the motions of the planets.

equatorial mount A mount for holding a telescope in which the telescope tube is attached to a shaft pointing to the celestial pole; this mounting provides for the tracking of a particular star throughout the night.

equinox One of the two times during the year when the sun crosses the equator, making night and day of equal length in all parts of the earth.

erode To wear away by abrasion or solution.

erosional mountain (residual mountain) A mountain which has been carved out by extensive erosion, usually from a plateau.

erratics Boulders in glacial till that are not like the bedrock under them.

escape velocity The speed an object must travel to free itself from the gravitational pull of a planet, moon, etc.

esker A long, winding, narrow ridge of sand and gravel, probably deposited by a stream flowing in or under glacial ice.

evaporation The process of changing a liquid into a vapor without boiling.

exfoliation A weathering process by which thin slabs or flakes of rock are removed from large domes or boulders.

extinct volcano A volcano for which there are no historical records of any eruptions.

extrusive igneous rock Igneous rock that solidified above the earth's surface.

eye The calm, clear area at the center of a hurricane.

Fahrenheit scale A temperature scale on which 32° marks the freezing point of water and 212° marks the boiling point of water.

fallacy A mistake in reasoning.

fault A crack in a rock along which there has been movement (slippage).

fault-block mountain A mountain bounded by at least one fault.

fiducial points The fixed points on a thermometer that indicate the freezing and boiling points of water.

fiord A glacially deepened inlet or arm of the sea.

fireball A large, brilliant meteor.

firn Granular ice formed by the melting and refreezing of snow.

first law of thermodynamics The principle that energy is not now being created or destroyed but is only transformed from one form to another.

first quarter The phase of the moon when the western half is lighted and the eastern half is dark.

flame test A test to identify a chemical element by its color when heated in a flame.

flood plain A plain bordering a stream and composed of sediment deposited by the stream during floods.

flowstones A cave formation resulting from deposits precipitated from a thin film of water flowing over the sides and floor of a cave rather than dripping from the ceiling.

Glossary

fluorescent   Having the property of emitting visible light when exposed to ultraviolet rays.

focus (*pl.,* foci)   The point at which light rays come together after being bent by a lens or curved mirror; the real center of an earthquake, generally some distance below the surface; one of two points used in drawing an ellipse.

fold mountain   A mountain apparently formed by the folding of rocks.

foliated metamorphic rock   Rock that has a banded or layered appearance, such as gneiss.

forked lightning   Lightning formed when a stepped leader branches on the way to the ground.

fossil   Any trace or remains of a living organism that has been preserved by natural means.

fossil fuel   Altered remains of living organisms that can be used as a source of energy; includes coal, petroleum (oil), and natural gas.

fossil graveyard   An assortment of fossils embedded in hardened sediment, evidently the result of a catastrophe.

Foucault pendulum   A pendulum used by Jean Foucault in 1851 to demonstrate that the earth rotates on its axis; any similar pendulum.

fracture   The characteristic manner in which a mineral breaks when it does not exhibit cleavage.

fragmental sedimentary rock   Rock formed by the cementing of rock fragments.

Frasch process   A method of mining sulfur in which hot water is fed into the deposits, melting the sulfur so that it can be forced to the surface by compressed air.

freeze   To change state from a liquid to a solid.

freezing nuclei   Small particles of clay or dust shaped like ice crystals around which an ice crystal may form in a cloud.

freezing rain   Supercooled water that falls as rain and then freezes on the surface it contacts.

fringing reef   A coral reef formed close to the shoreline with no navigable channel between.

front   Boundary between air masses that do not mix.

frost   Ice crystals formed on a surface when the cooler surface cools a nearby film of air to a below-freezing dew point.

frost heaving   The pushing of rocks upward in soil by repeated freezing (expansion) and thawing of soil water.

full moon   A phase in which the moon's entire near side is lighted.

fumarole   A fissure or vent in the ground from which steam and hot gases issue.

galaxy   Groups of millions of stars, usually elliptically arranged.

Galilean moons   Jupiter's four largest moons, named after their discoverer, Galileo Galilei.

gas giants   The planets Jupiter, Saturn, Uranus, and Neptune, which have large, gaseous atmospheres that are so deep that space probes have been unable to locate the planets' surfaces.

geocentric theory   The false theory that the earth is the center of the solar system.

geologic time scale   The history of the earth according to evolutionists.

geology   The study of the earth's structures and processes.

geostationary   The orbit of a satellite which stays over the same spot on the earth's surface by orbiting the earth once every twenty-four hours in the same direction as the earth's rotation.

geosyncline   An elongated syncline.

geosyncline theory   A theory that attempts to account for the formation of a mountain range by the accumulation of sediment in a gigantic trench or geosyncline.

geothermal   Of or having to do with the internal heat of the earth.

geyser   A spring that sends a column of hot water and steam into the air at intervals.

geyserite   A whitish deposit of silica around the opening of a geyser.

glacier   A mass of ice, made by the melting and refreezing of snow, that moves under the influence of gravity.

glacier ice   A form of ice consisting of interlocking crystals, produced by the recrystallization of snow under pressure.

glowing avalanche   A volcanic mixture of hot, solid particles suspended in water vapor or other gases that is so heavy that it falls down the volcano's slope instead of rising into the air.

gnomon A device which astronomers used to determine the time of day, the time of year, and the position and motion of heavenly bodies from the shadows cast in sunlight.

gradient The slope of a stream. A high-gradient stream has a relatively steep slope; a low-gradient stream has a gentle slope.

granite A common, coarse-grained intrusive igneous rock.

granule A cell in the sun's photosphere thought to result from convection currents bringing up heated gases from beneath the surface.

Great Red Spot A reddish colored, oval-shaped area on Jupiter; it may be due to an atmospheric disturbance or storm.

greenhouse effect Warming of the lower layers of the atmosphere by infrared radiation given off from the earth after it has been heated by the sun.

ground moraine Debris strewn over the whole area that a glacier occupied.

ground water Water at the depth where all the available spaces between rock particles are filled by water.

guyot A submerged island with a flattened top.

hailstone An ice pellet produced when strong updrafts carry raindrops to elevations cold enough to freeze them.

hanging valley A small valley that enters a glaciated valley from high on its sides and was formed by tributaries of the stream that occupied the main valley before the glacier formed.

hardness test The comparative capacity of one substance to scratch or be scratched by another substance; the degree of hardness of a mineral is expressed with reference to a scale ranging from 1 to 10 (talc to diamond).

harvest moon The full moon nearest to the autumnal equinox, about September 21.

head The nucleus and coma of a comet.

headwaters The highest point of a stream.

heat lightning Flashes of lightning from clouds too far away for the thunder to be heard.

heliocentric theory The accepted theory that the sun is the center of the solar system, with the earth and the other planets revolving around it.

heterosphere The gas layers above the homosphere; the layers of oxygen, helium, and hydrogen which are located several hundred miles above the earth's surface.

historical geology Branch of geology that deals with the history of the earth.

homosphere The layer of the atmosphere nearest the earth's surface which consists of a homogeneous mixture of gases.

honeycomb mirror A telescope mirror molded over a honeycomb-shaped structure to reduce the mirror's weight.

hook A spit with a sharp bend in it.

horizon A layer or zone of the soil.

horn A jagged mountain peak resulting from the erosion of several cirques against one headland, such as the Matterhorn in the Alps.

horse latitudes Permanent high-pressure areas that are caused by descending cold air and result in no horizontal wind, which is dangerous for sailing ships.

hot spring A natural spring from which heated water issues.

humus Decayed organic matter constituent of soil which is rich in nutrients.

hunter's moon The next full moon after the harvest moon.

hurricane Giant windstorms that form over the tropical oceans near the equator.

hydrologic cycle A cycle in which water evaporates from oceans, lakes, and rivers to form clouds that move over the land areas, then precipitates, and returns to the oceans, lakes, and rivers.

hydrosphere The water that covers nearly four-fifths of the earth's surface.

hygrometer An instrument used to measure relative humidity by using the change in a human hair's length to show the humidity.

ICBM Intercontinental ballistic missile; a guided missile of extreme range (8,000 km [5,000 mi.] or more).

Glossary

ice cap A large, permanent ice sheet with a raised center, especially one covering the top of a mountain or a plateau.

ices Frozen materials such as methane, ammonia, and water found in the heads of comets and in the atmospheres of outer planets.

ice sheet A thick layer of ice covering an extensive area for a long period.

igneous rock Rock that appears to have been molten in the past.

impermeable Not permitting the passage of fluid because of the absence of pores, spaces, and cracks.

index fossil A fossil that evolutionists use to date rock strata.

inertia The tendency of all objects in the universe to remain at rest if at rest, or, if moving, to continue moving in the same direction unless acted upon by some outside force.

inferior planet A planet whose orbit is inside the earth's orbit.

intrusive igneous rock A type of igneous rock that solidified beneath the earth's surface.

ion An electrically charged atom.

ionize To remove electrons from atoms or to add electrons to atoms.

ionosphere The outer part of the earth's atmosphere, extending from 80 km (50 mi.) to 400 km (250 mi.) and consisting of layers of ionized atoms of gas.

irons A type of meteorite containing 85 to 95 per cent iron.

island arc A long, curved chain of islands such as the Aleutians, West Indies, Philippines, or the Ryukyu (off the southern tip of Japan).

isobar A line on a weather map connecting stations having the same barometric pressure.

isotherm A line on a weather map connecting stations having the same temperature.

jet stream A path of high-speed wind in the stratosphere.

joint A large crack in a rock along which there has been no movement (slippage).

Jovian (See **gas giants.**)

kame A short ridge formed by stratified glacial drift; a low mound or hill composed of sand or gravel.

karst topography Topography typified by caverns, natural bridges, streamless valleys, and sinkholes.

kettle A depression in the surface of glacial drift formed by a melting block of ice.

lahar A mudslide caused by water from snow melted during a volcanic eruption.

land breeze A breeze that blows from shore to sea, usually during the night.

landslide The rapid downward movement of a mass of soil or rock on a steep slope.

lapse rate The rate that temperature drops as altitude increases in the troposphere, 6.4° C/km (3.5° F/1,000 ft.).

last quarter (See **third quarter.**)

lateral moraine Rocks and debris on the sides of valley glaciers.

latitude The distance north or south of the equator measured in degrees.

lava Molten rock flowing from a volcano or fissure in the earth; the rock formed by cooling of this molten rock.

law of gravitation The force that makes all bodies in the universe tend to move toward one another.

leap year An extra day added to the solar calendar every four years to keep the calendar in step with the seasons.

Leonids A shower of meteors occurring about November 17 which appears to be coming out of the constellation Leo.

levee A ridge of soil, often present on both sides of a stream, where it was deposited by stream flooding.

lightning An electrical discharge that occurs either between clouds or between a cloud and the ground.

lightning rod A metal rod attached to the highest point of a building's roof which can conduct lightning to the ground with metal conductor cables.

light-year A unit of distance for objects outside the solar system such as stars and galaxies; the distance light travels in one year, about 9.6 trillion km (6 trillion mi.).

limb The edge of the sun's disk.

lithosphere The solid part of the earth.

loam An especially fertile soil which contains about equal parts sand and silt and about half as much clay.

lodestone A stone that attracts iron as a magnet does; a kind of magnetite.

longitude The distance east or west of Greenwich, England, measured in degrees.

longshore current A current parallel to the shore produced by waves striking a beach at an oblique angle.

lunar calendar A calendar with months that correspond to the length of the moon's cycle but not to any particular season.

lunar eclipse When the moon passes into the earth's shadow.

lunisolar calendar A calendar which takes into account both the solar year and the lunar month.

luster The quality and intensity of light reflected from a mineral's surface.

L waves The slow-moving waves caused by an earthquake which travel along the surface; the last waves of an earthquake to arrive at a distant seismic station.

mackerel sky Cirrocumulus clouds which form in groups or lines that resemble the scales of fish.

magma Molten rock beneath the surface of the earth.

magnetism The characteristic of attracting iron and certain other materials; it is related to a force field produced by the alignment of atoms and movement of electrons.

magnetosphere A zone that encircles the earth and consists of electrons and protons from the sun trapped in the earth's magnetic field; it protects living things from cosmic radiation.

magnitude The measure of the brightness of a star; the measure of the energy of an earthquake.

mantle The portion of the earth's interior lying between the crust and the core.

mare (*pl.,* maria) A dark, flat lowland region of the moon.

mares' tails Cirrus clouds which are arranged in bands across the sky.

maritime air mass An air mass that forms over an ocean.

mass A measure of the amount of material an object contains, irrespective of gravity.

mass wasting The downhill movement of large masses of soil or rocks under the influence of gravity.

matrix The rock in which a gem, mineral, or fossil is enclosed or embedded.

maximum thermometer A thermometer that records the highest temperature over a certain period of time.

meander A loop in a stream's course.

mean sea level The level of the ocean's surface halfway between high tide and low tide.

mechanical weathering The breakdown of rocks into smaller pieces by the action of physical forces, such as by the freezing action of water, wind, or growing plant roots.

medial moraine The merging of lateral moraines when two valley glaciers join.

melt To change from the solid to the liquid state.

meniscus mirror A telescope mirror so thin that it requires computer-controlled devices to keep the mirror in the proper shape.

mercurial barometer A barometer that works by the pressure of the atmosphere supporting a column of mercury.

mesa A small, isolated, high plateau with a flat top and steep sides; common in arid regions of the western and southwestern United States.

mesosphere The layer of the atmosphere above the stratosphere where temperature steadily decreases with increasing altitude.

metamorphic rock Rock that has been altered since its creation or formation by agents such as heat and pressure.

meteor A mass of stone or metal that enters the earth's atmosphere from space and glows as it falls through the atmosphere; a "shooting star."

meteorite A meteor that survives the fall through the earth's atmosphere and hits the ground.

meteoroid A mass of stone or metal that orbits the sun and which can become a meteor if it enters the earth's atmosphere.

meteorology The science of the atmosphere.

mid-ocean ridge A submerged mountain range rising from the depths of an ocean.

Milky Way The galaxy in which the sun is located.

millibar A metric unit of barometric pressure equal to 1/1,000 of an average barometer reading.

mineral A naturally occurring, inorganic, crystalline solid.

minimum thermometer A thermometer that records the lowest temperature over a certain period of time.

minor planet An asteroid.

mixture Two or more substances mixed together but not chemically combined.

model A simplified picture used by a scientist to represent the phenomenon he is studying.

Mohorovičić discontinuity (Moho) The boundary between the earth's crust and mantle, the depth of which varies from approximately 5 km (3 mi.) under ocean basins to 60 km (37 mi.) under the mountain chains.

Mohs scale A scale for classifying the relative hardness of minerals from talc (1) to diamond (10).

monadnock An isolated mountain that was resistant to erosion while the area around it was eroded to a flat plain.

monocline A rock formation or fold having a single oblique incline.

monsoon A wind system that reverses directions periodically and thus brings periodic changes in climate over a large region.

moraine An accumulation of stones, sand, or other debris on the surface or side of a glacier or at its foot.

mountain glacier A valley glacier.

mountain range A series of mountains arranged in a line and connected by more or less elevated ground.

mountain system A group of mountain ranges.

mouth The lowest point to which a stream extends.

native mineral A mineral which contains only one kind of atom and is therefore a pure element.

natural bridge A stone arch formed by erosion; it can be the remains of a cave whose roof on either side of the arch has collapsed.

natural gas The gaseous form of fossil fuel.

neap tide The lowest possible high tide; it occurs when the moon is at first quarter and last quarter.

nebula (pl., nebulae) Clouds of gas and dust in space.

neck cutoff The new route of a river when floodwater cuts across the neck of a meander.

neutrino A subatomic particle emitted by the sun that travels at the speed of light.

neutron star An extremely dense, small star in which atomic particles (electrons and protons) combine to form neutrons.

new moon The phase of the moon when its position is closest to the sun's position in the sky.

nitrogen A colorless, odorless, tasteless gas that forms approximately 78 per cent of the air by volume.

nonfoliated metamorphic rock Metamorphic rock that is not banded or layered, such as quartzite.

normal fault A fault where the landmass that is wider at the top of the slanted fault moves down and the landmass that is wider below the slant moves up.

nova A star which explodes and increases up to ten magnitudes in brightness; it may return to normal after the explosion and may explode again later.

nucleus The relatively dense central part of a comet's head.

occluded front The arrangement when a cool air mass and a cold air mass trap a warm air mass between them—the warm air mass rises over the other air masses and loses all contact with the ground.

occult The eclipsing of a heavenly body such as a star or a planet by the moon or another planet.

oil The liquid form of fossil fuel; petroleum.

organic Containing carbon atoms.

outer planets Those planets beyond the orbit of Mars.

outwash plain Deposits of sand and gravel that meltwater carries far away from a glacier.

overthrust A fault where rocks on the upper side of the fault are pushed over the rocks on the lower side of the fault.

oxbow lake A water-holding, by-passed meander of a stream.

oxygen A colorless, odorless, tasteless gas that forms approximately 21 per cent of the air by volume.

ozone layer A layer of concentrated ozone located 20 to 50 km (12 to 31 mi.) above the earth's surface; it shields the earth from harmful ultraviolet light.

panning A method for collecting gold nuggets by washing away the lighter materials in a shallow pan.

parallax An apparent shift in position caused by a change in the point of observation; it is used to determine distances to nearby stars and as proof of the earth's revolution.

partial eclipse The cutting off of a portion of the light reaching an astronomical body by another astronomical body.

pedologist A scientist who studies soil.

penumbra The light outer part of a shadow; the light outer part of a sunspot.

perched water table A second water table resting on an impermeable layer located above the general water table in the area.

perigee The point nearest to the earth in the orbit of the moon or a manmade satellite's orbit.

perihelion The point nearest to the sun in the orbit of a planet or comet.

period The time it takes for the moon to complete one orbit around the earth.

periodic comet A comet that keeps returning because of an elliptical orbit.

permeable Able to transmit fluids such as water.

Perseids A shower of meteors occurring each August which appears to be coming out of the constellation Perseus.

phases The apparent changes of shape of the illuminated part of the moon as viewed from the earth.

philosophy An inquiry other than through observation or experimentation.

phosphorescent Having the property of emitting visible light *after* removal from a light source.

photosphere The visible surface of the sun.

piedmont glacier A glacier formed by the union of two or more valley glaciers; it is generally located on the plains below the mountains from which its feeding glaciers flow.

pilot balloon A balloon set aloft and observed to determine the direction of upper winds.

placer deposits Fine deposits of gold or other minerals found in stream deposits.

planet One of the nine most massive bodies orbiting the sun.

plasma A state of matter formed at extremely hot temperatures that is neither solid, liquid, nor gas.

plateau A large, high plain.

plate tectonics theory The theory which states that the earth's crust is made of several large, flat pieces called tectonic plates.

plucking A process in which glacial ice breaks up bedrock; some of the glacial ice melts then refreezes in cracks and pores in the bedrock; adhering chunks are then torn out of the bedrock when the glacier moves.

polar air mass An air mass that forms over cold areas.

polar easterlies Consistent winds blowing from the poles which bring cold, dry air to the northern part of North America.

polar orbit An orbit in which an earth satellite passes over or near the earth's poles.

polystrate fossil A fossil, such as a tree trunk, which extends through several rock strata.

porous Having many open spaces within.

porphyry Intrusive igneous rock containing both large and small crystals.

potassium-argon method A radioactive dating method based on the amount of argon-40 in a sample compared to its content of potassium-40; it is now discredited.

precipitation Any form of moisture falling from the atmosphere, such as rain, hail, snow, and sleet.

prevailing westerlies Consistent winds blowing towards the poles from 30° latitude.

prime hour circle The beginning line of celestial longitude extending from the north celestial pole to the south celestial pole through the point of the vernal equinox.

probe A space vehicle that is not placed into orbit but is used to explore regions of space.

Project Apollo U.S. space program that carried out the exploration of the moon.

Project Gemini U.S. space program where two men were carried in a space capsule for long-duration flights, preparing for Apollo flights.

Project Mercury U.S. manned space program that achieved the placing of man in orbit around the earth.

prominence Streams of material that rise into and fall from the sun's corona.

proper motion A star's apparent motion across the sky as we see it.

psychrometer A kind of hygrometer having wet- and dry-bulb thermometers; it is used to determine the relative humidity.

Ptolemaic theory The theory that incorrectly stated that the earth was the fixed center of the universe; geocentric theory.

P waves The primary waves caused by an earthquake which travel rapidly through the earth's interior, including the core; the first waves to arrive at a distant seismic station.

quadrant An instrument with a dial and movable sight used to measure a star's position by measuring the angle the star made with the horizon.

quasar A very distant, starlike object that is rapidly moving away from the earth and has strong radio emissions.

radar The method of determining the distance, speed, and topography of a body by reflecting radio waves from its surface.

radial motion A star's motion directly toward or away from the earth.

radiative zone The middle zone of the sun's interior where heat moves outward from the core by radiation.

radioactive The giving off of particles or radiation from the nucleus of an atom.

radiosonde An instrument package carried by balloons to study the atmosphere; most radiosondes consist of a thermometer, a barometer, a hygrometer, and a radio transmitter for sending the data back to a weather station.

radio telescope A radio receiver with an extensive antenna that focuses, amplifies, and analyzes radio waves from space.

rain gauge An instrument for measuring the amount of rainfall over a given period.

rawinsonde A pilot balloon that has a radio transmitter and is used to determine wind speeds when visibility is poor.

ray Any of the bright streaks radiating from some of the moon's craters and thought to have been formed by meteoritic impact.

recharge zone An area where rainwater or stream water seeps through to the water table to resupply ground water.

reflector telescope A telescope that uses a concave mirror to bring the light from an object to a focal point.

refraction The bending of a ray of light when it passes obliquely from one medium into another of different density.

refractor telescope A telescope that uses a lens to bring the light from an object to a focal point and then magnifies the light with an eyepiece.

relative humidity The percentage of water the air is holding compared to the amount that it could hold at a given temperature.

relief A term used in discussing extremes of elevation; the difference in the height of a region between its highest and its lowest points.

relief map A map that shows the different heights of a surface by using contour lines, shading, colors, or some other device.

residence time The time interval between an atom's entering the ocean and its removal from the ocean water.

residual mountain (See **erosional mountain.**)

resolution The ability to see detail in an image.

retrograde motion The occasional apparent backward movement of the superior planets from east to west.

return stroke Lightning discharge from the ground to the cloud.

reverse fault A fault where a wide-topped landmass moves up and the wide-bottomed landmass moves down.

revolve To orbit around a point.

Richter scale An open-ended scale for indicating the magnitude of earthquakes.

right ascension The measurement of a celestial object's position in hours and minutes east of the prime hour circle; celestial longitude.

rills Long, narrow valleys on the moon.

rip current A strong surface current that courses through a gap in the breakers.

rock A natural combination of one or more minerals or organic materials found in the earth's crust.

rocket A device that moves by pushing material (usually hot gases) out its end.

rock glacier A ridge of rock fragments extending down the valley of a mountainous region and moving downhill because of ice in the spaces between rocks.

rock slide A sudden catastrophic slippage caused by weakness between layers of bedrock.

rotate To spin on an axis.

salt dome A vertical, pipelike mass of salt that has been pushed upward through sediments.

sand dune A mound or ridge of loose sand heaped up by the wind.

satellite An object which orbits another, usually larger, object.

schist A common metamorphic rock which splits easily.

science The study of observable facts or events in the physical universe; the total collection of knowledge gained through man's observations of the physical universe.

scientific satellite A satellite which is used mainly for scientific study.

sea A part of the ocean that is more or less surrounded by land.

sea arch An arch of eroded rock formed along a seacoast by wave action.

sea breeze A breeze that blows from the sea to the shore, usually during the day.

sea cave A cavity in a cliff along a seacoast formed by wave action.

sea level The level of the ocean's surface; it changes with every tide.

seamount A submerged hill or mountain rising from the seafloor.

second law of thermodynamics The principle that things tend toward a state of disorder.

sediment Earthy matter suspended in or deposited by water, wind, or ice.

sedimentary rock Rock consisting of particles of sediment that have been bonded together by natural cements; or solids that have settled out from water solutions.

segmented mirror A telescope mirror that consists of several smaller mirrors that fit together to make the larger mirror.

seismograph An instrument for detecting and recording earth vibrations.

seismologist A scientist who studies earthquakes.

shield A flat, rounded structure attached to a cave ceiling and composed of calcium carbonate.

shield volcano A volcano that is built up from smooth lava flows and is spread out with gently sloping flanks.

shower meteors Meteors that fall from an orbit which intersects the earth's orbit.

sill A flat sheet of intrusive igneous rock that has forced its way between layers of existing rock.

sinkhole A depression in the ground caused by the collapse of a cave roof.

sleet Small, rounded ice pellets that form when rain falls through a layer of cold air.

sling psychrometer A wet-bulb, dry-bulb psychrometer that has a better circulation of air around the wet bulb because of its being whirled in the air.

sluicing The use of water flowing down a long, sloping trough to wash gold or other minerals from sand, dirt, or gravel.

snow Ice crystals formed in clouds when water vapor sublimates to become solid.

snowfield A large stretch of snow-covered land above the snow line.

snow line The line above which there is perpetual snow.

soil Sand, silt, and clay mixed with organic material.

solar calendar A calendar which corresponds to the solar year and ignores the lunar cycle.

solar cell A small, waferlike device which converts light from the sun directly to electricity.

solar eclipse An eclipse in which the moon passes between the sun and the earth.

solar flare A severe, suddenly occurring storm on the sun that emits both rays and particles and can disrupt radio transmissions on the earth by disrupting the ionosphere.

solar wind High-speed particles, mostly protons and electrons, traveling outward from the sun's corona.

solstice One of the two times of the year when the direct rays of the sun reach farthest north or south of the equator.

solution A type of erosion in which water dissolves minerals from rocks and soil.

sounding An environmental vertical probe of the atmosphere.

sounding rocket Probe launched into the atmosphere to gather information about the upper atmosphere.

source The highest point of a stream.

source region A region with uniform temperature and humidity over which air masses form.

space The apparently unbounded expanse of the universe in which the solar system, stars, and galaxies are located.

space shuttle A reusable space vehicle used in earth orbit.

specific gravity A comparison of the weight of a mineral to an equal volume of water.

spectroscope An instrument which separates light into its component wavelengths, permitting an identification of the elements in the light source.

spelunker A person who explores and maps caves as a hobby.

spicule A pointed jet of gases from the top of the sun's chromosphere extending into the corona.

spin casting A process for forming a telescope mirror in which molten glass is molded over a honeycomb-shaped structure by spinning and allowing the centrifugal force to mold the concave shape.

spit A sandbar extending into a bay from a headland or island.

sporadic meteor Any one of the meteors which come from random directions and can fall any time of the year.

spring A place, usually on a hillside, where the water table crops out at the surface of the ground, often providing water continuously.

spring tide The highest tide, occurring when the phase of the moon is full or new.

squall line A line of violent thunderstorms that sometimes accompanies an advancing cold front.

stack A mass of rock that has been cut off from the mainland by water erosion.

stage A segment of a larger rocket made by stacking two or more smaller rockets.

stalactite An icicle-shaped formation of calcium carbonate hanging from the ceiling of a cave and deposited by dripping water.

stalagmite A calcium carbonate deposit that grows upward from the floor of a cave, generally somewhat shorter and thicker than a stalactite.

star cluster A group of stars that appear to be near each other and have the same radial and proper motions.

stationary front A zone of contact between two dissimilar air masses, neither of which is displacing the other, and usually resulting in no weather change.

station model An abbreviated method of showing the weather conditions of a weather station on a weather map; a location circle with the conditions of the station recorded in assigned positions around the circle.

stepped leader A barely visible lightning discharge that jumps in a series of steps from the cloud to the ground.

stones (stony meteorites) Meteorites that contain 85 to 90 per cent silicate minerals and 10 to 15 per cent iron and nickel; the most common type of meteorite.

stony-irons Meteorites composed of approximately half silicate (stony material) and half iron.

storm swell The first signs of an approaching hurricane; waves that break onto the shore several hundred kilometers ahead of a hurricane.

strata (*sing., stratum*) Layers of sedimentary rock; they are usually horizontal but can be tilted to almost any angle by movements of the earth's crust.

stratosphere A region of the atmosphere between the troposphere and mesosphere located between 12 and 50 km (7.4 and 31 mi.) above the earth.

streak A mineral identification test made by rubbing a specimen across an unglazed porcelain tile and observing the color of the mark; if the mineral is harder than porcelain, the mineral is ground up and the color of the powder is observed.

streak plate A piece of unglazed porcelain on which a mineral is rubbed in testing the streak.

stream A body of water that flows either continuously or seasonally on the surface or underground.

streamless valley An abandoned streambed caused when a stream was diverted underground.

strewn field The elongated area where scattered meteorite fragments from an exploded fireball are found.

striations Parallel scratch marks in rocks over which a glacier has moved.

strike-slip fault A fault along which horizontal movement occurs.

sublimation The process of changing from the solid state directly to the vapor state or from a vapor to a solid, without an intervening liquid state; snow or ice changing directly into water vapor, and water vapor changing to snow or frost.

submarine canyon Deeply eroded valley in a continental slope.

subpolar low A low-pressure area formed at 60° N when the prevailing westerlies rise above the polar easterlies.

summer solstice The time when the sun appears to be directly over the Tropic of Cancer (about June 21).

sunspot Relatively small, cooler dark area on the sun's surface believed to be associated with the sun's magnetic field.

supercooled water Water contained in some clouds with temperatures below the freezing point of water; it freezes on airplane wings and causes ice storms.

superior planet A planet whose orbit is outside the earth's orbit.

supernova A star that may increase its brightness by twenty magnitudes in an explosion that practically destroys the star.

surface gravity The downward pull of an astronomical body on objects located at its surface.

surge The intermittent movement of a glacier.

S waves The secondary waves caused by an earthquake which travel through the earth's interior, but not the core, and arrive at a distant seismic station after the P waves but before the L waves.

synchronous orbit The orbit of a satellite above the earth's equator that completes an orbit every twenty-four hours, thus remaining over the same point on the earth.

syncline Sedimentary strata folded downward in the shape of a trough.

synoptic weather charts The four principle weather maps or charts prepared by the National Weather Service: Surface Weather Map, 500-Millibar Height Contours Map, Highest and Lowest Temperature Chart, and Precipitation Areas and Amounts Chart.

tail The long, tenuous streamer behind the head of a comet.

talus A sloping pile of rock that has fallen from a cliff.

tarn A glacially produced mountain lake.

tectonic plate Large broken sections of the earth's crust.

temperature The intensity of heat in a mass.

terminal moraine A moraine deposited at the end of a glacier.

terminator The line dividing the light side of the moon from the dark side.

terrestrial planets Planets that are the earth's size or smaller and about the same density as the earth; Mercury, Venus, Earth, Mars, and probably Pluto are terrestrial planets.

theodolite An instrument used for tracking a pilot balloon during its ascent; it is used in determining speeds of winds aloft.

thermal gradient The average increase in temperature (30° C) for each kilometer of depth into the ground.

thermograph An instrument that records temperature on a graph.

thermometer An instrument for measuring temperature.

thermometer shelter A small structure at a weather station used to protect thermometers with a top to provide shade from the sun, an airtight bottom to shield from convection currents, and latticed sides to allow air circulation.

thermoscope A thermometer invented by Galileo; air temperature changes in a glass bulb caused water to rise or fall in a long, thin glass tube.

thermosphere The uppermost layer of the earth's atmosphere where temperature rises rapidly with altitude, just above the mesosphere.

third quarter The phase of the moon in which the eastern half is lighted and the western half is dark.

thrust fault A reverse fault with a slant of less than 45°.

thunderhead A towering cumulonimbus cloud that rises rapidly to an altitude of about 7,600 m (25,000 ft.) and results in heavy showers, lightning, and thunder.

till Stiff, stony, unstratified glacial drift; it is found in all regions of extended glacial action, and it composes moraines and drumlins.

tombolo A beach of sand or gravel connecting two islands or connecting an island with the mainland.

tornado A narrow, funnel-shaped cyclonic windstorm extending down from a cumulonimbus cloud.

total eclipse An eclipse in which the light of one astronomical body is completely cut off by another astronomical body.

trade winds Consistent winds in the subtropics and tropics once used by ships sailing from Europe to the New World.

train The lighted trail behind a fireball.

transit The passage of an inferior planet across the sun's disk; the passage of a star across the meridian.

travertine A white or light-colored form of limestone deposited in caves and at hot springs.

trench A deep valley in the ocean floor, usually near an island arc that is near a continent.

tributary A stream that flows into a larger stream.

tropical air mass An air mass that forms over warm areas.

Tropic of Cancer The imaginary line on the earth's surface located at $23\frac{1}{2}°$ N latitude.

Tropic of Capricorn The imaginary line on the earth's surface located at $23\frac{1}{2}°$ S latitude.

troposphere The lowest layer of the atmosphere where continual changes occur in temperature, pressure, wind, humidity, and precipitation; it extends up to 11 km (6.8 mi.).

trough The lowest part of a wave.

tsunami A seismic sea wave.

turbidity current A density current which arises

from the sinking of muddy water and the rising of clear water.

type I tail   A comet's tail that is mainly gas and is pushed away from the sun by the solar wind; it forms rapidly and is almost straight.

type II tail   A comet's tail that is mainly dust and is pushed away from the sun by the pressure of sunlight; it forms slowly and is curved.

typhoon   Name given to hurricanes that occur in the Pacific region.

umbra   The dark inner part of a shadow; the dark inner part of a sunspot.

uniformitarianism   The doctrine that "the present is the key to the past" and that geological change is caused by gradual processes rather than sudden catastrophes; it is not accepted by creationists.

upwelling   The movement of cold, nutrient-rich bottom water up to the surface along the western coasts of some continents.

uranium-lead method   A radioactive dating method based on the amount of lead isotopes in the sample compared to its content of uranium isotopes.

valley glacier   A glacier found in valleys.

vaporization   The change from liquid to vapor by heating (boiling).

varve   A thin layer of sediment that forms at the bottom of lakes fed by glacial meltwater.

vent   A cylindrical opening that connects the earth's surface with a source of magma below.

vernal equinox   The equinox that occurs about March 21.

Viking   Space probes, I and II, that have searched for life on Mars.

volcano   A landform built up by molten rock that has come to the earth's surface through a vent.

waning crescent   The decreasing phase of the moon during the last week of the lunar cycle.

waning gibbous   The moon phase during the third week of the lunar cycle; when the western

edge of a full moon is gradually engulfed in darkness.

warm air mass   An air mass that is warmer than the surface over which it moves.

warm front   The leading edge of a warm air mass.

waterspout   A tornado occurring at sea.

water table   The level below which the ground is saturated with water.

wave base   The depth to which a wave reaches below the surface of the water; it is equal to half the wavelength.

wave height   The vertical distance from the crest to the trough of a wave.

wavelength   The horizontal distance from one wave crest to the next wave crest.

waxing crescent   The phase of the moon the first week after a new moon when it appears as a thin crescent.

waxing gibbous   The phase of the moon the second week after a new moon when the lighted portion of the moon is between the first quarter and full moon.

weather   The condition of the atmosphere at any given time.

weathering   The degenerative processes which contribute to the breaking up and alteration of rock materials.

weather satellite   An earth satellite with an instrument package used to determine the locations and movements of clouds.

weight   The gravitational pull exerted on an object.

wind-chill factor   The apparent temperature drop due to wind.

wind vane   An instrument that determines the direction from which the wind is coming.

winter solstice   The time when the sun appears to be directly over the Tropic of Capricorn (about December 21).

zone of accumulation   The part of a glacier that is above the snow line where snow accumulates to increase the glacier.

zone of aeration   The ground above the water

table in which the spaces are filled with air, not water.

zone of flow The lower zone of a glacier that flows over the terrain because of the tremendous pressure of the ice above it.

zone of fracture The upper layer of a glacier that consists of brittle ice that cannot adjust to the glacier's motion and relieves the stress of the glacier's motion by breaking to form crevasses.

zone of saturation The ground below the water table that has all spaces filled with water.

zone of wastage The part of a glacier that is below the snow line where the glacier melts and evaporates or flows away.

Index

Index

Index

Index

Index

Photograph Credits

The following agencies and individuals have furnished materials to meet the photographic needs of this textbook. We wish to express our gratitude to them for their important contribution.

Academy of Natural Sciences of Philadelphia
Advanced Water Systems
Alexander Turnbull Library, Wellington, New Zealand
American Museum of Natural History
American Science and Engineering, Inc.
David Anderson
Arecibo Radio Observatory, National Astronomy and Ionosphere Center
Australian Overseas Information Service
David Batchelor
Bausch and Lomb Co.
British Museum
Clifford Burdick
California Institute of Technology
Dan Calnon
Carolina Precious Metals
Doug Chaffee
Clemson University, Electron Microscope Facility; Department of Entomology, Cooperative Extension Service
Harold Coffin
George R. Collins
Grace C. Collins
Colorado Travel Section
Conservation and Renewable Energy Inquiry and Referral Service
Consulate General of Israel
Corning Glass Works
Stewart Custer
Department of the Army
Department of the Navy
Department of the Treasury, U.S. Mint
Dennis di Cicco, Sky and Telescope
Dupont Co.
Eastman-Kodak Co.
Dave Fisher
Gene Fisher

French Embassy
Evert Fruitman
Sam Frushour
Geological Survey of Canada
Goddard Collection, Clark University
Joseph Henson
Mary M. Hill for International Development Association
Institute for Creation Research
International Silver Co.
Japan Information Center
Brian D. Johnson
Keck Observatory, Mauna Loa, Hawaii
Breck P. Kent
Timothy Keesee
Joseph Larson
Library of Congress
Lick Observatory
Litton Itek Optical Systems
Lowell Observatory
Luray Caverns, Virginia
Mammoth Cave National Park
Randy McKay
Montana Promotional Division
John D. Morris
Mount Washington Observatory
Musées Nationaux–Paris
Museum of Science and Industry
National Aeronautics and Space Administration (NASA)
National Archives
National Center for Atmospheric Research (NCAR)
National Geophysical Data Center
National Institute of Standards and Technology
National Oceanic & Atmospheric Administration (NOAA)
National Optical Astronomy Observatories

National Radio Astronomy Observatory
National Science Foundation (NSF)
National Weather Service (NWS)
New Zealand Tourist and Publicity Office
Novosti Photo
Ocean Drilling Program, Texas A & M University
Oregon State Highway Department
A. Post
Pacific Gas and Electric Co.
Peabody Museum of Salem
J. Norman Powell
Ed Richards
Sacramento Peak Observatory for Research in Astronomy, Inc.
Al Salter Photography, Inc.
Schmidt-Thomsen and the Westfälisches Amt für Denkmalpflege
Scripps Institution of Oceanography
Robert Sheaffer
Smithsonian Institute
Marty Snyderman
Soil Conservation Service
South African Information Service
South Dakota State Historical Society
Tass Photographs
Taylor Instrument Co.
Texas Gulf, Inc.
USDA Soil Conservation Service
United States Air Force
United States Department of the Interior
United States Geological Survey (USGS)
United States Naval Observatory
United States Navy Photographic Center
Unusual Films, Bob Jones University
USAir
Ward's Scientific Co.
Woods Hole Oceanographic Institute
Yerkes Observatory

Cover

Breck Kent (bkgd, lm, r); Brian D. Johnson (tl); Unusual Films (bl)

Title pages

Brian D. Johnson i, iii (inset, right panel); Breck Kent ii-iii

Unit 1 Opener

Lick Observatory xiv-1; NASA 1 (inset)

Chapter 1

Keck Observatory ix (l); Clemson University ix (r); Library of Congress x; Unusual Films xii; NASA 2, 11 (b), 16; US Naval Observatory 3; Yerkes Observatory 7 (observatory); Lowell Observatory 10-11 (br); Musées Nationaux–Paris 11 (bl); George R. Collins 13; Smithsonian Institution 15

Chapter 2

Lick Observatory 25, 48, 52, 53, 54-55, 56 (both), 57 (l); Peabody Museum of Salem, photo by Mark Sexton 26; Smithsonian Institution 28 (l), 30 (b); Gene Fisher 26-27; Courtesy of David Batchelor 30 (t); Yerkes Observatory 32, 38; Corning Glass Works 34; Litton Itek Optical Systems 36; Dennis di Cicco 37 (l); American Science & Engineering, Inc. 37; Arecibo Radio Observatory and Ionosphere Center 37; David Anderson 39 (t); National Radio Astronomy Observatory 39 (b); National Optical Astronomy Observatories 57 (r)

Chapter 3

Breck Kent 59; Bausch & Lomb 63; Lick Observatory 64; NASA 65, 68 (both), 69 (first, second, fifth); Sacramento Peak Observatory 66 (r), 69 (third, fourth); Conservation & Renewable Energy Inquiry & Referral Service 71

Chapter 4

NASA 74, 81, 82-83 (all), 84-85 (all), 87 (both), 90-91, 93 (b), 94-95; Lowell Observatory 86 (all), 93 (t); Robert Sheaffer 88 (both); George R. Collins 97

Chapter 5

Dennis di Cicco 100; Yerkes Observatory 101-2; British Museum 105 (t); Lick Observatory 105 (b), 106, 109; NASA 108; Smithsonian Institution 115 (tl), 116 (all), 118; Neg. #314786, Courtesy Department of Library Services, American Museum of Natural History 115 (tr); Academy of Natural Sciences of Philadelphia 115 (b); USGS 117 (t); Geological Survey of Canada 117 (bl, br)

Chapter 6

NASA 120, 123, 124 (m, b), 125, 126 (l, br), 127, 128, 134; Lick Observatory 124 (t), 126 (tl), 130-31 (all); Yerkes Observatory 132, 135

Chapter 7

U.S. Air Force 140; NASA 142 (inset), 144 (r), 149 (b), 150 (all), 151, 154 (both), 155, 156 (bkgd), 158, 159, 162-63 (all), 164; Goddard Collection/Clark University 142; Tass 144 (l); Novosti 144 (m), 149 (t); Unusual Films, Courtesy of Doug Chaffee 156-57

Unit 2 Opener

Breck Kent 166-67 (both)

Chapter 8

Breck Kent 168; Dept. of Entomology, Clemson University Cooperative Extension Service 171; NASA 175, 181; B. Donald Johnson 178 (both)

Chapter 9

Breck Kent 183, 188 (bl), 191; Unusual Films 184; USAir 186; NOAA 188 (tl), 196 (all), 197 (l); Brian D. Johnson 188 (tr), 189 (all), 190 (both); David Anderson (br); George R. Collins 192; Courtesy of Schmidt-Thomsen and the Westfälisches Amt für Denkmalpflege 195 (both); USDA Photo by Joseph Larson 197 (tr, br)

Chapter 10

NOAA 199, 208, 211 (all), 212, 213 (both), 215 (b), 217 (all); NOAA/NWS 202, 210 (both), 215 (t); George R. Collins 205; Evert Fruitman 209; NCAR/NSF 212

Chapter 11

Breck Kent 220, 229 (r), 235; Taylor Instrument Co. 222-23 (all), 226 (l), 229 (l); NOAA 226 (br), 231; Smithsonian 226 (tr); Mount Washington Observatory 228 (both); NCAR/NSF 230 (both); NOAA/NWS 234 (all); Unusual Films 236-237 (all), 232

Unit 3 Opener

Brian D. Johnson 240-241; George R. Collins 241 (inset)

Chapter 12

Unusual Films 242, 250; J. Norman Powell 245; Lick Observatory 246 (both); Brian D. Johnson 247

Chapter 13

Brian D. Johnson 254, 256, 266-267 (t); NASA 255 (l); George R. Collins 255 (r), 261 (r), 263 (l); Ocean Drilling Program, Texas A & M University 258 (t), 259; Scripps Institution of Oceanography 258 (b); Breck Kent 261 (l), 269; Unusual Films 262 (l); David Anderson 262 (r); J. Norman Powell 263 (r); Consulate General of Israel 265; USGS, W.W. Vaughn 267 (b); Colorado Travel Section 268

Chapter 14

Breck Kent 271, 274 (l, tr), 284 (tl), 289 (r), 291 (bl); Unusual Films 275, 277 (b), 279 (all), 283, 288 (all); Unusual Films, Courtesy of Dr. Stewart Custer 272 (all), 273 (tm, tr, bl, br), 276 (tl), 277 (r), 280 (all), 293 (inset); Unusual Films, Courtesy of Dr. Joe Henson 273 (tl), 274 (br) 276 (bl), 277 (l); Unusual Films, Courtesy of Carolina Precious Metals 282 (l), 283 (r), 284 (tr); Ward's 275 (both), 276 (br,tr), 291 (tl), 292 (r); Clemson University 284 (bl); NASA 284 (br); Library of Congress

285; South Dakota State Historical Society 286; Courtesy of Eastman Kodak 287 (inset); International Silver 287 (b); National Institute Standards and Technology 289 (l); South Africa's Information Service 290 (t, m); Smithsonian Institute 290 (b); Texas Gulf 291 (r); Montana Promotional Division 292 (l); Al Salter Photography 293

Chapter 15

Breck Kent 295, 296 (l), 297 (tr), 302 (m), 310 (l, r), 312 (r); USGS, G.K. Gilbert 296 (inset); Unusual Films, Courtesy of Dr. Joe Henson 297 (tl), 298 (lt), 308 (t), 311 (t), 312 (b inset); USGS, J.R. Shay 297 (bl); Brian D. Johnson 297 (br), 299 (t), 301 (t, b), 302 (t, b), 303 (l inset), 309 (b), 313 (l); Unusual Films, Courtesy of Dr. Stewart Custer 298 (lb), 299 (b); Ward's 298, 301 (m), 303 (r inset); Neg. # 315932, 310705, 310110, Courtesy Department of Library Services, American Museum of Natural History 303 (t), 304 (both); Randy McKay 305; Harold Coffin 306 (t); Institute for Creation Research 306 (bl, br), 307; Dept. of the Navy 308 (b); George R. Collins 309 (t); USGS, H.E. Malde 310 (m); Tim Keesee 312 (tl); Dave Fisher 312 (Lincoln); Unusual Films 313 (r)

Chapter 16

Breck Kent 315, 325, 329; U.S. Dept. of the Interior 317; Dan Calnon 318 (t); Alexander Turnbull Library, Wellington, New Zealand 318 (b); Japan Information Center 321 (t); Colorado Travel Section 321 (b); Ward's 322, 324; George R. Collins 323 (tl, tr), 326, 328; Brian D. Johnson 323 (b)

Chapter 17

USGS 331, 335 (l), 338, 339; National Archives 335 (r); Ward's 336, 344 (t), 348; National Geophysical Data Center 341, 342 (all), 345 (m, b); NOAA/National Geophysical Data Center 344 (all); Hamilton, W.B. 345 (t); Institute for Creation Research 346 (t); Oregon State Highway Dept. 346 (b); Brian D. Johnson 347 (t); Breck Kent 347 (b); New Zealand Tourist & Publicity Office 349 (t); Pacific Gas & Electric 349 (l)

Chapter 18

Brian D. Johnson 351, 353 (t), 368 (t); Ward's 352 (all), 355 (b), 359 (b); USGS, Carrara, P. 353 (b), 359 (t); Breck Kent 354 (l), 355 (inset), 357 (r), 359 (r); George R. Collins 354 (rt), 364, 366 (bkgd, t); J. Norman Powell 354 (rb); USDA Soil Conservation Service 356, 357 (t), 362 (r), 363 (l); Institute for Creation Research 357 (b), 367 (l); USGS, W.W. Atwood 358; U.S. Dept. of the Interior 360; USDA 362 (l), 363 (r), 367 (r); Mary M. Hill for International Development Assoc. 362 (m); Dept. of the Army 365; Courtesy of Clifford Burdick 366; USGS 368

Unit 4 Opener

Marty Snyderman 370-71; Breck Kent 371

Chapter 19

George R. Collins 372, 378 (bl), 381, 384 (tr); USGS 374 (r); Dow Chemical Co. 374 (b), 375 (l); Dupont 375 (r); Breck Kent 378 (tr, mr), 384 (tl, b); French Embassy 378 (br); Ward's 382, 383 (b), 394 (r); USGS 383 (r); U.S. Navy Photographic Center 392; Woods Hole Oceanographic Institute 393 (all); Courtesy of the Australian Consulate, David Stahl 394 (l); Marty Snyderman 395

Chapter 20

Breck Kent 397, 398, 399 (t), 407 (tr), 408 (t, inset); USGS 399 (b), 409 (m, b); Institute for Creation Research 400 (all); U.S. Navy 401, 403 (r), 404 (all); National Archives 402 (l); Woods Hole Oceanographic Institute 402 (r), 403 (l); George R. Collins 406, 407 (tl); Ed Richards 407 (br); Grace Collins 408 (b); Brian D. Johnson 409 (t); A. Post 410

Chapter 21

George R. Collins 413, 417, 426 (b); Brian D. Johnson 415; Unusual Films 416 (both), 425 (all); Dept. of the Army 418, 426 (m); Advanced Water Systems 420; Luray Caverns, VA 421 (both); Ward's 423 (t); Mammoth Cave National Park 423 (b); Sam Frushour 426 (t inset)